Happy Birthday, Authors

Finding Your Place Among Writers

Howard Denson

Amazon Create Space / Kindle

Disclaimer

The birthdates of the authors enclosed come from dozens of sources. Like actors, writers may have occasion to lie about their ages or (in an identity-theft world) to put forth information to mislead crooks.

COVER PHOTOGRAPH:
Chelsea Whiteman Photography
http://www.chelseawhitemanphotography.com
chelseawhitemanphotography@yahoo.com

Title ID: 6235631
ISBN-13: 978-1532957406
ISBN-10: 1532957408

Printed in the United States of America

DEDICATION

To the aspiring, probably frustrated writer who is still turning out his or her apprenticeship work of 1-2 million words.

Books by Howard Denson
(available from Amazon.com or Barnes & Noble)

Novels and Fiction
Mowbray & the Sharks
Mowbray and the Baron
The Case of the Anniversary Libation
Mowbray and the Wolves*
Mowbray and the Catacombs*
Mowbray and the Ghosts*
A Grievance with Death
Clare and the Country People and Other Stories

Humor and fables
A Quandary of Fibbles
Fibble-Fabbles

Humor and opinion
Shoot-Out with a Wild-Eyed Moderate
Gunfight with a Wild-eyed Moderate
Duel with a Wild-Eyed Moderate*

Nonfiction
The Wrong Stuff: Findings of a Forensic Grammarian
The Cosmic God Cup*

*Available soon

CONTENTS

Introduction: Joining the Writing Community

We erect mortar-and-brick temples to education and expound at length about the importance of learning . . . and reading . . . and writing. Yet, when youngsters declare they wish to dedicate their lives to fiction, poetry, playwriting, etc., parents and friends often dig in their heels and demand, "What do you want to do THAT for? You can't make a living at it!"

Sure, J. K. Rowling wrote Potter novels and became as rich as the Queen until she started giving away much of her fortune to help others (as she herself had been given support when a single mother). In the U.S., Stephen King, Tom Clancy, and a few others have done very well thank you very much at selling their books.

An adage about acting, singing, wrestling, and other activities also applies to ink-slingers: "You can't make a living at it, but you may make a killing."[1]

The end result? Parents and close friends often tell aspiring writers that they should go into insurance, banking, or even cross-country trucking.

Consequently, young poets, lyricists, and prose-writers fail to develop a sense of community with others of their kind. They look around for other birds with feathers like their own and hope to flock together. All too often, they end up sighing at their isolation.

True, throughout the world, you may find occasional, informal writers' colonies, where established writers discuss mutual problems and youngsters, or those merely young at art, absorb the attitudes and perspectives as they develop their own sense of how a writer thinks. The young at art may also notice that their local masters give conflicting advice. One novelist, for example, insists that she outlines the entire book and knows exactly where it is going. Another novelist disagrees with the approach and may simply begin with a concept that will be fun to unravel. Still another writes the final chapter and, in essence, develops the novel as a back-story.

---

[1] For every Elvis, George Clooney, or Hulk Hogan, you may have hundreds and thousands of wanna-be's who find themselves using the short form when filling out their federal income taxes.

A major problem for most North Americans is that we really don't know the names of that many writers. Thanks to "A Christmas Carol," we do have Charles Dickens as part of our cultural knowledge. Ditto for Edgar Allan Poe with his gothic horrors. In more recent years, we may hear individuals mentioning Stephen King, Jo Rowling, Tom Clancy, and maybe Zane Grey or Louis L'Amour, Agatha Christie, or Barbara Cartland. Nine names, but only two of the scribblers are above ground.

How many people in the U.S. make their living entirely from writing? Not many. Maybe 3,000 out of a population of 311 million. In fact, for centuries, writers could not leave their day jobs. Shakespeare, for example, ran a theatre, acted occasionally, and wrote plays for his company. Others received stipends or honoraria from the government, the church, or special patrons. In the U.S., they worked as, say, ambassadors or port employees. Poor Edgar Allan Poe worked his tail off as editors of reviews and literary magazines and wrote prolifically during his short life. Jealous publishers often resented his successes and fired him, allegedly because of his drinking.

Today, and in recent decades, writers are often on faculties of colleges and universities. The basic paycheck and the time off during the summer enable them the luxury to work on their writing.

Teaching is not for everyone, however. T. S. Eliot thought teaching would dovetail nicely with his poetry compositions. It didn't. Instead, he found he was going to the same well of inspiration for both activities.

What makes drudges compile an extensive list of, say, the birthdays of famous composers . . . or stockcar drivers . . . or in this case writers, poets, playwrights, and other wordsmiths?

The genesis of this book began simply. For over a couple of decades, I have been editing and compiling a monthly newsletter called *The Write Stuff*. When it was only a paper version, we often needed filler for page 13 or 14. If the newsletter was for April, I automatically thought of including a blurb wishing William Shakespeare a happy birthday. I didn't even think about the other thirty-five writers born on April 23. Later, when a writers' birthday calendar came my way, I saw that it might mention six writers born in all of January, and I would dutifully use those as an article.

When a new year arrived, another writer's calendar might add some new people, but (surprise, surprise) it might have different birthdays for some of the writers on the older calendars. These had to be checked out and, when corrected, added to a modest template.

Eventually, a set of *The Encyclopaedia Britannica* from the 1960s was useful . . . thanks to the tedious turning of each page to find the writers and then jot them down.

"Famous persons" lists on the internet were handy, except they often threw writers in with sports figures, politicians, and even porn stars (grumble, grumble).

When the birthdays for each month became too long to include in the now e-newsletter of *The Write Stuff*, we switched to a quick link, to my homepage, where the curious could click on their particular month.

Meanwhile, any writer or editor may hear a nagging voice: "You ought to do something with all this stuff." At other times, that voice drowns out the other voices screaming, "You ought to get naked, sprinkle sauerkraut on yourself and go door to door as Barney Bratwurst." I ignored the voices and figured the neighbors would be happier if the project simply turns into a book listing the belly-button days of various wordsmiths.

So that is what we began with.

For several reasons, all such books are incomplete. First, we may not know when a writer was born. We do know that Ovid was born on March 20 in 43 BCE. Carl Reiner and Spike Lee were also born on March 20. However, we strike out trying to figure out the birthdays of Herodotus, Sophocles, Thomas Aquinas, or Harriet Tubman. Each was born and became noteworthy only as an adult.

Second, with many notables, we know only the year in which they were born. Thomas Aquinas, for example, was born in 1225. What device could accommodate writers with no definite belly-button days?

Two quick solutions emerged as possibilities:

First, those without actual birthdays could be assigned to Feb. 30 and 31. That approach might accommodate about fifty writers per page.

A second approach seems more realistic. We could create two brand new months, one called Groucho and the other called Zsa Zsa. Maybe a future edition will figure out an ideal approach.

Hundreds or thousands of writers today worry about identify theft and may refuse to publicize their complete birth information. Such precautions are understandable, but the absence of the month and day means that the writers don't get included in this collection. More seriously, they aren't included in newspapers' features about "What Happened on This Day" (or a similar title).

Since writers often use pen-names, they could use "pen-birthdays," if they want to head off any identity thieves.

Writers who are curmudgeons or idealists scoff at this whole business. "It's no one's damned business when I was born . . . Let my work speak for itself . . . Foolish nonsense . . . I'll not give any personal information to identity thieves . . . I'm going to scream if another naked nut covered in sauerkraut knocks on my door and says he is Barney Bratwurst."

Speaking of pen-names, entries in this collection will give the pen-name first and then the actual name in parentheses: O. Henry (William Sydney Porter) . . . George Eliot (Mary Anne Evans) . . . John le Carré (David John Moore Cornwell) . . . George Orwell (Eric Blair). John Creasey had twenty-eight pen-names, so *Happy Birthday, Authors* didn't try to list his aliases. Erle

Stanley Gardner used that name on his Perry Mason novels but called himself A. A. Fair on the Cool and Lam detective series.[2]

It may take a couple of editions to standardize the appearance of writers who have initials in their name. We generally list, say, A. E. Housman as Alfred Edward "A. E." Housman and A. A. Milne as Alan Alexander "A.A." Milne.

When a writer only uses part of his or her full name, the book will put parentheses around the name to be ignored, as with Eudora (Alice) Welty and Richard (Dafydd Vivian) Llewellyn (Lloyd).

This collection will differ from the newsletter lists in a couple of ways. First, hundreds of additional names have been discovered and added to the list. Second, this edition has eliminated most duplicates to be found in the e-list (Cervantes and historian David Eisenhower were listed on two days). Third, the e-list left out lyricists. Originally it had no qualms including Cole Porter, Irving Berlin, Stephen Foster, et al., but, when logic said it should also include rock lyricists, even from among the garage-rock bands, then the editor refused to go that direction.[3]

Does *Happy Birthday, Authors* restrict its focus to Great Literature and Writers for the Ages? In short, do we have a big umbrella or a small one? It's definitely inclusive, meaning that the project will need to continue for years to do a good job of recognizing writers, poets, and journalists.

This collection has tried to exclude "authors" who relied on ghost-writers or those whose bylines were followed by "as told to Sam Smith." When key elections are on the horizon, many politicians will have books on the market. We do know that Lincoln, Teddy Roosevelt, Hoover, Kennedy, Nixon, Carter,[4] Clinton, Obama, and others liked to write. Some other political scribes may have fallen through the cracks in this first edition. Actors and entertainers also rely heavily on ghost-writers, but David Niven, Peter Ustinov, Stephen Fry, Hugh Laurie, and most of the Python crew are skilled with the pen or keyboard.

An afterthought developed into an agonizing project: the quotations. For decades, each issue of *The Write Stuff* included an adage or an axiom by a writer. By and by, as each quotation was used, that bit of advice was included in a list (to make sure we didn't use it again). The list also included quotes that could be used for two or three years in the future. Notice the problem:

---

[2] Gardner also used the pennames Kyle Corning, Charles M. Green, Carleton Kendrake, Charles J. Kenny, Les Tillray and Robert Parr, but ESG was the money-maker name.

[3] This collection will include the classic lyricists but exclude drummer Brian XYZebra, who penned, "Do it, do it, do it, do it, do it," for the Razor's Kumquat.

[4] Jimmy Carter is the first president to write and publish a novel, thanks to *The Hornet's Nest: A Novel of the Revolutionary War* (New York: Simon & Schuster, 2003).

In ten years, you will have only 120 quotations.

Now . . .

It seemed logical for each day in this collection to include three axioms from writers born on that day. That decision meant that 366 days (remember Feb. 29) times three would require 1,098 quotations.

Luckily, such readers as Wendy Geiger of Jacksonville, Florida, had sent in suggested quotations, but the master list often included five to ten different quotations each for Hemingway, O'Connor, or Faulkner. That meant we might have only seventy usable quotes in our list and over a thousand more quotations to add.

Finally, if you are a wendiferous reader and kind of heart, you may notice errors of commission or omission in this collection . . . or possibly an outstanding quotation that begs to be included in a future edition. If so, send in your recommendations to hd3nson@hotmail.com or mail them to 1511 Parrish Place, Jacksonville, FL 32205.

For the quotations themselves, the original intent was to focus on observations about the creative process: the writing of novels, plays, poems, etc.; the discipline or schedules that authors use. Often the writer left us his or her work but no comments about the process. Many times, the quotations from various websites were merely excerpts from novels, plays, memoirs, or short stories.[5]

Yours in the word,

hd3

Jacksonville, Florida

---

[5] At some point, it was best to follow the advice of a sergeant at Fort Polk, Louisiana, in 1964: "Do like the folks in Georgia: the best you can with what you've got."

Born in January

Jan. 1—Antoinette du Ligier de la Guard Deshoulieres (1638), Elkanah Settle (1648), Soame Jenyns (1704), Kristijonas Donelaitis (1714), Maria Edgeworth (1767), Rebecca Rush (1779), Arthur Hugh Clough (1819), Sándor Petőfi (1823), Paul Hamilton Hayne (1830), Ludovic Halévy (1834), James Ryder Randall (1839), James Frazer (1854), Aleko Konstantinov (1863), Charles Edward "C. E." Montague (1867), Mariano Azuela (1873), André Savignon (1878), Edward Morgan "E. M." Forster (1879), Ernest Jones (1879), Sholem Asch (1880), Carry van Bridges (1881), Federigo Tozzi (1883), Catherine Drinker Bowen (1897), Russ Bender (1910), Inez Asher (Inez Harriett Silverberg) and Audrey Wurdemann (1911), Eliot Janeway and Norman Rosten (1913), François Bondy (1915), Jerome David "J. D." Salinger (1919), Roger Peacock (1920), Florence Mars (1923), Roberts Blossom (1924), Gina Berriault (1926), Ernest R. Tidyman (1928), John Kingsley "Joe" Orton (1933), Alison Gordon (1943), Terry C. Johnston (1947), Peter Dormer and (Douglas) George Fetherling (1949), James Richardson (1950), Ashfaq Hussain (1951), Christopher Moore (1957), Tory Dent (Victorine Dent) (1958), Meg Waite Clayton (1959), Gil(lian) Adamson (1961), Anwar Mansoor Mangrio and Bryan Thao Worra (1973).

Nothing in language is immutably fixed: the best writers are constantly changing it. Absolute government by dictionary would mean the arrest of this healthy process of change and growth.—C. E. Montague

Writing comes more easily if you have something to say.— Sholem Asch

Writing is a kind of double living. The writer experiences everything twice. Once in reality and once in that mirror which waits always before or behind.—Catherine Drinker Bowen

What really knocks me out is a book that, when you're all done reading it, you wish the author that wrote it was a terrific friend of yours and you could call him up on the phone whenever you felt like it. That doesn't happen much, though.—J.D. Salinger

Jan. 2—Philip Freneau (1752), Henry Kingsley (1830), Justin Winston (1831), Mendele Moykher Sforim (1836), Abdülhak Hamid (1852), Gilbert Murray (1866), Ernst Barlach (1870), William Lyon Phelps and Johannes L. "Jan" Walch (1879), Jacques Chardonne (1884), Moyshe-Leyb Halpern (1886), Robert (Gruntal) Nathan (1894), Rene Etiemble (1909), Ulrich Becher and Srirangam Srinivasarao (1910), Charles (Ray) Willeford (III) (1919), Isaac Asimov and Anna Langfus (Anna-Regina Szternfinkiel) (1920), Gerhard Amanshauser and Daisaku Ikeda (1928), Charles Beaumont (1929), Jean Little (1932), Leonard Michaels and Morimura Seiichi (1933), Robert Harris Frank (1945), David Shapiro (1947), Mark Frutkin, Tony Robert Judt, and Judith Miller (1948), Christopher (Ferdinand) Durang (1949), Jimmy Santiago Baca (1952), Colleen Taylor (1984).

I divide all readers into two classes; those who read to remember and those who read to forget.—William Lyon Phelps

It seems to me that I have always wanted to say the same things in my books: that life is one, that mystery is all around us, that yesterday, today and tomorrow are all spread out in the pattern of eternity, together, and that although love may wear many faces in the incomprehensible panorama of time, in the heart that loves it is always the same.—Robert Nathan

Individual science fiction stories may seem as trivial as ever to the blinder critics and philosophers of today—but the core of science fiction, its essence has become crucial to our salvation if we are to be saved at all.—Isaac Asimov

I cannot say this too strongly: Do not compare yourselves to others. Be true to who you are, and continue to learn with all your might.—Daisaku Ikeda

Jan. 3—Marcus Tullius Cicero (106 BCE), Pietro Metastasio (1698), Charles Palissot de Montenoy (1730), Douglas William Jerrold (1803), Henry Handel Richardson (1870), William Whittingham "Jack" Lyman Jr. (1885), John G(ould) Fletcher (1886), John Ronald Reuel "J. R. R." Tolkien (1892), Pierre Drieu La Rochelle (1893), Roman Brandstaetter (1906), Victor Borge (b. Børge Rosenbaum) (1909), Renaude Lapointe (1912), Morten Nielsen and Anne Szumigalski (1922), Jaroslav Hasek (1923), Marcel Dubé (1930), Anne Stevenson (1933), Betty Rollin (1936), Marcia Haufrecht (1937), Blanche d'Alpuget (1944), Jim Dunlap (1945), Charlotte Gray (1948), Erik Larson and Robert Olmstead (1954), Connie May Fowler (1960), Francesca Lia Block and Ulrike Lang (1962), Alex Wheatle (1963).

A room without books is like a body without soul.—Cicero

Criticism—however valid or intellectually engaging—tends to get in the way of a writer who has anything personal to say. A tightrope walker may require practice, but if he starts a theory of equilibrium he will lose grace (and probably fall off).—J.R.R. Tolkien

Humor is something that thrives between man's aspirations and his limitations. There is more logic in humor than in anything else. Because, you see, humor is truth.—Victor Borge

Jan. 4—Paul-Louis Courier (1772), Jacob Grimm (1785), Casimiro de Abreu (1837), Langdon Smith (1858), Sven Fleuron (1874), Alfred Edgar Coppard (1878), Wilhelm Lehmbruck (1881), Max F. Eastman (1883), Yumeno Kyūsaku (1889), Everett Dirksen (1896), Cyril Lionel Robert "C. L R." James (1901), Benito Perez Galdos (1920), Lois (Cook) Utz (1932), Phyllis Reynolds Naylor (1933), Gao Xingjian (1940), Doris Kearns Goodwin (1943), Elżbieta "Lisa" Appignanesi and Ramsey Campbell (1946), Harlan Coben and Michael France (1962), David Berman (1967), Andrew Pyper (1968), Nabila Jamshed (1988).

[The true poet] is like a man who is happy anywhere, in endless measure, if he is allowed to look at leaves and grass, to see the sun rise and set. The false poet travels abroad in strange countries and hopes to be uplifted by the mountains of Switzerland, the sky and sea of Italy. He comes to them and is dissatisfied. He is not as happy as the man who stays at home and sees the apple trees flower in spring, and hears the small birds singing among the branches.—Jacob Grimm

A poet in history is divine, but a poet in the next room is a joke.—Max Eastman

The past is not simply the past, but a prism through which the subject filters his own changing self-image.—Doris Kearns Goodwin

Jan. 5—Andre H. C. van Hasselt (1806), Rudolf Christoph Eucken (1846), Khristo Botev (1848), Gustaf af Geijerstam (1858), Herbert Bayard Swope (1882), Humbert Wolfe (1885), Paula Ludwig (1900), Jean Dixon (1918), Thomas "Tom" Harper (1919), Friedrich Dürrenmatt (1921), William De Witt "W. D." Snodgrass (1926), Umberto Eco (1932), Florence King (1936), Ngũgĩ wa Thiong'o (1938), Michael O'Donoghue (1940), Terenci Moix and Charlie Rose (1942), Ian Young (1945), Tananarive Priscilla Due (1966), Neamat Imam (1971), Philipp Meyer (1974).

The secret of a successful newspaper is to take one story each day and bang the hell out of it. Give the public what it wants to have and part of what it ought to have whether it wants it or not.—Herbert Bayard Swope

Usually the recipe for a bestseller is to give people what they want. My challenge is and was: Give them what they do not expect. Be severe with them. The world of media is full of easy answers, wash-and-wear philosophies, instant ecstasies, what-we-worry Epiphanies. Probably readers want a little more.—Umberto Eco

Writers who have nothing to say always strain for metaphors to say it in.—Florence King

Any good humor is sophomoric. 'Sophomoric' is the liberal word for funny.—Michael O'Donoghue

Jan. 6—Helius Eobanus Hessus (1488), Domingos dos Reis Quita (1728), Matija A. Reljkovic (1732), Ion Heliade-Radulescu (1802), Herman Grimm (1826), Kanagaki Robun (Bunzo Nozaki) (1829), Louis J. Stellmann (1877), Carl Sandburg (1878), Khalil Gibran (1883), Ludwig Berger (1892), Jan Filip Boon (1898), Eric Frank Russell (1905), Benedict Vilakazi (1906), Keith Davis (1909), Wright (Marion) Morris (1910), Joey Adams and Jacques Cesar Ellul (1911), Frederick (Feikema) Manfred (1912), John C. Lilly and Alan Watts (1915), Vincent Serventy (1916), Guillermo Rosario (1917), Caspar M.B. "Cas" Baas (1918), Jacques Laurent (Jacques Laurent-Cély) (1919), Jacobo Timerman (1923), Stuart E. "Stoo" Hample (1926), Denis Pitts (1930), Edgar Lawrence "E. L." Doctorow (1931), François (Roland) Truffaut (1932), John (Joseph) Wieners (1934), Osvaldo Soriano (1943), Henry Kravis (1944), Allen Appel and Barry (Holstein) Lopez (1945), Carolyn Delores "C. D." Wright (1949), Rowan Atkinson and Elizabeth Strout (1956), Themos Anastasiadis (1958), Nigella Lawson (1960), Antonya Nelson (1961), Muhammed al-Ahari (1965), Karin Slaughter (1971), Andrew (Paul) Britton (1981).

Writing is a socially acceptable form of schizophrenia.—E.L. Doctorow
Everyone who works in the domain of fiction is a bit crazy. The problem is to render this craziness interesting.—François Truffaut
The clear problem of the outlawing of insult is that too many things can be interpreted as such. Criticism, ridicule, sarcasm, merely stating an alternative point of view to the orthodoxy, can be interpreted as insult.—Rowan Atkinson

Jan. 7—James Harrington (1611), Pavao Vitezovic (1652), Joseph Kirkland and Frank A(lexander) Montgomery (1830), Julia (Thompson von Stosch) Schayer (1842), Louise Imogen Guiney (1861), Charles Péguy (1873), Zora Neale Hurston (1891), Albrecht Haushofer (1903), Richard Arès and Faiz Ahmed Faiz (1910), Robert Duncan (1919), Chester Simon Kallman (1921), William Peter Blatty (1928), Allen Grossman (1932), Ann Susan Hills (1941), Hayford Peirce (1942), Shobha De (1947), Dionne Brand (1953), Nicholson Baker (1957), Tina Anderson (1971), Billy Merrell (1982).

A word is not the same with one writer as with another. One tears it from his guts. The other pulls it out of his overcoat pocket.— Charles Péguy

I want a busy life, a just mind, and a timely death.—Zora Neale Hurston

But a myth, to speak plainly, to me is like a menu in a fancy French restaurant: glamorous, complicated camouflage for a fact you wouldn't otherwise swallow, like maybe lima beans. — William Peter Blatty

Jan. 8—Ivan (Dzivo F.) Gundulic (1589), Baltasar Gracián y Morales (1601), Francisco González Bocanegra and Wilkie Collins (1824), James Milton Carroll (1852), John (Gneisenau) Neihardt (1881), Storm Jameson (1891), Roger Vercel (Roger Cretin) (1894), Manuel Rojas Sepulveda (1896), Dennis (Yates) Wheatley (1897), Edmond Vandercammen (1901), Peter (Matthew Hillsman) Taylor (1917), Iva Michiels (Rik Ceuppens) and Joseph Weizenbaum (1923), Charles Thomlinson (1927), Gaston Miron (1928), Ko Un (1933), Alexandra Ripley (1934), Robert Littell (1935), Leon (Richard) Forrest (1937), Graham Chapman (1941), Stephen Hawking (1942), Terence Dean "Terry" Brooks (1944), Don Bendell, David Bowie (David Robert Jones), David Gates (1947), Karen Tei Yamashita (1951), Alan Cumyn (1960).

A synonym is a word you use when you can't spell the other one.—**Baltasar Gracián**

This is the story of what a Woman's patience can endure, and what a Man's resolution can achieve.—**Wilkie Collins**

You can tell a man is clever by his answers—you can tell a man is wise by his questions.—**Peter Taylor**

Jan. 9—Thomas Warton (1728), Per Daniel Amadeus Atterbom (1790), Catharine Parr (Strickland) Traill (1802), Gilbert Abbott à Beckett (1811), Thomas William Robertson (1829), Félix-Gabriel Marchand (1832), Anton Askerc and Lizette Woodworth Reese (1856), Henry B(lake) Fuller (1857), Hayyim Nahman Bialik (1873), Hans Bethge (1876), Lascelles Abercrombie and Giovanni Papini (1881), Karel Capek and Kurt Tucholsky (1890), August Gailit and Grace Zaring Stone (1891), Richard Halliburton (1900), Simone (Lucie Ernestine Marie Bertrand) de Beauvoir (1908), Louise McNeill and Stafford William Somerfield (1911), Richard Milhous Nixon (1913), Lucien Bodard (1914), Herbert Huncke (1915), William Morris Meredith Jr. (1919), Lister Sinclair (1921), Abdelhamid Benhadugah (1925), Judith Krantz (1928), Brian Friel and Heiner Muller (1929), Algi(rda)s (Jonas) Budrys and Paul Mantee (Paul Marianetti) (1931), Sonia Garmers and Wilbur Smith (1933), Anne Rivers Siddons (1936), K. Schlesinger (1937), Pierre Combescot (1940), Joan Baez (1941), John Dunning (1942), Robert Drewe (1943), George Mitchell (1944), Paul Levine (1948), Morris Gleitzman (1953), Normand Chaurette (1954), Michiko Kakutani (1955), Oliver Goldstick (1961), Christopher R. Mwashinga Jr. (1965), Hal Niedzviecki (1971).

Write for yourself, not for a perceived audience. If you do, you'll mostly fall flat on your face, because it's impossible to judge what people want. And you have to read. That's how you learn what is good writing and what is bad. Then the main thing is application. It's hard work.—Wilbur Smith

Laughter nibbled at my lips like tiny fish in warm water.—Anne Rivers Siddons

It seems to me that those songs that have been any good, I have nothing much to do with the writing of them. The words have just crawled down my sleeve and come out on the page.—Joan Baez

Jan. 10—Carolus Linnaeus (1778), Annette von Droste-Hülshoff (1797), Aubrey de Vere (1814), John Acton (1834), Peter J. Blok (1855), Charles G(eorge) D(ouglas) Roberts (1860), Enrica Freiin von Handel-Manzetti (1871), Olive Higgins Prouty (1882), Aleksei Tolstoi (1883), Robinson Jeffers (1887), Dumas Malone (1892), Samuel Simon Krafsur (1913), Émile Danoën and Clarice Lispector (1920), Ingeborg Drewitz (1923), Philip Levine (1928), Peter Barnes (1931), Stephen Ambrose (1936), Jared Carter, David Horowitz, and William Levy (1939), Elspeth (MacGregor) Cameron (1943), Baxter Black (1945), O. Niemand/Susan Doenim (George Alec Effinger) (1947), James (Elliot) Lapine (1949), Dorianne Laux (1952), Antonio Muñoz Molina (1956), Fran Walsh (1959).

> That public men publish falsehoods
> Is nothing new. That America must accept
> Like the historical republics corruption and empire
> Has been known for years.
> —Robinson Jeffers

I only achieve simplicity with enormous effort.—Clarice Lispector

It's ironic that while I was a worker in Detroit, which I left when I was twenty six, my sense was that the thing that's going to stop me from being a poet is the fact that I'm doing this crummy work . . . . The irony is, going to work every day became the subject of probably my best poetry.—Philip Levine

Jan. 11—Joseph Gwilt (1784), Bayard Taylor (1825), William James (1842), Gustav Falke (1853), Marie Bashkirtseff (1860), Thomas Frederick Dixon Jr. (1864), John Callan O'Laughlin (1873), Antonio Beltramelli (1879), Oswald de Andrade (1890), Hans Rudolf Krik (1898), Mohammed Abed Elhai (1901), Alan Patton (1903), Ellery Queen co-author Manifred B. Lee (Emanuel Benjamin Lepofsky) (1905), John Myers Myers (1906), Jill Churchill (Janice Young Brooks) (1943), Joseph Franklin Pippen Jr. (1947), Bille Brown and Carla Harryman (1952), Jasper Fforde (1961), Katharina Hacker (1967), Robert Joseph Greene (1973).

There is only one thing a philosopher can be relied upon to do, and that is to contradict other philosophers.—William James
If you wrote a novel in South Africa which didn't concern the central issues, it wouldn't be worth publishing.—Alan Patton
Whereas story is processed in the mind in a straightforward manner, poetry bypasses rational thought and goes straight to the limbic system and lights it up like a brushfire. It's the crack cocaine of the literary world.—Jasper Fforde

Jan. 12—Andreas Alicatus (1492), Peter Scriverius (1576), Charles Perrault (1628), Frances Brooke (1724), Edmund Burke (1729), Jacob M. R. Lenz (1751), François Edouard Joachim Coppée (1842), Robert Underwood Johnson (1853), Marika Stiernstedt (1875), John Griffith "Jack" London (b. John Griffith Chaney) (1876), Kyle Onstott (1887), Ferenc Molnar (1878), Ben Seijes (1908), Martin Agronsky and Paul Jarrico (1915), Tadeusz Żychiewicz (1922), Leopold Ahsen (1927), Jennifer P. Johnston (1930), Alain Teister (1932), Helmut Eisendle and Jacobus M. "Jacques" Hamelink (1939), William Nicholson (1948), Haruki Murakami (1949), Rush Limbaugh (1951), Walter (Ellis) Mosley (1952), Rockne S. O'Bannon (1955), Joe Quesada (1962), François Girard (1963), Jack Coughlin (1966), Heather Mills and Van Allen Plexico (1968).

Don't loaf and invite inspiration; light out after it with a club, and if you don't get it you will none the less get something that looks remarkably like it.—Jack London

A short story I have written long ago would barge into my house in the middle of the night, shake me awake and shout, 'Hey, this is no time for sleeping! You can't forget me, there's still more to write!' Impelled by that voice, I would find myself writing a novel. In this sense, too, my short stories and novels connect inside me in a very natural, organic way.—Haruki Murakami

A good short story crosses the borders of our nations and our prejudices and our beliefs. A good short story asks a question that can't be answered in simple terms. And even if we come up with some understanding, years later, while glancing out of a window, the story still has the potential to return, to alter right there in our mind and change everything.—Walter Mosley

Jan. 13—Matteo Palmieri (1406), Mark Alexander Boyd (1562), Richard Hurd (1720), Friedrich Müller (1749), Samuel Woodworth (1784), Eduard von Bauernfeld (1802), Victor de Laprade (1812), Nathaniel Harrington Bannister (1813), Ethel Lynn Beers (b. Ethelinda Eliot) (1827), Horatio Alger Jr. (1832), Karl Bleibtreu (1859), Kostis Palamas (1859), Frederick George H. "Fred" Williams (1863), George Ivanovich Gurdjieff (1866), Johannes Elsensohn (1884), Clarke Ashton Smith (1893), Anton Betzner (1895), Kaj Munk (1898), Alfred Bertram "A. B." Guthrie Jr. and Mieczysław Żywczyński (1901), Lewis B(yford) Patten (1915), Ted Willis (1918), Dachine Rainer (1921), Amanda Cross (Carolyn Heilbrun) (1926), Pamela M. Cunnington (1926), Michael Bond (1926), William Porter "Bill" Lawrence (1930), Kenneth Robeson et al. (Ron Goulart) (1933), Carolyn (Laws) See (1934), Edmund (Valentine) White (III) (1940), Joy Chant (Eileen Joyce Chant Rutter) (1945), Frank E(dward) Peretti (1951), Titus M. Mafolo and John Barrett "Jay" McInerney (1955), Claudia Emerson and Marie Lorena "Lorrie" Moore (1957), Michael Hollinger (1962), Shonda Rhimes (1970).

If you understand everything you have read in your life, you would already know what you are looking for now.—George Ivanovich Gurdjieff

What is, therefore, our task today? Shall I answer: "Faith, hope, and love"? That sounds beautiful. But I would say—courage. No, even that is not challenging enough to be the whole truth. Our task today is recklessness. For what we Christians lack today is not psychology or literature . . . what we lack is a holy rage—the recklessness which comes from the knowledge of God and humanity.—Kaj Munk

There ought to be more grants that go to people in their late twenties and early thirties. That's a crucial age, although it's very hard to judge who is worth supporting and who is not. Looking back on my own life, I see that was the period when I was closest to giving up as a novelist and when I most needed some encouragement.—Edmund White

You never stopped thinking of yourself as a writer biding his time in the Department of Factual Verification. But between the job and the life there wasn't much time left over for emotion recollected in tranquility.—Jay McInerney

Jan. 14—Isaac da Costa (1798), Harmen S. Sytstra (1817), Zacharias Topelius (1818), Vladimir Stasov (1824), Pierre Loti (1850), J. F. Archibald (1856), Wilhelm von Polenz (1861), Catharina A. M. de Savornin Lohman (1868), Thornton Waldo Burgess (1874), Albert Schweitzer (1875), Victor Segalen (1878). Hendrik W. van Loon (1882), Hugh Lofting (1886), George Richard Samways (1895), John Dos Passos (1896), Carlos Romulo (1899), F. C. Terborgh (Reijnier Flaes) (1902), Emily Hahn (1904), Anatoly Rybakov (1911), Tillie Olsen (1913), Dudley Randall (1914), Andre Frossard (1915), John Oliver Killens (1916), Yukio Mishima (1925), Lenore Kandel (1932), Kay (Oldham) Cornelius (1933), (Horace) Julian Bond (1940), Nina Totenberg (1944), Taylor Branch (1947), Lawrence (Edward) Kasdan and Mary (Cennamo) Robison (1949), Maureen Dowd (1952), Rosina Lippi(-Green) (1956), Anchee Min/Min Anqi and David Bergen (1957), Steven Soderbergh (1964), Glenda Goertzen (1967).

A satirist is a man whose flesh creeps so at the ugly and the savage and the incongruous aspects of society that he has to express them as brutally and nakedly as possible in order to get relief.—John Dos Passos

Unlike men writers who marry, most [women] will not have the societal equivalent of a wife—nor (in a society hostile to growing life) anyone but themselves to mother their children. —Tillie Olsen

It takes a lot of adrenaline and fear to make me actually write.— Maureen Dowd

Jan. 15—Molière (Jean-Baptiste Poquelin) (1622), Prosper Jolyot de Crébillon (1674), John Aikin (1747), Willem de Clerq (1795), Alexandr Griboyedov (1795), Thomas Crofton Croker (1798), Marjory Fleming (1803), Pierre-Joseph Proudhon (1809), Peter Christen Asbjørnsen (1812), Mikhail Saltykov (1826), Mihail Eminesco (Eminovici) (1850), Archibald Gracie IV (1858), Adolph Goldschmidt (1863), Arsen Kotsoyev (1872), Max Adler (Austrian) (1873), Mazo de la Roche (1879), Huang Yuanyong (1885), Rex Ingram (Reginald Ingram Montgomery Hitchcock) (1892), Stringfellow Barr and Xu Zhimo (1897), Goodman Ace (1899), Edna Staebler (1906), Esther (Etty) Hillesum (1914), Mikki Doyle (1916), Raymond (Holmes) Souster (1921), Ivor Cutler (1923), Michael Collins (Dennis Lynds) (1924), Martin Luther King Jr. (1929), Thomas Hoving (1931), Ernest Gaines (1933), Robert Silverberg (1935), Frank Conroy (1936), Bonnie Burnard (1945), Andrew Jordan "Andy" Jones (1948), Jose Dalisay Jr. (1954), Dawn-Michelle Baude (1959), Raegan Butcher (1969).

When deeds speak, words are nothing.—Pierre-Joseph Proudhon

Every word born of an inner necessity—writing must never be anything else.—Etty Hillesum

Today I must write a paragraph or a page better than I did yesterday.—Ernest Gaines

Jan. 16—Dorthe Engelbrechtsdatter (1634), Louis de Rouvroy, duc de Saint-Simon (1675), Richard Savage (1697), Conte Vittorio Alfieri (1749), Frank Bacon (1864), Robert W(illiam) Service (1874), Henry DeWitt "Harry" Carey II and Robert Garbe (1878), Margaret Wilson (1882), George (Edward) Kelly (1887), Osip Brik (1888), Nat Schachner (1895), Ruth Rose (1896), Carlos Pellicer (1897), Laura Riding (Laura Reichenthal Jackson) (1901), Clement Greenberg (1906), Hubert Creekmore and Alexander Knox (1907), Mario Tobino (1910), Franz Tumler (1912), Nel Benschop and Stirling Silliphant (1918), Anthony (Evan) Hecht (1923), William (Joseph) Kennedy (1928), Norman Podhoretz (1930), Vladimir Skutina (1931), Susan Sontag (1933), Jô Soares (1938), Magdalen Nabb (1947), Brian Castro (1950), Paul Fericano (1951), Roberta Baskin and Julie Anne Peters (1952), Mary Karr (1955), Ivan Safronov (1956), Garth Ennis (1970), Lin-Manuel Miranda (1980).

When anger rushes unrestrained to action, like a hot steed, it stumbles on its way. The man of thought strikes deepest and strikes safely.—Richard Savage

Volume depends precisely on the writer's having been able to sit in a room every day, year after year, alone.—Susan Sontag

Never get so fascinated by the extraordinary that you forget the ordinary.—Magdalen Nabb

Jan. 17—Leonhard Fuchs (1501), Pedro Calderón de la Barca (1600), Gerard van Loon (1683), Archibald Bower (1686), Benjamin Franklin (1706), James Hall (1761), Charles Brockden Brown (1771), Ellen Wood (1814), Anne Brontë (1820), Antanas Baranauskas (1835), Tomas Carrasquilla (1858), Florencio Sánchez (1875), Olga Fastrova (1876), May Gibbs (1877), Compton Mackenzie (1883), E. Ball-Hennings (1885), Ronald Firbank (1886), Evelyn Scott (1893), Nevil Shute (1899), Robert Maynard Hutchins (1899), Jyoti Prasad Agarwala (1903), William (Edgar) Stafford (1914), Robert Cormier (1925), Richard Michael Hills (1926), Paul O. Williams (1935), John Bellairs (1938), Gary L. Bennett and Oswald Mbuyiseni Mtshali (1940), Ita Buttrose (1942), Jan (Oskar Sverre Lucien Henri) Guillou (1944), Barry (Edward) Dempster (1952), Kevin Canty (1953), Robert F. Kennedy Jr. (1954), Warren Leight and Ann Nocenti (1957), Liz Balmaseda and Tom Cain (David Thomas) (1959), Brian Helgeland (1961), Sebastian Junger (1962), Ilja Leonard Pfeijffer (1968), Lukas Moodysson (1968), Leigh Whannell (1977).

He that can compose himself, is wiser than he that composes books.—Benjamin Franklin

All our talents increase in the using, and every faculty, both good and bad, strengthens by exercise: therefore, if you choose to use the bad, or those which tend to evil till they become your masters, and neglect the good till they dwindle away, you have only yourself to blame.—Anne Brontë

It's no good going on living in the ashes of a dead happiness.— Nevil Shute

To solve a problem it is necessary to think. It is necessary to think even to decide what facts to collect.—Robert M. Hutchins

Jan. 18—Antoine Houdar de la Motte (1672), Charles de Montesquieu (1689), Constantin von Tischendorf (1815), Louis van Haecke (1829), Jan van Droogenbroeck (1835), (Henry) Austin Dobson (1840), Ioan Slavici (1848), Rubén Darío (1861), Paul Leautaud (Maurice Boissard) (1872), Alan Alexander "A. A." Milne (1882), Arthur Ransome (1884), Clifford Martin "C. M." Eddy Jr. and Hans H. Holm (1896), Leane Zugsmith (1903), Jacob Bronowsky (1908), William Sansom (1912), Gwethalyn Graham (1913), Arno Schmidt (1914), Shelby Hearon (1931), Robert Anton Wilson (1932), Jon Stallworthy and Raymond Briggs (1935), David French (1939), Steven Moffat (1961), Dave Attell (1965), Seamus O'Regan (1972), Michael Dumanis (1976).

My spelling is Wobbly. It's good spelling but it Wobbles; and the letters get in the wrong places.—A. A. Milne

Every animal leaves traces of what it was; man alone leaves traces of what he created.—Jacob Bronowski

I know this is going to sound very self-serving, and I apologize for it, but if you can write comedy, you can pretty much write anything, because it's the hardest. It's the most technically demanding, the most precisely evaluated form of writing. People know if it works or not. There's a big button marked "fail," and that's when nobody laughs.—Steven Moffat

Jan. 19—Mohammed (570), Noel Alexandre (1639), Jacques Henri Bernardin de Saint-Pierre (1737), Isaiah Thomas (1749), Michel Bibaud (1782), Per Daniel Amadeus Atterbom (1790), Auguste Comte (1798), Sarah Helen Power Whitman (1803), Edgar Allan Poe (1809), Augustine Birrell (1850), Eugene Brieux (1858), Alice Eastwood (1859), Gustav Meyrink (1868), Eugene Manlove Rhodes (1869), Hans E. Blaich (1873), Marie Koenen and Boris Savinkov (1879), Alexander Woollcott (1887), Philip Albert Child (1898), Heinrich Schmist-Barrien (1902), Phyllis Flowerdew and Rex Ingamells (1913), (John Clifford) Brion Gysin (1916), John H. Johnson (1918), Patricia Highsmith (1921), Nina (Mary) Bawden and (Elsie) Jean (McGivney) Boese (1925), Libera Carlier (1926), Robert MacNeil (1931), George Macbeth (1932), Charlotte Vale-Allen (1941), Pat Mora (1942), Anthony John Herrera (1944), Julian Barnes (1946), Ann Compton (1947), Martin Bashir (1963), Eden (Victoria Lena) Robinson (1968), Edwidge Danticat (1969), John Corey Whaley (1984).

A short story must have a single mood and every sentence must build towards it.—Edgar Allan Poe

An ordinary man can . . . surround himself with two thousand books . . . and thenceforward have at least one place in the world in which it is possible to be happy.—Augustine Birrell

Nothing risque, nothing gained.—Alexander Woollcott

My imagination functions much better when I don't have to speak to people.—Patricia Highsmith

Jan. 20—Susanna van Baerle (1622), Michiel de Swaen (1654), Giovanni Vincenzo Gravina (1664), Jean-Jacques Barthélemy (1716), Eugène Sue (1804), Nathaniel Parker "N. P." Willis (1806), Richard Le Gallienne (1866), Johannes V. Jensen (1873), Henry Bernstein (1876), A(braham P.) Merritt (1884), Ethel Davis Wilson (1888), Frank Lawrence Owsley (1890), Kaj Birket-Smith (1893), George Burns (Nathan Birnbaum) (1896), Elmer R. Diktonius (1896), Sybil Marion Rosenfeld (1903), Theodore Brameld (1904), Abram Hill and Joy Adamson (1910), C. W. Ceram (Kurt Wilhelm Marek) (1915), Thorleif Schjelderup (1920), Bernt Engelmann and Jacques Ferron (1921), Ottis Dewey "Slim" Whitman (1923), Kevin Andrews (1924), Ernesto Cardenal (1925), William "Bill" Keith (1929), Mel Hague (1943), Eugen Gomringer (1925), Jamiluddin Aali and Qurratulain Hyder (1926), Nancy Kress (1948), Robert Olen Butler (1945), Edward Hirsch (1950), Ruth Elizabeth "Roo" Borson (1952), Sheryl McFarlane (1954), Samuel Arthur "Samm-Art" Williams (1946), Edward Hirsch (1950), Bill Maher (1956), Tami Hoag (Tami Mikkelson) (1959), Kazushige Nojima (1964), Nina Arsenault (1974), Emily Kendal Frey (1976), Diana Peterfreund (1979).

A writer's mind seems to be situated partly in the solar plexus and partly in the head.—Ethel Wilson

I honestly think it is better to be a failure at something you love than to be a success at something you hate.—George Burns

You must learn to be three people at once: writer, character, and reader.—Nancy Kress

Jan. 21—John I Pontanus (1571), Isaac Hawkins Browne (1705), Tsjalling Hiddes Halbertsma (1792), John Gelinde van Blom (1796), Eliza Roxcy Snow (1804), Imre Madách (1825), Ludwig Thoma (1867), Joaquín Álvarez Quintero (1873), Caridad De la Luz, a.k.a. "La Bruja" (1977), Egon Friedell (1878), Olav Aukrust (1883), Richard P. "R. P." Blackmur (1904), John Putz (1906), Donald Cuthbert Coleman (1920), Judith Merril (Josephine Juliet Grossman) (1923), Barry (Samuel) Broadfoot (1926), Mary Ellen McAnally (1939), Patrick Robinson (1940), Vincent Placoly (1946), Carolyn Zonailo (1947), Louis Menand (1952), Cris Cab (Cristian Cabrerizo) (1993).

Both Eliot and Pound condense; their best verse is weighted—Pound's, with sensual experience primarily, and Eliot's with beliefs. Where the mind's life is concerned the senses produce images, and beliefs produce dramatic cries. The condensation is important.—R. P. Blackmur

Science fiction is not necessarily either fiction or anything to do with science.—Judith Merril

Quotable quotes are coins rubbed smooth by circulation. — Louis Menand

Jan. 22—Ibn Taymiya (1263), Francis Bacon (1561), Richard Blackmore (1654), G. E. Lessing (1729), Lord Byron (George Gordon Byron) (1788), Ludger Duvernay (1799), Hermann von Lingg (1820), Samuel Muller Fzn (1848), August Strindberg (1849), Maurice Henry Hewlett (1861), Francis Picabia (b. Francis-Marie Martinez de Picabia) (1879), Louis Pergaud (1882), Helen Hoyt (Lyman)(1887), Ben van Eysselsteijn (1898), Guido Kisch (1899), Arkady Gaidar (1904), Robert E. Howard (1906), James Sinclair Ross (1908), Carl F. H. Henry (1913), Harilal Upadhyay (1916), Herwig Hensen (Flor Mielants) (1917), Piet Van Lishout (1920), Howard Moss (1922), Tom Blackburn (1926), Joseph Wambaugh (1937), James Carroll (1943), Michael (Ivan) Cristofer and (1945), Edward Lynn "Ed" Ayers (1953), Jane Christmas (1954), Francis (James Baird) Wheen (1957), Kenneth J(oseph Thomas) Harvey (1962), Subhash Ram Prajapati (1980).

Write down the thoughts of the moment. Those that come unsought for are commonly the most valuable.—Francis Bacon
If I don't write to empty my mind, I go mad.—Lord Byron
But whatever my failure, I have this thing to remember—that I was a pioneer in my profession, just as my grandfathers were in theirs, in that I was the first man in this section to earn his living as a writer.—Robert E. Howard

Jan. 23—John Barclay (1582), Friedrich von Matthison (1761), Christian A. Vulpius (1762), Stendhal (Marie-Henri Beyle) (1783), Agnes Maule Machar (1837), Herbert David Croly (1869), Oton Zupancic (1878), Ernest (Cook) Poole (1880), Freda Utley (1898), Joseph Nathan Kane (1899), Anya Seton and Louis Zukofsky (1904), Hubert Nicholson (1908), Pak Saleman Siswowitono (1908), Ernie Kovacs (1919), Erbet Pawel (1920), Walter M(ichael) Miller Jr. (1923), Derek Walcott (1930), Pierre Bourgault (1934), Jerry Kramer (1936), Frederick James "Fred" Wah (1939), Alan (Stuart) Cheuse (1940), Bruce Larkin and Lou Schuler (1957), S(teven) Craig Zahler (1973).

Only great minds can afford a simple style.—Stendhal

Television: A medium. So called because it's neither rare nor well done.—Ernie Kovacs (similar to a quote by Fred Allen)

One never knows whether the Poet is speaking fact, fancy, or allegory. If fancy is clever enough, I doubt that the Poet would admit a difference between fancy and fact.—Walter M. Miller Jr.

Jan. 24—Charles Sackville (1638), John Vanbrugh (1664), William Congreve (1670), Frances Brooke (1724), Pierre Augustin Caron de Beaumarchais (1732), Wybo Fijnje (1750), Antony C. W. Staring (1767), Ernst Theodor Amadeus "E. T. A." Hoffmann (1776), Karl von Holtei (1798), Charles Egbert Craddock (Mary Noailles Murfree) (1850), Robert Grant (1852), Edith Wharton (1862), Ethel Turner (1872), Eugen Roth and Albin Zollinger (1895), Catherine Lucille "C. L." Moore (1911), Nora Beloff (1919), Richard (Heath) Rohmer (1924), Henri (Jozef Machiel) Nouwen (1932), Stanisław Grochowiak (1934), Elizabeth Thornton (Mary Forrest Baxter George) (1940), David Gerrold (Jerrold David Friedman) (1944), John Harrison (1946), Steven McCaffery (1947), Isabella Russell-Ides (1948), Benjamin Urrutia (1950), Vince Russo (1961), Lynn Coady (1970), Sheila Callaghan (1973).

How prone poor Humanity is to dam up the minutest remnants of its freedom, and build an artificial roof to prevent it looking up to the clear blue sky.—E. T. A. Hoffmann

There are two ways of spreading light: to be the candle or the mirror that reflects it.—Edith Wharton

When I was a kid, my favorite movies were the George Pal version of 'War of the Worlds,' 'Them,' and 'Invasion of the Body Snatchers.' Those movies were scary! They haunted my nightmares for years, so when I started writing, I wanted to write a story that was just as big and just as scary.—David Gerrold

Jan. 25—Robert Boyle (1627), Robert Burns (1759), Arne Garborg (1851), Julije Kempf (1864), W. Somerset Maugham (1874), Emil Ludwig (1881), Virginia Woolf (1882), Kitahara Hakushū (1885), Diego Valeri (1887), Josephine (Lyons Scott) Pinckney (1895), Yojiro Ishizaka (1900), Gerard P. M. Knuvelder (1902), Frans Goedhart (1904), Edwin Newman (1919), Russell Reading Braddon (1921), Raymond Baxter and Jules P. de Palm (1922), Kenneth George Mills and Eva Zeller (1923), Tanya Savicheva (1930), Paavo J. Haavikko (1931), Alden Albert Nowlan (1933), James Gordon "J. G." Farrell (1935), Kathleen Tynan Halton (1937), Silvio Blatter (1946), Ann Fisher-Wirth (b. Ann Carolyn Welpton) (1947), John Cooper Clarke (1949), Gloria Naylor (1950), Timothy White (1952), Mark Bamford (1967), Stephen Chbosky (1970), Geoff Johns (1973), Alicia Keys (Alicia Augello Cook) (1981).

There are three rules for writing the novel. Unfortunately, no one knows what they are.—W. Somerset Maugham

A woman must have money and a room of her own if she is to write fiction.—Virginia Woolf

I saw no African people in the printed and illustrated Sunday school lessons. I began to suspect at this early age that someone had distorted the image of my people. My long search for the true history of African people the world over began.—John Cooper Clarke

Jan. 26—Florent Chrestien (1541), Ugo Foscolo (1778), Achim Arnim (1781), F. Clinton Barrington (Joseph Holt Ingraham) (1809), Mary Mapes Dodge (1831), Samuel Hopkins Adams (1871), Ilya G. Ehrenburg (1891), May Miller (1899), Menno ter Braak (1902), Kaye Webb (1914), Philip José Farmer (1918), John Logan Gorlay (1920), Michael Bentine (1922), Jules Feiffer (1929), Ronald Allison (1932), Brian (Francis Wynne) Garfield (1939), Susan Griffin (1943), Angela (Yvonne) Davis (1944), Thom Jones (1945), Gene Siskel (1946), Jonathan (Samuel) Carroll (1949), Nick Flynn (1960), Shannon Hale (1974).

Imagination is like a muscle. I found out that the more I wrote, the bigger it got.—Philip José Farmer

Artists can color the sky red because they know it's blue. Those of us who aren't artists must color things the way they really are or people might think we're stupid.—Jules Feiffer

. . . I get the most angry at American movies, when they just so cynically manipulate the audience without even trying to give a good story.—Gene Siskel

Jan. 27—Samuel Foote (1720), Johann A. Cramer (1723), Lewis Carroll (Charles Lutwidge Dodgson) (1832), Leopold von Sacher-Masoch (1836), Rafael Obligado (1851), Neel (Cornelia H.) Doff (1858), Léon (Eugène) Frapié (1863), Beatrice Hastings (Emily Alice Haigh) (1879), Giuseppe Prezzolini (1882), Ilja Ehrenburg (1891), Philip Duffield "Phil" Stong (1899), Lawrence Durrell (1912), Fritz Spiegl (1926), Nancy Dickerson (1927), Gastón Suárez (1929), John Hopkins and Mordecai Richler (1931), D. M. Thomas (1935), Ismail Kadare (1936), Clarissa Pinkola Estés (1945), Ethan Mordden (1949), Alexander Stuart (1955), Frank Miller (1957), James Grippando (1958), Emmanuel Aquin (1968), Patton Oswalt (1969).

When you are describing,
A shape, or sound, or tint;
Don't state the matter plainly,
But put it in a hint;
And learn to look at all things,
With a sort of mental squint.
　　　　—Lewis Carroll
Music is only love looking for words.—Lawrence Durrell
If you don't want to be in a story, don't know a writer. — Ethan Mordden

Jan. 28—John Barclay (1582), Johann Elias Schlegel (1719), António Feliciano de Castilho (1800), Henry Stanley (1841), Jose Martí y Perez (1853), Colette (Sidonie-Gabrielle Colette) (1873), Marthe Bibesco (1886), Harvey Fergusson (1890), Camille Melloy (1891), Valentin Katayev (1897), Wies Moens (1898), Hermann Kesten (1900), Allan Walker (1906), Hans (Hendrik A. J.) Tiemeijer (1908), Verda Bryant (1910), David John Lodge and Manuel dos Santos Lima (1935), Alan Alda (1936), Barbara Parker (1947), Rick Warren (1954), Robert von Dassanowsky (1960), Lynda Boyd and Robert (von) Dassanowsky (1965), Mo Rocca (1969), David Zingler (1975).

Sit down, and put down everything that comes into your head and then you're a writer. But an author is one who can judge his own stuff's worth, without pity, and destroy most of it.—Colette

Be brave enough to live life creatively. The creative place where no one else has ever been.—Alan Alda

Hypocrisy is great fodder for comedy.—Mo Rocca

Jan. 29—Johann Georg Graevius (1632), Hubert K. Poot (1689), Thomas Paine (1737), J. G. Seume (1763), Vasili A. Zjukovski (1783), Henry Neele (1798), Ion Luca Caragiale (1852), Anton Chekhov (1860), Romain Rolland (1866), Vicente Blasco Ibáñez (1867), Owen Gould Davis Sr. (1874). Muna Lee (1895), Karl Bjarnhof (1898), Willem F. K. Hussem (1900), Viña Delmar (b. Alvina Croter) (1903), Jacob "Jaap" Balk (1912), Daniel Taradash and Peter von Zahn (1913), Frederic Ramsey Jr. and Halfdan Rasmussen (1915), Barbara Skelton (1916), Norman F. Simpson (1919), Paddy Chayevsky (1923), Edward (Paul) Abbey (1927), Christopher Collier and John Junkin (1930), Hans Plomp (1944), Grazyna Miller (1957).

Don't tell me the moon is shining; show me the glint of light on broken glass.—Anton Chekhov
It is the artist's business to create sunshine when the sun fails.— Romain Rolland
Artists don't talk about art. Artists talk about work. If I have anything to say to young writers, it's stop thinking of writing as art. Think of it as work.—Paddy Chayefsky

Jan. 30—Walter Savage Landor (1775), Adelbert von Chamisso (1781), George Alfred Townsend (1841), Gelett Burgess (1866), Anton Hansen Tammsaare (1878), Jaishankar Prasad (1899), H E Nossak (1901), Saul (David) Alinsky (1909), Barbara Tuchman (1912), Jarl Andre Bjerke (Bernhard Borge) (1918), Nikolay Glazkov (1919), Lloyd (Chudley) Alexander, Margaret Beda Nicholson, and Margaret Yorke (1924), Lloyd Alexander (1924), Jack Spicer (1925), John Worthen "Jack" Germond and Andrew Salkey (1928), Allan W. Eckert and Shirley Hazzard (1931), Richard Brautigan (1935), twins James and Gregory Benford (1941), Michael (Anthony) Dorris (1945), Jean-Paul Daoust (1946), Les Barker (1947), John Dufresne (1948), Philip Lee Williams (1950), Judith Tarr (1955), Polly Horvath (1957).

Every great writer is a writer of history, let him treat on almost any subject he may.—Walter Savage Landor

Always remember the first rule of power tactics; power is not only what you have but what the enemy thinks you have.—Saul Alinsky

Books are the carriers of civilization. Without books, history is silent, literature dumb, science crippled, thought and speculation at a standstill.—Barbara Tuchman

It's a nervous work. The state that you need to write in is the state that others are paying large sums to get rid of.—Shirley Hazzard

Jan. 31—Jane Johnston Schoolcraft (b. Bamewawagezhikaquay) (1800), Antony Winkler Prins (1817), Emil Strauss (1866), Zane Grey (Pearl Zane Gray) (1872), Freya Stark (1893), Marie Luise Kaschnitz (1901), John (Henry) O'Hara (1905), Robert (Emmett) Cantwell (1908), Thomas Merton (1915), Norman (Kingsley) Mailer (1923), Kenzaburō Ōe (1935), Ajip Rosidi (1938), Anton Korteweg and Juan M. Vasquez (1944), Albert Goldbarth (1948), Janice (Silverman) Rebibo (1950), Di Brandt (1952), Laura Lippman (1959), Grant Morrison (1960), Lisa (Gluskin) Stonestreet (1968).

These critics who crucify me do not guess the littlest part of my sincerity. They must be burned in a blaze. I cannot learn from them.—Zane Grey

Art enables us to find ourselves and lose ourselves at the same time.—Thomas Merton

Writing can wreck your body. You sit there on the chair hour after hour and sweat your guts out to get a few words.—Norman Mailer

Born in February

Feb. 1—Abraham Emanuel Fröhlich (1796), James A. Herne (1839), Abdülhak Hamid (1852), Hugo von Hofmannsthal (1874), Charles Nordhoff (1887), Stephen Potter (1900), (James Mercer) Langston Hughes (1902), Georg Rendl (1903), Sidney Joseph "S. J." Perelman (1904), Michael Kanin (1910), Muriel Spark (1918), H. Richard Hornberger (1924), Galway Kinnell (1927), David Antin (1932), Reynolds Price (1933), Terence Graham Parry "Terry" Jones (1942), Frank Jennings Tipler (1947), Meggin Patricia "Meg" Cabot (1967).

We Negro writers, just by being black, have been on the blacklist all our lives. Censorship for us begins at the color line.—Langston Hughes

Learning is what most adults will do for a living in the 21st century.—S. J. Perelman

I like my stories once removed.—Terry Jones

Feb. 2—Anna Roemers Visscher (1583), Hans E. Schack (1820), Pavol Országh Hviezdoslav (1849), Havelock Ellis (1859), James Joyce (1882), William Rose Benét (1886), Frank Gruber (1904), Angéline (Roy) Hango and Ayn Rand (1905), Bernardas Brazdzionis (1907), Abba Eban and Evert Werkman (1915), Hella (S. Lelyveld) Haasse (1918), James Dickey and Mary Elizabeth "Liz" Smith (1923), Nydia M. E. Ecury (1926), Judith Viorst (1931), Rachel English (1939), Thomas M(ichael) Disch (1940), Joy Williams (1944), Josephine Humphreys (1945), Ina Garten and Jessica Savitch (1948), Ha Jin (Jīn Xuěfēi) (1956), Michel Marc Bouchard (1958), Dan Schneider (1965), R(ichard) Scott Bakker (1967).

It is the little writer rather than the great writer who seems never to quote, and the reason is that he is never really doing anything else.—Havelock Ellis

I've put in so many enigmas and puzzles that it will keep the professors busy for centuries arguing over what I meant, and that's the only way of insuring one's immortality.—James Joyce

A creative man is motivated by the desire to achieve, not by the desire to beat others.—Ayn Rand

Feb. 3—Caroline von Wolzogen (von Lengefeld) (1763), Horace Greeley (1811), Sidney (Clopton) Lanier (1842), Ernest von Wildenbruch (1845), Abel Hermant (1862), Ada Negri (1870), Gertrude Stein (1874), Clarence E(dward) Mulford (1883), Georg Trakl (1887), Nick Kenny (1895), Johannes Urzidil (1896), Lao She (1899), James A. Michener (1907), M. Vasalis (Margaretha Droogleever Fortuyn-Leenmans) (1909), Jann Willem Holsbergen (1915), George G(ideon) Blackburn (1917), Richard Yates (1926), Joan Lowery Nixon (1927), Ira Cohen (1935), Eric McCormack (1938), Paul Auster (1947), Henning Mankell (1948), Stephen Euin Cobb and Kirsty Wark (1955), Lee (Mark) Ranaldo (1956), Lizzie Borden (1958), Carmen Borgia (1959), Sarah Kane (1971), Daniel Allen Cox (1976), Sarah Lewitinn (1980).

Literature—creative literature—unconcerned with sex, is inconceivable.—Gertrude Stein

I'm not a very good writer, but I'm an excellent rewriter.—James Michener

Many words will be written on the wind and the sand, or end up in some obscure digital vault. But the storytelling will go on until the last human being stops listening. Then we can send the great chronicle of humanity out into the endless universe.—Henning Mankell

Feb. 4—Luis de Camões (1524), Hans A. Freiherr von Abschatz (1646), George Lillo (1693), Samuel I. Wiselius (1769), William Harrison Ainsworth (1805), Josef Kajetán Tyl (1808), Frederick Goddard Tuckerman (1821), Frederick James Furnivall (1825), Georg Brandes and Vasili O. Klyutshevski (1842), Francois-Victor-Jean Aicard (1848), Jean Richepin (1849), Constance Gore-booth Markiewicy (1868), Edwin John Dove "E. J." Pratt (1882), Henry/Henri Malherbe/Croisilles and Edward Brewster (Ned) Sheldon (1886), Ugo Betti (1892), Annie Romein-Verschoor (1895), Friedrich Glauser (1896), Edwin (Orr) Denby (1903), (Benjamin) MacKinlay Kantor (1904), Uys Krige (1910), Alfred Andersch and Hazel (Freeman) Brannon Smith (1914), Harry Whittington (1915), Gavin Buchanan Ewart and Colin Morris (1916), Ida Lupino (1918), Betty Friedan (1921), Russell Hoban (1925), John Edward Caulwell Hearne (1926), Robert Lowell Coover and Ivan Davis (1932), Kent Broadhurst (1940), Jean Bedford (1946), Keigo Higashino (1958) and Werner Schwab (1958), Tomasz Pac (1958), Siobhan Dowd and Jonathan Larson (1960), Stewart O'Nan (1961), Benjamin S. Lerner (1979).

Truth is truth, though from an enemy, and spoken in malice.—George Lillo
She would rather be an old man's darling than a young man's warling.—William Harrison Ainsworth
Why we write.
Because art blows life into the lifeless, death into the deathless. Because art's lie is preferable, in truth, to life's beautiful terror. Because as time does not pass (nothing, as Beckett tells us, passes) it passes the time. Because Death, our mirthless master, is somehow amused by epitaphs. Because epitaphs well struck give Death, our vorcious master, heartburn. Because fiction imitates life's beauty, thereby inventing the beauty life lacks . . . . —Robert Coover

Feb. 5—Giovanni de' Bardi (1534), Honorat de Brueil seigneur de Racan (1589), Esteban Manuel de Villegas (1589), Marie de Rabutin-Chantal, marquise de Sévigné (1626), Margaretha J de Neufville (1775), Johan Ludvig Runeberg (1804), Robert Montgomery Bird (1806), Abram Joseph Ryan (1838), Joris-Karl Huysmans (Charles-Marie-Georges Huysmans) (1848). Jovan Ducic (1871), Frederick Leonard Lonsdale (1881), George Saiko (1892), Adlai E. Stevenson II (1900), William S. Burroughs (1914), Margaret Millar (1915), Andrew M. Greeley (1928), Taitetsu Unno (1929), William Childress (1933), John Guare (1938), Stephen J. Cannell and Jane Bryant Quinn (1941), Susan Hill and Janine Pommy Vega (1942), Michael John Hollingsworth (1950), Karen Lawrence (1951), Giannina Braschi (1953), Han Ong (1968), Terézia Mora (1971).

An editor is someone who separates the wheat from the chaff and then prints the chaff.—Adlai Stevenson II

Language is a virus from outer space.—William S. Burroughs

I finally get to the place where the book has matured in my mind and I can hardly wait to start writing it. Then I just sit down and I start. I hit the go button. I have an outline, which is 70 pages, but I don't look at it. I never have to look at it.—Stephen J. Cannell

Feb. 6—Dzore Drzic (1461), Christopher Marlowe (1564), Daniel Georg Morhof (1639), Evariste Desire Desforges chevalier de Parny (1753), Ugo Foscolo (1778), José María de Pereda (1833), Johan (Eliza J.) de Meester and Henriette Dessaulles (1860), John Henry Mackay (1864), Theodor Lessing (1872), Wilhelm Schmidtbonn(-Schmidt) (1876), Anne Spencer (b. Annie Bethel Bannister) (1882), Siegfried Kracauer (1889), Melvin B(eaunorus) Tolson (1898), Rudolf Vornlund (1900), Louis Nizer (1902), Pieter G. Buckinx (1903), Wyatt Rainey "W. B." Blassingame (1909), Irmgard Keun (1910), Lothar-Günther Buchheim and Louis Dudek (1918), Paolo Volponi and Jin Yong (1924), Tom Brokaw (1940), Eliot Weinberger (1949), Robert Townsend (1957), William David "Billy" Lane (1970).

Words of comfort, skillfully administered, are the oldest therapy known to man.—Louis Nizer

It's all storytelling, you know. That's what journalism is all about.—Tom Brokaw

If you don't do it excellently, don't do it at all. Because if it's not excellent, it won't be profitable or fun, and if you're not in business for fun or profit, what the hell are you doing there?—Robert Townsend

Feb. 7—Thomas More (1478), Thomas Killigrew (1512), Jean-Francois Regnard (1655), Alexander Harris (1805), Charles Dickens (1812), Abel Beach (1829), Ricardo Palma (1833), James Augustus Henry Murray (1837), Raf(ael) Verhulst (Koen Ravestein) (1866), Laura Ingalls Wilder (1867), Jindrich S. Baar (1869), (Harry) Sinclair Lewis (1885), Milton Krims (1904), Paul Nizan (1905), Frederick Benjamin "Fred" Gipson (1908), David Ignatow and Ralph Whitlock (1914), H. Eisenreich (1925), Robert Newton Peck (1928), Gay Talese (1932), Crawford Kilian (1941), Eric Foner (1943), Ian Jack (1945), Joe Shea (1947), Karen Joy Fowler (1950), Brian Morton (1954), Sy Montgomery and Matthew White "Matt" Ridley (1958), Ashok (Kumar) Banker (1964), Emma McLaughlin (1974), Kristopher Reisz (1979), Adrianne Calvo (1984).

An absolutely new idea is one of the rarest things known to man.—Thomas More

It is impossible to discourage the real writers—they don't give a damn what you say, they're going to write.—Sinclair Lewis

Better that you should take the chance of trying something that is close to your heart, you think is what you want to write, and if they do not publish it, put it in your drawer. But maybe another day will come and you will find a place to put that.—Gay Talese

Feb. 8—Agrippa d'Aubigné (1552), Robert Burton (1577), Samuel Butler (1612), Gabriel Daniel (1649), Charles Jean François Hénault (1685), John Ruskin (1819), Maxime Du Camp (1822), Jules Verne (1828), Kate Chopin (b. Katherine O'Flaherty) (1851), Nikolai Garin (Michailovski) (1852), Henry Roth (1906), Elizabeth Bishop and Henri Knap (1911), Gypsy Rose Lee (b. Rose Louise Hovick) (1914), Lisel Mueller (1924), Philip D. Appleman and Neal Cassady (1926), Averil Cameron (1940), Ted Koppel (1940), John (Ray) Grisham Jr (1955), Nancy Oliver (1955).

They lard their lean books with the fat of others' works.—Robert Burton
When a man is in doubt about this or that in his writing, it will often guide him if he asks himself how it will tell a hundred years hence.—Samuel Butler
If after I read a poem the world looks like that poem for 24 hours or so I'm sure it's a good one—and the same goes for paintings.—Elizabeth Bishop

Feb. 9—Ali Sjir Neva'i (Fani) (1441), Adriaan Kluit (1735), Vasili A. Zjukovski (1783), Felix (Ludwig Julius) Dahn (1834), Anthony Hope (Hopkins) (1863), George Ade (1866), Franc S. Finzgar (1871), Amy Lowell (1874), Jacques Bainville (1879), Frederik Gerretson (Geerten Gossaert) (1884), Vital Celen (1887), Helen Muir and David (Harry) Walker (1911), Brendan Behan (1923), Roger Mudd (1928), James Baar (1929), Jovette Marchessault (1938), John Maxwell "J. M." Coetzee (1940), Alice (Malsenior) Walker (1944), Eamon Duffy (1947), Janet Issaca Ashford (1949), Susan G. Cole (1952), Mary Jo Duffy (1954), Nancy Holmes (1959), Lori L. Lake (1960).

It's easy to write books. It requires pen and ink and the ever-patient paper. It is a little more difficult to print books, because genius so often rejoices in illegible handwriting. It's more difficult still to read books, because of the tendency to go to sleep. But the most difficult task of all that a mortal man can embark on is to sell a book.—**Felix Dahn**

Only the more rugged mortals should attempt to keep up with current literature.—**George Ade**

For books are more than books, they are the life, the very heart and core of ages past, the reason why men worked and died, the essence and quintessence of their lives.—**Amy Lowell**

In my work and in myself I reflect black people, women and men, as I reflect others. One day even the most self-protective ones will look into the mirror I provide and not be afraid.—**Alice Walker**

Feb. 10—John Suckling (1609), Aaron Hill (1685), Henry James Pye (1744), Charles Lamb (1775), Rafael Altamira Crevea (1866), William Allen White (1868), Anne Anema (1872), Percy Jewett Burrell (1877), (Fran J.) Vital Celen (1887), G. Ungaretti (1888), Howard Spring (1889), Hugh Abercrombie Anderson and Boris Pasternak (1890), Elliot (Harold) Paul (1891), Bertolt Brecht (1898), Armand Bernier (1902), Henry Phelps Brown (1906), Alexander Comfort (1920), Jakov Lind (1927), Elaine Lobl "E. L." Konigsburg (1930), Thomas Bernhard (1931), Mary McGarry Morris (1943), Roxanne Pulitzer (1951), John Shirley (1953), George Stephanopoulos (1961), Glenn (Lee) Beck and John Shea (1964), Åsne Seierstad (1970).

Love is the fart Of every heart: It pains a man when 'tis kept close, And others doth offend, when 'tis let loose.—John Suckling

The teller of a mirthful tale has latitude allowed him. We are content with less than absolute truth.—Charles Lamb

Hungry man, reach for the book: it is a weapon.—Bertolt Brecht

Feb. 11—Honoré d'Urfé (1568), Bernard Fontenelle (1567), Marie Joseph de Chénier (1764), Lydia Maria Francis Child (1802), Hermann Allmers (1821), Rachilde (Marguerite Vallette-Eymery) (1860), Else Lasker-Schüler (1869), Agnes Christina Laut (1871), Feodor Chaliapine (1873), Elsa Beskow (1874), Johan C. P. Alberts (1893), Beb (Elizabeth) Vuyk (1905). Ernest William "E. W." Swanton (1907), Sutan Takdir Alishahbana (1908), Joseph L. Mankiewicz (1909), Roy Fuller (1912), Patrick Leigh Fermor (1915), Sidney Sheldon (b. Sidney Schechtel) (1917), Daniel F(rancis) Galouye (1920), Larry Merchant (1931), Freda Ahenakew (1932), Jane (Hyatt) Yolen (1939), Joy Williams (1944), John Ellis "Jeb" Bush (1953), Wesley Strick (1954), Zain Verjee (1974).

Women react differently. A French woman who sees herself betrayed by her husband will kill his mistress. An Italian will kill her husband. A Spaniard will kill both; and a German will kill herself.—Bernard Le Bovier Fontenelle

I was gravely warned by some of my female acquaintances that no woman could expect to be regarded as a lady after she had written a book.—Lydia Maria Child

There's this sense of excitement because you invent and control the characters. You decide whether they live or die. I find this type of creative process tremendously stimulating.—Sidney Sheldon

Feb. 12—Thomas Campion (1567), Casparus Barleaus (1584), Caspar Bartholin (1585), Cotton Mather (1663), Charles Pinot Duclos (1704), William Whitehead (bapt. 1715), Friedrich de la Motte Fouqué (1777), Abraham Lincoln (1809), Charles Darwin (1809), Otto Ludwig (1818), William Wetmore Story (1819), George Meredith (1828), Lou (Andreas-) Salome (1861), Kazimierz P. Tetmajer (1865), Hedwig Courths-Mahler (1867), John L. Lewis (1880), Hatcher Hughes (1881), Mary Craig (Kimbrough) Sinclair (1882), S(amuel) Foster Damon (1893), Jean Effel (1908), Frank Hercules (1911), R. F. Delderfield (1912), Alan Dugan (1923), Hans Berghuis (1924), Gerhard Rohm (1930), Janwillem (Lincoln) van de Wetering (1931), Axel Jensen (1932), Juanita (Ruth) Coulson (1933), (Marilyn Marie Coco) "Dede" Wilson (1937), Judy Blume (Judith Sussman) (1938), Robert Graysmith (Robert Gray Smith) (1942), Jackie Torrence (1944), David Small (1945), Raymond Kurzweil (1948), George Elliott Clarke and Andrey Veter (Nefedov) (1960), Jacqueline Woodson (1963), Deborah Garrison (1965), Darren Aronofsky (1969).

Books serve to show a man that those original thoughts of his aren't very new at all.—Abraham Lincoln
The man of science is nothing if not a poet gone wrong.— George Meredith
Let children read whatever they want and then talk about it with them. If parents and kids can talk together, we won't have as much censorship because we won't have as much fear.—Judy Blume

Feb. 13—Hartmann Schedel (1440), John C. Hespe (1557), Ivan Krylov (1759), Rufus Wilmot Griswold (1815), Julius H. M. Busch (1821), Lev A. Mej (1822), Gerard Keller (1829), Frank van de Goes (1859), Uchimura Kanzo (1861), Stephen Lucius Gwynn (1864), Joseph C(rosby) Lincoln (1870), Kate Roberts (1891), Georges Simenon (1903), Pauline Frederick (1908), Theodore Odrach (Theodore Sholomitsky) (1912), Henk van Galen Last and Leonard Frank Meares (1921), Jan Arends (1925), Robert (Marshall Blount) Fulford (1932), Ali El-Maak (1937), Friedrich Christian "F. C." Delius (1943), Walter Wangerin Jr. (1944), Sarah Sheard (1953), Vijay Seshadri (1954), Henry Rollins (b. Henry Lawrence Garfield) (1961), Iván González (1975).

I have always tried to write in a simple way, using down-to-earth and not abstract words.—Georges Simenon

When a man gets up to speak, people listen [and] then look. When a woman gets up, people look; then, if they like what they see, they listen.—Pauline Frederick

If I lose the light of the sun, I will write by candlelight, moonlight, no light. If I lose paper and ink, I will write in blood on forgotten walls. I will write always.—Henry Rollins

Feb. 14—Christianus Adrichomius (1533), Sybilla Schwarz (1638), Pierre-Claude Nivelle de La Chaussée (1692), Richard Owen Cambridge (1717), Frederick Douglass (1817), Edmond François Valentin About (1824), François Haverschmidt (1835), Jan van Rijswijck (1853), Frank Harris (1856), Charles Rann Kennedy (1871), Frederick Philip Grove (1879), William John Gruffydd (1881), George Jean Nathan (1882), Kostas Varnalis (1884), Oscar Odd "O. O." McIntyre (1884), Lewis Allan (Abel Meeropol) (1903), Abraham Moses "A. M." Klein (1909), Edmund George Love (1912), Albert "Ab" Visser (1913), Harry Mathews (1930), Alexander Kluge (1932), Robert (Joseph) Shea (1933), Harvey Hess (1939), Phillip Hamilton (1961), Danai Jekesai Gurira (1978).

A little learning, indeed, may be a dangerous thing, but the want of learning is a calamity to any people.—**Frederick Douglass**
I am, really, a great writer; my only difficulty is in finding great readers.—**Frank Harris**
Criticism is the art of appraising others at one's own value.—**George Jean Nathan**

Feb. 15—Claude Prosper (1707), Johann Jakob Wilhelm Heinse (1746), Jeremy Bentham (1748), Jens Immanuel Baggesen (1764), Thomas Malthus (1766), Abraham de Amorie van der de Have (1821), Silas Weir Mitchell (1829), Alfred North Whitehead (1861), Joseph Hergesheimer (1880), Pearl Lenore Curran (1883), Sax Rohmer (1886), Matthew Josephson (1899), Ypk fan der Fear (1908), Miep Gies (1909), George Mikes (1912), Paul Ferris (1915), Piet van Aken (1920), Radha Krishna Choudhary (1921), Herman Kahn (1922), Susan Brownmiller (1935), Gregory Mcdonald (1937), Jack Tinker (1938), Jo Clayton (1939), Richard Alan Fortey (1946), Matt Groening (1954), Steve Farhood (1957), Chrystine Brouillet (1958), Brigitte France (Fourneron) Byrd (1959), Trevor (William) Cole (1960), Richard Blanco (1968), Josh Marshall (1969).

I have suffered a great deal from writers who have quoted this or that sentence of mine either out of its context or in juxtaposition to some incongruous matter which quite distorted my meaning, or destroyed it altogether.—Alfred North Whitehead

There are few states, I suppose, which exact so severe a toll from one's nervous system as the anticipation of calamity.—Sax Rohmer

Women are all female impersonators to some degree. — Susan Brownmiller

Feb. 16—Ordericus Vitalis (1075), Phineas Parkhurst Quimby (1802), Clara (Sophia) Jessup (Bloomfield-)Moore (1824), Joseph V. von Scheffel (1826), Sarah Anne (Ellis) Dorsey (1829), Nikolai Leskow (1831), Henry B. Adams (1838), Octave Mirbeau (1850), William Scarborough (1852), Vyacheslav I. Ivanov (1866), George Macauley Trevelyan (1876), Maurits H. E. Uyldert (1881), Elizabeth Craig (1883), Van Wyck Brooks (1886), Albert (Maurice) Hackett (1900), Hal Porter (1911), Bob Tadema Sporry (1912), Joseph Langland (1917), Hubert van Herreweghen (1920), Desmond Cory (Shaun Lloyd McCarthy) (1928), A. Kolleritsch (1931), A. Appelfeld (1932), Paul Bailey and Lionel (John) Kearns (1937), Richard Ford (1944), Eckhart Tolle (1948), Iain Banks (1954), Guy Gallo and Elizabeth Wellburn (1955), Natalie Angier (1958), Warren Ellis (1968), Zoe Whittall (1976).

No one means all he says, and yet very few say all they mean, for words are slippery and thought is viscous.—Henry Brooks Adams

No man should ever publish a book until he has first read it to a woman.—Van Wyck Brooks

Literature has as one of its principal allures that it tells you something about life that life itself can't tell you. I just thought literature is a thing that human beings do.—Richard Ford

Feb. 17—Friedrich M. Klinger (1752), John Pinkerton (1758), Rose Terry Cooke (1827), Gustavo Adolfo Bécquer (1836), Louisa Lawson (1848), Samuel Sidney McClure (1857), Langdon Elwyn Mitchell and Mori Ōgai (1862), Fyodor Sologub (1863), Andrew Barton "Banjo" Paterson (1864), Isabelle Eberhardt and Henri Vandeputte (1877), Dorothy Canfield Fisher (1879), Ronald Aburthnott Knox (1888), Georg Britting (1891), Theodor Plievier (1892), Charles B. Timmer (1907), Walter L "Red" Barber (1908), Ai Qing (1910), Andre Norton et al. (Alice Mary Norton) and Virginia (Eggertsen) Sorensen (1912), Per-Jakez Helias and Albert Westerlinck (1914), William Bronk (1918), Elleston Trevor (1920), Margaret Truman (1924), John Thomas "J. T." Edson (1928), Chaim Potok (1929), Ruth Rendell (1930), David Meltzer (1937), (Harold) Wayne Greenhaw (1940), Jack Rudloe (1943), Dallas Adams (1947), Mo Yan (Guan Moye) (1955), Allison Silverman (1972).

Our imaginations seem to have been torn open . . . as by a charge of dynamite.—Dorothy Canfield Fisher

What I have in advance are people I want to write about and a problem or problems that I see those people encountering and that I want to explore—it all proceeds sentence by sentence, paragraph by paragraph, and scene by scene.—Chaim Potok

I always write about subjects which attract me because if I didn't, it would be awful, a failure.—Ruth Rendell

Feb. 18—Leon B. Alberti (1404), Charles-Irénée Castel de Saint-Pierre (1658), Wilson Barrett (1846), Alexander L. Kielland (1849), Sholem Aleichem (Solomon Rabinowitz) (1859), Betsy Ranucci-Beckmann (1877), Nikos Kazantzakis (1883), Wendell (Lewis) Wilkie (1892), Andre Breton (1896), Arthur Bryant (1899), Wallace (Earle) Stegner (1909), Grace Beacham Freeman (1916), Helen Gurley Brown and Juhan Smuul (1922), Chin Shunshin or Chen Shunchen (1924), Jack Gilbert (1925), Archie Randolph "A. R." Ammons (1926), Leonard Cyril Deighton (1929), Joel Lester Oppenheimer (Jacob Hammer) (1930), Toni Morrison (1931), Andre Lorde (b. Audrey Geraldine Lorde) (1934), Jean M(arie) Auel, Timothy John "T. J." Binyon, and Paul (James) Hemphill and Marin Sorescu (1936), Elke Erb (1938), Graeme Garden (1943), Bebe Moore Campbell (1950), Daniel David Moses and Alan R. Shapiro (1952), Miles Tredinnick (1955), Henry Winter (1963), David Biespiel (1964), Peter Martini (1965), Wes Funk (1969).

When you die, others who think they know you, will concoct things about you . . . . Better pick up a pen and write it yourself, for you know yourself best.—Sholom Aleichem

When I was twenty I was in love with words, a wordsmith. I didn't know enough to know when people were letting words get in their way. Now I like the words to disappear, like a transparent curtain.—Wallace Stegner

I always know the ending; that's where I start.—Toni Morrison

I started writing to please myself, a story I would like to read, and that is still true.—Jean M. Auel

Feb. 19—Sadiq Hidajat (3 CE), David Garrick (1717), Tiphaigne de la Roche (1722), Vincenzo Monti (1754), William Dunlap (1766), Mark Prager Lindo (1819), Adrian van Oordt (1865), Paul Zech (1881), Jose Eustasio Rivera (1889), André Breton (1896), Yury Olesha (1899), Giorgos Seferis (1900), Kay Boyle (1902), Adolf Rudnicki (1912), Carson McCullers (1917), Jaan Kross (1920), Ross Thomas and William Weintraub (1926), Carole Eastman (1934), Frederick Seidel (1936), Stephen Dobyns (1941), Thomas Brasch and Clifton Taulbert (1945), William Messner-Loebs (1949), Amy Tan (1952), Siri Hustvedt (1955), Helen Fielding and Theresa Rebeck (1958), Laurell K. Hamilton (1963), Jonathan Allen Lethem and Dmitri Lipskerov (1964), Jeffrey Patrick "Jeff" Kinney (1971), Andrew Ross Sorkin (1977).

You are indebted to your imagination for three-fourths of your importance.—David Garrick

Words to me were magic. You could say a word and it could conjure up all kinds of images or feelings or a chilly sensation or whatever. It was amazing to me that words had this power.—Amy Tan

I always market research my books before I hand them in by showing them to five or six close friends who I trust to be honest with me, so they are very heavily re-written already.—Helen Fielding

Feb. 20—Henry James Pye (1745), Johann Heinrich Voss (1751), William Carleton (1794), Gilbert Buote (1833), Joshua Slocum (1844), Nérée Beauchemin (1850), Nikolai Garin (Michailovski), (1852), Pieter Cornelis Boutens (1870), Jacques d'Adelswärd-Fersen (1880), Shiga Naoya (1883), Hesketh Pearson (1887), Georges Bernanos (1888), Russel Crouse (1893), René Jules Dubos (1901), Jascha Golowanjuk (1905), Mary Durack (1913), Arnold Sheldon Denker (1914), Pramudya Ananta Tur (1925), Richard (Burton) Matheson (1926), Ardath (Frances Hurst) Mayhar (1930), Adrian Cristobal (1932), Ellen Gilchrist (1935) Alan Furst (1941), Andrew Bergman (1945), David Israel Kertzer (1948), (Owen) Kenn(eth Glenn) Nesbitt (1962), Camilla Gibb (1968), Julia Franck (1970).

Your garrulous book teaches many things new and true: If only the true were new, if only the new were true!—Johann Heinrich Voss
The State of the rest of the world changed. Now what? Any Communist countries accommodate capitalism. The cold war no longer exists. I myself remain as before, against injustice and oppression. Not just oppose, but fight back! Against abuse of humanity. I did not change.—Pramudya Ananta Tur
I had to write about realistic circumstances. That's the way my brain works. And I think that gave me a sort of place in the field.—Richard Matheson

Feb. 21—Justus van Effen (1684), Willem van Haren (1710), Louis-Pierre Anquetil (1723), Charles L Fournier (1730), Karl A. Varnhagen von Ense (1785), Jose Zorrilla y Moral (1817), (James) Burner Matthews (1852), Karel Matěj Čapek-Chod (1860), Jacob D. du Toit (Totius) (1877), Waldemar Bonsels (1880), Sacha Guitry (1885), Clemence Dane (1888), Winifred (Estella) Bambrick (1892), Arthur D. Nock (1902), Raymond Queneau and Anais Nin (b. Angela Anaïs Juana Antolina Rosa Edelmira Nin y Culmell) (1903), Armand Preud'homme (1904), Wystan Hugh "W. H." Auden (1907), Roderick Langmere Haig-Brown (1908), Hermanus P. "Piet" Mulder (1914), Hans Andreus (Johan W. van der Zant) (1926), Erma Bombeck (Erma Fiste) (1927), Leonard Melfi (1932), Victor Sokolov (1947), Kevin Robinson (1951), Jeffrey M. "Jeff" Shaara (1952), Victor L. Martinez (1954), Charles Michael "Chuck" Palahniuk and David Foster Wallace (1962), Ha Jin (Jīn Xuěfēi) (1956), Jacob M. Appel (1973), Eric Baus (1975), Jonathan Safran Foer (1977), Bryan Lee O'Malley (1979).

Poetry is the clear expression of mixed feelings.—W. H. Auden

If you do not breathe through writing, if you do not cry out in writing, or sing in writing, then don't write, because our culture has no use for it.—Anaïs Nin

Great short stories and great jokes have a lot in common. Both depend on what communication-theorists sometimes called exformation, which is a certain quantity of vital information removed from but evoked by a communication in such a way as to cause a kind of explosion of associative connections within the recipient.— David Foster Wallace

Feb. 22—Tahmasp I, shah of Persia (1514), George Washington (1732), William Barnes (1801), Sarah Adams (1805), James Russell Lowell (1819), Francis Pharcellus Church (1829), Leon Vanderkindere (1842), Affonso de Escragnolle Taunay (1842), Jules Renard (1864), Edna St. Vincent Millay (1892), Paul Van Ostaijen (1896), Sean O'Faolain (John Whelan) and Giorgios Seferis (1900), Stefan Lorant (1901), Morley Callaghan (1903), Nicholas Monsarrat (1910), Hugh Garner (1913), Jane Bowles (1917), Wayne Booth (1921), Edward Gorey and Gerald Stern (1925), Emory King (1931), (Philip) Christopher Ondaatje (1933), Joanna Russ (1937), Ishmael (Scott) Reed and Pierre Vallières (1938), Richard Greenberg (1958).

The story I am writing exists, written in absolutely perfect fashion, some place, in the air. All I must do is find it, and copy it.—Jules Renard

A person who publishes a book willfully appears before the populace with his pants down.—Edna St. Vincent Millay

There is only one trick that marks the writer. He is always watching. It is a trick of the mind and he is born with it.—Motley Callaghan

Books, Cats, Life is Good.—Edward Gorey

Feb. 23—Samuel Pepys (1633), Richard Price (1723), Margaret Deland (b. Margaretta Wade Campbell) (1857), William Edward Burghardt "W. E. B." Du Bois (1868), Jozef E. Stokvis (1875), Agnes M. Royden (1876), Erich Kästner (1899), William L. Shirer (1904), Walter Ernest Allen (1911), Heinrich Schirmbeck (1915), David Wright (1920), Gery Florizoone (1923), Gerry Davis, Jef Geeraert, and Paul (Noden) West (1930), Donna J. Stone (1933), Haki R. Madhubuti (b. Don L. Lee) (1942), John Sandford (John Roswell Camp) (1944), John McWethy (1947), John Pielmeier (1949), Rebecca (Newberger) Goldstein and Neil Jordan (1950), Simon Rose (1961).

Then to the King's Theatre, where we saw Midsummer's Night's Dream, which I had never seen before, nor shall ever again, for it is the most insipid ridiculous play that ever I saw in my life.—Samuel Pepys

A classic is a book that doesn't have to be written again. —W. E. B. Du Bois

As a poet, it's fair to say that I was a "late bloomer." My youngest had published two poems by the age of nine. Isn't that amazing? I was a little older when I saw my first poem in print— almost 40 years older. Now my little boy is my editor, and I wouldn't have it any other way. I'm the only writer I know who used to burp her editor.—Donna J. Stone

Feb. 24—Muhammad ibn Battutah (1304), Sixt(us) Birck (Xystus Betulius (1501), Matthias C Sarbiewski (1595), Vincent Voiture (1597), Johannes Clauberg (1622), Wilhelm Grimm (1786), Samuel Lover (1797), Charles de Bernard (1804), Arrigo Boito (1842), Teófilo Braga (1843), (Charles) Grant (Blairfindie) Allen (1848), George A. Moore (1852), Daniel Berkeley Updike (1860), Herman Teirlinck (1879), Juliusz Kaden-Bandrowski and Ernest Pérochon (1885), Jacob Presser (1899), Alexis Curvers (1906), August William Derleth (1909), (Harry) Weldon Kees (1914), Ludvig Aschkenazy (1921), David Mourao-Ferreira (1927), Michael Harrington (1928), Brenda Maddox (1932), Daryl Hine (1936), David K. Williamson (1942), (Alan) Kent Haruf (1943), Rupert Holmes (David Goldstein) (1947), Jane Hirshfield (1953), Gillian Schieber Flynn (1971), David K. Williamson (1975).

When once the itch of literature comes over a man, nothing can cure it but the scratching of a pen. But if you have not a pen, I suppose you must scratch any way you can.—Samuel Lover

Taking something from one man and making it worse is plagiarism.—George A. Moore

Children accept many things adults will not accept, since the world of a child is a constant revelation without any need for knowledge of cause and effect.—August Derleth

Feb. 25—Friedrich von Spee (1591), Pierre Antoine Motteux (1663), Karl Ludwig, Freiherr von Pöllnitz (1692), Carlo Goldoni (1707), Simon Stijl (1731), Clement Anselm Evans (1833), Karl May (1842), John Watson (1847), Benedetto Croce (1866), George Samuel Schuyler (1895), John C(hipman) Farrar (1896), Leo J. Weisgerber (1899), Adelle Davis (1904), Mary Coyle Chase (1906), Frank G. Slaughter (1908), John Evan "Jasper" Weston Mather and Edgar Pangborn (1909), Frank Bonham (1914), Lauran (Bosworth) Paine (Lawrence Kerfman Duby Jr.) (1916), Anthony Burgess (1917), F. de Jong Edz (1919), Gérard Bessette (1920), Larry Gelbart and Richard G(ustave) Stern (1928), Erica Pedretti (1930), John Leonard (1939), Frank Chin (1940), John Saul and Cynthia Voigt (1942), Campbell Armstrong (1944), Shiva Naipaul (1945), F. Xaver Kroetz (1946), Gregory "Greg" Hollingshead (1947), Aldo Busi (1948), Amin Maalouf (1949), Garrett Glaser (1953), Thomas Wharton (1963), Sam Bourne (Jonathan Saul Freedland) (1967), Rashida Jones (1976).

Eat breakfast like a king, lunch like a prince, and dinner like a pauper.—Adelle Davis

[Elwood P. Dowd speaking] Doctor, I've wrestled with reality for 40 years and I'm happy to say that I've finally won out over it.—Mary Chase

Reading about imaginary characters and their adventures is the greatest pleasure in the world. Or the second greatest.—Anthony Burgess

One doesn't have a sense of humor. It has you.—Larry Gelbart

It is safer to assume that every writer has read every word of every review, and will never forgive you.—John Leonard

Feb. 26—Anthony Ashley-Cooper (1671), James Hervey (1714), Victor Hugo (1802), Horace Binney Wallace (1817), John George Nicolay (1832), (William Benjamin) Basil King (1859), Arthur Stringer (1874), Henri Fauconnier (1879), Stefan Grabinski (1887), Ivor Armsrong "I. A." Richards (1893), Julien de Valckenaere (1898), Vercors, (Jean Bruller), (1902), Leela Majumdar (1908), George G. Barker and Hermann Lenz (1913), Theodore Sturgeon (b. Edward Hamilton Waldo) (1918), Lucjan Wolanowski (1920), Judith Saint George (1931), Robert Novak (1934), Tim Lander (1938), Clark Coolidge (1939), Adriaan van Dis (1942), Charles "Red" Lillard (1944), Sharyn McCrumb (1948), (Susan) Elizabeth George (1949), Harry Kondoleon (1955), Reginald McKnight (1956), Michel Houellebecq (Michel Thomas) (1956/1958), Atiq Rahimi (1962), Irene Latham (1971).

To learn to read is to light a fire; every syllable that is spelled out is a spark.—Victor Hugo

A good science fiction story is a story with a human problem, and a human solution, which would not have happened with its science content.—Theodore Sturgeon

Plotting is difficult for me, and always has been. I do that before I actually start writing, but I always do characters, and the arc of the story, first . . . . You can't do anything without a story arc. Where is it going to begin, where will it end.—Elizabeth George

Life is painful and disappointing. It is useless, therefore, to write new realistic novels. We generally know where we stand in relation to reality and don't care to know any more.—Michel Houellebecq

Feb. 27—Johan van Heemskerk (1597), Edward Cave (1691), Elias Annes Borger (1784), Henry Wadsworth Longfellow (1807), Alfred Pollard Edward (1832), Richard Garnett (1835), Laura Elizabeth Howe Richards (1850), Marah Ellis Ryan (1860/66), Alice Hamilton (1869), Angelina Weld Grimké (1880), Allison Danzig (1898), John (Ernst) Steinbeck (Jr.) (1902), James T(homas) Farrell (1904), Peter De Vries (1910), Lawrence Durrell and Kusumagraj (1912), Paul Ricœur and Irwin Shaw (b. Irwin Gilbert Shamforoff) (1913), Mervyn Jones (1922), Richard A. F. M. Auwerda and Kenneth Koch (1925), Peter Stone (1930), Edward Lucie-Smith (1933), Roland Henry Flint and N(avarre) Scott Momaday (1934), André Roy (1944), Brad E. Leithauser (1953), Thylias (Rebecca Brasier) Moss (1954), Michael A. Burstein (1970).

With many readers, brilliancy of style passes for affluence of thought; they mistake buttercups in the grass for immeasurable gold mines under ground.—Henry Wadsworth Longfellow

If there is a magic in story writing, and I am convinced that there is, no one has ever been able to reduce it to a recipe that can be passed from one person to another. The formula seems to lie solely in the aching urge of the writer to convey something he feels important to the reader. If the writer has that urge, he may sometimes but . . . find the way to do it.—John Steinbeck

I love being a writer. What I can't stand is the paperwork. — Peter De Vries

Feb. 28—Michel de Montaigne (1533), Reinier C. Bakhuizen van de Brink (1810), Ernest Renan (1823), Hermann Schell (1850), Arthur Symons (1865), Vyacheslav I. Ivanov (1866), Jose Gutierrez Solana (1886), Ben Hecht (1894), Marcel Pagnol (1895), Laura Z. Hobson (1900), Rudolf W. Nilsen (1901), Glyn Jones (1905), Milton Caniff (1907), Ketti Frings (Katherine Hartley) and Stephen Spender (1909), Amir Hamzah (1911), Virginia Hamilton Adair (1913), John Bouber (1921), Don Coldsmith (1926), Bernard Frank (1927), Walter S(tone) Tevis (1928), John Montague (1929), Bruce Dawe (1930), Jack Thieuloy (1931), Alice May Brock (1941), Colin Nutley (1944), Paul Krugman (1953), Robert "Bobby" DeLaughter (1954), Donna (Elizabeth Hazouri) Deegan (1961), Colum McCann (1965), Lemony Snicket (David Handler) (1970), Tristan Louis (1971).

I write to keep from going mad from the contradictions I find among mankind—and to work some of those contradictions out for myself.—Michel de Montaigne

When you read and understand a poem, comprehending its rich and formal meanings, then you master chaos a little . . . . Great poetry is always written by somebody straining to go beyond what he can do.—Stephen Spender

If writers wrote as carelessly as some people talk, then adhasdh asdglaseuyt(bn(pasdlgkhasdfasdf.—Lemony Snicket

Feb. 29—John Byrom (1692), Emmeline B. Wells (1828), William A. Wellman (1896), Dorris Alexander "Dee" Brown (1908), Fyodor Abramov and Howard Nemerov (1920), Vance Haynes (1928), Paolo Eleuteri Serpieri (1944), Jirō Akagawa, Hermione Lee, and Patricia A(nne) McKillip (1948), Sharon Dahlonega Raiford Bush and Tim Powers (1952), J. Randy Taraborrelli (1956), Tony Robbins (1960), Howard Tayler and Frank Woodley (1968).

You just don't give up. There have been times when everything seemed to conspire against getting a book done or printed, and I would feel like turning my back on the whole thing. But I came back and persisted.—Dee Brown

Yeah, there's some unlikely beasts in the world, and it's best to stay near the ones that you've bought drinks for.—Tim Powers

The only limit to your impact is your imagination and commitment.—Tony Robbins

Born in March

Mar. 1—Martial (40 C.E.), Po Tjiu-I (772), Rudolph Goclenius (1547), Johann B. Schup (Schuppius) (1610), Vittorio Bersezio (Carlo Nugelli) (1828), Ion Creanga and William Dean Howells (1837), Henry Harland (1861), Lytton Strachey (1880), Percival Wilde (1887), Ryunosuke Akutagawa (1892), Mercedes de Acosta (1893), Moriz Seeler (1896), Sara (Powell) Haardt (1898), Basil (Cheesman) Bunting and Yorgos Seferis (1900), Pol le Roy (1905), David Niven (1910), Paul Murray Kendall (1911), Ralph Ellison (1914), Robert (Traill Spence) Lowell (IV) (1917), Richard (Purdy) Wilbur (1921), Kuczka Péter (1923), Jacques Chessex (1934), Camille E. Baly and Jean-Edern Hallier (1936), Michael J(oseph) Kurland (1938), Tom Clark and Robert L. Hass (1941), Franz Hohler (1943), Steven Barnes (1952), Mark (Gerald) Kingwell (1963), Darin Strauss (1970).

I make two movies a year to take care of the butcher and the baker and the school fees. Then I try to write, but it's not that easy. Acting is what's easy.—David Niven

On the trail of another man, the biographer must put up with finding himself at every turn; any biography uneasily shelters an autobiography within it.—Paul Murray Kendall

Eclecticism is the word. Like a jazz musician who creates his own style out of the styles around him, I play by ear.—Ralph Ellison

It is true that the poet does not directly address his neighbors; but he does address a great congress of persons who dwell at the back of his mind, a congress of all those who have taught him and whom he has admired; they constitute his ideal audience and his better self.—Richard Wilbur

Mar. 2—George Sandys (1578), Camille Desmoulins (1760), Evgeny Baratynsky (1800), Janos Arany (1817), Multatuli (1820), John Jay Chapman (1862), Dr. Seuss (Theodor Seuss Geisel) (1904), Marcus Samuel "Marc" Blitzstein (1905), Jan Fabricius (1909), Godfried (Jan Arnold) Bomans (1913), David (Loeb) Goodis (1917), Orrin Keepnews (1923), Oliver Roosevelt (1927), Philip K. Dick (1928), Thomas Kennerly "Tom" Wolfe Jr. (1931), Daniel J. Kevles (1939), John Irving (1942), Peter (Francis) Straub (1943), Michael Schmidt (1947), Mark Evanier (1952), Michael Troughton (1955), Morioka Hiroyuki and Michael Salinger (1962), Charles Perez (b. Charles Dabney) (1963), Glenn Rubenstein (1976).

I start drawing, and eventually the characters involve themselves in a situation. Then in the end, I go back and try to cut out most of the preachments.—Dr. Seuss

I am basically analytical, not creative; my writing is simply a creative way of handling analysis.—Philip K. Dick

I still believe nonfiction is the most important literature to come out of the second half of the 20th century.—Tom Wolfe

It's my experience that very few writers, young or old, are really seeking advice when they give out their work to be read. They want support; they want someone to say, "Good job."—John Irving

Mar. 3—Edward Herbert (1583), Edmund Waller (1606), Thomas Otway (1652), William Godwin (1756), Charles Sealsfield (1793), Vissarion Belinsky (1811), Eduard Douwes Dekker (Multatuli) (1820), Fred Burnaby (1842), Alain (Emile-Auguste Chartier) (1868), Colonel Edward Thomas (1878), Floris H. L. Prims (1882), Tore Ørjasæter (1886), Grace Lumpkin (1891), Beatrice Wood (1893), Juri Olescha (1899), Rabbe A. Enckell (1903), Artur Lundkvist and Krishnarao Shiva Shelvankar (1906), Aar van de Werfhorst (Pieter G. Jansen) (1907), Kenton Kilmer (1909), Roger Caillois (1913), Bert van Aerschot (1917), James (Ingram) Merrill (1926), Don Gibson and G. Pausewang (1928), Hans Pieter Verhagen (1939), Owen Spencer-Thomas (1940), Roger Swaybill (1943), Elisabeth Young-Bruehl (Elisabeth B. Young) (1946), Max Allan Collins (1948), Ronald Chernow (1949), Eric Robert Walters (1957), Stephen Belber (1967) .

He that cannot forgive others, breaks the bridge over which he must pass himself; for every man has need to be forgiven.— Edward Herbert

First of all, I'd like to say here the fact that I'm not naturally a craftsman has made me work very hard.—Beatrice Wood

And, as I have said, it's made me think twice about the imagination. If the spirits aren't external, how astonishing the mediums become! Victor Hugo said of his voices that they were like his own mental powers multiplied by five.—James Merrill

Mar. 4—Lauritz de Thurah (1706), Charles Dibdin (1765), Johann Wyss (1782), Hardin E(dwards) Taliaferro (1811), Kristian Mandrup Elster (1841), Josip Jurcic (1844), Toru Dutt (1856), Brand Whitlock (1869), Thomas Sturge Moore (1870), Guy Wetmore Carryl (1873), Léon-Paul Fargue (1876), Bernhard Kellermann (1879), Channing Pollock (1880), Thomas Sigismund "T. S." Stribling (1881), Emilio Prados (1899), Herbert Biberman (1900), Jean-Joseph Rabearivelo (1901/03), George Gamow (1904), Meindert DeJong (1906), Boris N. Poveloi (Kampov) (1908), Taos Amrouche (1913), Giorgio Bassani (1906), Patrick Moore (1923), Alan Sillitoe (1928), Wally Bruner (1931), Richard B. Wright (1937), David Robert Plante (1940), Eleanor Millard (1942), Dieter Meier (1945), David Franzoni (1947), Lee Earle "James" Ellroy (1948), Ofelia Medina (1950), Theresa Hak Kyung Cha (1951), Daniel Woodrell (1953), Mark Chorvinsky (1954), Jim Dwyer (1957), Andrew Collins and Khaled Hosseini (1965), Dav Pilkey (1966), Andrew Osmond (1967), Max Vergara Poeti (1983).

Break free, my soul, good manners are thy tomb!—Thomas Sturge Moore

I put on such a good show, the story is outrageous, and people don't want to hear that I'm basically a reasonable human being. As long as it continues to get me print, I'll continue to perform in an exuberant manner.—James Ellroy

Why resurrect it all now. From the Past. History, the old wound. The past emotions all over again. To confess to relive the same folly. To name it now so as not to repeat history in oblivion. To extract each fragment by each fragment from the word from the image another word another image the reply that will not repeat history in oblivion.—Theresa Hak Kyung Cha

Mar. 5—Vasily Kirillovich Trediakovsky (1703), Jacob Wallenberg (1746), Wilhelm von Giesebrecht (1814), Anna Cora Mowatt (Ritchie) (1819), Constance Fenimore Woolson (1840), Hugh Antoine d'Arcy (1843), Isabella Gregor (1852), Howard Pyle (1853), Benjamin Franklin "Frank" Norris Jr. (1870), Arthur van Schendel (1874), (Charles) Marius Barbeau (1883), Friedrich Schnack (1888), Fritz Usinger (1895), Julian Przybos (1901), Irving Fiske (1908), Joseph Tomelty (1911), Winifred Hamrick Farrar (1923), Charles H. Fuller (Jr.) (1939), Michael D(iamond) Resnick (1942), Roy Gutman (1944), Leslie Marmon Silko (1948), Robin Hobb/Megan Lindholm (Margaret Astrid Lindholm Ogden) and Jim Simmerman (1952), Mark Handley (1956), David Fury (1959), Mark Z. Danielewski (1966), Yuri Lowenthal (1971), Nelly Arcan (Isabelle Fortier) (1973).

The stories of childhood leave an indelible impression and their author always has a niche in the temple of memory from which the image is never cut out to be thrown on the rubbish heap of things that are outgrown and outlived.—Howard Pyle

I write with great difficulty. . . . Don't like to write, but like having written. Hate the effort of driving pen from line to line, work only three hours a day, but work every day.—Frank Norris

To spend one's life being angry, and in the process doing nothing to change it, is to me ridiculous. I could be mad all day long, but if I'm not doing a damn thing, what difference does it make?—Charles Fuller

Mar. 6—Michelangelo di Lodovico Buonarroti Simoni (1475), Jean Luis Vives (1492), Luigi Alamanni (1495), Jan Zoet (1615), Cyrano de Bergerac (1619), Francis Atterbury (1663), John Alberti (1698), Giovanni Meli (1740), Elizabeth Barrett Browning (1806), David Bates (1809), George du Maurier (1834), Johan Bojer (1872), Herbert Kaufman (1878), John Cournos (b. Ivan Grigorievich Korshun) (1881), Ring Lardner (1885), Hugh Williams (1904), Will Eisner (1917), Roger Price, (1920), Gabriel García Márques (1927), William F(rancis) Nolan (1928), Cor Van den Heuvel (1931), Teru Miyamoto (1947), Connie Gault (1949), Jan Kjærstad (1953).

The greater danger for most of us lies not in setting our aim too high and falling short; but in setting our aim too low, and achieving our mark.—Michelangelo

At painful times, when composition is impossible and reading is not enough, grammars and dictionaries are excellent for distraction.—Elizabeth Barrett Browning

How can you write if you can't cry?—Ring Lardner

In journalism just one fact that is false prejudices the entire work. In contrast, in fiction one single fact that is true gives legitimacy to the entire work. That's the only difference, and it lies in the commitment of the writer. A novelist can do anything he wants so long as he makes people believe in it.—Gabriel García Márques

Mar. 7—Guillaume du Vair (1556), Jean Lebeuf (1687), Ewald Christian von Kleist (1715), Rebecca Hammond Lard (1772), Alessandro Manzoni (1785), Frantisek L Celakovsky (1799), Franz Grave von Pocci (1807), Judocus Smits (1813), Olegario Victor Andrade (1841), William Rockhill Nelson (1841), Luther Burbank (1849), Matilde Serao (Tuffolina) (1856), Paul Ernst (1866), Ben Ames Williams (1889), Vera Fjodorova Panova (1905), Mircea Eliade (1907), Greta Schoon (1909), Leo Malet (1909), Mochtar Lubis (1919), John Patrick Gillese (1920), Kobo Abe (1924), Jean-Paul Desbiens (1927), Robert (Sampson) Elegant (1928), Frederick (William) Nolan (1931), Georges Perec (1936), Harald Gerlach (1940), Paul Preuss (1942), Jorgen Theobaldy (1944), Stanley Schmidt (1944), David Boyd (1951), Robert Harris (1957), Rick Bass (1958), Bret Easton Ellis (1964).

For those who do not think, it is best at least to rearrange their prejudices once in a while.—Luther Burbank

The Persians were right, in their poetry, to compare women's hair to snakes.—Mircea Eliade

Writing a novel—unlike operating a piece of heavy machinery, say, or cooking a chicken—is not a skill that can be taught. There is no standard way of doing it, just as there is no means of telling, while you're doing it, whether you're doing it well or badly. And merely because you've done it well once doesn't mean you can do it well again.—Robert Harris

I'm not a big believer in disciplined writers. What does discipline mean? The writer who forces himself to sit down and write for seven hours every day might be wasting those seven hours if he's not in the mood and doesn't feel the juice. I don't think discipline equals creativity.—Bret Easton Ellis

Mar. 8—Christopher Pearse Cranch (1813), Ede Szigligeti (1814), João de Deus (1830), Kenneth Grahame (1859), M. Lichnowsky (1879), Stuart Chase (1888), Gene Fowler (1890), Eric (Robert Russell) Linklater (1899), Elmer (Merrifield) Keith (1899), R. W. Schnell (1916), Leslie (Aaron) Fiedler and A. Marja (ATE Mooy) (1917), (John) Douglass Wallop (III) (1920), H. Kipphardt (1922), Sembene Ousmane (1923), Victor "Toby" Neuberg (1924), Jonathan Williams (1929), John McPhee (1931), Neil Postman (1931), Sylvia Fraser (1935), Richard (George) Fariña (1937), George William Reed (1939), Jim Bouton (1939), Arimasa Osawa (1956), Jeffrey (Kent) Eugenides (1960).

Monkeys . . . very sensibly refrain from speech, lest they should be set to earn their livings.—Kenneth Grahame

I find it difficult to believe that words have no meaning in themselves, hard as I try. Habits of a lifetime are not lightly thrown aside.—Stuart Chase

Writing is easy: All you do is sit staring at a blank sheet of paper until drops of blood form on your forehead.—Gene Fowler

To read a group of novels these days is a depressing experience. After the fourth or fifth, I find myself thinking about "The Novel" and I feel a desperate desire to sneak out to a movie.—Leslie Fiedler

Mar. 9—Friederike C. Neuber (1697), Honore Mirabeau (1749), William Cobbett (1763), Taras Shevchenko (1814), Umberto Saba (1883), David Garnett (1892), Joseph Weinheber and Vita Sackville-West (1892), Frank Arnau (1894), Robert Menzies McAlmon (1895), Laurence Henry Scott (1896), Peter C. Quennell and Rex Warner (1905), Kenneth (Carter) Benton (1909), Ed(uard) Hoornik (1910), Ger(ar)da Brautigam (1913), Frank Morrison "Mickey" Spillane (1918), Herbert Gold (1924), Lore (Groszmann) Segal (1928), Marie Cardinal (1929), Heere Heeresma (1932), Keri Hulme (1947), Michael Kinsley (1951), Keven Wade (1954), Shashi Tharoor (1956), Jack Kenny (1958), and Michael Patrick MacDonald (1966).

Among the many problems which beset the novelist, not the least weighty is the choice of the moment at which to begin his novel.—Vita Sackville-West

If you're a singer, you lose your voice. A baseball player loses his arm. A writer gets more knowledge, and if he's good, the older he gets, the better he writes.—Mickey Spillane

I don't go by my caste, creed or religion. My works speak for me.—Shashi Tharoor

Mar. 10—Constantine Huygens Jr. (1628), Lorenzo da Ponte (1749), Georg F. Creuzer (1771), Friedrich von Schlegel (1772), Joseph Freiherr von Eichendorff (1788), Samuel Ferguson (1810), Louis-Ovide Brunet (1826), Ina Donna Coolbrith (1841), Henry Watson Fowler (1858), Tekahionwake/E. Pauline Johnson (Emily Pauline Johnson) (1861), Pim (Willem J. H.) Mulier (1865), Jakob Wassermann (1873), David M. Chumaceiro (1877), Karel van de Woestijne (1878), Nancy Cunard (1896), Heywood Hale Broun (1918), Boris Vian (1920), Manolis Anagnostakis (1925), Georges Dor and John (Francisco) Rechy (1931), Hugh Nissenson (1933), Alfredo Zitarrosa (1936), David (William) Rabe (1940), Laurie Langenbach (1947), Johanna (Helen Howard) Lindsey (1952), Juliusz Machulski (1955), Anne MacKenzie (1960), David Grann (1967), Felice Arena and John Miller (1968), Rodrigo (Salago) Bascuñán and Nicholas Stoller (1976).

Man is a creative retrospection of nature upon itself.—Karl Wilhelm Friedrich Schlegel

In the march up the heights of fame there comes a spot close to the summit in which man reads nothing but detective stories.— Heywood Hale Broun

Choosing to write a play is some kind of surrender. I don't make an outline. I sit and work, and suddenly the door opens, and out it comes.—David Rabe

Mar. 11—Torquato Tasso (1544), Hendrik L. Spieghel (1549), Isaac Elsevier (1596), Robert Bage (1730), Jan F. Willems (1793), Pearl Rivers (Eliza Jane Poitevent Holbrook Nicholson) (1843), Antonio C. G. Crespo (1846), Wobbe de Vries (1863), Jan Lemaire (1884), Josef Martin Bauer (1902), Dorothy Schiff and Ronald Syme (1903), Maurits Wertheim (1904), Fitzroy Maclean (1911), Robert Clifford Latham (1912), Karl Krolow (1915), Ezra Jack Keats (1916), D. J. Enright (1920), Francis Marion "F. M." Busby Jr. and Barbara "Elizabeth" Linington (1921), A. X. Gwerder (1923), Ad(rianus C.) de Besten (1923), Adrienne Keith Cohen (1926), Rupert Murdoch (1931), Sam Donaldson (1934), Antonin Gregory Scalia (1936), Douglas Adams (1952), D. J. MacHale and Cyrus Mistry (1956), Flemming Rose (1958), Dejan Stojanović (1959), Martha Elizabeth "Libba" Bray (1964), Deborah (Elizabeth) Copaken (1966), Delia Gallagher (1970), and Christopher Rice (1978).

And really, the basis, I think, of achieving some success in what I want to do today comes from my mother's push to get me to read and to make something of myself from the standpoint of an education.—Sam Donaldson

I seldom end up where I wanted to go, but almost always end up where I need to be.—Douglas Adams

There was a story out there and we had to cover it. We just chose to cover it in a different way, according to the principle: don't tell it, show it.—Flemming Rose

Mar. 12—Johann Heinrich Hottinger (1620), John Aubrey (1626), Richard Steele (1672), George Berkeley (1685), Louis-Prosper Gachard (1800), Thomas Buchanan Read (1822), Adolf A. Wolfschoon (1863), Gabriele D'Annunzio (1863), Stewart Edward White (1873), Jackson Gregory (1882), Philip Guedalla (1889), Þórbergur Þórðarson (1889), A. Evert Taube (1890), Irving (Peter) Layton and Kylie Tennant (1912), Jack Kerouac (1922), Harry (Max) Harrison (b. Henry Maxwell Dempsey) (1925), John Clellon Holmes (1926), Edward (Franklin) Albee (1928), U Win Tin (1929), Virginia (Esther) Hamilton (1934), John Gross (1935), M. A. Numminen (1940), Peter Whalley (1946), Sandra (Lynn) Brown (1948), Mary Alice Williams (1949), Susan Musgrave (1951), Eliézer Niyitegeka and Naomi Shihab Nye (1952), Carl Hiaasen (1953), Randall Kenan (1963), Steve Levy (1965), Karen Marie Connelly and Jake Tapper (1969), Dave Eggers (1970), and Simon Young (1976).

Reading is to the mind what exercising is to the body.—Richard Steele

Write in recollection and amazement for yourself.—Jack Kerouac

Good writers define reality; bad ones merely restate it. A good writer turns fact into truth; a bad writer will, more often than not, accomplish the opposite.—Edward Albee

Mar. 13—John Theophilus Desaguliers (1683), Charles Bonnet (1720), Karl F. Schinkel (1781), Oswald Garrison Villard (1872), Balthazar H. Verhagen (1881), Emanuel Stickelberger (1884), Oskar Loerke and Hugh S. Walpole (1884), Janet Flanner and Joseph Peyré (1892), Dorothy Aldis (1896), Marcel Thiry (1897), Jan Lechoń (1899), Giorgos/George Seferis (Georgios Seferiades) (1900), Margaret Craven (1901), Albert Hughes Williams (1907), L(aFayette) Ron Hubbard (1911), Sergey Mikhalkov (1913), Willliam Ormond "W. O." Mitchell (1914), Pierre Gascar (Pierre Fournier) (1916), Maria Vlamynck (1917), Jim Rodger (1922), Charles Sickman Corsen (1927), Ellen (Ermingard) Raskin (1928), J. D. Slater and Linnea Eleanor "Bunny" Yeager (1929), Marc Dessauvage (1931), Barry Hughart (1934), Michael Walzer (1935), Mahmoud Darwish (1941), Andre Techine (1943), Didier Decoin (1945), Charles Krauthammer and Stephen Reid (1950), Ridley Pearson (1953), Cynthia Tucker Haynes (1955), Yuri Andrukhovych (1960), Robert Lanham (1971).

I almost think there is no wisdom comparable to that of exchanging what is called the realities of life for dreams.—Hugh Walpole

One tends to overlook the fact that all during the 30's and actually during the late 40's I was a highly successful writer and a great many properties accumulated during that period of time.—L. Ron Hubbard

Sometimes I feel as if I am read before I write. When I write a poem about my mother, Palestinians think my mother is a symbol for Palestine. But I write as a poet, and my mother is my mother. She's not a symbol.—Mahmoud Darwish

Mar. 14—Friedrich Gottlieb "F. G." Klopstock (1803), Théodore de Banville (1823), Alexandru Macedonski (1854), Algernon Blackwood (1869), Johannes Carl Andersen (1873), Isadore Gilbert Mudge (1875), Carel T. Scharten (1878), Albert Einstein (1879), John P. Strijbos (1891), Maria Valtorta (1897), Arnold Chikobava (1898), William R(obert) Cox (1901), Maurice (Jean Jacques) Merleau-Ponty (1908), André Pieyre de Mandiargues (1909), Horton Foote (1916), Macha Louis Rosenthal (1917), Max Shulman (1919), Colin Fletcher (1922), John Barrington Wain (1925), Joop F. Wolff (1927), Michael Caine (Maurice J. Micklewhite) (1933), Bertrand Blier (1939), Geoffrey Ursell (1943), Peter Paul Zahl (1944), Herman(us J.) van Veen (1945), Pam Ayres (1947), Lynn Collins Emanuel and Michael Stedman (1949), Andrew Robinson (1957), Tad Williams (1957), Kevin Williamson (1965).

I used to tell strange, wild, improbable tales akin to ghost stories, and discovered a taste for spinning yarns.—Algernon Blackwood

A writer has an inescapable voice. I think it's inherent in the nature, and I think that we don't control it anymore than we control what we want to write about.—Horton Foote

Comedy is underrepresented in every actor's life, because it's so bloody difficult to write.—Michael Caine

Mar. 15—Johann Jakob Breitinger (1701), Branko Radicevic (1824), Harriet E. Wilson (1825), Paul (Johann Ludwig) von Heyse (1830), Richard Henry Boyd (1843), Augusta Gregory (1852), Rodrigues Ottolengui (1861), Sui Sin Far (Edith Maude Eaton) (1865), Lionel Pigot Johnson (1867), John C(unyus) Hodges (1892), Gilberto Freye (1900), An Rutgers van der Loeff-Basenau (1910), Louis Paul Boon (1912), Leonard Byron "Len" Peterson (1917), Richard Ellmann (1918), Lawrence Sanders (1920), Madelyn Pugh (1921), Louis Boon (1922), Juij Bondarew (1924), Robert Nye and Jack Whyte (1939), Margo Coleman (1940), Jacques Doillon (1944), Mark J. Green (1945), Kate Bornstein (1948), Ken Ludwig (1950), Brian F. Haig and Heather Graham/Shannon Drake (Heather Graham Pozzessere) (1953), Ben Okri (1959), Jennifer 8. Lee and Jose Sanchez Zolliker (1976), Adel Iskandar (Adel Iskandar Farag) (1977), F.V.A. Morriello (1985).

From *Merlin*: "The old, endless, approachable and always answering Sorrow," says my father Lucifer. "For who calls on me never goes unanswered. Only prayers to God go without answers." — Robert Nye

Square wheels are hard to sell— Jack Whyte

I used to, when I was younger, be into personal growth.— Jennifer 8. Lee

Mar. 16—Pieter Corneliszoon Hooft (1581), Gerbrant A. Bredero (1585), René Le Bossu (1631), Marie Madeleine La Fayette (1634), Bengt Lidner (1757), Peter Ernst von Lasaulx (1805), Ernest Feydeau (1821), Camilo Castelo Branco (1825), René François Armand (Sully) Prudhomme (1839), Maxim Gorki (1868), F. A. Forbes (1869), Ethel Anderson (1883), Irita Bradford Van Doren (1891), Francisco Ayala (1906), Samael Aun Weor (1917), Albert Sidney "Sid" Fleischman (1920), Geoffrey Freeman Allen and Harding Lemay (1922), Jerry Lewis (Joseph Levitch) (1926), Daniel Patrick Moynihan (1927), Don (Richard) Carpenter (1931), Edna Buchanan (1939), Margaret (Edith) Weis (1948), Alice Hoffman (1952), Kate Worley (1958), R. Quin Edmonson Hillyer (1964), David Liss (1966), Tracy K. Smith (1972).

If I had a lover who wanted to hear from me every day, I would break with him.— Marie Madeleine de La Fayette

People think I'm against critics because they are negative to my work. That's not what bothers me. What bothers me is they didn't see the work. I have seen critics print stuff about stuff I cut out of the film before we ran it. So don't tell me about critics.—Jerry Lewis

I always felt and still feel that fairy tales have an emotional truth that is so deep that there are few things that really rival them.—Alice Hoffman

Mar. 17—Daniel van Papenbroeck (1628), Alexander Knox (1757), Ebenezer Elliott (1781), Karl Ferdinand Gutzkow (1811), Jean Ingelow (1820), Oskar Peschel (1826), Corra Mae Harris (1869), Kristian Elster (1881), Urmuz (Demetru Dem. Demetrescu-Buzău) (1883), Frank (Howard) Buck (1884), Wilbur Daniel Steele (1886), Paul Green (1894), Boris N. Poveloi (Kampov) (1908), Bayard Rustin (1910), Arthur Basil Cotle (1917), Ennis (Samuel) Rees (Jr.) (1925), Siegfried Lenz (1926), Kenneth S. Goldstein (1927), Nancy Sheehan (1927), Penelope (Margaret) Lively (1933), Louise Armstrong (1937), John Thompson (1938), James Morrow (1947), William (Ford) Gibson (1948), Peter Robinson (1950), Lawrence Christopher Patrick "Ytzhak" Braithwaite (1963), William Patrick "Billy" Corgan Jr. (1967), Marc Gunn (1972), Zachery "Zach" Kouwe (1978).

I'd luv to kiss ya, but I just washed my hair.—Paul Green
To be afraid is to behave as if the truth were not true.—Bayard Rustin
Language is to the mind more than light is to the eye.—William Gibson

Mar. 18—Cornelis Ketel (1548), Manuel de Faria e Sousa (1590), Matthew Decker (1679), Friedrich Hebbel (1813), William Cosmo Monkhouse (1840), Stéphane Mallarmé (1842), Michael G. de Boer (1867), Bernard Cronin (1884), Marianne (Goudeket-)Philips (1886), Margaret (Frances) Culkin Banning (1891), Robert P(eter) T(ristram) Coffin (1892), Wilfred Owen (1893), Srečko Kosovel (1904), William Hutchinson Murray (1913), Richard (Thomas) Condon (1915), Bob Broeg (1918), Egon Bahr (1922), George (Ames) Plimpton (1927), Christa Wolf (1929), John Updike (1932), Unita (Brown) Blackwell (1933), Hans Peter Bleuel (1936), Mark Medoff (1940), Wolfgang Bauer (1941), Joy Fielding (1945), Patrick Barlow (1947), Richard Kretchmer (1950), Franz Wright (1953), Luc Besson (1959), and Max Barry (1973).

It is also one of the pleasures of oral biography, in that the reader, rather than editor, is jury.—George Plimpton

I want to write books that unlock the traffic jam in everybody's head.—John Updike

I might not write fiction in the literary sense. But I write very well. My characters are good. My dialogue is good. And my stories are really involving.—Joy Fielding

Mar. 19—Benedetto Varchi (1503), Tobias Smollett (1721), Zacharias H. Alewijn (1742), Richard Francis Burton (1821), Patricius Walker (William Allingham) (1824), Ulrika "Minna" Cant-Johnstown (1844), Willem H. de Beaufort (1845), James Otis (James Otis Kaler) (1848), Peter Joseph Hamilton (1859), Josef Albers (1888), L. O'Flaherty (1897), Patrick Quentin/Q. Patrick/Jonathan Stagge (Hugh Callingham Wheeler) (1912), Irving Wallace (Wallechinsky) (1916), Kjell Aukrust (1920), FrancEyE (Frances Dean Smith) (1922), Jacqueline S. "Jackie" Moore (1926), Philip Roth (1933), Renée Taylor (1933), Borge Andersen (1934), Lynne Sharon Schwartz (1939), Bigas Luna (1945), Kristjana Gunnars (1948), Robert (Frederic) Schenkkan (Jr.) (1953), Jill Ellen Abramson (1954), Jorma Taccone (1977).

Some folks are wise and some are otherwise.—Tobias Smollett
Every man can transform the world from one of monotony and drabness to one of excitement and adventure.—Irving Wallace
The road to hell is paved with works-in-progress.—Philip Roth

Mar. 20—Ovid (Publius Ovidius Naso) (43 BCE), Anne (Dudley) Bradstreet (1612), Friedrich Hölderlin (1770), Karl August Nicander (1799), Thomas Cooper (1805), Mary Elizabeth Hewitt (1807), Ned Buntline (Edward Zane Carroll Judson) (c1813), Carel Vosmaer (1826), Henrik Ibsen (1828), Auguste Bender (1846), Louis Marie Émile Bertrand (1866), Obe Postma (1868), Karin Michaelis (1872), Börries von Münchhausen (1874), S. V. Vegesack (1888), (John) Hugh MacLennan (1907), Kathryn Forbes (Kathryn Anderson McLean) (1908), Jerre Mangione (1909), Donald Featherstone (1918), Ray Goulding and Carl Reiner (1922), Shaukat Siddiqui (1923), David Malouf (1934), Elizabeth Gille, Jeremy Larner, and Lois (Ann Hammersberg) Lowry (1937), Gerard Malanga (1943), Jonathan "John" de Lancie and Jay Ingram (1945), John Eastburn Boswell (1947), Ronni Sanlo (1948), Curt Smith (1951), Liana Kanelli and Louis Sachar (1954), Sheldon Jackson "Spike" Lee (1957), Mary Roach (1959), Kathryn Harrison (1961), Maggie Estep (1963), William Dalrymple (William Hamilton-Dalrymple) (1965), Touré (1971), Andrzej Pilipiuk (1974).

Habits change into character.—Ovid

A thousand words will not leave so deep an impression as one deed.—Henrik Ibsen

A lot of times, we censor ourselves before the censor even gets there.—Spike Lee

Mar. 21—Jean Paul (1763), Neith Boyce (Hapgood) (1872), Geoffrey Dearmer (1893), Richard Leslie Hill (1901), William Downie Forrest (1902), Phyllis McGinley (1905), John Paxton (1911), Peter Bull (1912), Frank Hardy (1917), Geoffrey Pinnington (1919), Peter Brook and Madison (Percy) Jones (1925), Andre Delvaux and Virginia Weidler (1926), Peter Hacks (1928), Hubert Fichte (1935), Michael Dibdin (1947), Lesley Choyce (1951), Pearl Luke (1958), Mark Waid (1962).

In Australia, not reading poetry is the national pastime.—Phyllis McGinley

I've always worked a bit like a cook in a big restaurant, where you've got lots and lots of things laid out and you go and look into one cauldron and you look into the other and you see what's coming to the boil.—Peter Brook

Imagine living in a country where the cops are all people who're cut out for the job.—Michael Dibdin

Mar. 22—Antonio Francesco Grazzini (1503), Edward Moore (1712), Anton Raphael Mengs (1728), Heinrich D Zschokke (1771), Theodor Birt (1852), Arnold Sauwen (1857), Ellen Glasgow (1874), Giulia D. De Albertis (1896), Ellin MacKay Berlin (1902), Jochen Klepper and Maurice Valency (1903), Albrecht Goes and Louis (Dearborn) L'Amour (1908), Jack Popplewell and Gabrielle Roy (1909), Nicholas Monsarret (1910), Georgiy Zhzhonov (1915), Stewart Stern (1922), Dmitri Antonovitch Volkogonov (1928), Stephen (Joshua) Sondheim (1930), Igor Hajek (1931), Leslie Thomas (1931), William Shatner (1931), Alan Bleasdale and Dean Faulkner Wells (1936), William James "Billy" Collins (1941), Rudy/Rudolf (von Bittner) Rucker (1946), Érik Orsenna (Érik Arnoult) and James (Brendan) Patterson (1947), Wolf Blitzer (1948), Diane Mott Davidson (1949), James "Jim" McManus (1951).

I suppose I am a born novelist, for the things I imagine are more vital and vivid to me than the things I remember.—Ellen Glasgow

Failure is very difficult for a writer to bear, but very few can manage the shock of early success.—Maurice Valency

The basic quality that any great story must have is a story that illustrates the human condition.—William Shatner

I'm trying to write poems that involve beginning at a known place, and ending up at a slightly different place. I'm trying to take a little journey from one place to another, and it's usually from a realistic place, to a place in the imagination.—Billy Collins

Mar. 23—John Bartram (1699), Jeronimo de Bosch Kemper (1808), Aleksej F. Pisemski (1821), Eduard Schlagintweit (1831), Alexandru D. Xenopol (1847), Thomas Chapais (1858), Madison Cawein and Paul Leicester Ford (1865), Roger Martin du Guard (1881), Robert N. Bradbury (1886), Encarnacion Alzona (1895), Erich Fromm (1900), H(enry) Beam Piper (1904), Eleanor Frances (Butler) Cameron (1912), Francis Berry (1915), H. C. Allen (1917), Wolfgang Altendorfer (1921), Barry Cryer (1936), Jim Trelease (1941), Walter Rodney (1942), Winston (Francis) Groom Jr. and Nils-Aslak Valkeapää (1943), Kim Stanley Robinson (1952), Bruce William "B. W." Powe (1955), Julia Glass and Steven Saylor (1956), (Oscar) Michael Moore and Terry Sweeney (1960), Gary Whitehead (1965), Mitch Cullin (1968).

You can never properly predict the future as it really turns out. So you are doing something a little different when you write science fiction. You are trying to take a different perspective on now.—**Kim Stanley Robinson**

Even the crudest, most derivative novel is an expression of the author's hopes and fears and ideas about good and evil.—**Steven Saylor**

I've always felt so grateful that I dropped out of school, that I never had to do a thesis. I wouldn't know how to organise and structure myself to film so that B follows A and C follows B.—**Michael Moore**

Mar. 24—Arai Hakuseki (1657), Jose F. de Isla (Francisco de Salazar) (1703), Thomas Rowley (1721), Joel Barlow (1754), Robert Hamerling (1830), William Morris and John Wesley Powell (1834), Honoré Beaugrand (1848), Silas Hocking (1850), Olive Schreiner (1855), Harry Houdini (Erich Weiss) (1874), Top Naeff (Anthonetta van Rhijn-N-Naeff) (1878), John Knittel (1891), Gianna Manzini (1896), Malcolm Muggeridge (1903), Andre Christiaens and Pura Santillan-Castrence (1905), John Cameron Swayze (1906), Janet Harmon Bragg and Lydia Korneevna Chukovskaya (1907), Donald Hamilton (1916), Lawrence Ferlinghetti (1919), Mary (Slattery) Stolz (1920), Wilson Harris (1921), Dario Fo (1926), Martin Walser (1927), Peter Bichsel (1935), John Robert Colombo and David (Takayoshi) Suzuki (1936), Ian Hamilton and David Irving (1938), Pieter W. Coetzer (1947), Irina Ratushinskaya (1954), José Rivera (1955), Taj Matthews (1976).

It took me years to understand that words are often as important as experience, because words make experience last.—William Morris

People do not believe lies because they have to, but because they want to.—Malcolm Muggeridge

Constantly risking absurdity and death whenever he performs above the heads of his audience, the poet, like an acrobat, climbs on rhyme to a high wire of his own making.—Lawrence Ferlinghetti

Mar. 25—Maria Tesselschade Roemers Visscher (1594), Louis Moréri (1643), Paul de Rapin (1661), Paulin Paris (1800), Jose de Espronceda y Delgado (1808), Alexander Ivanovich Herzen (1812), Gustaaf D. F. L. Schamelhout (1869), Alphonse (Van Bredenbeck) de Châteaubriant (1877). Louis Dosfel (1881), Mary Gladys Webb (1891), Veit Valentin (1885), Marten Baersma (M. H. Bottema) (1890), Jacques Audiberti and Bella Spewack (1899), Alan J. P. Taylor (1905), Marthe Robert (1914), Paul Mark Scott (1920), Mary Douglas (1921), Douglas Lochhead (1922), Roberts (Scott) Blossom and David Ferry (1924), Theodore (Vernon) Enslin and Flannery O'Connor (1925), Carter Curtis Revard (1931), Gloria Steinem (1934), Hoyt (Wayne) Axton (1938), Toni Cade Bambara (Miltona Mirkin Cade) (1939), Jacqueline Lichtenberg and Richard O'Brien (1942), Stephen Hunter (1946), Paul Levinson (1947), Thom Loverro and Elli Stai (1954), Jim Uhls (1957), Fred Goss (1961), Katrina Elizabeth "Kate" DiCamillo (1964).

Everywhere I go I'm asked if I think the university stifles writers. My opinion is that they don't stifle enough of them. There's many a bestseller that could have been prevented by a good teacher.
—Flannery O'Connor

Without leaps of imagination, or dreaming, we lose the excitement of possibilities. Dreaming, after all, is a form of planning.—Gloria Steinem

However, there's three reasons for doing things in this particular world. One is love, one is prestige and the other's money. If you get all three together, that's fine.—Richard O'Brien

Mar. 26—Conrad Gessner (1516), William Wollaston (1659), Nathaniel Bowditch (1773), Louise Otto (1819), Eliza Laurillard (1830), Betsy Perk (Christina E.) (1833), Edward Bellamy (1850), Alfred Edward "A. E." Housman (1859), Serafín Álvarez Quintero (1871), Robert Frost (1874), Duncan Hines (1880), Jozef Arras (1890), James B. Connant (1899), Joseph Campbell (1904), Viktor Emil Frankl (1905), Betty MacDonald (Anne E. Campbell Bard) (1908), Thomas Lanier "Tennessee" Williams (1911), Sterling Hayden (Sterling Relyea Walter) (1916), Bob Elliott (1923), Gregory (Nunzio) Corso (1930), Leonard Nimoy (1931), Patrick Lane (1939), Richard Dawkins (1941), Larry Butler and Erica (Mann) Jong (1942), Robert Woodward (1943), Patrick Süskind (1949), Martin Short (1950), Chris Hansen (1959), Natsuhiko Kyogoku (1963), Martin McDonagh (1970), Andrew Ervin (1971).

Nature, not content with denying him the ability to think, has endowed him with the ability to write.—A. E. Housman

A poem . . . begins as a lump in the throat, a sense of wrong, a homesickness . . . . It finds the thought and the thought finds the words.—Robert Frost

You see a lot of smart guys with dumb women, but you hardly ever see a smart woman with a dumb guy.—Erica Jong

There have to be moments when you glimpse something decent, something life-affirming even in the most twisted character. That's where the real art lies. See, I always suspect characters who are painted as lovely, decent human beings. I would always question where the darkness lies.—Martin McDonagh

Mar. 27—Benjamin Neukirch (1665), Francesco Antonio Zaccaria (1714), Michael Bruce (1746), Alfred V Comte de Vigny (1797), A. Glabbrenner (1810), Frank Frost Abbott (1860), Patty Smith Hill (1868), Heinrich Mann (1871), Marie Under (1883), Yakup Kadri Karaosmanoglu (1889), (James) Thorne Smith (Jr.) (1892), Gloria (May Josephine) Swanson (1897), Jacques (Izaak) den Haan (1908), Golo Mann (Angelus Gottfried Thomas Mann) (1909), Seymour Wilson "Budd" Schulberg (1914), Denton Welch (1915), Simon van Collem (1919), Stefan Wul (1922), Shusaku Endo and Louis (Aston Marantz) Simpson (1923), Francis Russell "Frank" O'Hara (1926), Anthony Lewis (1927), Bob den Uyl (1930), Abelardo Castillo (1935), Joanne Dobson, Michael (James) Jackson, and Michael York (1942), Bebu Silvetti (Juan Fernando Silvetti Adorno) (1944), Walt Mossberg (1947), Julia Alvarez (1950), Dana Stabenow (1952), Patrick McCabe (1955), Clare Lucy Madeleine Evans and Jess Mowry (1960), Quentin Tarantino (1963), Pauley Perrette (1969), Dorothea Lasky (1978).

I'll be eighty this month. Age, if nothing else, entitles you to set the record straight before I dissolve. I've given my memoirs far more thought than any of my marriages. You can't divorce a book.—Gloria Swanson

Silence is the sure sign that you're on your way out in Hollywood.—Budd Schulberg

The First Amendment is very important, but it's not everything.—Anthony Lewis

I think that you have to believe in your destiny; that you will succeed, you will meet a lot of rejection and it is not always a straight path, there will be detours—so enjoy the view.—Michael York

Mar. 28—Arnold Houbraken (1660), William Byrd (1674), Andrew Kippis (1725), Sophie Mereau (1770), Henry (Rowe) Schoolcraft (1793), Georg Heinrich Pertz (1795), Alexandre Herculano de Carvalho e Araújo (1810), Arsène Houssaye (1815), James Darmesteter (1849), Maxim Gorky (Alexei Maximovich Peshkov) (1868), Karel MJF Cruysberghs (1891), Nelson Algren (1909), J. L. Austin and Myfanwy Piper (1911), A(rthur) Bertram Chandler (1912), Edward Anhalt and Bohumil Hrabal (1914), Gerhart Fritsch (1924), Frederick Earl "Fred" Exley (1929), Amelia Rosselli (1930), Jane (Vance) Rule (1931), Sven Oskar Lindqvist (1932), Mario Vargas Llosa (1936), Russell Banks (1940), Daniel (Clement) Dennett (III) (1942), Peter (John) Hennessy (1947), Lisa Moore (1964), Taylor McDowell Mali (1965), Iris Chang (1968), Ada Limón (1976), Lauren Weisberger (1977).

You must write for children in the same way as you do for adults, only better.—**Maxim Gorky**

The hard necessity of bringing the judge on the bench down into the dock has been the peculiar responsibility of the writer in all ages of man.—**Nelson Algren**

Naturally, I mine my girlfriends' lives for good anecdotes and stories—so many of their experiences find their way into my books.—**Lauren Weisberger**

Mar. 29—Vitsentzos Kornaros (1553), John Lightfoot (1602), Alexander Chalmers (1759), Constantine S. Aksakov (1817), Amelia Edith Huddleston Barr (1831), Joseph Schmidlin (1876), Howard Lindsay (1889), Ivan Goll (1891), Cecil Lewis (1898), Frans U. Kailas (1901), Marcel Aymé (1902), Yvonne Waegemans (1909), Ronald Stuart "R. S." Thomas (1913), Julia Montgomery Walsh (1923), Sheila Kitzinger (1929), Jacques Brault (1933), Judith Guest (1936), Eric Idle (1943), John Suchet (1944), Edward Richard Holmes (1946), Nick Brune (1952), Elizabeth Hand (1957), Jo Nesbø (1960), Santiago (Rafael) Roncagliolo Lohmann (1975).

But the lover's power is the poet's power. He can make love from all the common strings with which this world is strung.—Amelia Barr

I shall give you hunger, and pain, and sleepless nights. Also beauty, and satisfactions known to few, and glimpses of the heavenly life. None of these you shall have continually, and of their coming and going you shall not be foretold.—Howard Lindsay

I think the special thing about Python is that it's a writers' commune. The writers are in charge. The writers decide what the material is.—Eric Idle

Mar. 30—Maimonedes (Moshe ben Maimon) (1135), Jethro Tull (1674), John Hawkins (1719), Anna Sewell (1820), John Fiske (Edmund Fisk Green) (1842), Paul M. Verlaine (1844), Sean O'Casey (1880), Erwin Panofsky (1892), Jean Giono (1895), Heinz Risse (1898), Sharadindu Bandyopadhyay (1899), Andrew Rodger Waterson (1912), McGeorge Bundy (1913), Milton Acorn and Herbert Asmodi (1923), Symmes Chadwick "Chad" Oliver and Tom Sharpe (1928), Ted Morgan (1932), Jon Hassler (1933), Gerrit Komrij (1944), Ron Miksha (1954), Stephen Francis Tomajczyk (1960), Efstratios Grivas (1966).

Do not consider it proof just because it is written in books, for a liar who will deceive with his tongue will not hesitate to do the same with his pen.—Maimonides

My doctrine is this, that if we see cruelty or wrong that we have the power to stop, and do nothing, we make ourselves sharers in the guilt.—Anna Sewell

All the world's a stage and most of us are desperately unrehearsed.—Sean O'Casey

Mar. 31—René Descartes (1596), Andrew Marvell (1621), Edward FitzGerald (1809), Nikolay Przhevalsky (1839), Andrew Lang (1844), Borisav "Bora" Stanković (1876), Bertram (Richard) Brooker (1888), Ion Pillat and Esther Kreitman (Hinde Ester Singer Kreytman) (1891), Vardis A Fisher (1895), Robert Brasillach (1909), William (Julius) Lederer (Jr.) (1912), Octavio Paz (1914), Marga (Sara Voeten-) Minco (1920), Leo Buscaglia (1924), John Fowles (1926), John Jakes (1932), Nichita Stănescu (1933), Richard Chamberlain and Judith (Perelman) Rossner (1935), Marge Piercy (1936), Israel Horovitz (1939), Valerie Curtin (1945), David Eisenhower (1948), Beverle Graves Myers (1951), Gabriel Alberro (1976).

The reading of all good books is like a conversation with the finest minds of past centuries.—René Descartes

But at my back I always hear Time's wingéd chariot hurrying near.—Andrew Marvell

Be persistent. Editors change; tastes change; editorial markets change. Too many beginning writers give up too easily.—John Jakes

I knew I'd have to go to work in real estate or something else or I could never finish my novel.—Judith Rossner

Born in April

Apr. 1—John Wilmot, 2nd Earl of Rochester (1647), Antoine François Prévost (1697), Martha Wadsworth Brewster (1710), Joseph de Maistre (1753), Fredrik Cygnaeus (1807), Nikolai Gogol (1809), Arnold Aletrino (1858), Gaetano Mosca (1859), Marie Jungius (1864), Edmond Rostand (1868), Peter A. Egge (1869), Edgar Wallace (1875), Carl Sternheim (1878), Leonard Bloomfield (1887), Roger Bastide and Pola Gojawiczynska (1898), Whittaker Chambers (1901), Maria Polydouri (1902), Juan Gil-Albert (1904), Abraham H. Maslow (1908), Evert H. "Bep" Bakhuys and (Henry/Hanson) Orlo Miller (1911), Toshiro Mifune (1920), William Manchester (1922), Anne (Inez) McCaffrey (1926), Dimitri Frenkel Frank (1928), Milan Kundera (1929), Rolf Hochhuth (1931), Samuel R(ay) Delany Jr. (1942), Francine Prose (1947), Bruce Andrews (1948), Gill Scott-Heron (1949), Tom Gabbay (1953), David Kessler (1957), Brad Meltzer (1970).

Before I got married I had six theories about bringing up children; now I have six children, and no theories.—John Wilmot

My pessimism goes to the point of suspecting the sincerity of the pessimists.—Edmond Rostand

Long before the idea of a writer's conference was a glimmer in anyone's eye, writers learned by reading the work of their predecessors. They studied meter with Ovid, plot construction with Homer, comedy with Aristophanes; they honed their prose style by absorbing the lucid sentences of Montaigne and Samuel Johnson. —Francine Prose

Apr. 2—Onno Zwier van Haren (1713), Giacomo Girolamo Casanova (1725), Francisco Balagtas (1788), August Heinrich Hoffmann von Fallersleben (1798), Hans Christian Andersen (1805), Émile Zola (1840), Mary Raymond Shipman Andrews (1860), John Squire (1884), Roberto Arlt (1900), Kurt Adler (1905), Helen Bevington (1906), Joeri German (1910), John Marlyn (1912), George MacDonald Fraser (1925), Edward Merton "Ed" Dorn and Catherine Gaskin (1929), Howard Engel (1931), Rochelle (Bass) Owens (1936), Peter Haining (1940), Jay Parini, Joan (Carol) D(ennison) Vinge, and Anne Waldman (1948), Thierry Le Luron (1952), Mark Shulman (1962).

Worthy or not, my life is my subject, and my subject is my life.—Giacomo Casanova

It may be tripe, but it's my tripe—and I do urge other authors to resist encroachments on their brain-children and trust their own judgment rather than that of some zealous meddler with a diploma in creative punctuation who is just dying to get into the act.—George MacDonald Fraser

Each time, storytellers clothed the naked body of the myth in their own traditions, so that listeners could relate more easily to its deeper meaning.—Joan D. Vinge

Apr. 3—Lieven van der Maude (Ammonius) (1485), George Herbert (1593), Mark Catesby (1683), George Edwards (1693), Julien de Lallande Poydras (1740), Washington Irving (1783), John Banim (1798), Ivan Kireevsky (1806), Edward Everett Hale (1822), Harriet (Elizabeth) Prescott Spofford (1835), John Burroughs (1837), Frederik W. van Eeden (1860), Jose Juan Tablada (1871), Margaret M.J. "Daisy" Ashford (1881), Douwe Kalma (1896), Peter Huchel (1903), Kathleen Tillotson (1906), Isaac Deutscher (1907), Herb Caen (1916), Daniel (Gerard) Hoffman (1923), Reginald (Charles) Hill (1936), Jeff Barry (1938), Jonathan Lynn (1943), Arlette Cousture (1948), Michael Burleigh (1955).

The land of literature is a fairy land to those who view it at a distance, but, like all other landscapes, the charm fades on a nearer approach, and the thorns and briars become visible.—Washington Irving

I am only one, but I am one. I cannot do everything, but I can do something. And I will not let what I cannot do interfere with what I can do.—Edward Everett Hale

Bernard always had a few prayers in the hall and some whiskey afterwards as he was rather pious.—Daisy Ashford

Apr. 4—William Strachey (1572), Bettina von Arnim (1785), Dorothea Dix (1802), James Freeman Clarke (1810), Thomas Mayne Reid (1818), Margaret Oliphant (1828), Jose Echegaray y Elizaguirre (1832), Comte de Lautréamont (1846), Remy de Gourmont (1858), George P. Baker (1866), Henry Bataille (1872), Zdzisław Żygulski Sr. (1888), Robert Sherwood and Tristan Tzar (Samuel Rosenfeld) (1896), Louise L. de Vilmorin and Stanley G. Weinbaum (1902), Ernestine Gilbreth Carey (1908), Chaim Grade (1910), Jerome Weidman (1913), Marguerite Duras (Marguerite Donnadieu) (1914), Lars G. Ahlin and Jan Drda (1915), Emmett Williams (1925), Maya Angelou (Marguerite Johnson) (1928), Monty Norman (1928), Denis Frank Owen (1931), Trevor Griffiths (1935), Ian St. James (1937), Frances Mayes (1940), Kitty Kelley (1942), Paulette Jiles(-Johnson) (1943), Katherine Neville (1945), Larry Beckett (1947), Dan Simmons (1948), Charles Bernstein (1950), José Acquelin and David E. Kelley (1956), Pamela Ribon (1975).

Temptations come, as a general rule, when they are sought. —Margaret Oliphant

Women are the simple; and poets the superior; artisans of language. . . . [T]he intervention of grammarians is almost always bad.—Remy de Gourmont

People forget that unauthorized does not mean untrue and authorized does not mean authentic.—Kitty Kelley

Apr. 5—Thomas Hobbes (1588), Nadar (Félix Tournachon) (1820), Sydney Thompson Dobell (1824), Mary Jane Holmes (1825), Alexander Muir (1830), Frank (Richard)Stockton (1834), Algernon Charles Swinburne (1837), Booker T(aliaferro) Washington (1856), David Pinski (1872), Richard (Ghormley) Eberhart (1904), Mary Hemingway (1908), Frederick Angus Armstrong (1914), Robert (Albert) Bloch (1917), Rafique Zakaria (1920), Arthur Hailey (1920), Robert Q. Lewis (1921), Hugo Claus (1929), Larry Felser (1933), David Helwig (1938), Ann (Elizabeth) Maxwell (1944), Paul C. McKain and Guy Clarence Vanderhaeghe (1951), Charles Cumming (1971), Mary Katharine Ham (1980).

Words are the money of fools.—Thomas Hobbes
I had my share of critics, and I wash my hands of the whole lot.—Frank Stockton
The man who can smile when things go wrong has thought of someone else he can blame it on.—Robert Bloch

Apr. 6—Stjepan Gradić (1613), Jean-Baptiste Rousseau (1671), James Mill (1773), John Pierpont (1785), Philip Gosse (1810), Aasmund Olavsson Vinje (1818), (Joseph) Lincoln Steffens (1866), Erich Mühsam (1878), Mien Labberton (1883), Daniel Andersson (1888), Gabriela Mistral (1889), Lowell Thomas (1892), Robert Myron Coates (1897), Leo Robin (1900), Willem Pelemans (1901), Charles R(eginald) Jackson (1903), John Betjeman (1906), Marie (Birmingham) Ponsot (1921), Willis Hall (1929), John Pepper Clark (1935), Homero Aridjis (1940), Randy Paul Gage (1959), Vincent "Vince" Flynn (1966), Jack Canfora (1969).

Readiness of speech is often an inability to hold the tongue. —Jean-Baptiste Rousseau
Nothing fails like success.—Lincoln Steffens
Too many people in the modern world view poetry as a luxury, not a necessity like petrol. But to me it's the oil of life.—John Betjeman

Apr. 7—John Sheffield (1648), Hugh Blair (1718), William Wordsworth (1770), William Ellery Channing (1780), Flora Tristan (1803), J. P. Jacobsen (1847), Marjory Stoneman Douglas (1890), Gerald Brenan (1894), Walter Winchell (1837), Robert Charroux (1909), Roger Lemelin (1919), Johannes Mario Simmel and Lucien Stryk (1924), James White (1928), Donald Barthelme (1931), Preston Jones (1936), David Frost (1939), Megas (Magnús Þór Jónsson) (1945), Herménégilde Chiasson (1946), William Alfred "Bill" Whittle (1959), Artemis Gounaki (1967).

Fill your paper with the breathings of your heart.—William Wordsworth

I take advantage of every thing I can—age, hair, disability—because my cause [saving the Everglades] is just.—Marjory Stoneman Douglas

I write a lot—every day, seven days a week—and I throw a lot away. Sometimes I think I write to throw away; it's a process of distillation.—Donald Barthelme

The most important advice you can give anyone about to appear on TV is incredibly prosaic—be yourself.—David Frost

Apr. 8—Phienas Fletcher (1582), Jose B. da Gama (1741), Dionysios Solomos (1798), Margaret Ayer Barnes (1886), Jo Swerling (1897), Hans Scherfig (1905), Helen B. M. Fennell Joseph (1905), Charles J. B. Jonckheere (1906), John Fante (1909), Harriet Huntington Doerr (1910), Emil Mihai Cioran (1911), Glendon (Fred) Swarthout (1918), Frédéric Back (1924), Anthony Farrar-Hockley (1924), Fred Ebb (1928), Renzo de Felice (1929), William K. Everson (1929), Seymour Hersh (1937), Eduard Visser (1942), Michael Bennett (1943), Christoph Hein (1944), Bradford Morrow (1951), Barbara Kingsolver (1955), Jim Piddock (1956), Daniel Olivas (1959), Charles David "Chuck" Todd (1972), Nnedi Okorafor-Mbachu (1974), Mehran Ghassemi (1977).

I'm a better American than 99% of the guys in the White House.—Seymour Hersh

Close the door. Write with no one looking over your shoulder. Don't try to figure out what other people want to hear from you; figure out what you have to say. It's the one and only thing you have to offer.—Barbara Kingsolver

I'm an old school actor in the sense. More and more now, I play myself as I get older. Even as a writer, I never got typecast. I've always bounced from project to project or initiated my own things. —Jim Piddock

Apr. 9—Philippe Néricault Destouches (1680), Fisher Ames (1758), Étienne Aignan (1773), Charles (Pierre) Baudelaire (1821), Maria Susanna Cummins (1827), Gyula Reviczky (1855), J(ames) William Fulbright (1905), Lew Kopelew (1912), Johannes Bobrowski (1917), Carl Amery (1922), William Price Fox (1926), Thomas Andrew "Tom" Lehrer (1928), Paule Marshall (b. Valenza Pauline Burke) (1929), Bill Gilbert (1931), Barrington J(ohn) Bayley (1937), Thomas Archibald "Tom" Marshall (1938), Ken Kalfus (1954), Joolz Denby and Kate Heyhoe (1955), Charles Joseph "Joe" Scarborough (1963), Rachel (Sarah) Specter (1980).

What is conceived well is expressed clearly.—Philippe Néricault Destouches

No one ever became, or can become truly eloquent without being a reader of the Bible, and an admirer of the purity and sublimity of its language.—Fisher Ames

Always be a poet, even in prose.—Charles Baudelaire

Remember why the good Lord made your eyes, Pla-gi-a-rize! —Tom Lehrer

Apr. 10—Balthazar Huydecoper (1695), Benjamin Heath (1704), William Hazlitt (1778), George Lippard (1822), Lewis "Lew" Wallace (1827), Louise Chandler Moulton (1835), Forceythe Willson (1837), Joseph Pulitzer (1847), Alfred Kubin (1877), Montague Summers (1880), Simon F. H. J. Berkelbach Van der Sprenkel (1882), Bernardo A Houssay (1887), Horace Gregory (1898), Fray Angelico Chavez and Paul Sweezy (1910), Maurice Schumann (1911), Stefan Heym (1913), Leo Vroman (1915), Marcel van Maele (1931), Robert Rhodes James (1933), David Halberstam, Richard Peck, and Vladimir Posner (1934), Bella Akhmadulina (1937), Barbara D'Amato (1938), Clark Blaise and Mick Burrs (1940), Paul (Edward) Theroux (1941), Nick Auf der Maur and Stuart Dybek (1942), Norman Dubie (1945), Barry M. Riemer (1950), David Helvarg (1951), Anne Lamott (1954), John M(ilo) Ford (1957), Moez Surani (1979), Kendra Morris (1981).

Rules and models destroy genius and art.—William Hazlitt
Beauty is altogether in the eye of the beholder.—Lew Wallace
**I don't think anyone wants a reader to be completely lost—
certainly not to the point of giving up—but there's something to be
said for a book that isn't instantly disposable, that rewards a second
reading.—John M. Ford**

Apr. 11—Antoine Coypel (1661), Christopher Smart (1722), Manuel Jose Quintana (1772), Nicolaas C. Kist (1793), Edward Everett (1794), Claude Tillier (1801), Henry Rawlinson (1810), Edward S(ylvester) Ellis (1840), R(ichard) Austin Freeman (1862), Bernard O'Dowd (1866), Frank Oliver Call (1878), Caspar Neher (1897), Léo-Paul Desrosiers (1898), Sandor Marai (1900), Glenway Wescott (1901), József Attila (1905), Leo Rosten (1908), David Westheimer (1917), Jean-Claude Servan-Schreiber (1918), Marlen Haushofer (1920), Antoine Blondin (1922), Harold Louis "H. L." Humes Jr. (1926), Clive Exton (1930), Tony Brown (1933), Ralph Compton and Mark Strand (1934), Thomas Harris (1940), Ellen Goodman (1941), John Milius and Liza Cody (1944), Dorothy Allison (1949), Ann Diamond and James Patrick Kelly (1951), Ethel Morgan Smith (1952), Jeremy Clarkson (1960), Jon Evans (1973), Scott O. Brown and Walid Soliman (1975).

A writer writes not because he is educated but because he is driven by the need to communicate. Behind the need to communicate is the need to share. Behind the need to share is the need to be understood.—Leo Rosten

Poetry is, first and last, language—the rest is filler.—Mark Strand

You can fire your secretary, divorce your spouse, abandon your children. But they remain your co-authors forever.—Ellen Goodman

Apr. 12—Joachim Camerarius (Liebhard Kammerer) (1500), Muretus (Marc Antoine Muret) (1526), Caspar Burman (1695), Guillaume Thomas François Raynal (1713), Charles Burney (1726), Ik Marvel (Donald Grant Mitchell) (1822), Aleksandr Ostrovsky (1823), José Gautier Benítez (1848), William M. Conway (1856), Raul d'Avila Pompeia (1863), John Murray Gibbon (1875), Frederick G. Melcher (1879), Gladys (Bagg) Taber (1899), Guy Mazeline (1900), Hardie Gramatky (1907), Jorgen Rausch (1910), Emil (Theodore) Petaja (1915), Beverly Cleary and Brian Connell (1916), Carol Emshwiller (1921), George Adam Herman Jr. (1928), Henry Eric Beissel (1929), Bryan Magee (1930), Leonid Derbenyov (1931), Jack Gelber (1932), Alan Ayckbourn and William M(oses) Hoffman (1939), Charles Ludlam (1943), Peter L. de Baan (1946), Tom Clancy and Scott (Frederick) Turow (1949), Emily Mann, Gary (Anthony) Soto, and Ralph Wiley (1952), Tama Janowitz (1957).

Quite often somebody will say, "What year do your books take place?" and the only answer I can give is, in childhood.—Beverly Cleary

As a writer one is allowed to have conversations with oneself.— Alan Ayckbourn

Success is a finished book, a stack of pages each of which is filled with words. If you reach that point, you have won a victory over yourself no less impressive than sailing single-handed around the world.—Tom Clancy

Apr. 13—Peter Faber (1506), Roger de Rabutin, Comte de Bussy (1618), Jonathan Carver (1710), Thomas Percy (1729), Thomas Jefferson (1743), Heinrich F. L. Rellstab (1799), Alphonse Wauters (1817), Thomas D'Arcy McGee (1825), Juan Montalvo (1832), William Henry Drummond (1854), A. Roda Roda (1872), Demjan Bednyi (1883), Nellallitea "Nella" Larsen (1891), Jacques (Marie Émile) Lacan (1901), Samuel Beckett (1906), Eudora (Alice) Welty (1909), Reuel Denney (1913), Stephan Hermlin and Albert L. F. "Bert" Peleman (Dirk Dyckmans) (1915), Phyllis Fraser Cerf Wagner (1916), Audrey Barker (1918), Roland Gaucher (1919), Maxwell Henley Harris (1921), John Braine (1922), Michael Burchill and Beverley Cross (1931), Barney Simon (1932), Lanford Wilson (1937), Seamus (Justin) Heaney (1939), Jean-Marie Gustave "J. M. G." Le Clézio (1940). Ataol Behramoglu (1942), Bill Pronzini (1943), Rae Armantrout (1947), Amy Robinson (1948), Marilyn Bowering (1949), Charles Patrick "Chuck" Pfarrer III (1957), Francis Chalifour (1977), Colleen (Smith) Clinkenbeard (1980).

James Joyce was a synthesizer, trying to bring in as much as he could. I am an analyzer, trying to leave out as much as I can.
—Samuel Beckett

Writing a story or a novel is one way of discovering sequence in experience, of stumbling upon cause and effect in the happenings of a writer's own life.—Eudora Welty

Writing poetry involves luck, skill, dedication, patience, and disappointment. The poet throws the bait of his experience into the sea of language and waits and works for the right collection of words to attach themselves to it.—Seamus Heaney

Apr. 14—Christian Huygens (1629), George Grey (1812), René Boylesve (René M. A. Tardiveau) (1867), Daniel Plooy (1877), James Branch Cabell (1879), Anton Wildgans (1881), Moritz Schlick (1882), Ernst R. Curtius and Edward C. Tolman (1886), Horace McCoy (1897), Martin Kessel (1901), Belinda Quirey (1912), Scott (Alexander) Young (1918), William Darling (1923), Frank Daniel (1926), Fredric Jameson (1934), Erich von Däniken (1935), Tom Monteleone (1946), (Michael) Bruce Sterling (1954), Margaret Murphy (1959), Tina Rosenberg (1960), Peter Gibson (1971).

Poetry is man's rebellion against being what he is.—James Branch Cabell

Let's go sit and hate a bunch of people.—Horace McCoy

I like to get paid for doing basic research, so it's pleasant to write some nonfiction about it.—Bruce Sterling

Apr. 15—Leonardo da Vinci (1452), Claudius Salmasius (Claude Saumaise) (1588), Friedrich Bouterwek (1766), Étienne Geoffroy Saint-Hilaire (1772), John Lothrop Motley (1814), Wilhelm Busch (1832), Henry James (1843), Emile Durkheim (1858), Bliss Carman (1861), Klaziena "Ina" Boudier-Bakker (1875), Robert Walser (1878), Melville Henry Cane (1879), Giovanni Amendola (1882), Nikolay Gumilyov (1886), Maximilian Kronberger (1888), Wallace Reid (1891), Corrie ten Boom (1892), Corrado Alvaro (1895), Fernando Pessa (1902), Erich Arendt (1903), Gerald Abrahams (1907), Ernest Borneman (1915), Louis O(sborne) Coxe (1918), Meriol Trevor (1919), John Grigg (1924), Tomas (Gösta) Tranströmer (1931), Boris Strugatski (1933), Earl Russell (1937), Bennie Lee Sinclair (1939), Jeffrey Archer (1940), Albert Frank "A. F." Moritz (1947), Craig Zadan (1949), Heloise II (Kiah Michelle Cruse) (1951), Dolores Gordon-Smith, Anne Michaels, and Benjamin Zephaniah (1958), Emma Thompson (1959), Rollin Jarrett (Rollin William Jewett) (1960), Bobby Pepper (1963), Jaime Clarke (1971).

The poet ranks far below the painter in the representation of visible things, and far below the musician in that of invisible things.—Leonardo da Vinci

The only reason for the existence of a novel is that it does attempt to represent life.—Henry James

If you're actually allowing your creative part to control your writing rather than a more commercial instinct or motive, then you'll find that all sorts of interesting things will bubble up to the surface.—Emma Thompson

Apr. 16—John Luyken (1648), Charles Montagu (1661), Georg Curtius (1820), Octave Crémazie (1827), Anatole France (1844), Herbert Baxter Adams (1850), Grace Livingston Hill (1865), John Millington Synge (1871), Alice Corbin Henderson (1881), Gertrude Chandler Warner (1890), Germaine Guèvremont (1893), Robert Dean Frisbie (1895), John B. Glubb (1897), Bep (Elisa H.) Bakhuis (1906), Herman Uyttersprot (1909), Gerard McLarnon (1915), Peter Ustinov (1921), Kingsley Amis and Christopher Samuel Youd (1922), Marion Montgomery (1925), Sarah Kirsch (1935), Sandra Djwa and Diane (Helen Wood) Middlebrook (1939), Ewald Vanvugt (1943), Margot Adler (1946), Ioan Mihai Cochinescu (1951), J. Neil Schulman (1953), Essex Hemphill (1957), Bert Archer (1968), Tracy K. Smith (1972), Amelia (Holt) Atwater-Rhodes (1984).

There are no bad books, any more than there are ugly women.—Anatole France

I'm a good scholar when it comes to reading but a blotting kind of writer when you give me a pen.—John Millington Synge

The first time I called myself a 'Witch' was the most magical moment of my life.—Margot Adler

Apr. 17—John Ford (1586), Henry Vaughan (1622), François Valentijn (1666), Robert Blair (1699), William Gilmore Simms (1806), Samuel Austin Allibone (1816), David Gravson (Ray Stannard Baker) (1870), Ian Hay (1876), Anton Wildgans (1881), Isak Dinesen (Karen Blixen-Finecke) (1885), Antonius F. "Anton" Coolen and Thornton N(iven) Wilder (1897), Edward Chodorov (1904), Humphrey Sims Moore (1909), Ivan Goff (1910), Jean-Pierre Herve Bazin (1911), Bengt N. Anderberg and (Marie-Charlotte Élisabeth) Edmonde Charles-Roux (1920), Lloyd Biggle Jr., Norman Potter, and Harry Reasoner (1923), Cynthia Ozick (1928), Han J. A. Hansen (Jansen) (1932), Penelope Lively (1933), Louis Daniel Brodsky (1941), Peter Michalke and Erin Mouré (1955), Nick Hornby (1957), John M(cLaughlin) Higgins (1961).

All sorrows can be borne if you put them into a story or tell a story about them.—**Isak Dinesen**

Seek the lofty by reading, hearing and seeing great work at some moment every day.—**Thornton Wilder**

If we had to say what writing is, we would define it essentially as an act of courage.—**Cynthia Ozick**

Apr. 18—Thomas Middleton (1580), Pieter 't Hoen (1744), George Henry Lewes (1817), Henry François Becque (1837), Henry Clarence Kendall (1839), Abraham Bredius (1855), Clarence S. Darrow (1857), Richard Harding Davis (1864), Didericus G. van Epen (1868), Oskar Ernst Bernhardt (1874), Ivana Brlić-Mažuranić (1875), Vicente Sotto (1877), Lord Leatherland (Charles Edward Leatherland) (1898), Clara Eggink (Ebbele) (1906), Stephen Longstreet (1907), Claire Martin (1914), Joy Gresham Lewis (1915), Jake Copass (1920), Leif Panduro (1923), Raf de Linde (Raphael van Hecke) (1924), Richard Bausch (1945), Kathy Acker (Karen Lehmann) (1947), Conan (Christopher) O'Brien (1963), Niall Ferguson (1964), Keith R. A. DeCandido and C. Dale Young (1969), Ilya Kaminsky (1977).

Well, I think writing is basically about time and rhythm. Like with jazz. You have your basic melody and then you just riff off of it. And the riffs are about timing.—Kathy Acker

When all else fails there's always delusion.—Conan O'Brien

Oral history is a recipe for complete misrepresentation because almost no one tells the truth, even when they intend to.—Niall Ferguson

Apr. 19—Jacques Lelong (1665), Francsco Albergati Capacelli (1728), Louis Amédée Achard (1814), José Echegaray y Eizaguirre (1832), Andrea Bezzola (1840), Lucien Levy-Bruhl (1857), Warden Oncle (Edward Vermeulen) (1861), Melville Davisson Post (1869), Ricardo Bacchelli (1891), Richard (Arthur Warren) Hughes (1900), Etheridge Knight and Walter Stewart (1931), Etheridge Knight (1933), Sharon Pollock (1936), Frank(land Wilmot) Davey (1940), Frits Castricum (1947), Stuart McLean (1948), Barry Brown and Pierre Lemaitre (1951), Neil (Devindra) Bissoondath (1955), Steven H. Silver (1967), Craig McNeil (1968).

Do your bit to save humanity from lapsing back into barbarity by reading all the novels you can.—Richard Hughes

To write a blues song is to regiment riots and pluck gems from graves.—Etheridge Knight

What I learned about journalism there was that it was a suspect craft, dominated by hypocrisy, exaggeration, and fakery. At the Tely, we toadied to advertisers, eschewed investigative reporting, slanted our stories gleefully to fit the party line (Conservative) and to appeal to the one man who counted—the publisher . . . .—Walter Stewart

Apr. 20—Jafar Sadiq (702), John Agricola (Schneider) (1494), John Eliot (1592), Louis Bertrand (1807), Dina M. Craik (1826), Hermann Bang and Charles L. P. "Philip" Zilcken (1857), Maulvi Abdul Haq (1870), William Henry "W. H." Davies (1871), Robert Lynd (1879), Adolf Hitler (1889), Hermann Ungar (1893), Martinus Nijhoff (1894), G(eorge) Herbert Sallans (1895), Bernard Verhoeven (1897), Dagmar Edqvist (1903), Soewarsil Djojopoespito (1912), Patricia "Pat" Janus (1932), Lindsay Oliver John Boynton (1934), George (Hosato) Takei (1937), Peter S. Beagle and Wayson Choy (1939), Jan Cremer (1940), Ian Watson (1943), Andrew Tobias (1947), Stephen Michael "Steve" Erickson (1950), Toine van Benthem (1952), Sebastian Faulks (1953), Evan Solomon (1968), Rebecca Makkai (1978).

If you tell a big enough lie and tell it frequently enough, it will be believed.—Adolf Hitler

I began composing the next poem, the one that was to be written next. Not the last poem of those I had read, but the poem written in the head of someone who may never have existed but who had certainly written another poem nonetheless, and just never had the chance to commit it to ink and the page.—Steve Erickson

Most stories we tell in real life are under 500 words . . . . So my advice would be this: Don't get all up in your head thinking short-short stories have to be poetry without the line breaks. Don't put on your beret. Just tell a story, an actual story. Quick, while they're still listening.—Rebecca Makkai

Apr. 21—John Capgrave (1393), Ulrich von Hutten (1488), Catherine II, the Great (Sophia Augusta Frederica) (1729), Charlotte Brontë (1816), Josh Billings (Henry Wheeler Shaw) (1818), John Muir (1836), Benjamin A. Jesurun (1867), Robert (Welch) Herrick (1868), Henry (Marie Joseph Frédéric Expedite Millon) de Montherlant) (1896), Gladys Mitchell (1901), Bernard J. H. "Ben" Stroman (1902), Sanora Babb and Dorothy (Dodds) Baker (1907), Rollo May (1909), Norman Panama (1914), Andrew Glaze (1920), John (Clifford) Mortimer (1923), William Lee Brammer (1929), Elaine May (1932), Helen Prejean (1939), Patrick Rambaud (1946), Michael Zarnock (1958), John Cameron Mitchell (1963).

The human heart has hidden treasures, In secret kept, in silence sealed; The thoughts, the hopes, the dreams, the pleasures, Whose charms were broken if revealed.—Charlotte Brontë

Don't mistake vivacity for wit, thare iz about az much difference az thare iz between lightning and a lightning bug.—Josh Billings

The only rule I have found to have any validity in writing is not to bore yourself.—John Mortimer

Apr. 22—Henry Fielding (1707), Madame de Staël (1766), Georg Hermes (1775), Jurgen Engebretsen Moe (1813), Philip James Bailey (1816), Margaret Murray Robertson (1823), Nikolai Lenin (Vladimir Ilich Ulyanov) (1870),) Ole Edvart Rølvaag (1876), James Norman Hall (1887), Ludwig Renn (1889), Vladimir (Vladimirovich) Nabokov (1899), Robert Choquette (1905), Ivan Efremov (1907), Indro Montanelli (1909), Hans Baumann, Jan de Hartog, and Charles Hubert Sisson (1914), Leo Abse (1917), William Jay Smith (1918), Paula Fox (1923), Jeffrey (Peter) Hart (1930), Joseph Ceravolo (1934), Jason Miller (1939), Sandra (Louise Birdsell (Sandra Bartlette) (1942), Janet Evanovich (b. Janet Schneider) and Louise (Elisabeth) Glück (1943), Jancis Robinson (1950), Ana María Shua (1951), Marie Uguay (1955).

Loafing is the most productive part of a writer's life.—James Norman Hall

I think like a genius, I write like a distinguished author, and I speak like a child.—Vladimir Nabokov

I don't know what makes a writer's voice. It's dozens of things. There are people who write who don't have it. They're tone-deaf, even though they're very fluent. It's an ability, like anything else, being a doctor or a veterinarian, or a musician.—Paula Fox

Apr. 23—Julius Caesar Scaliger (1484), Alexander Alesius (Aless/Alane) (1500), Georg Fabricius (1516), William Shakespeare (1564), Friedrich von Hagedorn (1708), Thomas Wright (1810), James Anthony Froude (1818), Edwin Markham (b. Charles Edward Anson Markham) (1852), Thomas Nelson Page (1853), Simon Abramsz (1867), Arthur Moeller van den Bruck (1876), Charles Gilman Norris (1881), Marcel L'Herbier (1890), Minus van Looi (Benjamin van der Voort) (1892), Richard Huelsenbeck (1892), Ngaio Marsh (1895), Margaret Kennedy (1896), Edwin E. Dwinger (1898), Halldór (Kiljan) Laxness (Halldór Guðjónsson) (1902), Maria Arnoldo (Adrianus Broeders) (1906), Margaret Avison and Maurice Druon (1918), Margaret Avison (1918), Avram Davidson and James Kirkup (1923), James Colin Ross Welch (1924), James Patrick "J. P." Donleavy (1926), Okke Jager (1928), (Francis) George Steiner (1929), Jim Fixx (1932), Rod McKuen (1933), Coleman Barks and Victoria Glendinning (1937), Richard Monaco (1940), (Howard) Barry Hannah (1942), Charles R(ichard) Johnson and Pascal Quignard (1948), Eugene Joseph "E. J." Dionne Jr. and Alice Persons (1952), Arthur Phillips (1969), Pierre Labrie (1972), Noah Falck (1977).

Suit the action to the word, the word to the action.—William Shakespeare

Writing is turning one's worst moments into money.—J. P. Donleavy

Not until you have a sufficiently rich sentence structure and enough words to define the third cousin four times removed of the mother's uncle can you have incest and kinship rules. So that grammar, in a way, is a necessary condition for basic moral law.—George Steiner (commenting on Claude Lévi-Strauss)

Apr. 24—John Trumbull (1750), Nikolaj A Bestuzhev (1791), Karl Leberecht "K. L." Immermann (1796), John Francis Hamtramck Claiborne (1809), Vincente F. Lopez (1814), Anthony Trollope (1815), Robert Michael Ballantyne (1825), Carl Spitteler (1845), Marcus Clarke (1846), Eduardo Acevedo Diaz (1851), Maurice Constantin-Weyer (1881), Jaroslav Hasek (1883), Kurt Pinthus (1886), Allen Saunders (1899), Siegfried F. Nadel (1903), Robert Penn Warren (1905), George Oppen (1908), (Charles) William Goyen (1915), Stanley Kauffmann (1916), Clement Freud (1924), Leon (Midas) C(almet) Standifer Jr. (1925)), Patrick Bowles and Pasqualino de Santis (1927), Dorothy (Goldstein) Uhnak (1930), Maxie Clarence Maultsby Jr. (1932), Patricia Bosworth (1933), Shirley MacLaine (1934), Sue (Taylor) Grafton (1940), Thomas King and David Morrell (1943), Eric Bogosian (1953), Eliot Kleinberg (1956), Kevin Powell (1966), Eric Kripke (1974), Siarhey Balakhonau (1977).

The habit of reading is the only enjoyment in which there is no alloy; it lasts when all other pleasures fade.—Anthony Trollope

Life is what happens while you are busy making other plans.—Allen Saunders

The poem is a little myth of man's capacity of making life meaningful. And in the end, the poem is not a thing we see—it is, rather, a light by which we may see—and what we see is life.—Robert Penn Warren

Ideas are easy. It's the execution of ideas that really separates the sheep from the goats.—Sue Grafton

Apr. 25—Roger Boyle (1621), Giuseppe Marc' Antonio Baretti (1719), Georg Sverdrup (1770), Antonio Fogazzaro (1842), Refugitta et al. (Constance Cary Harrison) (1843), Clarín (Leopoldo Alas y Ureña) (1852), Walter De La Mare (1873), Elsa Maxwell (1883), Sally Salminen (1906), Ross (Franklin) Lockridge Jr. and Claude Mauriac (1914), William Goyen (1915), James H. Robb (1918), Jean Mogin (1921), George Frederick Morgan (1922), James U(nderwood) Cross (1925), Jose Angel Valente (1929), Paul Mazursky (1930), Theodore Victor "T. V." Olsen (1932), J(ay) Anthony Lukas (1933), Robert Jacob Alexander, Ted Kooser, and Rex Miller (b. Rex Miller Spangberg) (1939), Peter T. Wild (1940), James Fenton (1949), Padgett Powell (1952), Francine Pelletier (1959), Dinesh D'Souza (1961), Darcey Steinke (1962), Anne Fleming (1964), Chris Lilley (1975).

All day long the door of the sub-conscious remains just ajar; we slip through to the other side, and return again, as easily and secretly as a cat.—Walter de La Mare

Someone said that life is a party. You join in after it's started and leave before it's finished.—Elsa Maxwell

Life is a sandwich of activity between two periods of bed-wetting.—Padgett Powell

Apr. 26—Caesar Marcus Aurelius Antoninus Augustus (121), Giovanni P. Lomazzo (1538), David Hume (1711), Ludwig Uhland (1787), Martha Finley (1808), Alice Cary (1820), Frederick Law Olmsted (1822), Martha Farquharson (Martha Finley) (1828), Artemus Ward (Charles Farrar Browne) (1834), Wilhelm Scherer (1841), Arno Holz (1863), Robert Herrick, U.S. (1868), Otto zur Linde (1873), Ğabdulla Tuqay (1886), Anita Loos (1888), Ludwig Wittgenstein (1889), Vicente Aleixandre (1898), Niven Busch (1903), Gwen Frostic (1906), Theun de Vries (1907), Johan Doorn (1910), Alfred Elton "A. E." van Vogt (1912), Horace Leonard Gold and Bernard Malamud (1914), Morris L. West (1916), Dorothy Salisbury Davis (1916), Richard Mitchell (1929), Bruce Jay Friedman (born April 26, 1930), Paul Almond (1931), Joan Haggerty (1940), Marilyn Nelson (1946), Natasha Trethewey (1966), Lisa Unger (1970), Joanne Gobure (1982).

If it is not right, do not do it; if it is not true, do not say it.— Marcus Aurelius

I have already given two cousins to the war and I stand ready to sacrifice my wife's brother.—Artemus Ward

You write by sitting down and writing. There's no particular time or place—you suit yourself, your nature. How one works, assuming he's disciplined, doesn't matter.—Bernard Malamud

Don't sell your soul to buy peanuts for the monkeys.—Dorothy Salisbury Davis

Apr. 27—Adamantios Korais (1748), Mary Wollstonecraft Godwin (1759), Herbert Spencer (1820), Ulysses S. Grant (Hiram Ulysses Grant) (1822), Gerben Colmjon (1828), Jules Lemaître (1853), Johan M. Skjoldborg (1861), Andre Baillon (1875), Claude Farrère (Frédéric-Charles Bargone) (1876), Hubert Harrison (1883), Jessie Redmon Fauset (1884), Ludwig Bemelmans (1898), Frank Belknap Long (1901), Cecil Day-Lewis and Ragnar Skrede (1904), Julian Stryjkowski (1905), Yórgos Theotokás (1906), Muriel C. Bradbrook (1909), Franz Weyergans (1912), Albert Soboult (1914), John Alfred Scali (1918), Edwin Morgan (1920), Frances Spotswood (1921), Martin Gray (1922), Timothy F. "Tim" LaHaye (1926), Burton Nathan Raffel (1928), Gilbert Sorrentino (1929), Jean Valentine (1934), Donald Thomas "Don" Evans (1938), Doug Beardsley and Jennings Michael Burch (1941), August Wilson (1945), Michael (Arvaarluk) Kusugak (1948), Russell T. Davies (1963), Jason Whitlock (1967), Talitha Cummins (1980).

[L]et us not overlook the further great fact, that not only does science underlie sculpture, painting, music, poetry, but that science is itself poetic. The current opinion that science and poetry are opposed is a delusion . . . . On the contrary science opens up realms of poetry where to the unscientific all is a blank. Those engaged in scientific researches constantly show us that they realize not less vividly, but more vividly, than others, the poetry of their subjects. —Herbert Spencer

I don't keep any copy of my books around . . . . They would embarrass me. When I finish writing my books, I kick them in the belly, and have done with them.—Ludwig Bemelmans

Poetry is partly sympathy, don't you think? If it's any good, it gets people to think about others' points of view.—Edwin Morgan

I don't write particularly to effect social change. I believe writing can do that, but that's not why I write.—August Wilson

Apr. 28—Charles Cotton (1630), James Monroe (1758), Ezra Abbot (1819), Karl Kraus (1874), Franz Arnold (1879), Bruno Apitz (1900), Johan Borgen (1902), Pierre (Louis) Boileau, Kurt Gödel, and Paul Sacher (1906), Sam Merwin Jr. (1910), Lee Falk (Leon Harrison Gross) (1911), Robert (Woodruff) Anderson and Joop Waasdorp (1917), Rowland Evans (1921), Alistair MacLean (1922), (Nelle) Harper Lee (1926), Lois Duncan and Diane Johnson (1934), Iryna Zhylenko (1941), Jim Northrup (1943), Terry Pratchett (1948), Brian Brett (1950), Roberto Bolaño (1953), Jeremy John Beadle (1956), Ian Rankin (1960), Elizabeth Willis (1961).

A writer is someone who can make a riddle out of an answer.—Karl Kraus

In an abundant society where people have laptops, cell phones, iPods and minds like empty rooms, I still plod along with books.—Harper Lee

Reading is more important than writing.—Roberto Bolaño

Apr. 29—Taliesin (534), John Arbuthnot (1667), Charles Nodier (1780), Addie Lucia Ballou (1838), Edward Rowland Sill (1841), Henri Poincaré (1854), Edouard Rod (1857), Joseph Alexander Altsheler (1862), Constantine P. Cavafy (1863), Louis William Stern (1871), Rafael Sabatini (1875), Egon E. Kisch (1885), H(enry James O'Brien) Bedford-Jones (1887), Elisaveta Bagrjana (Beltsheva) (1893), Walter Mehring (1896), George Osborne Sayles (1901), Jack (Stewart) Williamson (1908), Daniel Raphael Mayer (1909), John Beavan (1910), Terence de Vere White (1912), Lawrence Earl (Lawrence Earl Wiezel) (1915), Edward Blishen and Charles Guenther (1920), Hugo (Lafayette) Black Jr. (1922), David S(aul) Landes (1924), Elmer (Stephen) Kelton (1926), Walter Kempowski (1929), Robert Adams "Bob" Gottlieb (1931), Rodney Marvin "Rod" McKuen (1933), Jill Paton Walsh (1937), Yusef Komunyakaa (James William Brown) (1941), Ian Kershaw (1943), Paul Hendrickson (1944), Olavo de Carvalho (1947), David Icke (1952), Robert J. Sawyer (1960), Kamran Jawaid (1982).

He was born with a gift of laughter and a sense that the world was mad. And that was all his patrimony.—Rafael Sabatini

It's amazing . . . how perfectly honest people who would starve rather than steal sixpence, will steal books without compunction. —Jill Paton Walsh

The truth is that editing lines is not necessarily the same as editing a book. A book is a much more complicated entity and totality than the sum of its lines alone. In structural integrity, the relation and proportions of its parts, and its total impact could escape even a conscientious editor exclusively intent on vetting the book line by line.—Bob Gottlieb

Naturally, one does not normally discuss plans to commit murder with the intended victim.—Robert J. Sawyer

Apr. 30—William Lilly (1602), Mathurin Jacques Brisson (1723), Rosalie Amstein (1846), Alfred von Berger (1853), Frans Netscher (1864), Juhan Liiv (1864), Cyriel Verschaeve (1874), Trijntje "Nine" van de Schaaf (1882), John Crowe Ransom (1888), Watze Cuperus (1891), Ringuet (Philippe Panneton) (1895), Humberto Mauro (1897), Jannetje Fisherman-Roosendaal (1899), Martha Mott Kelley (1906), Luise Rinser and John-Baptist J. Walgrave (Henricus/ Humanus) (1911), Edith Fowke (1913), Harry (Peter McNab) Brown (Jr.) (1917), Valeer (Valerius V) van Kerkhove (1919), George Byatt (1923), Sheldon Harnick (1924), Edmund Cooper (1926), Hugh Hood (1928), Helen Vendler (1933), Laurence van Cott "Larry" Niven (1938), Edward "Ed" Kleban (1939), Annie Dillard and Claude van de Berge (Rony M.F. Pauwels) (1945), Craig Lucas (1951), Nicolas Hulot (1955), Aviva Chomsky (1957), Charles Berling (1958), Paul Gross and W. Thomas Smith Jr. (1959), John Boyne (1971).

When critics are waiting to pounce upon poetic style on exactly the same grounds as if it were prose, the poets tremble.—John Crowe Ransom

SF isn't a genre; SF is the matrix in which genres are embedded, and because the SF field is never going in any one direction at any one time, there is hardly a way to cut it off.—Larry Niven

The sensation of writing a book is the sensation of spinning, blinded by love and daring. It is the sensation of a stunt pilot's turning barrel rolls, or an inchworm's blind rearing from a stem in search of a route. At its worst, it feels like alligator wrestling, at the level of the sentence.—Annie Dillard

Born in May

May 1—Franciscus Junius (Francois du Jon) (1545), Joseph Addison (1672), Aleksey Khomyakov (1804), Jose Amador de los Rios (1818), Jose M. de Alencar (1829), Laza Lazarević (1851), Harry Leon Wilson (1867), Conrad Weiss (1880), Ignazio Silone (1900), Antal Szerb (1901), Giovanni Guareschi (1908), Janis Ritsos (1909), Yannis Ritsos (1909), Louis G. "Lo" van Hensbergen (1917), Jack (Harold) Paar (1918), George Ault "Tad" Mosel Jr. (1922), Joseph Heller (1923), Terry Southern (1924), Roland Verhavert (1927), Alette Beaujon (1934), Ray Aranha and Max Robinson (1939), Bobbie Ann Mason (1940), Sergio Infante (1947), Patrick (March) Dearen and Sally Mann (Sally Turner Munger) (1951), Joel Rosenberg (1954), Ray Buttigieg (1955), Ruth Picardie (1964), Wes Anderson (1969).

Every writer I know has trouble writing.—Joseph Heller
The important thing in writing is the capacity to astonish. Not shock—shock is a worn-out word—but astonish.—Terry Southern
I'm a simple man. All I want is enough sleep for two normal men, enough whiskey for three, and enough women for four.—Joel Rosenberg

May 2—William Camden (1551), Friedrich Christoph Oetinger (1702), Novalis (Georg Philipp Friedrich Freiherr von Hardenberg) (1772), Henrik Steffens (1773), John Galt (1779), Charles Heavysege (1816), Henry Martyn Robert (1837), Albion Winegar Tourgée (1838), Jerome K(lapka) Jerome (1859), Theodor Herzl and D'Arcy Thompson (1860), Clyde Fitch (1865), Hedda Hopper (Elda Furry) (1885), Gottfried Benn (1886), E. E. "Doc" Smith et al. (Edward Elmer Smith) (1890), Stephen W. Meader (1892), Peggy Bacon and Alfred Kurella (1895), Jef (Josephus C. F.) Last (1898), Lev N. Lunts and Willi Bredel (1901), Charlotte Armstrong (Lewi) (1905), Marten Toonder (1912), Otto Buchsbaum (1920), Abraham Michael "A. M." Rosenthal (1922), Jamal Abro (1924), Ruth Fainlight and Martha Grimes (1931), Maury Allen (1932), Lewis P. Turco (1934), Gisela Elsner and Lorenzo Music (1937), Howard Cruse and Franz Innerhofer (1944), Florian Henckel von Donnersmarck (1973).

There is no fun in doing nothing when you have nothing to do.—Jerome K. Jerome

Two of the cruelest, most primitive punishments our town deals out to those who fall from favor are the empty mailbox and the silent telephone.—Hedda Hopper

If you don't have a sensation of apprehension when you set out to find a story and a swagger when you sit down to write it, you are in the wrong business.—A. M. Rosenthal

May 3—Niccolo Machiavelli (1469), John A. "Joannes" Antonides van der Goes (1647), August (Friedrich Ferdinand) von Kotzebue (1761), Giuseppe Acerbi (1773), Hermanus W. Witteveen (1815), Edouard A. Drumont (1844), Jacob Riis (1849), Edgar Watson "E. W." Howe (1853), Andy Adams (1859), (Nicoline) Magdalene Anchor-Roll (1873), B. Traven (Otto Feige or Ret Marut) (1890), Tadeusz Peiper (1891), Konstantine Gamsakhurdia (1893), Earnest Kantorowicz (1895), Cornelius Van Til (1895), Dodie Smith (1896), Joan Appleton (1901), Seton I. Miller (1902), Harry Lillis "Bing" Crosby Jr. (1903), Mary Astor (Lucile Vasconcellos Langhanke) (1906), Earl Wilson (1907), Eleanore Marie "May" Sarton (1912), Earl Blackwell (1913), William M(otter) Inge (1913), Pierre Emmanuel (1916), Betty Comden (1917), Yehuda Amichai (1924), Jaharna Imam (1929), Robert Osborne (1932), Steven Weinberg (1933), Nélida Piñon (1937), Dave Marash (1942), John Costello (1943), Ian Peter Leslie Smith (1944), Tatyana Tolstaya (1951), Benjamin Charles "Ben" Elton (1959), Daryl F. Mallett (1969).

The wise man does at once what the fool does finally.—Niccolo Machiavelli

The creative person should have no other biography than his works.— B. Traven

If you wouldn't write it and sign it, don't say it.—Earl Wilson

I used to write stories a lot because you had to fill your hours some other way than watching television. So my imagination was vivid, and I used to write a lot of stories. I wrote a novel, which I still have, which is so awful.—Robert Osborne

May 4—Abd-Allah Ansari (1006), Richard Graves (1715), Johann Friedrich Herbart (1776), Karl Christian Friedrich Krause (1781), Horace Mann and William H. Prescott (1796), Cornelius Ambrosius Logan (1806), Thomas Henry Huxley (1825), Mynona (1871), Harold Bell Wright (1872), Ramiro de Maeztu y Whitney (1875), Wilhelm Lehmann (1882), Johan W. F. Werumeus Buning (1891), Cola (Nicolas) Debrot (1902), Lincoln (Edward) Kirstein and Maxence Van der Meersch (1907), Jeroom Verten (Jozef F. Vermetten) (1909), Emmanuel Robles (1914), Thomas Mead (1918), Heloise I (Heloise Bowles Cruse) (1919), Assi Rahbani (1923), Peter Blum (1925), Gerlind Reinshagen (1926), Eric Wright (1929), Thomas Stuttaford (1931), Carlos Monsiváis (1938), Amos Oz (1939), Robert Brian "Robin" Cook (1940), George F. Will (1941), Monika van Paemel and Narasimhan Ram (1945), Marele Day (1947), Graham Swift (1949), Donald (Nelson) Gallinger (1953), David Guterson (1956), Alice Randall (1959), Ishita Bhaduri (1961), Gail Carriger (Tofa Borregaard) (1976), Shaenon K. Garrity (1978).

Each cursed his fate that thus their project crossed; How hard their lot who neither won nor lost!—Richard Graves

Science and literature are not two things, but two sides of one thing.—Thomas Huxley

Look, three love affairs in history, are Abelard and Eloise, Romeo and Juliet and the American media and this President at the moment. But this doesn't matter over time. Reality will impinge. If his programs work, he's fine. If it doesn't work, all of the adulation of journalists in the world won't matter.—George Will

May 5—Philippe Quinault (1635), Jacob Kats (1804), Søren Kierkegaard (1813), Eugene-Marin Labiche (1815), Karl Marx (1818), Thomas Edward Brown (1830), Hubert Howe "H. H." Bancroft (1832), Henryk Sienkiewicz (1846), Max Elskamp (1862), Frederik A Stoett (1863), Nellie Bly (Elizabeth Cochran Seaman) (1864), Douglas Malloch (1877), Christopher Morley (1890), J(oseph) Dewey Soper (1893,), Freeman Gosden (1899), James Beard (1903), Kenneth Muir (1907), Miklos Radnoti (1909), George Sessions Perry (1910), Richard H. Rovere (1915), Edward Crumly (1916) Roger O. Hirson (1926), Douglas Turner Ward (1930), Greg (Achille Talon) (1931), Michael Palin (1943), Richard Holmes (1945), Linda Fairstein and Burt Joseph Kimmelman (1947), Deborah Wiles (1953), Kaye Gibbons (1960), Tom Reiss (1964), Naomi Klein (1970), Morgan Pehme (1978), Catherynne M. Valente (b. Bethany L. Thomas) (1979), William Henry "Hank" Green (1980).

I must be free . . . free to do what I like, say what I like, write what I like, within the limits prescribed for me by my own sense of what is seemly and fitting.—Thomas Edward Brown

What a mysterious thing madness is. I have watched patients whose lips are forever sealed in a perpetual silence. They live, breathe, eat; the human form is there, but that something, which the body can live without, but which cannot exist without the body, was missing.—Nellie Bly

The most valuable writing habit I have is not to answer questions about my writing habits.—Christopher Morley

We are looking to brands for poetry and for spirituality, because we're not getting those things from our communities or from each other.—Naomi Klein

May 6—Lorenzo Lippi (Perlone Zipoli) (1606), Charles Batteux (1713), Francois G. J. S. Andrieux (1759), Arvir A. Afzelius (1785), Ludwig Borne (1786), Guido Gezelle (1830), Sigmund Freud (1856), Willem J. T. Kloos (1859), Radindranath Tagore (1861), Oscar (Wilder) Underwood (1862), Gaston (Louis Alfred) Leroux and Wladyslaw Stanislaw Reymont (1868), Joseph Cuvelier (1869), Christian Morgenstern (1871), Jose Ortega y Gasset (1883), Júlio César de Mello e Souza (1895), Paul Alverdes (1897), Harry Golden (1902), Harry Martinson (1904), Enrique Laguerre and Richmond (Alexander) Lattimore (1906), Antoon Breyne (1910), Barend Roest Crollius (1912), Randall Jarrell (1914), Orson Welles and Theodore H. White (1915), Erich Freid (1921), Henry Habibe (1940), Sergio Kokis (1944), Jerry Estrin (1947), Olga Broumas (1949), Jeffery Deaver (1950), Debra Ghigna (1955).

Sex in a woman's world has the same currency a penny has in a man's. Every penny saved is a penny earned in one world and in the next every sexual adventure is a literary experience.—Harry Golden

A novel is a prose narrative of some length that has something wrong with it.—Randall Jarrell

There are two kinds of editors, those who correct your copy and those who say it's wonderful.—Theodore White

If you want a happy ending, that depends, of course, on where you stop your story.—Orson Welles

May 7—Olympe de Gouges (1748), Joseph Joubert (1754), Dániel Berzsenyi (1776), Robert Browning (1812), José Valentim Fialho de Almeida (1857), Rabindranath Tagore (1861), Władysław Stanisław Reymont (1867), Willem Elsschot (Alfons J. de Ridder) (1882), Henri Pourrat (1887), Archibald MacLeish (1892), Vera Chapman (1898), Bauke Tuinstra (1900), Edwin Corle (1906), Ruth Prawer Jhabvala (1927), Horst Bienek (1930), Gene (Rodman) Wolfe (1931), William Dempsey "W. D." Valgardson (1939), Angela Carter (1940), Peter (Philip) Carey (1943), Almudena Grandes (1960), Johnny Lee Middleton (1963), Brian Clevinger (1978).

You will find poetry nowhere unless you bring some with you. —Joseph Joubert

The aim, if reached or not, makes great the life: Try to be Shakespeare, leave the rest to fate!—Robert Browning

Journalism wishes to tell what it is that has happened everywhere as though the same things had happened for every man. Poetry wishes to say what it is like for any man to be himself in the presence of a particular occurrence as though only he were alone there. —Archibald MacLeish

Reading a book is like re-writing it for yourself. You bring to a novel, anything you read, all your experience of the world. You bring your history and you read it in your own terms.—Angela Carter

May 8—Francis Quarles (1592), Alain R. Lesage (1668), Henry Baker (1698), Edward Gibbon (1737), Jean Henri Dunant (1828), Augusta Jane Evans Wilson (1835), Oscar Hammerstein (1846), John Meade Falkner (1858), Thomas B. Costain (1885), Fulton J. Sheen and Edmund Wilson (1895), Gertrud Fussenegger (Dorn) and George Woodcock (1912), Romain Gary (1914), Milton Meltzer (1915), Sloan Wilson (1920), Gary (Sherman) Snyder (1930), Julieta Campos (1932), Alistair Service (1933), Thomas (Ruggles) Pynchon (Jr.) (1937), Peter Benchley and Eddie Woods (1940), Ruth Holland (1942), Patricia Mary W. "Pat" Barker (Drake) (1943), Elizabeth Becker "Beth" Henley (1952), Roddy Doyle (1958), Robin Jarvis (1963), Kirk Lynn (1972), Christopher Meades (1974), Zygmunt Miłoszewski (1976).

I am convinced that all writers are optimists whether they concede the point or not . . . . How otherwise could any human being sit down to a pile of blank sheets and decide to write, say two-hundred thousand words on a given theme?---Thomas Costain

No two persons ever read the same book.—Edmund Wilson

"You fool you. There is a story. There are many stories and all deserve to be counted."—Julieta Campos

Hey, over here! Have your picture taken with a reclusive author! Today only, we'll throw in a free autograph! But wait, there's more! —Thomas Pynchon

May 9—Dante Alighieri (1265), Peter Pindar (John Wolcot) (1738), Johannes C. de Jonge (1793), August Pauly (1796), John Brougham (1814), James Matthew "J. M." Barrie (1860), David Edelstadt (1866), Howard Carter (1873), Frank Parker Day (1881), Jules Van de Leene (1887), Lucian Blaga (1895), Austin Clarke (1896), Walter Dehmel (1903), Eleanor Estes (1906), Baldur von Schirach (1907), Zola Helen Ross (1912), Richard (Milton) McKenna (1913), Josef Muller-Brockmann (1914), Richard Adams and William Tenn (Philip Klass) (1920), Daniel Berrigan and Mona (Jane) Van Duyn (1921), Bulat S. Okudzjava (1924), Georges Conchon (1925), Jean J. A. Girault and Gavin Lyall (1932), Alan Bennett (1934), Dušan "Charles" Simić (1938), Jorie Graham (1950), Christopher Dewdney (1951), Henri Cole (1956), Skye Regan (1988).

Art, as far as it is able, follows nature, as a pupil imitates his master; thus your art must be, as it were, God's grandchild.—Dante Alighieri

The world's perverse, but it could be worse.—Mona Van Duyn

The rabbits mingled naturally. They did not talk for talking's sake, in the artificial manner that human beings—and sometimes even their dogs and cats—do. But this did not mean that they were not communicating; merely that they were not communicating by talking.—Richard Adams

May 10—Jean Mairet (1604), Claude-Joseph Rouget de Lisle (1760), J. P. Hebel (1760), Jacques-Nicolas-Augustin Thierry (1795), James, 1st Viscount Bryce (1838), James Gordon Bennett Jr. (1841), Benito Pérez Galdós (1843), Jan Kalf (1873), Moses Schorr (1874), Ivan Cankar (1876), Fritz von Unruh (1885), Karl Barth (1886), Olaf Stapleton (1886), Jacobus C. Bloem (1887), Walter Lowenfels (1897), Ariel Durant (1898), Bella "Bel" Kaufman (1911), Harold Myers (1912), Monica Dickens (1915), Nayantara Sahgal (1927), Antonine Maillet and Peter C(harles) Newman (1929), June Knox-Mawer (1930), Ettore Scola (1931), William Alfred "Bill" Bauer (1932), Barbara Taylor Bradford (1933), Jeanine Basinger and Jayne Cortez (1934), Arthur (Lee) Kopit (1937), Jean Becker (1938), Pascal Lainé (1942), Caroline Cooney and Thomas Tessier (1947), John Solomon Sandridge (1950), John Diamond (1953), Jan Zwicky (1955), Vladislav Listyev (1956), Elizabeth S. "Lisa" Kron (1961), Suzan-Lori Parks (1963), Jon Ronson (1967), Geoffrey G. O'Brien and John Scalzi (1969), Elizabeth Bachinsky (1976), Katori Hall (1981), Jeremy Gable (1982).

Many a good newspaper story has been ruined by over verification.—James Gordon Bennett

Education is not a product: mark, diploma, job, money in that order; it is a process, a never ending one.—Bel Kaufman

I love writing and do not know why it is considered such a difficult, agonizing profession.—Caroline B. Cooney

May 11—Cornelis van Alkemade (1654), János Batsányi (1763), Robert Charles Sands (1799), Walter Goodman (1838), Henry Cuyler Bunner (1855), Carl Hauptmann (1858), Edward Lucas White (1866), Irving Berlin (Isadore Balin) (1888), William Richard "Will R." Bird (1891), Arthur Crew Inman and Jiddu Krishnamurti (1895), Mari Susette Sandoz (1896), Paulino Masip (1899), Mari Sandoz (1901), Kaarlo Sarkia (1902), Rose Ausländer (1907), Camilo Jose Cela (1916), Richard P. Feynman (1918), Gene Savoy and Zilpha Keatly Snyder (1927), Stanley L(awrence) Elkin (1930), Francisco Umbral (1935), Ulrich Berkes and Gwen Davis (1936), Michael Heller (1937), Margaret Visser (1940), Rachel Billington (1942), Michael Palmer (1943), Lubomir Stoykov (1954), Theresa Burke (1956), Liz Swaine (Elizabeth Swaine Culp) (1960), Hilly Hicks Jr. (1970).

Our attitudes control our lives. Attitudes are a secret power working twenty-four hours a day, for good or bad. It is of paramount importance that we know how to harness and control this great force.—Irving Berlin

I am going to be vague expressly; I could be altogether explicit, but it is not my intention to be so. For once a thing is defined, it is dead.—Jiddu Krishnamurti

Be who you are. / Give what you have.—Rose Ausländer

Poets say science takes away from the beauty of the stars—mere globs of gas atoms. I, too, can see the stars on a desert night, and feel them. But do I see less or more?—Richard P. Feynman

Poetry, ever sensitive to the nuances of its surroundings, must limn or bode forth the environmental conditions out of which it arises. That poets, those presumed antennae of the race, might be picking up the signals and putting them somehow into the work seems only too obvious.—Michael Heller

May 12—(Johannes) Carsten Hauch (1790), John Kearsley Mitchell (1798), J. V. Snellman (1806), Edward Lear (1812), Dante Gabriel Rossetti (1828), George Edward Woodberry (1855), Winthrop Pickard Bell (1884), Lorine Faith Niedecker (1903), Leslie Charteris (Leslie Charles Bowyer-Yin) (1907), May Sarton (Eleanore Marie Sarton) (1912). Bertus Aafjes (1914), Howard K. Smith (1914), Albert L. Murray (1916), Farley (McGill) Mowat (1921), Marco Denevi (1922), Giovanni Testori (1923), John Simon (1925), Andrey Voznesensky (1933), George Carlin (1937), Andrei Amalrik (1938), Rosellen Brown (1939), John (Henry) Lahr (1941), Timothy Hugh Brown and Barry B(rookes) Longyear (1942), Eva Demski (1944), Norma Cole, Bernadette Mayer, and Gayla Reid (1945), L. Neil Smith (1946), Michael Ignatieff, Micheline Lanctôt, and Catherine "Cal" Yronwode (Catherine Anna Manfredi) (1947), Simon Levy (1949), Carolyn Haines (1953), Rafael Yglesias (1954), Madeline Sonik (1960), Jennifer Moxley (1964), Jon Stock (1966).

I was much distressed by next door people who had twin babies and played the violin; but one of the twins died, and the other has eaten the fiddle, so all is peace.—Edward Lear

Conception, my boy, fundamental brain work, is what makes all the difference in art.—Dante Gabriel Rossetti

Democracy encourages the majority to decide things about which the majority is ignorant.—John Simon

May 13—Richard Simon (1638), Adrian Loosjes Pzn (1761), Alphonse Daudet (1840), Jos Panhuysen (1900), Alfred Earle Birney (1904), Daphne du Maurier and Austin Whitaker (1907), Wallace Breem (1926), Clive Barnes (1927), Adolf Muschg (1934), Stella Rimington (1935), Roch Carrier, Jerome Charyn, and Roger (Joseph) Zelazny (1937), Bruce Chatwin and Rachel (Holmes) Ingalls (1940), Leighton (David) Gage (1942), Betsy Finley Ashton, Brian Fawcett, and Armistead (Jones)Maupin (Jr.) (1944), Charles Baxter and Stephen R(eeder) Donaldson (1947), (William) Manning Marable (1950), Mark Abley (1955), Kia Corthron (1961), Kathleen Jamie (1962), Stephen Colbert (1964).

Women want love to be a novel, men a short story.—Daphne du Maurier

One of my standard—and fairly true—responses to the question as to how story ideas come to me is that story ideas only come to me for short stories. With longer fiction, it is a character (or characters) coming to visit, and I am then obliged to collaborate with him/her/it/them in creating the story.—Roger Zelazny

Thankfully, dreams can change. If we'd all stuck with our first dream, the world would be overrun with cowboys and princesses.—Stephen Colbert

May 14—Friedrich von Raumer (1781), Frantisek Palacky (1798), Alexander Kaufmann (1817), Hall Caine (1853), William Alexander Percy (1885), Louis Verneuil (1893), Hal Borland (1900), Edgar Wind (1900), Solange Chaput-Rolland (1919), Herbert W. Franke (1927), Barbara Branden (1929), María Irene Fornés (1930), George Lucas (1944), Karin Struck (1947), Robert Eria "Bob" Telson (1949), Jens Sparschuh (1954), Christine Brennan (1958), Eoin Colfer (1965), Amber Rose Tamblyn (1983).

As far as the functioning of your mind is concerned, it doesn't matter what you feel. It doesn't matter to anyone else, and it matters least of all to yourself.—Barbara Branden

A lot of people like to do certain things, but they're not that good at it. Keep going through the things that you like to do, until you find something that you actually seem to be extremely good at. It can be anything.—George Lucas

The thing about reading is that if you are hooked, you're not going to stop just because one series is over; you're going to go and find something else.—Eoin Colfer

May 15—Melchiorre Cesarotti (1730), Mary Wortley Montague (1762), Martinus W. van der Aa (1830), Eduard earl of Keyserling (1855), Graf Keyserling (1855), Lyman Frank Baum (1856), Arthur Schnitzler (1862), Albert Verwey (1865), Edwin Muir (1887), Katherine Anne Porter (1890), David Vogel (1891), Mikhail Bulgakov (1891), Xavier Herbert (1901), Clifton Fadiman (1904), Max Frisch (1911), Alexis Kagame (1912), Maurice B. Latey (1915), Hugh Henry Home Popham (1920), Jakucho Setouchi (1922), Jaime Garcia Terre (1924), twins Anthony (Joshua) Shaffer and Peter (Levin) Shaffer (1926), Norma Fox Mazer (1931), Donald (Anthony) Moffitt and Paul Zindel Jr. (1936), Harve Brosten (1943), Raymond Federman (1928), Julie Otsuka (1962), Laura Hillenbrand (1967), Bruce G. Blowers (1987).

No entertainment cheap as reading, nor any pleasure so lasting.—**Lady Mary Wortley Montague**

I shall try to tell the truth, but the result will be fiction. —**Katherine Anne Porter**

When you reread a classic, you do not see more in the book than you did before; you see more in you than was there before.—**Clifton Fadiman**

May 16—Friedrich Rückert (1788), Douglas Southall Freeman (1886), Jacob van Hoddis (1887), Herbert Ernest "H. E." Bates (1905), Arturo Uslar Pietri and Margret Rey (1906), Olga Berggolts (1910), Olaff J. de Landell (J.B. Wemmerslager van Sparwoude0 (1911), Louis "Studs" Terkel (1912), Edward T. Hall (1914), Juan Rulfo and Edward Thomas (1918), Richard Mason (1919), Frank F. Mankiewicz (1924), Adrienne (Cecile) Rich (1929), Peter Levi (1931), Bruce Norris (1960), Scott Albert (1975).

I've always felt, in all my books, that there's a deep decency in the American people and a native intelligence—providing they have the facts, providing they have the information.—Studs Terkel

As part-time advisor to Senator Gary Hart's . . . campaign in 1984 . . . I was struck by the minutiae of the press's questions. The authorship of a speech—the identity of the speechwriters—seemed far more important than its content . . . . Rarely if ever does the question turn on such things as "does he have the right ideas?" or "would he make a strong—or even good—president?"—Frank F. Mankiewicz

Art, whose honesty must work through artifice, cannot avoid cheating truth.—Adrienne Rich

May 17—Jien (1155), Martinus A. del Rio (1551), Martin Delrio (1551), Antoine Court (1691), Andreas Felix von Oefele (1706), Anna Brownell Jameson (1794), Robert Smith Surtees (1803), Virginie Loveling (1836), Julius Wellhausen (1844), Henricus P. Bremmer (1871), Henri Barbusse and Dorothy Miller Richardson (1873), Henri Barbusse (1873), Alban Collignon (1876), Joseph Morris (Bachelor) (1887), Alfonso Reyes (1889), Hannah Tillich (1896), John Patrick (Goggin) (1905), Frederic Prokosch (1906), Mark Schorer (1908), Peter B. Germano (1913), (Jean-)Guy Sylvestre (1918), Ronald Verlin "R. V." Cassill and Merle Miller (1919), Donald Cameron Watt (1928), Jean Vautrin (Jean Herman) (1933), (Alexandra) Sandra (Fraser) Gwyn and Dennis Christopher George Potter (1935), Lars Gustafsson (1936), Trinus Riemersma (1938), Gary (James) Paulsen (1939), Lyn Hejinian (1941), Joan Louise Barfoot and F. Paul Wilson (1946), Patricia McDowell (Patricia McDowell Aakhus) (1952), Yoko Shimada (1953), Rudy Amado Pérez (1958), Lise Lyng Falkenberg (1962), Davor Džalto (1980).

He that seeks popularity in art closes the door on his own genius: as he must needs paint for other minds, and not for his own.—**Anna Brownell Jameson**

Pain makes man think. Thought makes man wise. Wisdom makes life endurable.—**John Patrick**

The most valuable part of writing lies in challenging one's secret fears and testing to the utmost one's resources of spirit. It takes courage to write well.—**R.V. Cassill**

Most serious writers work slowly, and, thus, miss deadlines, sometimes several deadlines, publishers' deadlines, that is. A serious writer cannot have any deadline but his own.—**Merle Miller**

May 18—Omar Khayyám (1048), John Wilson (1785), Jan P. Veth (1864), Franiska zu Reventlow (1871), Bertrand (Arthur William) Russell (1872), Jérôme Tharaud (1874), Ernst Wiechert (1887), Gunnar Gunnarsson (1889), Rudolf Carnap (1891), Juan J. Domenchina (1898), (Robert) Meredith Willson (1902), Arthur van Schendel (1910), Charles Wintour (1917), John Paul II (Karol Wojtyla) (1920), Patrick Dennis (Edward Everett Tanner III) (1921), Robin (Francis) Blaser (1925), Barbara Goldsmith and Fred(erick Thomas) Saberhagen (1930), Winfried Georg "W. G." Sebald (1944), Stuart Gannes (1945), Diane E(lizabeth) Duane (1952), Martyn Wiley (1954), Lionel Shriver (1957), Jonathan Maberry (1958), Tina Fey (1970).

The moving finger writes, and having written moves on. Nor all thy piety nor all thy wit, can cancel half a line of it.—Omar Khayyam

There are two motives for reading a book: one, that you enjoy it; the other, that you can boast about it.—Bertrand Russell

Freedom consists not in doing what we like, but in having the right to do what we ought.—John Paul II

If you want to be a screenwriter, take an acting class to get a sense of what you're asking actors to do. Learning other skills will help you communicate with people and respect what they do.—Tina Fey

May 19—Johann G. Fichte (1762), Wilson Mizner (1876), Henricus W. J. M. Keuls (1883), Konstatin G. Paustovski (1892), Julius Evola (1898), Leonid Maksimovich Leonov (1899), T(homas) Harry Williams (1909), Malcolm X (Malcolm Little; el-Hajj Malik el-Shabazz) (1925), Swami Kriyananda (1926), Lorraine (Vivian) Hansberry (1930), Eric Davidson (1931), Paul Erdman (1932), Ruskin Bond and James Charles "Jim" Lehrer (1934), F. R. Fries (1935), Jane Brody and Nora Ephron (1941), Sarah Ellis (1952), Dennison Berwick (1956), Gregory Poirier (1961), Jodi (Lynn) Picoult (1966), Jordan Tannahill (1988).

I wrote a short story because I wanted to see something of mine in print other than my fingers.—**Wilson Mizner**
Never be afraid to sit a while and think.—**Lorraine Hansberry**
Real luxury is time and opportunity to read for pleasure.—**Jane Brody**
I try to write parts for women that are as complicated and interesting as women actually are.—**Nora Ephron**

May 20—Honoré de Balzac (1799), John Stuart Mill (1806), Emile Erckmann-Chatrian (Emile Erckmann) and Frederic Passy (1822), Hector H. Malot (1830), Hugh Cowan (1867), Grace Stone Coates (1881), Sigrid Undset (1882), Joseph Allan Nevins (1890), Adela Rogers St. John (1894), Hans Sahl (1902), Margery Allingham (1904), Gerrit Achterberg and William Mode "W. M." Spackman (1905), Gardner F(rancis) Fox and Annie M. G. Schmidt (1911), Richard Charles Cobb (1917), Wolfgang Borchert (1921), Samuel Selvon (1923), John Lucarotti (1926), Andre Carolus Cirino (1929), David Ray (1932), Clyde Edgerton (1944), Dave Thomas (1948), Sheldon Oberman (1949), W. Michael Gear (1955), William Michaelian and Douglas (Jerome) Preston (1956), Elizabeth S. "Lisa" Kron (1961), Christopher Sorrentino (1963).

An unfulfilled vocation drains the color from a man's entire existence.—Honoré de Balzac

A person may cause evil to others not only by his actions but by his inaction, and in either case he is justly accountable to them for the injury.—John Stuart Mill

I am one of those people who are blessed, or cursed, with a nature which has to interfere. If I see a thing that needs doing I do it.—Margery Allingham

May 21—Albrecht Dürer (1471), Alexander Pope (1688), Charles-Albert Gobat (1834), Thomas Cooper De Leon (1839), Emile A. G. Verhaeren (1855), Emil Ermatinger (1873), Everard Verachtert (1873), Tudor Arghezi (1880), Manuel Pérez y Curis (1884), John Peale Bishop (1892), Ilse Lagner (1899), Suzanne Lilar (Verbist) (1901), Manly Wade Wellman (1903), Romain Gary (1914), Harold Robbins (1916), Victor Henry Anderson and Jean-Louis Curtis (1917), Robert Creeley (1926), Adele Wiseman (1928), Gabriele Wohmann (1932), Urs Widmer (1938), Jack Lawrence Granatstein (1939), Janet Dailey (1944), Al Franken (1951), Taku Ashibe (1958), Tina Landau (1962), Richard Appel (1963), Jill Hartman (1974), James Clancy Phelan (1979), Kira (Lily) Peikoff (1985).

> Next o'er his books his eyes began to roll,
> In pleasing memory of all he stole.
> **—Alexander Pope**
> The pattern of the narrative never of necessity wants to end, it never has to.**—Robert Creeley**
> When you encounter seemingly good advice that contradicts other seemingly good advice, ignore them both.**—Al Franken**

May 22—Gérard de Nerval (Gérard Labrunie) (1808), Richard Wagner (1813), Catulle Mendès (1841), Judith Crist and Arthur Conan Doyle (1859), August Cuppens (1862), Alla Nazimova (1879), Francis de Miomandre (1880), Johannes Robert "J. R." Becher (1891), Clyde Brion Davis (1894), Robert Neumann (1897), Anne de Vries and Paul Viiding (1904), Hergé (Georges Prosper Remi) and Laurence Olivier (1907), Vance Packard (1914), Jean-Louis Curtis (Louis Laffitte) (1917), Judith Crist (1922), Peter Matthiessen (1927), Arnold Stark Lobel (1933), M. Scott Peck (1936), Bernard Shaw (1940), Donald (Harman) Akenson (1941), Lucie Brock-Broido (1956), Wayne Johnston (1958), Eliza Clark (1963), Andrew Zawacki (1972), Olympia Vernon (1973), Shane L. Koyczan (1976).

Mediocrity knows nothing higher than itself, but talent instantly recognizes genius.—Arthur Conan Doyle
I take a simple view of life: keep your eyes open and get on with it.—Laurence Olivier
Discipline is wisdom and vice versa.—M. Scott Peck

May 23—Juan Caramuel y Lobkowitz (1606), John Bartram (1699), William Hunter (1718), Giuseppe Parini (1729), Thomas Hood (1799), Henri A. Esquiros (1812), James Gleason (1882), Adrian Roland Holst (1888), Pär (Fabian) Lagerkvist (1891), Scott O'Dell (1898), Walter Reisch (1903), Margaret Wise Brown and Artie Shaw (Arthur Jacob Arshawsky) (1910), Barbara Ward (1914), Margaret Hayden Rector (1916), Naomi Replansky (1918), James (Benjamin) Blish (1921), Dennis Compton (1922), Walter Jackson Bate (1918), Friedrich Achleitner (1930), Joseph Robert Janes (1935), John Xavier "Jack" McCarthy and Robert A(rthur) M(orton) Stern (1939), David Arnason (1940), Susan Polis Schutz (1944), Ursula Hegi (1946), Gary "William" Bannerman and Jane Kenyon (1947), Patricia McCormick (1956), Mitchell David "Mitch" Albom (1958), Blake Schwendiman (1970, Rebecca Rosenblum (1978), Ty G. Allushuski (1986).

A certain portion of the human race has certainly a taste for being diddled.—Thomas Hood
In this modern world where activity is stressed almost to the point of mania, quietness as a childhood need is too often overlooked. Yet a child's need for quietness is the same today as it has always been—it may even be greater—for quietness is an essential part of all awareness. In quiet times and sleepy times a child can dwell in thoughts of his own, and in songs and stories of his own.—Margaret Wise Brown
The poet's job is to put into words those feelings we all have that are so deep, so important, and yet so difficult to name, to tell the truth in such a beautiful way, that people cannot live without it. —Jane Kenyon

May 24—William Whewell (1794), Cornelis E. van Koetsveld (1807), Abraham Geiger (1810), Robert Bontine Cunninghame Graham (1852), Arthur Wing Pinero (1855), James Oppenheim (1882), William F. Albright (1891), Kathleen Hale (1898), Henri Michaux (1899), Eduardo De Filippo (1900), Seishi Yokomizo (1902), Mikhail Sholokhov (1905), Michael Roberts (1908), Louis Fornberg and Guillermo Diaz-Plaja (1909), George Tabori (1914), William Trevor (1928), Gilbert Morris (1929), Earl Thompson (1931), Arnold Wesker (1932), Marian Engel (Marian Ruth Passmore) (1933), Iosif Aleksandrovich "Joseph" Brodsky (1940), Bob Dylan (Robert Allen Zimmerman) (1941), Ian Hamilton and Jeremy Treglown (1946), Lorna Crozier (1948), Michael Chabon (1963), Larry (Alex) Taunton (1967), Mo Willems (1968), Greg Berlanti (1972).

He who has rejected his demons badgers us to death with his angels.—Henri Michaux

Bad literature is a form of treason.—Joseph Brodsky

Everybody has their own idea of what's a poet. Robert Frost, President Johnson, T.S. Eliot, Rudolf Valentino—they're all poets. I like to think of myself as the one who carries the light bulb.—Bob Dylan

Louis Pasteur said, "Chance favors the prepared mind." If you're really engaged in the writing, you'll work yourself out of whatever jam you find yourself in.—Michael Chabon

May 25—Claude Buffier (1661), Ralph Waldo Emerson (1803), Jacob Burckhardt (1818), Jules de Geyter (1830), Naim Frashëri (1846), Jean Richard Bloch (1884), Miles Malleson (1888), Dirk Vansina (1894), Jan N. Bakhuizen van den Brink (1896), Bennett Cerf and Gustav Regler (1898), Kazi Nazrul Islam (1899), Alain Grandbois (1900), Herbert (Arthur) Krause (1905), Theodore (Huebner) Roethke (1908), Richard Dimbleby (1913), Douglas (Valentine) LePan (1914), Daniel Wolf (1915), Phyllis (Fay) Gotlieb (1926), Robert Ludlum (1927), John Gregory Dunne (1932), John Weitz (1933), David J. Burke (1934), William Patrick "W. P." Kinsella and Jay Wright (1935), David Levering Lewis (1936), Raymond Carver and Arturo Islas Jr. (1938), Jamaica Kincaid (Elaine P. Richardson) and James Stewart "Jim" Thayer (1949), Bob Gale (1951), Al Sarrantonio (1952), Eve Ensler (1953), Edward Lee (1957), Michel Pleau (1964), Poppy Z. Brite (Billy Martin; born Melissa Ann Brite) (1967), Michael B. Enyaer (1970), Kōtarō Isaka (1971).

I hate quotations. Tell me what you know.—Ralph Waldo Emerson

Writing is manual labor of the mind, like laying pipe.—John Gregory Dunne

I think when people begin to tell their stories, everything changes, because not only are you legitimised in the telling of your story and are you found, literally, like you matter, you exist in the telling of your story, but when you hear your story be told, you suddenly exist in community and with others.—Eve Ensler

I think a little menace is fine to have in a story. For one thing, it's good for the circulation.—Raymond Carver

May 26—Mary Wortley Montagu (1689), Nikolaus L. earl von Zinzendorf und Pottendorf (1700), Mary Wollstonecraft Godwin (1759), Alexander S. Pushkin (1799), Edmond de Goncourt (1822), Robert W(illiam) Chambers (1865), John Eigenhuis (1866), Jean Schlumberger (1877), Leonard Bacon (1887), Maxwell Bodenheim (1892), Otto E. Neugebauer (1899), Richard Maibaum (1909), Norman A(rnold) Fox (1911), Antonia Forest (1915), Moondog (Louis Thomas Hardin) (1916), Henriette Roosenburg (1916), Osvaldo Reyes Herrera and Peter Malcolm Gordon Raleigh (1919), Phyllis Gotlieb (1929), Edward Whittemore (1933), Lawson Fusao Inada, Lyudmila Petrushevskaya, and Darryl Ponicsan (1938), Brent Musburger (1939), Sam Posey (1944), Bronwen Wallace (1945), Piers Gray (1947), David R. Ignatius (1950), Alan Hollinghurst and Aritha van Herk (1954), Joey Green (1958), Phil Doyle (1967), David Reed (1982).

If you but knew the flames that burn in me which I attempt to beat down with my reason.—Alexander Pushkin

You don't go after poetry, you take what comes. Maybe the gods do it through me but I certainly do a hell of a lot of the work.—Phyllis Gotlieb

All families are silly in their own way.—Alan Hollinghurst

May 27—Ibn Khaldun (1332), Girolamo Mei (1519), William Petty (1623), Henry Parkes (1815), Julia Ward Howe (1819), Luigi Capuana (1839), Georges Eekhoud (1854), Arnold Bennett (1867), Richard von Schaukal (1874), Ferdynand Antoni Ossendowski (1876), Rudolf Pannwitz (1881), Max Brod (1884), Erich Kuttner and Emiel van der Straeten (1887), Louis-Ferdinand Céline (Louis-Ferdinand Destouches) and Dashiell Hammett (1894), Joanna (Maxwell) Cannan (1896), (John) Raymond Knister (1899), Uładzimir Zylka (1900), Émile Benveniste (1902), Rachel (Louise) Carson (1907), Torolf Elster (1911), John Cheever (1912), Herman Wouk (1915), Julia Ward Howe (1819), Sidney A. K. Keyes (1922), Henry Kissinger and David Derek Stacton (b. Arthur Lionel Kingsley Evans) (1923), Tony Hillerman (1925), Jan Blokker and Stephen Minot (1927), John Barth (1930), Linda Pastan (1932), Harlan (Jay) Ellison (1934), Frank Bidart and Sarah Cockburn Caudwell (1939), Robert H(alsall) Abel and Adriaan Venema (1941), Jocelyne Saucier (1948), Norma Jean Almodovar (1951), Steven Brill (1962), Ningeokuluk Teevee (1963), Kaur Kender (1971), Michael A. Buonauro (1979).

I've been as bad an influence on American literature as anyone I can think of.—Dashiell Hammett

My trouble is insomnia. If I had always slept properly, I'd never have written a line.—Louis-Ferdinand Céline

For me, a page of good prose is where one hears the rain [and] the noise of battle.—John Cheever

May 28—Xin Qiji (1140), Thomas Moore (1779), Bernard S. Ingemann (1789), Louis Agassiz (1807), Willem Doorenbos (Keerom) (1820), Claude Anet (Jean Schopfer) (1868), Gamel Woolsey (1895), Gaston Duribreux (1903), Frederick George Emmison (1907), Ian (Lancaster) Fleming (1908), John Schepens (Jean Baudoux) (1909), Roger Ikor and Patrick (Victor Martindale) White (1912), Anna Thilda May "May" Swenson (1913), Walker Percy (1916), Heinz G. Konsalik (1921), Francois Nourissier (1927), André Schwarz-Bart (1928), Stephen Birmingham (1931), José Montoya and Ronald (Burt) Ribman (1932), Fred (Davis) Chappell (1936), Guntram Vesper (1941), Marjorie May "Maggie" Siggins (1942), Adriaan T. "Ad" Zuiderent (1944), K. Satchidanandan and William (Hartley Hume) Shawcross (1946), Lynn Johnston (1947), Ian Bradley (1950), David Rambo (1955), Meg Wolitzer (1959), Marco (Antonio) Rubio (1971).

Every scientific truth goes through three states: first, people say it conflicts with the Bible; next, they say it has been discovered before; lastly, they say they always believed it.—Louis Agassiz

I was just on the edge of getting married, and I was frenzied at the prospect of this great step in my life after having been a bachelor for so long. And I really wanted to take my mind off of the agony, and so I decided to sit down and write a book.—Ian Fleming

A good title should be like a good metaphor; it should intrigue without being too baffling or too obvious.—Walker Percy

I've always felt that life is a novel, and part of it is written for you, and part of it is written by you. It's up to you to write the ending, ultimately.—Lynn Johnston

May 29—Patrick Henry (1736), Gilbert Keith "G. K." Chesterton (1874), Oswald Spengler (1880), Max Brand (Frederick Schiller Faust) (1892), Alfonsina Storni and Terence Hanbury "T. H." White (1906), Desmond Shawe-Taylor (1907), Neil R(onald) Jones (1909), John (B. M. R.) Hanlo (1912), John Fitzgerald Kennedy (1917), Bernard (Charles Henri) Clavel (1923), Paul R. Ehrlich (1932), André P. Brink (1935), George Amabile (1936), Brock Cole (1938), Nanette Newman (1939), Amon Liner (1940), Linden MacIntyre (1943), Melvin Dixon (1950), Louise Cooper (1952).

There is a great deal of difference between an eager man who wants to read a book and a tired man who wants a book to read. —G. K. Chesterton

Life is a serious problem to a man over thirty. To a man under thirty it is simply a game.—Max Brand

What use is Order without Chaos to challenge its rule? And by the same standard, what lies ahead for us if nothing opposes our ways?—Louise Cooper

May 30— Ann S(ophia) Stephens (1810), Alfred Austin (1835), Josephine Preston Peabody (1874), Ludwig Lewisohn (1882), Laurent Barré and Randolph Bourne (1886), Cornelia Otis Skinner (1901), Countee Cullen (Countee LeRoy Porter) (1903), Joseph Stein (1912), Julian Gustave Symons (1912), Guadalupe "Pita" Amor (1918), Harry Clement Stubbs (1922), Harry Clement "Hal" Stubbs (1922), Evelyn Wesler Zemel (1927), Arthur C. Jacobs (1937), Michael Piller (1948), Moyez G. "M. G." Vassanji 1950), Kelley Armstrong (1968), Young Jean Lee (1974).

One learns in life to keep silent and draw one's own confusions.—Cornelia Otis Skinner

There is no secret to success except hard work and getting something indefinable which we call 'the breaks.' In order for a writer to succeed, I suggest three things—read and write—and wait.— Countee Cullen

A writer is very much like the captain on a star ship facing the unknown. When you face the blank page and you have no idea where you're going. It can be terrifying, but it can also be the adventure of a lifetime.—Michael Piller

May 31—Ludwig Tieck (1773), Georg Herwegh (1817), Walter "Walt" Whitman (1819), John William De Forest (1826), Ernest Daudet (1837), James Jeffrey Roche (1847), Francis E. Younghusband (1863), Saint-John Perse/Saint-Leger Leger (Alexis Leger) (1887), Konstantin G(eorgiyevich) Paustovsky (1892), Fred Allen (John Florence Sullivan) (1894), George R(ippey) Stewart (1895), Johan Brouwer (1898), Norman Vincent Peale (1898), Leonid Leonow (1899), Helma Wolf-Catz (1900), Robert Arthur Ley (1921), Julian Beck (1925), Yaffa Eliach (Yaffa Sonenson) (1937), Al Young (1939), W(alter) Patrick Lang (Jr.) (1940), Bernard Goldberg (1945), Ted Baehr and Libby Scheier (1946), Phillip M. Hoose (1947), Svetlana (Alexandrovna) Alexievich (1948).

The words of my book nothing, the drift of it everything.—Walt Whitman
Some men borrow books; some men steal books; and others beg presentation copies from the author.—James Jeffrey Roche
I can't understand why a person will take a year or two to write a novel when he can easily buy one for a few dollars.—Fred Allen

Born in June

June 1—Johan Runius (1679), Carl von Clausewitz (1780), Ferdinand Raimund (1790), Caroline Lee (Whiting) Hentz (1800), William W. Campbell (1858), Antonio JdC Feijo (1862), John (Edward) Masefield (1878), Charles Kay Ogden (1881), John Drinkwater (1882), Elsie (Williamson) McWilliams (1896), John (William) Van Druten (1901), Bill Deedes (1913), William Sloane Coffin (1924), Philo (Rolf) Bregstein (1932), Willy Roggeman and Doris Buchanan Smith (1934), Clayton Eshleman (1935), Sandra Scoppettone (1936), Colleen McCullough (1937), Patrick Grainville (1947), Crad Kilodney (Lou Trifon) (1948), Kathleen Hirsch (1953), Ralph Morse (1955), Diann Blakely (1957), Ahron Bregman (1958), Adeena Karasick (1965), Sheri Holman (1966).

All action takes place, so to speak, in a kind of twilight, which like a fog or moonlight, often tends to make things seem grotesque and larger than they really are.—Carl von Clausewitz

Poetry is a mixture of common sense, which not all have, with an uncommon sense, which very few have.—John Masefield

It's a dead give away of an inexperienced writer if every character speaks with the same voice.—Colleen McCullough

June 2—Marquis de Sade (1740), Adrian van der Hoop Jr. (1802), Grace Aguilar (1816), Thomas Hardy (1840), Constantly A.M. Cap (1842), Karl Adolph Gjellerup (1857), Adolf Herckenrath (1879), Bokke R. S. Pollema (1883), Orrick Glenday Johns (1887), Dorothy West (1907), Xia Hong (1911), Barbara Pym (1913), George (Parks) Hitchcock (1914), Lester del Rey (1915), Kathryn Tucker Windham (1918), Michael James O'Hehir (1920), Juan Antonio Bardem (1922), June Callwood (1924), W. Watts Biggers and Phillip Burton (1927), John Anthony Bowden Cuddon (1928), Norton Juster (1929), Carol (Ann Warner) Shields (1935), Dorothy K. Fletcher (1940), Albert Innaurato (1948), Janice Kulyk Keefer (1952), Joël Pourbaix and Graham (Macdonald) Robb (1958), Lydia Lunch (b. Lydia Anne Koch) (1959), Jim Knipfel (1965), Salvatore Scibona (1975).

There is a condition worse than blindness, and that is, seeing something that isn't there.—Thomas Hardy

My thoughts went round and round and it occurred to me that if I ever wrote a novel it would be of the 'stream of consciousness' type and deal with an hour in the life of a woman at the sink.—Barbara Pym

Misinterpretation is the most deadly of human sins.—Lester del Rey

Books do not write themselves. One has to sit down and actually write them, even when inspiration is not present.—Dorothy K. Fletcher

June 3—Sydney Smith (1771), Caspar G. C. Reinwardt (1773), William Hone (1780), Charles Waterton (1782), Paul Lindau (1839), Eugeen van Oye (1840), Detlev (Freiherr Friedrich A. von) Liliencron (1844), Konstantin Dmitrievich Balmont (1867), Robert (Silliman) Hillyer (1895), Rosa Chacel (1898), Gerard den Brabander (Jan G. Jofriet) (1900), Mary Louise White Aswell (1902), Wilfred Thesiger (1910), William Douglas-Home (1912), Pedro Mir (1913), David Richard Holloway (1924), Gerhard Zwerenz (1925), Allen Ginsberg (1926), Marion (Eleanor) Zimmer (Breen) Bradley (1930), John Norman (John Frederick Lange Jr.) (1931), Irma Pamela Hall (1935), Larry McMurtry and David Nicholls (1936), Melissa Mathison (1950), Marjory Heath Wentworth (1958), Donald Mitchell "Don" Brown Jr. (1960), Anderson Cooper (1967), Tate Taylor (1969), Susan Abulhawa (1970).

I really would like to stop working forever—never work again, never do anything like the kind of work I'm doing now—and do nothing but write poetry and have leisure to spend the day outdoors and go to museums and see friends . . . . Just a literary and quiet city-hermit existence.—Allen Ginsberg

Science fiction encourages us to explore . . . all the futures, good and bad, that the human mind can envision.—Marion Zimmer Bradley

You expect far too much of a first sentence. Think of it as analogous to a good country breakfast: what we want is something simple, but nourishing to the imagination.—Larry McMurtry

June 4—Franz Xaver, Baron Von Zach (1754), Apollon Maykov (1821), Servaas Daems (Peeter Klein) (1838), Josef Sittard (1846), Frank N. D. Buchman (1878), Mabel Lucie Attwell and Theodor Haecker (1879), Karl Valentin (1882), Daan Boens (1893), Harry (Grew) Crosby (1898), Jacques Roumain and Patience Strong (1907), Walther Vanbeselaere (1908), Willy-August Linnemann (1914), Charles Collingwood (1917), Jack D. Hunter (1921), Elizabeth Jolley (1923), Doris Betts and Maurice Shadbolt (1932), Robert Fulgrum (1937), Daniel Topolski and Gordon Waller (1945), Bettina Gregory and James Kelman (1946), François Ricard (1947), Margaret Gibson (1948), Charles Dickinson and Wendy Pini (1951), Val McDermid and Paul Stewart (1955), Marie NDiaye (1967), Buddy Wakefield (1974).

There are, in actual fact, men who talk like books. Happily, however, there are also books that talk like men.—Theodor Haecker

I believe that imagination is stronger than knowledge. That myth is more potent than history. That dreams are more powerful than facts. That hope always triumphs over experience. That laughter is the only cure for grief. And I believe that love is stronger than death.—Robert Fulghum

A good idea for lyrics and a melody to expand on.—Gordon Waller

But some words to men and women, boys and girls alike: The quality of the work must merit the readers' time and money. Do it for yourself, but make yourself a member of your own audience. There is no other way to evaluate your own progress.—Wendy Pini

June 5—Pu Songling (1640), Adam Smith (1723), Christian August Lobeck (1781), Pat Garrett (1850), John Maynard Keynes (1883), Ivy Compton-Burnett (1884), Ruth Benedict (1887), Raden Mas Nato Suroto (1888), Roy Thomson (1894), Federico (del Sagrado Corazón de Jesús) García Lorca (1898), Barbara Gooden (1900), (William) Bruce Hutchison (1901), Hugo Huppert (1902), Rolf Bongs (1907), Beatrice de Cardi (1914), Alfred Kazin (1915), Alvin "Al" Fox and Jack Sutherland (1916), Richard McClure Scarry (1919), Cornelius Ryan (1920), Henry Kreisel (1922), Shirley Kaufman and Harry Mark Petrakis (1923), David (Russell) Wagoner (1926), Otto V. Walter (1928), Alifa Rifaat (1930), Jerzy Prokopiuk (1931), Christy Brown and Charlotte Fielden (1932), Bill D. Moyers (1934), Margaret Drabble and Laurali Rose Appleby "L. R." Wright (1939), Orlando Patterson (1940), Spalding Gray (1941), Ann Craft (1943), Matthew Lesko (1943), David Hare (1947), Ken Follett (1949), John Joseph "J. J." Bittenbinder and John Yau (1950), Suze Orman (1951), James Reasoner (1953), Margo Lanagan (1960), Richard Russell "Rick" Riordan Jr. (1964), Michael (Lewis) MacLennan (1968), Chuck Klosterman (1972), C. E. "Chris" Gatchalian (1974), Lauren Beukes (1976).

No society can surely be flourishing and happy, of which the far greater part of the members are poor and miserable.—Adam Smith

The writer writes in order to teach himself, to understand himself, to satisfy himself; the publishing of his ideas, though it brings gratification, is a curious anticlimax.—Alfred Kazin

Family life itself, that safest, most traditional, most approved of female choices, is not a sanctuary: It is, perpetually, a dangerous place.—Margaret Drabble

June 6—Pierre Corneille (1606), Claude-Jean Allouez (1622), Cornelis Loots (1765), Alexandr Sergeyevich Pushkin (1799), Timothy Shay Arthur (1809), Eliza Orzeszkowa (1841), (James Morrison) Steele MacKaye (1842), Gerben Postma (Ids) (1847), Henry John Newbolt (1862), Thomas Mann (1875), Dorothy Heyward (1890), Vladislac Vancura (1891), Will James (Ernest Dufault) (1892), (Peter) Dale Wimbrow (1895), Robert Sheriff (1896), Jan Struther (Joyce Anstruther et al.) (1901), Stefan Andres (1906), Isaiah Berlin (1909), Édouard Roditi (1910), Mignon McLaughlin (1913), Tom Scott (1918), Helen Forrester (June Bhatia) (1919), Cleo Virginia "V. C." Andrews (1923), Maxine Kumin (1925), Peter Spier (1927), Viktor Konezki (1929), Joy (Nozomi) Kogawa (1935), Stephen Dixon (1936), Alexander Cockburn (1941), Deborah Crombie (Darden) (1952), Harvey (Forbes) Fierstein and Cynthia Rylant (1954), Dana Carvey (1955), Richard Powers (1957), Elizabeth Wong (1958), François Avard (1968), Sarah Dessen (1970).

A writer is someone for whom writing is more difficult than it is for other people.—**Thomas Mann**

Words were the only net to catch a mood, the only sure weapon against oblivion.—**Jan Struther**

A critic can only review the book he has read, not the one which the writer wrote.—**Mignon McLaughlin**

June 7—Étienne Pasquier (1529), Paulus Voet (1619), Richard D. Blackmore (1825), Amelia Edwards (1831), Henry Ames Blood (1836), Samuel McChord Crothers (1857), Ernest William "E. W." Hornung (1866), Janet Ayer Fairbank (1878), William Walraven (1887), Elizabeth Bowen (1899), Jan (Johannes A.A.) Engelman (1900), Anthony David Machell Cox (1913), Gwendolyn Brooks (1917), Martin Carter (1927), Anthony Nicholas Maria Wahl (1928), Samuel Lipman (1934), Harry (Eugene) Crews (1935), Georgess McHargue (1941), Yolande Cornelia "Nikki" Giovanni Jr. (1943), Devra Lee Davis (1946), Welwyn Wilton Katz (1948), (Ferit) Orhan Pamuk (1952), (Karen) Louise Erdrich (1954), Hargurchet Singh "H. S." Bhabra (1955), Jesse Ball (1978).

A prose writer gets tired of writing prose, and wants to be a poet. So he begins every line with a capital letter, and keeps on writing prose.—**Samuel McChord Crothers**

I am a writer perhaps because I am not a talker.—**Gwendolyn Brooks**

What the artist owes the world is his work; not a model for living.—**Harry Crews**

June 8—Charles Reade (1814), Moriz Heyne (1837), Leo Birinski (1884), John G. Bennett (1897), Herman J. Friederic (H. J. Merlijn) (1900), Albe (Renaut A. Joostens) (1902), Gerrit C. Berkouwer (1903), Brian Coffey (1905), John W. Campbell (1910), N. Richard Nash (b. Nathan Richard Nusbaum) (1913), KuBa (1914), Ruth Stone (1915), Gwen Harwood (1920), Malcolm Boyd (1923), David (Adam) Cairns (1926), Monique Bosco and Jerry Stiller (1927), Kat(i)e (Gertrude Meredith) Wilhelm (1928), Ivan V. Lali (1932), Joan Rivers (Molinsky) (1933), Elizabeth A. Lynn and Alan John Scarfe (1946), Sara Paretsky (1947), Herb Greenberg (1952), Ginny Aiken (1955), Keenan Ivory Wayans (1958), Lutz Seiler (1963), Karin Alvtegen (1965), Gary Beers (1971), Rachel (Grace) Held Evans (1981).

Sow an act and you reap a habit. Sow a habit and you reap a character. Sow a character and you reap a destiny.—Charles Reade
What makes me laugh is, of course, the absurd, the horror—anything that upsets me.—Joan Rivers
Sometimes I panic and think I can't really write.—Sara Paretsky

June 9—Henricus Hondius (1573), Daniel Heinsius (1580), John Howard Payne (1791), Johnson J(ones) Hooper (1815), Bertha von Suttner (1843), Gerardus J.P.J. Bolland (1854), Rudolf Borchardt (1877), Johannes Clinge Doorenbos (1884), Samuel Nathaniel "S.M.: Behrman (1893), Curzio Malaparte (Kurt E. Suckert) (1898), Marcia Davenport (1903), Jose Luis Lopez Aranguren (1909), Isobel English (June Guesdon Braybrooke) (1920), Arthur Hertzberg (1921), George Axelrod and John Gillespie Magee Jr. (1922), (John) Keith Laumer (1925), Louise Maheux-Forcier (1929), Lin(wood) (Vrooman) Carter and Marvin Kalb (1930), Charles (Richard) Webb (1939), William Tremblay and Richard John "Dick" Vitale (1940), Charles North (1941), Joe (William) Haldeman (1943), Susan Swan (1945), John Gurda (1947), Denise Chong (1953), Gregory Maguire (1954), Jean M. Redmann (1955), Patricia Cornwell (b. Patricia Carroll Daniels) (1956), Louis Hamelin (1959), Steve Paikin (1960), Michael J. Fox and Aaron (Benjamin) Sorkin (1961).

The ability to laugh at its own pretensions and shortcomings is a true mark of the civilized nation, as it is of the civilized human.
—S. N. Behrman
Nothing is very important, and few things are important at all.
—Isobel English
I didn't invent forensic science and medicine. I just was one of the first people to recognize how interesting it is.—Patricia Cornwell

June 10—Fakhruddin 'Iraqi (1213), Esprit Fléchier (1632), Amable-G-P B. de Barante (1782), Edwin Arnold (1832), Constant A. Serrure (1835), Minot Judson Savage (1841), Jacques F. H. Perk (1859), Louis M. A. Couperus (1863), Gustave Vanzype (1869), Margit Kaffka (1880), Leo Weismantel (1888), Paul J. M. Lindemans (1890), Immanuel Velikovsky (1895), Henri Bruning (1900), Terence Rattigan (1911), Mary (Josephine) Lavin (1912), Saul Bellow (1915), Bill Waddington (1916), Prince Philip, Duke of Edinburgh (1921), Nat Hentoff and James Salter (James Arnold Horowitz) (1925), Willem Oltmans (1926), Maurice Sendak and Asher Wallfish (1928), Edward Osborne "E. O." Wilson (1929), F(rancis) Lee Bailey (Jr.) (1933), Brian (Harry) Freemantle (1936), Susan Howe (1937), Janet Kauffman (1945), Mensje F. van Keulen-van der Steen (1946), Kate Snow (1969).

I don't think I would ever want to be a writer of detective stories—but I would like to be a detective and there is a large deal of detection in the short story.—Mary Lavin

You never have to change anything you got up in the middle of the night to write.—Saul Bellow

I don't enjoy writing, and I certainly would not do it for a living. Some people do, but some people enjoy flagellation.—Prince Philip, Duke of Edinburgh

Whenever I see that kind of story, where everybody agrees, I know there's something wrong.—Nat Hentoff

June 11—Barnabe Googe (1540), Ben Jonson (1572), George Wither (1588), Francesco A. Vallotti (1697), Edward Capell (1713), Jan H. Leopold (1865), Alfred L. Kroeber (1876), Renee Vivien (1877), Joseph Lewis (1889), Edward B. B Shanks (1892), Bruno Frei (1897), Yasonari Kawabata (1899), Anton D. Hildebrand (1907), Jacques-Yves Cousteau (1910), Josephine (Louise) Miles (1911), Hendrik Berkhof (1914), Irving Howe (1920), Michael Meyer and Beatrice "Fiet" van Ommeren-Samson (1921), Erving Goffman (1922), William (Clark) Styron (Jr.) (1925), David "Brother Dave" Gardner (1926), George (Palmer) Garrett (1929), (Jean-Paul) Frédérick (Baron) Tristan (1931), Athol Fugard (1932), Gene Wilder (Jerome Silbermann) (1933), Christina Crawford (1939), Robert (Norman) Munsch (1945), Eduardo (Oscar) Machado (1953), Mark Anthony Jarman (1955), Nathaniel Philbrick (1956), Hugh Laurie (1959).

> Give money me, take friendship whoso list,
> For friends are gone, come once adversity,
> When money yet remaineth safe in chest,
> That quickly can thee bring from misery.
> —Barnabe Googe

The good writing of any age has always been the product of *someone's* neurosis, and we'd have a mighty dull literature if all the writers that came along were a bunch of happy chuckleheads.— William Styron

I write funny. If I can make my wife laugh, I know I'm on the right track. But yes, I don't like to get Maudlin. And I have a tendency towards it.—Gene Wilder

June 12—Harriet Martineau (1802), Parson Lot (Charles Kingsley Jr.) (1819), Johanna Spyri (1829), James Oliver "Jim" Curwood (1878), Djuna Barnes, (Viola) Blanche Evans Dean, and John Donald Robb (1892), Hendrik J. Elias (1902), Sandro Penna (1906), Max Tailleur (1908), Bill Naughton (1910), Milovan Djilas (1911), Jameel Jalibi (1912), H. C. Artmann (1921), James Houston (1921), Christopher Derrick (1921), Paul Howe Shepard Jr. (1925), Henry Slesar (1927), Anne Frank (1929), Brigid Brophy (1929), Trevanian (Rodney William Whitaker) (1931), Rona Jaffe (1932), Christoph Meckel (1935), Harry Glasper (1946), Tess Gerritsen (1953), Ella Joyce (Cherron Hoye) (1954), Jim Goad (1961), Michael Redhill (1966), Icíar Bollaín (1967), Julie Orringer (1973), Josh Dies (1983).

You had better live your best and act your best and think your best today; for today is the sure preparation for tomorrow and all the other tomorrows that follow.—Harriet Martineau

Except a living man, there is nothing more wonderful than a book.—Charles Kingsley Jr.

If I read a book that impresses me, I have to take myself firmly in hand before I mix with other people; otherwise they would think my mind rather queer.—Anne Frank

Whenever people say we mustn't be sentimental, you can take it they are about to do something cruel. And, if they add, we must be realistic, they mean they are going to make money out of it.—Brigid Brophy

June 13—Adrien Baillet (1649), Giuseppe Cerutti (1738), Fanny Burney (Frances d'Arblay) (1752), Thomas Arnold (1795), Bernard ter Haar (1806), Dwight B. Waldo (1864), William Butler Yeats (1865), Leopoldo Lugones (1874), Étienne Gilson (1884), Bruno Frank (1887), Fernando A. Nogueira de Seabra Pessoa (1888), Dorothy L(eigh) Sayers (1893), Leo Kanner and Mark van Doren (1894), Paavo Johannes Nurmi (1897), Lode Zielens (1901), Gonzalo Torrente Ballester (1910), Hector de Saint-Denys Garneau (1912), Etienne Leroux (1913), Jean Villain (1928), Robert (Anthony) Inman and Irvin D(avid) Yalom (1931), Claire Harris (1937), John Newlove (1938), Whitley Strieber (1945), Peter Balakian (1951), Lise Tremblay (1957), Helen Humphreys (1961), Hannah Storm (1962), Audrey Niffenegger (1963), Marcel (Raymond) Theroux (1968), Johannes Grenzfurthner (1975), Anis Mojgani (1977).

Traveling is the ruin of all happiness! There's no looking at a building after seeing Italy.—Fanny Burney

The creations of a great writer are little more than the moods and passions of his own heart, given surnames and Christian names, and sent to walk the earth.—William Butler Yeats

The great advantage about telling the truth is that nobody ever believes it.—Dorothy L. Sayers

June 14—Giglio Gregorio Giraldi (1479), Alexander Keith McClung and Harriet Beecher Stowe (1811), John Bartlett (1820), Lucien Cerfaux (1883), Louis Finkelstein (1895), Kawabata Yasunari (1899), George Wylie Henderson (1904), Margaret Bourke-White (1906), Nicolas Bentley and René Char (1907), Vladimir Soloukhin (1924), Barbara Hammer Avedon and Pierre Salinger (1925), Hermann Kant (1926), Jerzy Kosinski (b. Józef Lewinkopf) (1933), John Edgar Wideman (1941), Laurie Colwin (1944), Carolyn (Penny) Chute (1947), Harry Turtledove (1949), Leon Wieseltier (1952), Mona Elizabeth (Jandali) Simpson (1957), Michael Gerber and Peter Hessler (1969), Diablo Cody (1978).

The past, the present and the future are really one: they are today.—Harriet Beecher Stowe

Not everyone can write a book or paint a picture or write a symphony, but almost anyone can fall in love. There is something almost miraculous in that.—Laurie Colwin

I know white clothing is supposed to enhance that summer glow, but writers don't tan.—Diablo Cody

June 15—Samuel Apostool (1638), François-Xavier Garneau (1809), Edward Channing (1856), William Wilfred Campbell (1858?), Konstantin Dmitriyevich Balmont (1867), Eduard R. Verkade (1878), William McFee (1881), Ramon Lopez Velarde (1888), Willem Scheps (1898), Peter Shankland (1901), Wilbert Vere "W. V." Awdry (1911), Amy Clampitt (1920), James Emanuel (1921), Erland Josephson (1923), Jaime Sabines (1925), Ibn-e-Insha (1927), George (Edwin) Starbuck (1931), Pierre Billon, Ray Coleman, and Lola Lemire Tostevin (1937), Stephen Breyer and Brian Jacques (1939), Xaviera Hollander (DeVries) (1942), Ana Castillo (1953), Adam Rapp (1968).

If you are going to be a pioneer . . . you cannot be faint of heart.—William Wilfred Campbell

Women who are inclined to write poetry at all are inspired by being mad at something.—Amy Clampitt

I wrote about a bird that cleaned a crocodile's teeth. The story was so good that my teacher could not believe that a ten-year-old could write that well. I was even punished because my teacher thought I'd lied about writing it! I had always loved to write, but it was then that I realized that I had a talent for it.—Brian Jacques

June 16—John Cheke (1514), John Cleveland (1613), Adam Smith (1723), Mary Katharine Goddard (1738), Salawat Yulayev (1754), Fritz Schulz and Theo(dorus J.) Thijssen (1879), Murray Leinster (William Fitzgerald Jenkins) (1896), John Hadfield (1907), Victor Canning (1911), John Howard Griffin, Isabelle (Christian) Holland, and Geoffrey (Ernest) Jenkins (1920), Joachim Nowotny (1933), August Willemsen (1936), Erich Segal (1927), Erich (Wolf) Segal (1937), Torgny Lindgren and Joyce Carol Oates (1938), Mumtaz Hamid Rao (1941), J(acqueline) Jill Robinson (1955), Isobelle (Jane) Carmody (1958), Scott Alexander (1963), Gabriel Gudding and Adrienne Shelly (1966), Rajiv Joseph (1974).

Our own tung shold be written cleane and pure, vnmixt and vnmangled with borrowing of other tunges.—John Cheke

Short stories do not say this happened and this happened and this happened. They are a microcosm and a magnification rather than a linear progression.—Isobelle Carmody

Any kind of creative activity is likely to be stressful. The more anxiety, the more you feel that you are headed in the right direction. Easiness, relaxation, comfort—these are not conditions that usually accompany serious work.—Joyce Carol Oates

June 17—John B. Wesley (1703), James Nelson Barker (1784), Alexandre Vinet (1797), Henrik Wergeland (1808), Ferdinand Freiligrath (1810), Henry Lawson (1867), Nicolae Iorga and James Weldon Johnson (1871), Philipp A. Kohnstamm (1875), Carl Van Fight and Carl Van Vechten (1880), William Lindsay White (1900), Michail Swetlow (1903), Maurice Cloche (1907), Jacob "Jimmy" Herman Huizinga (1908), Viktor P. Nekrasov (1911), Felix Hartlaub (1913), John R(ichard) Hersey (1914), Kingman Brewster and Max Dendermonde (Henk Hazelhoff) (1919), Gotthold Gloger (1924), Harry Browne (1933), Hanna Johansen (1939), George Akerlof (1940), Ron Padgett (1942), Peter Rosei (1946), Kerry Greenwood (1954), Gail Jones and Alan Shaw Taylor (1955), Will Forte (1970).

The majority of writers ought to translate themselves; there are but few thoughts that are born translated, that is, clothed with the power best fitted alike to express and transmit them. What we have in the first instance written for ourselves, should be written a second time for others.—Alexandre Vinet

To be a writer is to sit down at one's desk in the chill portion of every day, and to write; not waiting for the little jet of the blue flame of genius to start from the breastbone—just plain going at it, in pain and delight. To be a writer is to throw away a great deal, not to be satisfied, to type again, and then again, and once more, and over and over.—John Hersey

Because we were stranded together and because I stuttered, we read. There is no refuge so private, no asylum more sane. There is no facility of voices captured elsewhere so entire and so marvellous. My tongue was lumpish and fixed, but in reading, silent reading, there was a release, a flight, a wheeling off into the blue spaces of exclamatory experience, diffuse and improbable, gloriously homeless.—Gail Jones

June 18—Gabriello Chiabrera (1552), Thomas Overbury (1581), Royall Tyler (1757), Frances Sargent (Locke) Osgood (1811), Ivan Goncharov (1812), Pavel Annenkov (1813), Edward Wyllis Scripps (1854), Jose FdT Coelho (1861), George Essex Evans (1863), Leonid Nikolaevich Andreev (1871), S. S. Van Dine (William Huntingdon Wright) (1888), Hans Ruin (1891), Philip Barry (1896), Raymond Radiguet (1903), John Gardener (1905), Anahareo (Gertrude Moltke Bernard) (1906), Sylvia Porter (1913), Inez J. Baskin (1916), Mary Ward Brown (1917), Aster Berkhof (Louis Van de Bergh) (1920), Donald L. Keene (1922), William Humphrey (1924), Rex Collings (1925), John Phillipps Kenyon (1927), Rodolfo "Corky" Gonzáles (1928), Leland (Mosley) Hawes Jr. (1929), Della Smith (1931), Geoffrey Hill (1932), Gail (Kathleen) Godwin (1937), Patricia Dobler (1939), Roger Ebert and (James) Paul McCartney (1942), Winfried Georg "W. G." Sebald (1944), Russell Ash (1946), Carol (Ann) Windley (1947), William Randolph Hearst III and Chris Van Allsburg (1949), Christopher Largen (1969), Crystal Renn (1986).

The detective himself should never turn out to be the culprit. —S. S. van Dine

When I write, I fall into the zone many writers, painters, musicians, athletes, and craftsmen of all sorts seem to share: In doing something I enjoy and am expert at, deliberate thoughts fall aside and it is all just there. I think of the next word no more than the composer thinks of the next note.—Roger Ebert

Dreams say what they mean, but they don't say it in daytime language.—Gail Godwin

June 19—Annibale Caro (1507), James I (James Stuart) (1566), Thomas Fuller (1608), Blaise Pascal (1623), Hugues F. R. de Lamennais (1782), Gustav Schwab (1792), Louise Clarke Pyrnelle (Elizabeth Louise Clarke Parnell) (1850), Elbert Hubbard (1856), Sam Walter Foss (1858), Jose Protasio Rizal (1861), Sutton E(lbert) Griggs (1872), Johann Sigurjonsson (1880), Georges Ribemont-Dessaignes (1884), Robert Herberigs (1886), Laura Z(ametkin) Hobson (1900), Earl W. Bascom (1906), Osamu Dazai (1909), Pauline Kael (1919), Maris Soule (1939), Tobias (Jonathan Ansell) Wolff (1945), Salman Rushdie and John Ralston Saul (1947), Steven Naifeh (1952), Kimberley Leston (1959), Leo McKay Jr. (1964).

When we read too fast or too slowly, we understand nothing.—Blaise Pascal

This will never be a civilized country until we expend more money for books than we do for chewing gum.—Elbert Hubbard

A mistake in judgment isn't fatal, but too much anxiety about judgment is.—Pauline Kael

Everything has to be pulling weight in a short story for it to be really of the first order.—Tobias Wolff

June 20—George Hickes (1642), Nicholas Rowe (1674), Hans Adolph Brorson (1694), Adam Ferguson (1723), Anna Laetitia Barbauld (1743), Moses Waddel (1770), Marceline Desbordes-Valmore (1786), Charles Timothy Brooks (1813), John Godfrey Saxe I (1816), Charles W(addell) Chesnutt (1858), Ivans (Jacob van Schevichaven) (1866), (Joseph) Trumbull Stickney (1874), Kurt Schwitters (1887), S. M. Tretjakow (1892), George Delacorte (1894), Elisabeth Hauptmann (1897), Rupert Croft-Cooke (1903), Lillian Hellman (1905), Stanley Burnshaw and Catherine Cookson (1906), Joan Harrison (1909), Josephine Winslow Johnson (1910), Anthony Buckeridge (1912), Lillian Jackson Braun (1913), Celia (Margaret) Fremlin (1914). Zoltán Sztáray (1918), Bruce Gordon (1919), Peter Gay (Peter Joachim Fröhlich) (1923), Audie Murphy (1924), Catherine Aird (Kinn Hamilton McIntosh) (1930), Robert Ivanovich Rozhdestvensky (1932), Claire Tomalin (Claire Delavenay) (1933), Paul Muldoon (1951), Vikram Seth (1952), Robert Crais (1953), E(verette) Lynn Harris (1955), Tim Weiner (1956), Derek McCormack (1969), Jason Robert Brown (1970).

The dead of midnight is the noon of thought.—Anna Letitia Barbauld

If you believe, as the Greeks did, that man is at the mercy of the gods, then you write tragedy. The end is inevitable from the beginning. But if you believe that man can solve his own problems and is at nobody's mercy, then you will probably write melodrama.—Lillian Hellman

Revision has its own peculiar pleasures and its own peculiar frustrations. The ground rules are already established; the characters already exist. You don't have to bring the characters to life, but you do have to make them more convincing.—Vikram Seth

June 21—Wolfgang Menzel (1798), W. E. Aytoun (1813), William Stubbs (1825), Joaquim M. Machado de Assic (1839), Machado de Assis (1839), Johannes Schlaf (1862), Damrong Rajanubhab (1862), Heinrich Wölfflin (1864), Henry M. Tomlinson (1873), Fjodor W. Gladkow (1883), Fyodor Gladkov (1883), Reinhold Niebuhr (1892), Milward Kennedy (1894), Donald C. Peattie (1898), Jean Paul Sartre (1905), Aleksandr Tvardovsky (1910), Ford Worth (Manning Lee Stokes) (1911), Mary (Therese) McCarthy (1912), Irving Shulman (1913), James Bysse Joll (1918), Gérard Pelletier (1919), Patricia Goedicke (1931), Wulf Kirsten (1934), Françoise Sagan (Quoirez) (1935), William (Frederick) Blinn and Silver Donald Cameron (1937), John W. Dower (1938), Joe Flaherty (1941), Henry S. Taylor (1942), Adam Zagajewski (1945), Trond Kirkvaag (1946), Ian McEwan and Andrzej Sapkowski (1948), (Mary) Elizabeth (Anania) Edwards and Jane Urquhart, (1949), Anne Carson (1950), Robert Menasse (1954), Katherine Jean "Kate" Ross (1956), Gosho Aoyama (1963), Alisyn Camerota (1968), Gretchen Carlson (1968), Olen Steinhauer (1970), Alon Hilu (1972).

A good book is always a book about travel; it is about life's journey.—H. M. Tomlinson

In any work that is truly creative, I believe, the writer cannot be omniscient in advance about the effects tht he proposes to produce. The suspense of a novel is not only in the reader, but in the novelist, who is intensely curious about what will happen to the hero.—Mary McCarthy

Of course the illusion of art is to make one believe that great literature is very close to life, but exactly the opposite is true. Life is amorphous, literature is formal.—Françoise Sagan

There's just something about youth and comedy that go together. Maybe it's that foolishness, that silliness that you can get away with when you're younger, that you can't get away with when you're older.—Joe Flaherty

June 22—John Taylor (1704), Jacques Delille (1738), Nikoli A. Poveloi (1796), Countess Ida von Hahn-Hahn (1805), Julian Hawthorne (1846), H(enry) Rider Haggard (1856), Frank Heino Damrosch (1859), William MacLeod Raine (1871), Albert P. A. A. Besnard (1887), Julian S. Huxley (1887), Franz de Backer (1891), Norbert Elias (1897), Edmund A. Chester (1897), Erich Maria Remarque (1898), Anne Morrow Lindbergh and Billy Wilder (1906), Fuller Asbury Kimbrell (1909), Lilo Hardel (1914), Helen Norris Bell, Emil Ludwig Fackenheim, and Eugenia Price (1916), Hillary (Baldwin) Waugh (1920), Abbas Kiarostami (1940), Aude (Claudette Charbonneau-Tissot) and Octavia E(stele) Butler (1947), Kenneth Hale "Ken" Fortenberry and Jimmy Lerner (1951), Elliott Hayes and Tim Russ (1956), Jennifer Finney Boylan (b. James Boylan) (1958), Daniel "Dan" Brown (1964), Akhil Sharma (1971).

Man's cleverness is almost indefinite, and stretches like an elastic band, but human nature is like an iron ring. You can go round and round it, you can polish it highly, you can even flatten it a little on one side, whereby you will make it bulge out the other, but you will NEVER, while the world endures and man is man, increase its total circumference.—H. Rider Haggard

To speculate without facts is to attempt to enter a house of which one has not the key, by wandering aimlessly round and round, searching the walls and now and then peeping through the windows. Facts are the key.—Julian Huxley

You don't start out writing good stuff. You start out writing crap and thinking it's good stuff, and then gradually you get better at it. That's why I say one of the most valuable traits is persistence. —Octavia Butler

June 23—Justus G. Schottel (Schottelius) (1612), Giambattista Vico (1668), Matthijs Siegenbeek (1774), Irvin S. Cobb (1876), Anna Akhmatova (Anna Andreyevna Gorenko) (1889), Hans C. Branner and Anthony Veiller (1903), Wolfgang Koeppen (1906), Paulus Akkerman (Paul fen Nijenborn) (1908), Jean Anouilh (1910), Thomas Wakefield "Tom W." Blackburn II, Molly Harris, and Jacques Rabemananjara (1913), Thomas Rogers (1927), Michael Shaara (1928), Urs Jaeggi (1931), Richard Bach (1936), Roger McDonald (1941), Kjell Albin Abrahamson (1945), Darhyl S. Ramsey (1948), John Katzenbach (1950), Maggie Greenwald (1955), Steven Dietz (1958), David Leavitt (1961), Joseph Hill "Joss" Whedon (1964), Thea Dorn (Christiane Scherer) (1970), Kathryn Borel (Jr.) (1979).

If writers were good businessmen, they'd have too much sense to be writers.—Irvin S. Cobb

Talent is like a faucet, while it is open, one must write.—Jean Anouilh

Here is the test to find whether your mission on Earth is finished: if you're alive, it isn't.—Richard Bach

June 24—Juan de la Cruz (de Yepes) (1542), St. John of the Cross (1542), Robert Parsons (1546), Samuel Ampzing (1590), Johann Albrecht Bengel (1687), Jean-Baptiste de Boyer (1704), Henry Ward Beecher (1813), Ambrose Bierce (1842), Brooks Adams (1848), Aleksei M. Remizov (1877), George Shiels (1886), Bruce Marshall (1899), Kurt Kusenberg (1904), Arseny Tarkovsky (1907), Tullio Pinelli (1908), Ernesto Sábato (1911), Norman Cousins (1912), John Ciardi (1916), Miriam Mandel (1930), Pete Hamill (1935), Anita Mazumdar Desai (1937), Lawrence Block (1938), Julia Kristeva (1941), Gerhart Roth (1942), Kathryn Lasky (1944), Mercedes R(itchie) Lackey (1950), Eugen Ruge (1954), Connie McBride (1967), Louisa Leaman (1976), Brian Fitzgerald (1982).

The covers of this book are too far apart.—**Ambrose Bierce**

It makes little difference how many university courses or degrees a person may own. If he cannot use words to move an idea from one point to another, his education is incomplete.—**Norman Cousins**

You don't have to suffer to be a poet; adolescence is enough suffering for anyone.—**John Ciardi**

Writing is the hardest work in the world not involving heavy lifting.—**Pete Hamill**

I was actually very hesitant to write about Marie Antoinette. She seemed at first glance—well, I cannot think of any other term—an airhead of the first degree.—Kathryn Lasky

Remember, thinking about writing, planning to write and talking about writing isn't the same as WRITING. The best advice I was ever given as a writer is a bit crude, but I repeat it to myself often. "Just get it on paper. Even if it's a shitty first draft, you can edit it later. You can't edit what you don't write." So write on!—**Connie McBride**

June 25—Georges Courteline (Moineaux) (1858), Robert Erskine Childers (1870), Arthur Chapman (1873), George (Francis) Abbott (1887), Hans Marchwitza (1890), Josephine Tey and Gordon Daviot (Elizabeth Mackintosh) (1896), Izak D. du Plessis (1900), George Orwell (Eric A. Blair) (1903), Daniel Fuchs (1909), Peter Lind Hayes (1915), Theodore P. Toynbee (1916), Percy Howard "P. H." Newby (1918), Jean-Louis Bory (1919), Dorothy Gilman and Nicholas Mosley (1923), Ingeborg Bachmann (1926), Eric Carle (1929), Larry Kramer (1935), Paul Nowee (1936), Mirabel Morgan (1937), A. J. Quinnell (1940), Michel Tremblay (1942), Linda (Dickinson) Spalding (1943), Kerry Shawn Keys (1946), Barbara Gowdy (1950), Anthony Bourdain (1956), Ricky Gervais (1961), Mike Myers and Yann Martel (1963), Ariel Gore (1970), Leanne Shapton (1973).

If you think about the unthinkable long enough it becomes quite reasonable.—Josephine Tey

Writing a book is a horrible, exhausting struggle, like a long bout of some painful illness. One would never undertake such a thing if one were not driven on by some demon whom one can neither resist nor understand.—George Orwell

If something anticipated arrives too late it finds us numb, wrung out from waiting, and we feel—nothing at all. The best things arrive on time.—Dorothy Gilman

June 26—Hedwig Sophia Augusta (1681), Julius Rodenberg (Levy) (1831), Bernard Berenson (1865), Martin Andersen Nexø (1869), Andre Maurois (Emile Herzog) and Anna M. F. van Wageningen-Salomons (1885), Sidney (Coe) Howard and Vladislav Vancura (1891), Pearl S(ydenstricker) Buck and Henry Canova Vollam "H. V." Morton (1892), Gladys Hasty Carroll (1904), Stefan Andres (1906), Betty Askwith (1909), Laurie Lee (1914), Walter (Lorimer) Farley and Charlotte Zolotow (1915), Robert Kroetsch (1927), Colin Wilson (1931), Jeremy Wolfenden (1934), Edith Pearlman (1936), Luis Valdez (1940), Yves Beauchemin (1941), James Anderson (1953), Élise Turcotte (1957), (Andrew) Jonathan Bate (1958).

If you create an act, you create a habit. If you create a habit, you create a character. If you create a character, you create a destiny.—Andre Maurois

I don't wait for moods. You accomplish nothing if you do that. Your mind must know it has got to get down to work.—Pearl S. Buck

The perfect place for a writer is in the hideous roar of a city, with men making a new road under his window in competition with a barrel organ, and on the mat a man waiting for the rent.—H. V. Morton

. . . [H]alf the trouble in the world comes from people asking 'What have I achieved?' rather than 'What have I enjoyed?' I've been writing about a subject I love as long as I can remember—horses and the people associated with them, anyplace, anywhere, anytime. I couldn't be happier knowing that young people are reading my books. But even more important to me is that I've enjoyed so much the writing of them.—Walter Farley

June 27—Bankim Chandra Chattopadhyay (1838), Ivan Vazov (1850), Lafcadio Hearn (1850), Paul Laurence Dunbar (1872), Jean François van Royen (1878), Helen (Adams) Keller (1880), Eduard Spranger (1882), Gaston Bachelard (1884), Lewis Bernstein Namier (1888), Alexandra G. "Alja" von Hoyer-Rachmanova (1898), Vernon P. Watkins (1906), João Guimarães Rosa (1908), Robert Aickman and Alexander Pola (Abraham Polak) (1914), M. Carl Holman (1919), I. A. L. Diamond (Iţec [Itzek] Domnici) (1920), Herbert Ziergiebel (1922), Efua Theodore Sutherland (1924), Frank O'Hara (1926), Captain Kangaroo (Bob Keeshan) (1927), James Lincoln Collier (1928), Joachim Wohlgemuth (1932), Lucille Clifton (1936), Ivan Doig (1939), James P(atrick) Hogan (1941), Cornelis J. "Kees" Ouwens (1944), Alvin D. Hall and Douglas Unger (1952), Alice McDermott (1953), Barrett "Barry" Root (1954), Dan Jurgens (1959), Eric Simonson (1960), Simon (Jonathan) Sebag Montefiore (1965), Dawud Wharnsby (David Howard Wharnsby) (1972), Nekima Valdez Levy-Pounds (1976).

Literary success of any enduring kind is made by refusing to do what publishers want, by refusing to write what the public wants, by refusing to accept any popular standard, by refusing to write anything to order.—Lafcadio Hearn

People are taking it for granted that [the African-American] ought not to work with his head. And it is so easy for these people among whom we are living to believe this; it flatters and satisfies their self-complacency.—Paul Laurence Dunbar

The most pathetic person in the world is someone who has sight, but has no vision.—Helen Keller

Pain always produces logic, which is very bad for you.—Frank O'Hara

June 28—Giovanni della Casa (1503), Jean-Jacques Rousseau (1712), Otto Julius Bierbaum (1865), Luigi Pirandello (1867), Berthold Viertel (1885), Floyd (James) Dell (1887), Esther (Louise) Forbes (1891), Edward H. Carr (1892), Leon Kruczkowski (1900), Richard (Charles) Rodgers (1902), Safford Cape (1906), Eric Ambler (1909), David "Honeyboy" Edwards (1915), Bert Schierbeek (Lambertus) (1918), Aaron Edward "A. E." Hotchner (1920), Terje Stigen (1922), Mel Brooks (Melvin Kaminsky) and Robert Shelton Shapiro (1926), Theo van Tijn (1927), Harold Evans and Nicholas Anthony "Nick" Virgilio (1928), Maureen Howard (1930), Bette Greene (1934), Gisela Kraft (1936), Peter Hall (1936), Alan Coren (1938), Enid Dame (1943), Robert L(ynn) Asprin and Gilda Radner (1946), Mark Helprin (1947), Jean-Christophe Rufin (1952), Brad Fraser (1959), Aimee Bender (1969), Florian Zeller (1979), Alexx Calise (1985).

However great a man's natural talent may be, the act of writing cannot be learned all at once.—Jean-Jacques Rousseau

Every human being has hundreds of separate people living under his skin. The talent of a writer is his ability to give them their separate names, identities, personalities and have them relate to other characters living with him.—Mel Brooks

A humorist tells himself every morning, "I hope it's going to be a rough day." When things are going well, it's much harder to make the right jokes.—Alan Coren

I wanted a perfect ending. Now I've learned, the hard way, that some poems don't rhyme, and some stories don't have a clear beginning, middle and end.—Gilda Radner

June 29—Giacomo Leopardi (1798), Willibald Alexis (Georg Wilhelm Heinrich Häring) (1798), John Newton Brown (1803), Celia Laighton Thaxter (1835), James Harvey Robinson (1863), Antoon Schweigmann (1893), Fulgence Charpentier (1897), Antoine de Saint-Exupéry (1900), Robert Traver (John D. Voelker) (1903), Manuel Altolaguirre (1905), Paul Lebeau (1908), Frank (Henry) Loesser (1910), John Toland (1912), Frédéric Dard (1921), Vasko Popa (1922), Sidney "Cid" Corman and John (Meade) Haines (1924), Stokely Carmichael/Kwame Toure (1941), Oleg Korenfeld (1977).

The meaning of things lies not in the things themselves, but in our attitude towards them.—Antoine de Saint-Exupéry

It was that there are no simple lessons in history, that it is human nature that repeats itself, not history.—John Toland

There are several ways to be a fool, but the fool always chooses the worst.—Frédéric Dard

June 30—John Gay (1685), Thomas Lovell Beddoes (1803), Friedrich T. Vischer (1807), Stanko Vraz (Jakob Frass) (1810), Franz von Dingelstedt (1814), Joseph D. Hooker (1817), Hendrik Jan Schimmel (1823), Gerrit Kalff (1856), Georges Duhamel (1884), Harold (Joseph) Laski (1893), Charles Camproux and Winston (Mawdsley) Graham (1908), Juan Bosch (1909), Hannah Kahn and Czesław Miłosz (1911), Martha Blum (1913), Judson Crews (1917), Patrick Earl "Pat" McCauley (1927), Frank Ulrich Marcus (1928), James Goldman (1929), David John "Dave" Duncan (1933), Robert Ballard (1942), Yasuko (Nguyen) Thanh (1971).

Tell me and I forget. Show me and I remember. Involve me and I understand.—John Gay

Between the two windows stood the writing-table, covered with heaps of newspapers, stacks of letters, mountains of ledgers, bound in canvas or leather, and tipped with brass at the corners; a chaos for every eye and every hand but the master's.—Franz von Dingelstedt

The number of substitutes for fine and clear thinking the world provides positively gnaws at one's vitals.—Harold J. Laski

When a writer is born into a family, the family is doomed. —Czesław Milosz

Born in July

July 1—Hadrianus Junius (Adriaen de Jonghe) (1511), Joseph Hall (1574), Johann Heinrich Heidegger (1633), G. W. Leibniz (1646), Pedro R. de Campomanes (1723), Georg C(hristoph) Lichtenberg (1742), George Sand (Amantine Lucile Aurore Dupin) (1804), Jadwiga Łuszczewska (1834), Florence (Van Leer) Earle (Nicholson) Coates (1850), Robert Allen "Bob" Cole (1868), William Strunk Jr. (1869), Michel H. Campen (1874), Susan (Keating) Glaspell (1876), James M. Cain (1892), Pavel G. Antokolski (1896), Irna Phillips (1901), Bill Stern (1907), Paul Hardy (1908), Juan Carlos Onetti (1909), Roy McKelvie (1912), Jo Sinclair (1913), Jean Stafford (1915), Hans Bender (1919), Oakley (Maxwell) Hall (1920), François-Regis Bastide (1926), Claude Berri (1935), Wallace "Wally" Amos Jr. (1936), Denis (Hale) Johnson (1949), Harryette Mullen (1953), Dan Aykroyd (1952), Lisa Scottoline (1955), Louise Penny (1958).

I regard reviews as a kind of infant's disease to which newborn books are subject.—Georg C. Lichtenberg

I am not a writer except when I write.—Juan Carlos Onetti

It never occurs to her that she will not be a writer and only occasionally does it occur to her, depressingly, that she is going to grow into a woman, not a man.—Jean Stafford

When I'm not acting, I'm writing, building an inventory of scripts. Even if they sit on the shelf, I just keep stacking them up. —Dan Aykroyd

July 2—Samuel Penhallow (1665), Friedrich Gottlieb Klopstock (1724), Lili Braun (Amalie von Kretschmann) (1865), Hermann Hesse (1877), James Boyd (1888), Cor Hermus (1889), Richard Bruce Nugent (1906), Thurgood Marshall (1908), Hermann Bengtson (1909), Hans Gunther Adler (1910), Diego Fabbri (1911), Bert Decorte (1915), Pierre Dubois (1917), Jean (Carolyn) Craighead George (1919), Eliseo Diego (1920), Wisława Szymborska (1923), Charles Muñoz and Octavian Paler (1926), Pavel Kohout (1928), Ed Bullins (1935), M(ichael) A(nthony) Foster and Alexandros Panagoulis (1939), Irving Martin Abella and Lawrence James "L. J." Davis (1940), Larry David (1947), Lee Maracle (1950), Jack Gantos (1951), Kevin Michael Grace (1955), Cynthia Kadohata (1956), Terry Rossio (1960), Chris Lynch (1962), Mark Kermode (1963), Evelyn Lau (1971), Darren Shan (1972), Andy McDermott and Matthew John Reilly (1974), Tao Lin (1983).

Words do not express thoughts very well. They always become a little different immediately after they are expressed, a little distorted, a little foolish.—Hermann Hesse

Why does this written doe bound through these written woods? For a drink of written water from a spring. . .—Wisława Szymborska

When you're not concerned with succeeding, you can work with complete freedom.—Larry David

July 3—Claude Fauchet (1530), Increase Mather (1639), Edward Young (1683), Arnold Hoogvliet (1687), Nikoli A. Poveloi (1796), F. Kornberger (1851), Charlotte Perkins Gilman (1860), George M. Cohan (1878), Alfred Korzybski (1879), Franz Kafka (1883), John Mason Brown (1900), Francis Steegmuller (1906), Mary Frances Kennedy "M. F. K." Fisher and Thomas Narcejac (1908), João Saldanha (1917), Emmanuel Bankole Timothy (1923), Evelyn Anthony and G. B. Fuchs (1928), Andres Burnier (Catharina Dessaur) (1931), Manfred Bieler (1934), Tom Stoppard (1937), Anthony Piccione and Jay Tarses (1939), Geraldo Rivera (Gerry Rivers) (1943), Dave Barry (1947), Rohinton Mistry (1952), Franny Billingsley (1954), Faye Resnick (1957), Matthew Fraser and Charles Murray "Charlie" Higson (1958), Joanne Harris (1964).

Who knows if Shakespeare might not have thought less if he had read more.—Edward Young

Don't bend; don't water it down; don't try to make it logical; don't edit your own soul according to the fashion. Rather, follow your most intense obsessions mercilessly.—Franz Kafka

Don't you wish you had a job like mine? All you have to do is think up a certain number of words! Plus, you can repeat words! And they don't even have to be true!—Dave Barry

My heroes and heroines are often unlikely people who are dragged into situations without meaning to become involved, or people with a past that has never quite left them. They are often isolated, introspective people, often confrontational or anarchic in some way, often damaged or secretly unhappy or incomplete.
—Joanne Harris

July 4—Paul Scarron (1610), Christian F. Gellert (1715), Michel-Jean Sedaine (1719), Desire de Haerne (1804), Nathaniel Hawthorne (1804), Theodor W. Ahlwardt (1828), Edward Gailliard (1841), Alexander Byvanck (1884), Arthur George "A. G." Gaston (1892), Mao Dun (1896), Pilar Barbosa (1898), Malka Lee (1904), Lionel Trilling (1905), Howard Taubman (1907), Lynette Roberts (1909), Fred Grove (Frederick Herridge) (1913), Christine Lavant (1915), Abigail Van Buren (Pauline Esther "Popo" Friedman) and Ann Landers (Esther Pauline "Eppie" Friedman) (1918), Gerard Debreu (1921), George (Matthew) Elliott (1923), (Marvin) Neil Simon (1927), Paul de Wispelaere, Theodore "Ted" Joans, and Patrick Tilley (1928), Richard Lee Rhodes (1937), Gerald Michael "Geraldo" Rivera (1943), Jaimy Gordon (1944), Donald Alarie (1945), Katherine (Mary) Govier (1948), David L. Robbins (1950), Cristina García and Deon (Godfrey) Meyer (1958), Margaret "Maggie" Edson (1961), Tracy Letts (1965).

Easy reading is damn hard writing.—Nathaniel Hawthorne

The poet is in command of his fantasy, while it is exactly the mark of the neurotic that he is possessed by his fantasy.—Lionel Trilling

Everyone thinks they can write a play; you just write down what happened to you. But the art of it is drawing from all the moments of your life.—Neil Simon

July 5—Claudio M. da Costa (1729), Phineas Taylor "P. T." Barnum (1810), Ignacio Mariscal (1829), Mandell Creighton (1843), Andre Lhote (1885), Felix Timmermans (1886), Jean Cocteau (1889), Frederick Lewis Allen (1890), Tin Ujević (1891), Marcel Achard (1899), Frank Waters (1902), Harold Acton (1904), Naomi Long Madgett and Mitsuye Yamada (1923), W. M. Diggelmann (1927), John Gilmore (1935), Barry (Morley Joseph) Callaghan and Brooke Hayward (1937), Barbara Frischmuth (1941), Patrick (Frank) Friesen (1946), Meredith Ann Pierce (1958), Bill Watterson (1958), Veronica Guerin (1959), Nardwuar the Human Serviette (John Ruskin) (1968), Jenji Kohan (1969), Igor Semyonovich "Gary" Shteyngart (1972).

The poet is a liar who always speaks the truth.—Jean Cocteau
So often is the virgin sheet of paper more real than what one has to say, and so often one regrets having marred it.—Harold Acton
The purpose of writing is to inflate weak ideas, obscure pure reasoning, and inhibit clarity. With a little practice, writing can be an intimidating and impenetrable fog!—Bill Watterson

July 6—Peter Burmannus (Pieter Burman) (1668), Antoine de Jussieu (1686), Alexander Wilson (1766), William J. Hooker (1785), Albert von Kölliker (1817), William Clark Falkner (1825/26), (Karl Gustaf) Verner von Heidenstam (1859), Paul Keller (1873), Eino Leino (1878), Josef Winckler (1881), Mignon G(ood) Eberhart (1899), Richard Krautheimer (1897), Emil Barth and Frederica Sagor Maas (1900), Eleanor Clark (1913), Harold Norse (b. Harold Rosen) and Unica Zürn (1916), Bert (Lambertus H.) Voeten (1918), H. J. Heise and Françoise Mallet-Joris (F. Lilar) (1930), Wadih Saadeh (1948), John Byrne (1950), Lynda S(uzanne) Robinson (1951), Hilary (Mary) Mantel (Thompson) (1952), Kathi Appelt (1954), William Wall (1955), Peter (Simpson) Hedges (1962), Laurent Gaudé (1972), Amir-Abbas Fakhravar (1975).

Faith is a euphemism for prejudice and religion is a euphemism for superstition.—Paul Keller

Life is always struggle with eternal forces.—Eino Leino

I feel not unlike a small boy, waking from a bad dream to find reality not much of an improvement.—John Byrne

July 7—Michele Amari (1806), Albert Vandal (1853), Ludwig Ganghofer (1855), Abraham "Abe" Cahan (1860), Lion Feuchtwanger (1884), Vladimir Mayakovsky (1893), Miroslav Krleža (1893), Helene Johnson and Robert A(nson) Heinlein (1907), Harriette (Simpson) Arnow and Evert W. Beth, (1908), Gian Carlo Menotti (1911), Margaret Walker (Margaret Abigail Walker Alexander) (1915), Yvonne Mitchell (1925), Reinhard Baumgart and Marcel Liebman (1929), David Eddings (1931), Nancy Bauer (Nancy Luke) (1934), Nancy Farmer (1941), Joel Siegel (1943), Hasan Abidi and Howard Rheingold (1947), Stephen Ratcliffe and Kathleen Joan Toelle "Kathy" Reichs (1948), Tetsuo Takashima (1949), Martin Edwards (1955), Keith Reddin (1956), Jill (Collins) McCorkle (1958), Zoë (Kate Hinde) Heller (1965), Nilanjana Sudeshna "Jhumpa" Lahiri (1967), Jeff VanderMeer (1968), Andy Quan (1969).

Writing is not necessarily something to be ashamed of, but do it in private and wash your hands afterwards.—Robert A. Heinlein

When I was about eight, I decided that the most wonderful thing, next to a human being, was a book.—Margaret Walker

If you fight back and get hit, it hurts a little while; if you don't fight back, it hurts forever.—Joel Siegel

July 8—Jean de la Fontaine (1621), Fitz-Greene Halleck (1790), Ljudwit Gaj (1809), Maria White Lowell (1821), Pierre A. Vicomte de Ponson du Terrail (1829), William Vaughn Moody (1869), Marie C. of Seggelen (1870), Emil Bloch (1885), Walter Hasenclever (1890), Elisabeth Zernike (1891), Josef Hora (1891), Richard Aldington (1892), Claude-Henri Grignon (1894), Anton G. J. van de Velde (1895), Alec Waugh (1898), Petar Segedin (1909), John (Dudley) Ball (1911), Walter (Francis) Kerr (1913), James Farl "J. F." Powers (1917), Jean Cau (1925,), Elizabeth Kubler-Ross (1926), Shirley Ann Grau (1929), David Berry (1943), Wolfgang Puck (1949), Christopher G. Moore and Anna (Marie) Quindlen (1952), Rob Burnett (1962), Jeremy Bates and Dray Skky (AnDraya Skcih) (1978).

A man desires praise that he may be reassured, that he may be quit of his doubting of himself; he is indifferent to applause when he is confident of success.—Alec Waugh

Half the world is composed of idiots, the other half of people clever enough to take indecent advantage of them.—Walter Kerr

Everyone tells stories around here. Every place, every person has a ring of stories around them, a halo almost. People have told me tales ever since I was a tiny girl squatting in the front dooryard, in mud-caked overalls, digging for doodlebugs. They have talked to me, and talked to me. Some I've forgotten, but most I remember. And so my memory goes back before my birth.—Shirley Ann Grau

July 9—John van Hembyze (1513), Emanuel van Meteren (1535), Johannes a Sancto Thoma (Poinset) (1589), Alexis Piron (1689), Johann Nikolaus Götz (1721), Ann Ward Radcliffe (1764), Johanna Schopenhauer (1766), Matthew Lewis (1775), Henry Hallam (1777), Joseph Cowen and Johan P. van der Kellen (1831), Jan (Nepomuk) Neruda (1834), Franz Boas (1858), Samuel Eliot Morison (1887), Gerard Walschap (1898), Barbara Cartland (1901), Gerhard Pohl (1902), Lionel White (1905), Beene Dubbelboer (1906), Allama Rasheed Turabi (1908), Mervyn Peake (1911), Oliver Sacks (1933), Marianne Macdonald (1934), June Jordan (1936), Hermann Burger (1942), Glen (Charles) Cook (1944), Dean R(ay) Koontz (1945), Larry Brown (1951), Robin (McLaurin) Williams (1952), Diane (Mavis) Schoemperlen (1954), Thomas Ligotti and Fred Norris (1955), Tom Hanks (1956), Tim Kring and Paul Merton (1957), Vardis A. Fisher and Lars Gyllenhaal (1968), Masami Tsuda (1970), Kenneth Tam (1984).

Governments always tend to want not really a free press but a managed or well-conducted one.—Ann Ward Radcliffe

We romantic writers are there to make people feel and not think. A historical romance is the only kind of book where chastity really counts.—Barbara Cartland

With any hallucinations, if you can do functional brain imagery while they're going on, you will find that the parts of the brain usually involved in seeing or hearing—in perception—have become super active by themselves. And this is an autonomous activity; this does not happen with imagination.—Oliver Sacks

When I turned about 12 or 13, I realised that being funny wasn't about remembering jokes. It was about creating them.—Paul Merton

July 10—John Calvin (1509), Pierre d'Hozier (1592), Arthur Annesley, 1st Earl of Anglesey (1614), John Ernest Grabe (1666), Robert Chambers (1802), Benjamin Paul Akers (1825), Finley Peter Dunne (1867), Marcel Proust (1871), Gunther Weisenborn (1902), John Wyndham P. L. B. Harris (1903), Salvador Espriu (1913), Saul Bellow (1914), David Brinkley (1920), Jean Kerr and Derek Prouse (1922), G. A. Kulkarni (1923), Elwy (McMurran) Yost (1925), Moshe Greenberg (1928), George Clayton Johnson (1929), Julian May and Alice (Ann) Munro (1931), Jorgen Becker (1932), Qazi Anwar Hussain (1936), Ahmet Taner Kışlalı (1939), David G. Hartwell (1941), Charles G. Irion and Robert Priest (1951), Scott Adams (1952).

It don't make much difference what you study, so long as you don't like it.—**Finley Peter Dunne**

Our passions shape our books; repose writes them in the intervals.—**Marcel Proust**

Confronted by an absolutely infuriating review it is sometimes helpful for the victim to do a little personal research on the critic. Is there any truth to the rumor that he had no formal education beyond the age of eleven? In any event, is he able to construct a simple English sentence? Do his participles dangle? When moved to lyricism does he write "I had a fun time"? Was he ever arrested for burglary? I don't know that you will prove anything this way, but it is perfectly harmless and quite soothing.—**Jean Kerr**

I want my stories to be something about life that causes people to say, not, oh, isn't that the truth, but to feel some kind of reward from the writing, and that doesn't mean that it has to be a happy ending or anything, but just that everything the story tells moves the reader in such a way that you feel you are a different person when you finish.—**Alice Munro**

July 11—Bar Daisan (Bardesanes) (154), Robert Greene (1558), Luis de Góngora (1561), Jean-François Marmontel (1723), Thomas Bowdler (1754), Elizabeth Wetherell (Susan [Bogert] Warner) (1819), Alexander Aphanashev (1826), Henry Abbey (1842), Leon Bloy (1846), Richard Beer-Hofmann (1866), Clarence Budington "Bud" Kelland (1881), Herman de Man (Salomon H. Hamburger) (1898), Elwyn Brooks "E. B." White (1899), John Francis Boyd (1910), Cordwainer Smith (Paul Myron Anthony Linebarger) (1913), Claus Bremer (1924), (Carl) Frederick Buechner (1926), Harold Bloom (1930), Pai Hsien-yung (1937), James Reiss (1941), David Ross Huddle and Daphne (Buckle) Marlatt (1942), Allan Gurganus (1947), David Ives (1950), Stephen Lang (1952), Paul Nicholas Sussman (1966), Nilanjana Sudeshna "Jhumpa" Lahiri (1967), Kevin Powers (1980).

I acknowledge Shakespeare to be the world's greatest dramatic poet, but regret that no parent could place the uncorrected book in the hands of his daughter, and therefore I have prepared the Family Shakespeare.—Thomas Bowdler
No one can write decently who is distrustful of the reader's intelligence, or whose attitude is patronizing.—E.B. White
Shakespeare is the true multicultural author. He exists in all languages. He is put on the stage everywhere. Everyone feels that they are represented by him on the stage . . . . Shakespeare is universal.—Harold Bloom

July 12—Gaius Julius Caesar (or on the 13th) (100 BCE), Edward Benlowes (1602), Arnold Moonen (1644), Henry David Thoreau (1817), Nikolai Chernyshevsky (1828), Abraham Goldfaden (1840), William Osler (1849), Otto Schoetensack (1850), Cora Crane (b. Cora Ethel Eaton Howarth) (1865), Stefan George (1868), Max Jacob (1876), Ludwig Rubiner (1881), Bruno Schulz (1892), Oscar (Greeley Clendenning) Hammerstein II (1895), Fjodor Godunov-Tcherdynchev (1900), Gunther Anders (1902), Pablo Neruda (Ricardo Eliécer Neftalí Reyes Basoalto) (1904), Milton Berle (1908), Johanna Moosdorf (1911), Pierre (Francis de Marigny) Berton and Beah Richards (1920), Ellen Douglas (Josephine Ayres Haxton) and Trevor Illtyd Williams (1921), James E(dwin) Gunn (1922), Beah Richards (1926), Mary Jane Latsis (1927), Gordon Pinsent (1930), Donald E. Westlake (1933), Bill Cosby (1937), Phillip Adams (1939), Leslie "Les" Payne (1941), Voja Antonić and Robin (Clarkson) Hardy (1952), Timothy Garton Ash (1955), Adam Johnson (1967).

Not that the story need be long, but it will take a long while to make it short.—Henry David Thoreau
Poetry is an act of peace. Peace goes into the making of a poet as flour goes into the making of bread.—Pablo Neruda
Both class and race survive education, and neither should. What is education then? If it doesn't help a human being to recognize that humanity is humanity, what is it for? So you can make a bigger salary than other people?—Beah Richards

July 13—Wilhelm H. Wackenroder (1773), John Clare (1793), Gustav Freytag (1815), Sydney Webb (1859), Margaret (Alice) Murray (1863), Francis B. Young (1884), Fernando A. N. de Seabra Pessoa (1888), Isaak Emmanuilovich Babel (1894), Martin David (1898), Kenneth Clark (1903), George (Anthony) Weller (1907), Josephine "Josefina" Niggli (1910). Hans Blumenberg (1920), Louis R(udolph) Harlan (1922), Hélène Brodeur (1923), Amanda Cross (Carolyn Gold Heilbrun) (1926), Samuel Eldred "Sam" Greenlee Jr. (1930), David M. Storey and (Hugh Brennan) Scott Symons (1933), Akinwande Oluwole "Wole" Babatunde Soyinka (1934), Jack F. Kemp (1935), Jean-Pierre E. Plooij (1945), Michael Shea (1946), Tony Kornheiser (1948), Carolina Garcia-Aguilera (1949), Jane Haddam (Orania Papazoglou) (1951), Jane Hamilton (1957), Ian Hislop (1960), (William Graham) Tullian Tchividjian (1972), Steven Galloway (1975).

I am gennerally understood tho I do not use that awkward squad of pointings called commas colons semicolons etc.—John Clare

The inevitability of gradualness cannot fail to be appreciated. —Sidney Webb

I'm so picky. People hate going to the movies with me. —Margaret Murray

Children who are treated as if they are uneducable almost invariably become uneducable.—Kenneth Clark

July 14—Poliziano (Angelo Ambrogini) (1454), Pasquier Quesnel (1634), Caspar Abel (1676), William Oldys (1696), John Douglas (1721), Gavrila Romanovich Derzhavin (1743), Mordecai Manuel Noah (1785), John Gibson Lockhart (1794), Owen Wister (1860), Frank Raymond Leavis (1895), Irving S. Stone (b. Irving Tennenbaum) (1903), Isaac Bashevis Singer (1904), Chaim Raphael (1908), Peter Stadlen (1910), Northrop Frye (1912), Béatrix Beck (1914), Jerome Lawrence (Schwartz) (1915), Natalia Ginzburg (1916), Arthur Laurents (1917), Alfred "Alf" Van Hoose (1920), Leon Garfield (1921), John William Chancellor (1927), Ronald Sukenick (1932), Jerry Rubin (1938), George E. Slusser (1939), Susan Howatch (1940), Maulana Karenga (1941), Christopher Priest (1943), Pierre Joris (1946), Kat Martinet al. (Kathleen Kelly Martin) (1947), Nick Bantock (1949), Kenneth Lee Hutcherson (1952), L. Brent Bozell (1955), Joe Keenan (1958), Phil Rosenthal (1963), Brian Selznick (1966), Ranj Dhaliwal and Kirsten Sheridan (1976).

When you can't have what you choose, you just choose what you have.—Owen Wister

Every creator painfully experiences the chasm between his inner vision and its ultimate expression. The chasm is never completely bridged. We all have the conviction, perhaps illusory, that we have much more to say than appears on the paper.—Isaac Bashevis Singer

Basically, all novelists should want to tell a story, and if they don't want to, they shouldn't be novelists. I think story-telling is important and underrated.—Susan Howatch

July 15—Clement Clarke Moore (1779), Thomas Bulfinch (1796), Vilfredo F. D. Pareto (1848), Eduardo Gutiérrez (1851), Julia K(ein) Wetherill Baker (1858), Kunikida Doppo (1871), Walter Benjamin (1892), Donald Grant Creighton (1902), Walter D(umaux) Edmonds (1903), Rudolf Arnheim (1904), Richard (Willard) Armour (1906), (Ralph) Hammond Innes and Abraham Sutzkever (1913), Robert Conquest (1917), Iris Murdoch (1919), Kathryn Adams Doty (Kathryn Elizabeth Hohn) (1920), Jiri Lederer (1922), Driss Chraïbi (1926), Ann Jellicoe (1927), Clive Eric Cussler (1931), Carmen Thérèse Callil (1938), Lydia Davis (1947), Victor DiGenti (1948), Richard Russo (1949), Arianna Huffington (1950), Kate Kellaway (1957), Sandon Berg (1971).

To congratulate oneself on one's warm commitment to the environment, or to peace, or to the oppressed, and think no more is a profound moral fault.—Robert Conquest

Writing is like getting married. One should never commit oneself until one is amazed at one's luck.—Iris Murdoch

Sometimes my plot lines are so convoluted, I get calls from friends at 3 am saying; you SOB, you'll never pull this one off.—Clive Cussler

I've always thought of reading and writing as addictive behavior. Once they've hooked you, they'll never let you go .—Victor DiGenti

July 16—Mary Baker Eddy (1821), William Henry Rhodes (1822), Philipus J. Hoedemaker (1839), Eben E(ugene) Rexford (1848), Jens Otto Harry Jespersen (1860), George A. Birmingham (Rev. James Owen Hannay) (1865), Lambert McKenna (1870), Kathleen (Thompson) Norris (1880), Anna Vyrubova (1884), Carlyle Ferren MacIntyre (1890), Mauritius R. J. Dekker (Boris Robazki) (1896), James Still (1906), Geoffrey Bryan Bentley (1909), Anatole (Paul) Broyard (1920), Mari Evans (1923), Shirley Hughes (1927), Anita Brookner and Robert Sheckley (1928), Caroline Blackwood (1931), Hédi Bouraoui (1932), Anita Brookner (1938), Marion Pitt (1939), Reinaldo Arenas and Stanley Gebler Davies (1943), Esther M. Friesner(-Stutzman) and Jean-Luc Mongrain (1951), Susan Wheeler (1955), Anthony Robert "Tony" Kushner (1956), Alexandra Marinina (1957), Deb Caletti (1963), Johnny Vaughan (1966), Will Ferrell (1967).

Man is a classifying animal: in one . . . the whole process of speaking is nothing but distributing phenomena, of which no two are alike in every respect, into different classes on the strength of perceived similarities and dissimilarities. In the name-giving process we witness the same ineradicable and very useful tendency to see likenesses and to express similarity in the phenomena through similarity in name.—Otto Jespersen

Just the knowledge that a good book is waiting one at the end of a long day makes that day happen.—Kathleen Norris

It's surprising that authors should expect kindness to be shown to their books when they are not themselves known for kindness toward their characters, their culture or by implication their readers.—Anatole Broyard

You never know what you will learn till you start writing. Then you discover truths you never knew existed.—Anita Brookner

It is necessary to fear the revenge of a derided woman.— Alexandra Marinina

July 17—Richard Carew (1555), Isaac Watts (1674), Johannes H. van der Palm (1763), Alexander Beaufort Meek (1814), William John Courthope (1842), Jakob Christoph Heer and Luis Munoz Rivera (1859), Bart de Ligt (1883), Shmuel Yosef Agnon (1888), Erle Stanley Gardner (1889), Paul (Gerhardt) Hiebert (1892), Bruno Jasieński (1901), Christina Stead (1902), Michael (Francis) Gilbert and Art Linkletter (Gordon Arthur Kelly) (1912), Roger Garaudy (1913), James (Otis) Purdy (1914), Robert V(incent) Remini (1921), Donald Alfred Davie and Marjorie Kellogg (1922), Olive Ann Burns (1924), Charles Champlin (1926), Caroline Graham (1931), Karla Kuskin (Seidman) (1932), Rainer Kisch and Pat McCormick (1934), Jose Ignacio Cabrujas (1937), David (Samuel D'Arcy) Young (1946), Mark Robert Bowden (1951), Robert R(ick) McCammon (1952), J. Michael Straczynski (1954), Shelly Sanders (1964), Cory Doctorow (1971), Karen Russell (1981), Matthew Joseph Thaddeus "Mattie" Stepanek (1990).

The real trouble with the writing game is that no general rule can be worked out for uniform guidance, and this applies to sales as well as to writing.—Erle Stanley Gardner

Writing is like a battle. You're often so into it you don't have any high ideals. You're just doing it. I have all these boxing prints on my walls. I always feel that's what I am, a boxer. I get my brains knocked out every so often.—James Purdy

Writers get embarrassed sometimes in talking about how much fun writing can be, but drafting is often really enjoyable. Often, you're tumbling in the dark, and you don't know where the story is going to lead.—Karen Russell

July 18—Heinrich Bullinger (1502), Zacharias Ursinus (1534), Saverio Bettinelli (1718), Immanuel Hermann Fichte (1797), William Makepeace Thackeray (1811), Tristan Corbière (1845), Rose Hartwick Thorpe (1850), Ricarda Huch (1864), Laurence Housman (1865), Manuel Galvez (1882), Sydney Horler (1888), Herbert Marcuse (1898), Nathalie Sarraute (Natalia/Natacha Tcherniak) (1900), (Mary) Jessamyn West (1902), Samuel Ichiye "S. I." Hayakawa and Clifford Odets (1906), Harry Levin (1912), John G. Bearer (1914), Thomas Kuhn (1922), Margaret Laurence and Robert Sloman (1926), Ludwig Harig (1927), Simon Vinkenoog (1928), Aad Nuis and Yevgeny Yevtushenko (1933), Edward Bond (1934), Roald Hoffmann (b. Roald Safran) and Hunter S(tockton) Thompson (1937), Joseph John Ellis (1943), Janet Peery (1948), Hedwig Gorski (1949), John Gilbert "Jack" Layton (1950), Daniel Dion "Dan" O'Brien (1966), Elizabeth M. Gilbert (1969), Rigoberto González (1970), Alan Morrison (1974), Alfian bin Sa'at (1977), Jared Hess (1979).

There are thousands of thoughts lying within a man that he does not know till he takes up the pen and writes.—William Makepeace Thackeray

There is no royal path to good writing; and such paths as do exist do not lead through neat critical gardens, various as they are, but through the jungles of self, the world, and of craft.—Jessamyn West

Any idiot can face a crisis—it's day to day living that wears you out.—Clifford Odets

In a very real sense, people who have read good literature have lived more than people who cannot or will not read. . . . It is not true that we have only one life to live; if we can read, we can live as many more lives and as many kinds of lives as we wish.—S. I. Hayakawa

July 19—Heinrich Christian Boie (1744), Gottfried Keller (1819), William Shakespeare Hays (1837), F. A. Alphonse Aulard (1849), Ferdinand Brunetière (1849), Hermann Bahr (1863), Adriaan J. Zoetmulder (1881), Vladimir Mayakovsky (1893), A(rchibald) J. Cronin (1896), Marc Turfkruijer (1900), Robert Leslie Bellem (1902), Edgar P. Snow (1905), Ernest Buckler (1908), Eve Merriam (1916), Robert Pinget and Miltos Sachtouris (1919), Elizabeth Spencer (1921), Joseph Hansen and William A. Rusher (1923), Vassar Miller and Sybren Polet (Sijbe Minnema) (1924), Max Sordam (1926), Jan Myrdal (1927), John Bratby (1928), Larry Zolf (1934), Nicholas Bethell and Dom Moraess (1938), Jayson Stark (1951), Jayne Anne Phillips (1952), Jane Eaton Hamilton and Srđa Trifković (1954), Ethan (Andrew) Canin and David (Alton) Manicom (1960), Garth Nix (1963), Adriaan J. Zoetmulder (1972).

Worry never robs tomorrow of its sorrow, but only saps today of its strength.—A. J. Cronin

I tell my students that being a writer is like being a member of a medieval guild and that what we are doing is very subversive and very important.—Jayne Anne Phillips

Authors are influenced by everything they've ever read. If you've read widely enough, it helps you create your own mix.—Garth Nix

July 20—Imam Bukhari (810), Francesco Petrarch (1304), Arnaud d'Ossat (1537), Destutt de Tracy (1754), Thomas Lovell Beddoes (1803), John Sterling (1806), Ivan S. Gagarin (1814), Thomas C. Allbutt (1836), George Otto Trevelyan and Augustin Daly (1838), Blanche Willis Howard (1847), Frederic Jesup Stimson (1855), Erik Karlfeldt (1864), Hermann Alexander Graf Keyserling (1880), Gustave Charlier (1885), Richard Billinger (1893), Maurice Gilliams (1900), Dilys Powell and Cesare Zavattini (1902), Molly Mary Nesta Keane (1905), Cicely Veronica Wedgwood (1910), George Johnston and Andrew Long (1912), Stanisław Albinowski (1923), Thomas Berger and Hans Lodeizen (Johannes A. Frederik) (1924), Pavel Kohout (1928), Cormac McCarthy (b. Charles McCarthy) (1933), Henry Dumas, Uwe Johnson, and Ralph C. Rinzler (1934), Joseph Bathanti, Thomas Friedman, and Dan Shaughnessy (1953), Jess Walter (1965), Alistair MacLeod (1936), Ricardo "Rick" Sánchez (1958), Gregory Scofield (1966), Victor Heck (David Nordhaus) (1967).

Why do writers write? Because it isn't there.—Thomas Berger
I'm not interested in writing short stories. Anything that doesn't take years of your life and drive you to suicide hardly seems worth doing.—Cormac McCarthy
Optimists are usually wrong. But all the great change in history, positive change, was done by optimists.—Thomas Friedman

July 21—Al-Bukhari (810), Matthew Prior (1664), Anthony Collins (1676), Elizabeth Hamilton (1758), Vasile Alecsandri (1821), A. S. C. Wallis (Adele S. C. von Antal-Opzoomer) (1857), Frances Parkinson Keyes (1885), Anton Schnack (1892), Hans Fallada (1893), Hart Crane and Ernest (Miller) Hemingway (1899), Diana Trilling (1905), Alec Derwent "A. D." Hope (1907), (Herbert) Marshall McLuhan (1911), Brigitte Reimann (1933), John Gardner, U.S. (1933), Tess Gallagher (1943), Buchi Emescheta (1944), (Garretson Beekman) "Garry" Trudeau (1948), Michael Connelly (1956), Ed Greenwood (1959).

. . . [A] compensation is something which does not quite compensate . . .—Frances Parkinson Keyes

One must be drenched in words, literally soaked in them, to have the right ones form themselves into the proper pattern at the right moment.—Hart Crane

There is no rule on how to write. Sometimes it comes easily and perfectly; sometimes it's like drilling rock and then blasting it out with charges.—Ernest Hemingway

July 22—Jean-Noel/Joannes Natalis Paquot (1722), Mikhail Shcherbatov (1733), Karolina Pawlowa (1807), Emma Lazarus (1849), David D. Salas (1872), Lucien Febvre (1878), O. M. Graf (1894), Stephen Vincent Benét (1898), Edward Dahlberg (1900), Amy Vanderbilt (1908), Shaista Suhrawardy Ikramullah (1915), Megan Terry (1932), Tom Robbins (1936), Quincy (Thomas) Troupe (Jr.) (1939), Pete Dexter and Ira (Bruce) Nadel (1943), Albert Brooks (Albert Lawrence Einstein) (1947), Susan Eloise "S. E." Hinton (1948), Lisa Robertson (1961), Steve Albini (1962), David Spade (1964), Lauren Booth (1967), Arno Geiger (1968).

I am a journalist in the field of etiquette. I try to find out what the most genteel people regularly do, what traditions they have discarded, what compromises they have made.—Amy Vanderbilt

In fiction, when you paint yourself into a corner, you can write a pair of suction cups onto the bottoms of your shoes and walk up the wall and out the skylight and see the sun breaking through the clouds. In nonfiction, you don't have that luxury.—Tom Robbins

If you paint, write, do mosaics, knit—if it's solving that part of your brain saying, 'I need to do this,' you've won.—Albert Brooks

July 23—Sylvester Judd (1813), Coventry (Kersey Dighton) Patmore (1823), Edward John Armstrong (1841), Apolinario Mabini (1864), Salvador de Madariaga y Rojo (1886), Raymond Chandler (1888), Maurus H. Hulsman (1891), Karl A. Menninger (1893), Elspeth Josceline Huxley (1907), Ronald Ridout (1916), Davis Grubb (1919), Cyril M. Kornbluth (1923), Gavin Lambert (1924), Ludvik Vaculik (1926), Hubert Selby Jr. (1928), Guy Fournier (1931), John Treadwell Nichols (1940), Lisa Alther (1944), Rene Ricard and Larry (Howard) Shue (1946), Carl Phillips (1959), Thea Dorn (1970), Lauren Groff (1978).

To him that waits all things reveal themselves, provided that he has the courage not to deny, in the darkness, what he has seen in the light.—Coventry Patmore

At least half the mystery novels published violate the law that the solution, once revealed, must seem to be inevitable.—Raymond Chandler

The voice of the intelligence is drowned out by the roar of fear. It is ignored by the voice of desire. It is contradicted by the voice of shame. It is biased by hate and extinguished by anger. Most of all it is silenced by ignorance.—Karl A. Menninger

July 24—John Newton (1725), Elizabeth "Betje" Wolff-Bekker (1738), Alexandre Dumas, père (Dumas Davy de la Pailleterie) (1802), Timothy Titcomb (Josiah Gilbert Holland) (1819), Henrik Pontoppidan (1857), Johan A. de Sleeve (Adwaita) (1862), (Benjamin) Frank(lin) Wedekind (1864), Vicente Acosta and Frederic Benson (1867), Oswald Chambers (1874), Alice Jane Chandler "Jean" Webster (1876), Lord Dunsany (Edward J. M. D. Plunkett) (1878), Junichiro Tanizaki (1886), Amelia (Mary) Earhart (1897), Hermann Kasack (1896), Karl von Mechow (1897), Zelda Sayre Fitzgerald (1900), John D(ann) MacDonald (1916), Michel Brunet and John Hillaby (1917), Madeleine Ferron (1922), Ignacio Aldecoa (1925), Hedda J. Garza (1929), Aaron Elkins (1935), Albert Marrin (1936). Barry (Norman) Malzberg (1939), Michael Coveney and Geoffrey McQueen (1947), Marc Jampole (1950), Brad Watson (1955), Anthony Bidulka (1962), Banana Yoshimoto (1964), Colleen Doran (1968), Jennifer "Jen" Miller (1972).

We can easily manage if we will only take, each day, the burden appointed to it. But the load will be too heavy for us if we carry yesterday's burden over again today, and then add the burden of the morrow before we are required to bear it.—John Newton

Any fool can have bad luck; the art consists in knowing how to exploit it.—Frank Wedekind

Mr. Fitzgerald, I believe that is how he spells his name, seems to believe that plagiarism begins at home.—Zelda Fitzgerald

July 25—Jacques Peletier (du Mans) (1517), Geeraerdt Brandt (1626), Pieter Langendijk (1683), Immanuel J. Pyra (1715), Charlotte von Kalb (1761), David Belasco (1853), Charles Major (1856), Max Dauthendy (1867), Alfred Walton Hinds (1874), Benito Lynch (1885), Josephine (Lyons Scott) Pinckney (1895), Eric Hoffer (1902), Elias Canetti and Denys James Watkins-Pitchford (1905), Hubert Booi (1919), Maria Gripe (1923), Alice Parizeau (1930), George (Graf) Dickerson (Jr.) (1933), Claude Zidi (1934), Felix Ph. Ingold and Frances Susan (Hill) Itani (1942), Brian M(ichael) Stableford (1948), Barbara Haworth-Attard (1953), (Oeva) Jean (Wells) Koebernick (1955), Anne Elizabeth Appl ebaum (1964), Mur Lafferty and Chris Turner (1973), Jovica Tasevski-Eternijan (1976).

If you can't write your idea on the back of my calling card, you don't have a clear idea.—David Belasco

Propaganda does not deceive people; it merely helps them to deceive themselves.—Eric Hoffer

The process of writing has something infinite about it. Even though it is interrupted each night, it is one single notation.—Elias Canetti

July 26—George Catlin (1796), Winthrop Mackworth Praed (1802), George Bernard Shaw (1856), Charles Hale Hoyt (1859), George Barr McCutcheon (1866), George Louis Beer (1872), Carl Jung and Antonio Machado (1875), Andre Maurois (1885), Marcel Jouhandeau (1888), Jacques Pirenne (1891), Aldous L Huxley and Ludovicus J. Rogier (1894), Robert Graves (1895), Paul Gallico (1897), Danton Walker (1899), Jean Shepherd (1921), Blake Edwards (1922), Jan Berenstain and Bernice Rubens (1923), Ana María Matute (1926), Ibn-e-Safi (1928), Austin (Ardinel Chesterfield) Clarke (1934), James Michael Kacian (1953), Lawrence Watt-Evans (1954), Hart Hanson (1957), Rick Bragg (1959), Anne Provoost (1964), Ruth Ellen Kocher (1965).

The road to ignorance is paved with good editions.—George Bernard Shaw

Prose books are the show dogs I sell to support my cat.—Robert Graves

It is only when you open your veins and bleed onto the page a little that you establish contact with your reader. If you do not believe in the characters or the story . . . with all your mind, strength, and will, if you don't feel joy and excitement while writing it, then you're wasting good white paper, even if it sells . . . .—Paul Gallico

July 27—Jakob Aall (1773), Thomas Campbell (1777), Denis Davydov (1784), Alexandre Dumas fils (1824), Giosuè Carducci (1835), Vladimir Korolenko (1853), Joseph Hilaire Pierre Belloc (1870), Francesco Gaeta (1879), Joseph Moncure March (1899), Agnes Yarnall (1904), Jerzy Giedroyc (1906), Joseph (Quincy) Mitchell (1908), Bea Marcia Anastasia verbrook Christoforides (1910), Julien Gracq (Louis Poirier) (1910), Rayner Heppenstall (1911), Hilde Domin (1912), Eva Jones (1913), Vittorio Sereni (1913), Elizabeth Hardwick (1916), Norman Lear (1922), Vincent Canby (1924), Jack Higgins (Harry Patterson) (1929), George Ryga (1932), William "Bill" Pearson (1938), Bharati Mukherjee (1940), Robert Arthur Thornbury Campbell (1942), Bill Bradley (1943), Cat Bauer (1955), Wil Wheaton (1972), Alexei Maxim Russell (1976).

The harmonies of bound books are like the flowers of the field.
—Hilaire Belloc

The greatest gift is a passion for reading. It is cheap, it consoles, it distracts, it excites, it gives you a knowledge of the world and experience of a wind kind. It is moral illumination.—Elizabeth Hardwick

Life is made up of small pleasures. Happiness is made up of those tiny successes. The big ones come too infrequently. And if you don't collect all these tiny successes, the big ones don't really mean anything.—Norman Lear

Some ISPs are blocking all BitTorrent traffic, because BitTorrent can be used to share files in a piratical way. Hollywood lobbying groups are trying to pass laws which would force ISPs to block or degrade BitTorrent traffic, too. Personally, I think this is like closing down freeways because a bank robber could use them to get away.
—Wil Wheaton

July 28—Ibn al-'Arabi (1165), Jacopo Sannazaro (1456), Fabre d'Églantine (1750), Ludwig A. Feuerbach (1804), Gerard Manley Hopkins (1844), Beatrix Potter (1866), Charles Dillon Perrine (1867), George Morren (1868), Thomas P. Krag (1868), Ernst Cassirer and Alice Duer Miller (1874), Kenneth F. Fearing and Karl Raimund Popper (1902), Malcolm Lowry (1909), John (Lawrence) Ashbery (1927), Remco (Wouter) Campert and Jean Roba (1930), Natalie Babbitt (1932), Francis Veber and Anthony Ward (1937), Robert Hughes (Studley Forrest) (1938), Judy (Rae) Grahn (1940), Fahmida Riaz (1946), Randall Wallace (1949), Shahyar Ghanbari (1950), Carol Higgins Clark (1956), William T. Vollmann (1959).

I always knew in my heart Walt Whitman's mind to be more like my own than any other man's living. As he is a very great scoundrel this is not a pleasant confession.—Gerard Manley Hopkins

Thank goodness I was never sent to school; it would have rubbed off some of the originality.—Beatrix Potter

A determined soul will do more with a rusty monkey wrench than a loafer will accomplish with all the tools in a machine shop. —Robert Hughes

July 29—Simon Dach (1605), Nicolaas Heinsius (1620), Antonius van Gils (1758), Alexis de Tocqueville (1805), Johannes Schmidt (1843), Max Nordau (1849), Georg Kerschensteiner (1854), (Newton) Booth Tarkington (1869), Eric Alfred Knudsen (1872), August Stramm (1874), Don Marquis (1878), Porfirio Barba-Jacob (1883), Henri Liebrecht (1884), Karl Otten (1889), Michail M. Zosjtsjenko (1895), Eyvind Johnson (1900), Stanley (Jasspon) Kunitz (1905), Chester (Bomar) Himes (1909), Henry Brian Boyne (1910), Vladimir Dudentzev, Edwin O'Connor, and Mary Lee Settle (1918), Aled Eames (1921), Harry K. V. Mulisch (1927), Jean Baudrillard (1929), Leo Coughlin and Richard Curry Marius (1933), Pat(ricia Louise Tinmuth) Lowther (1935), Karen Swenson (1936), Peter Jennings (1938), Marilyn Tucker Quayle (1949), Ruud Janssen (1959), Didier Van Cauwelaert (1960), Chang-rae Lee (1965), Adele Griffin (1970), Abiola Abrams (1976).

In America the majority raises formidable barriers around the liberty of opinion; within these barriers an author may write what he pleases, but woe to him if he goes beyond them.—Alexis de Tocqueville

Arguments only confirm people in their own opinions.—Booth Tarkington

Writing a book of poetry is like dropping a rose petal down the Grand Canyon and waiting for the echo.—Don Marquis

July 30—Giorgio Vasari (1511), Samuel Rogers (1763), Emily Jane Brontë (1818), Emily Oliver Optic (William Taylor Adam) (1822), Gaston Calmette (1858), Leo van Puyfielde (1882), Jean Jacques Bernard (1888), Salvador Novo (1904), Cyril Northcote Parkinson (1909), Karl Guttmann (1913), William H(oward) Gass (1924), Alexander Trocchi (1925), Thomas Sowell (1930), Daniel Abdal-Hayy Moore (1940), Patrick Modiano (1945), Cherie Priest (1975).

Men of genius sometimes accomplish most when they work the least, for they are thinking out inventions and forming in their minds the perfect idea that they subsequently express with their hands.
—Giorgio Vasari

If I could I would always work in silence and obscurity, and let my efforts be known by their results.—Emily Brontë

The expression "to write something down" suggests a descent of thought to the fingers whose movements immediately falsify it.
—William Gass

July 31—Peter Rosegger (1843), Ignazio Guidi (1844), Munshi Premchand (1880), Grete Gulbransson (1882), Arthur Daley and Brett Halliday (Davis Dresser) (1904), Milton Friedman (1912), Curt Gowdy and Primo Levi (1919), Walter Vogt (1927), Lynne Reid Banks and Oriana Fallaci (1929), John Searle (1932), Elise Nada Cowen and Cees Nooteboom (1933), Theodore Weesner (1935), Robert Barnard (1936), William Bennett (1943), Salman Akhtar (1946), Jo Bannister and Louis McKee (1951), João Barreiros and Faye (Marder) Kellerman (1952), Kim (Addie) Addonizio (1954), J. K. Rowling/ Robert Galbraith (Joanne Rowling) (1965), Elizabeth Wurtzel (1967), Ahmad Akbarpour (1970).

I find writing for children much easier. I don't mean it's less demanding—you've got to have a talent for it and you've got to work very hard—but you don't have to pull your guts out and lay them on the line in quite the same way as when you're writing for adults. —Lynne Reid Banks

Where questions of style and exposition are concerned I try to follow a simple maxim: if you can't say it clearly you don't understand it yourself.—John Searle

I was set free because my greatest fear had been realized, and I still had a daughter who I adored, and I had an old typewriter and a big idea. And so rock bottom became a solid foundation on which I rebuilt my life.—J. K. Rowling

Born in August

Aug. 1—Claudius (Tiberius Claudius Caesar Augustus Germanicus) (10 BCE), Peter van Herenthals (1322), Andrew Melville (1545), Luís Vélez de Guevara (1579), Benedetto Marcello (1686), Francis Scott Key (1779), Lorenz Oken (1779), Richard Henry Dana (1815), Herman Melville (1819), Mary Harris "Mother" Jones (1837), Paul Barth (1858), Montague Rhodes James (1862), Stuart (Fitzrandolph) Merrill (1863), Emilie Rose Macaulay (1881), Aline Murray Kilmer (1888), Edward Streeter (1891), Constantly Burniaux (1892), Paul (George Vincent O'Shaughnessy) Horgan (1903), Anne Hébert (1916), Stanley Middleton (1919), Jeffrey Segal (1924), Ernst Jandl (1925), Robert James Waller (1939), Frederick Busch and Étienne Roda-Gil (1941), Paul Spencer Sochaczewski (b. Paul Spencer Wachtel) (1947), Frank Stanford (1948), Christopher Gilbert (1949), Jim Carroll (1951), Jan Burke (1953), James Gleick (1954), Madison Smartt Bell (1957), Carolyn Marie Souaid (1959), Richard Roeper (1960), Ross Gay (1974), Damien Saez (1977).

Say not always what you know, but always know what you say. —Claudius

It is impossible to talk or to write without apparently throwing oneself helplessly open.—Herman Melville

Only one hour in the normal day is more pleasurable than the hour spent in bed with a book before going to sleep, and that is the hour spent in bed with a book after being called in the morning. —Rose Macaulay

The most important sentence in a good book is the first one; it will contain the organic seed from which all that follows will grow. —Paul Horgan

Aug. 2—Theodor Zwinger (1533), Kaspar von Stieler (1632), Johann Jakob Scheuchzer (1672), Joan Lucaz (1746), Adolf Friedrich von Schack (1815), Francis Marion Crawford (1854), William Watson (1858), Duncan Campbell Scott (1862), Irving Babbitt (1865), Ernest C. Dowson (1867), Aino J. M. Kallas (1878), Ethel Mary Dell (1881), Johannes Tralow (1882), Alice (Erya) Gerstenberg (1885), Viktor Maksimovich Zhirmunsky (1891), John Kieran (1892), Charles Bennett and George Malcolm Thomson (1899), Albert Goodwin (1906), Mary Hamman (1907), Roger MacDougall and Lou Zara (1910), Oscar Fraley and Félix Leclerc (1914), Louis Pauwels (1920), James Baldwin (1924), Peter O'Toole (1932), Benjamin Barber (1939), François Weyergans (1941), Isabel Allende (1942), Rose Tremain (Rosemary Jane Thomson) (1943), James Howe (1946), Lawrence Wright (1947), Robert P. Holdstock (1948), James Fallows (1949), Anne Leuchars (1953), Caleb Carr (1955), Russell (Claude) Smith (1963), Aline Brosh McKenna (1967).

I am a part of all I have read.—John Kieran

The responsibility of a writer is to excavate the experience of the people who produced him.—James Baldwin

I have likened writing a novel to going on a journey, with some notion of the destination I will arrive at, but not the whole picture - which emerges gradually as a series of revelations, as the journey goes along.—Rose Tremain

Aug. 3—Étienne Dolet (1509), Paul A. Daum (1850), Henry Cuyler Bunner (1855), Vernon Louis Parrington (1871), Eugene Baie (1874), Rupert Brooke (1887), Lorne (Albert) Pierce (1890), Ernie Pyle (1900), Clifford D(onald) Simak (1904), Leonard Huizinga (1906), Walter Van Tilburg Clark (1909), Mel Tolkin (1913), Sal Santen (1915), Shakeel Badayuni and (William) Gordon Merrick (1916), James MacGregor Burns (1918), P. D. James (Phyllis Dorothy James White) (1920), Hayden Carruth (1921), Robert Sumner (1922), Roger Foulon (1923), Leon (Marcus) Uris (1924), James Komack (1930), Mario Montes de Oca (1932), Marvin Bell and Diane Wakoski (1937), Martha Stewart (1941), Steven Millhauser (1943), Reed Waller (1949), Frank Schaeffer (1952), Walter Kirn (1962).

In 1930s mysteries, all sorts of motives were credible which aren't credible today, especially motives of preventing guilty sexual secrets from coming out. Nowadays, people sell their guilty sexual secrets. —P. D. James

Writing, basically breaks down to relationships between people and that is what you write about.—Leon Uris

I have always wanted what I have now come to call the voice of personal narrative. That has always been the appealing voice in poetry. It started for me lyrically in Shakespeare's sonnets.—Diane Wakoski

Aug. 4—François Hédelin, abbé d'Aubignac (1604), Susanna Wright (1697), Thomas Blackwell (1701), Percy Bysshe Shelley (1792), Walter Pater (1839), Knut Hamsun (1859), Adrien Bertrand (1888), Erich Weinert (1890), Witold Gombrowicz (1904), Osbert Lancaster and Leslie Wilkinson (1908), Aleksandr Danilovich Aleksandrov (1912), Robert Hayden (b. Asa Bundy Sheffey) (1913), Sheldon Vanauken (1914), Patrick (John MacAllister) Anderson (1915), Iceberg Slim (Robert Beck) (1918), Helen Thomas (1920), Mushtaq Ahmad Yusufi (1923), John Gorman (1930), Rutger Kopland (Rutger van den Hoofdakker) (1934), Assia Djebar (1936), Donald L. Coburn (1938), Robert Grenier (1941), Richard Belzer (1944), Alison Light (1955), Brooks D. Simpson (1957), Allison Hedge Coke (1958), Tim Winton (1960), Barack (Hussein) Obama (II) (1961), Dennis Lehane (1965), John August (1970), Lee Mellor (1982).

Poetry is a sword of lightning, ever unsheathed, which consumes the scabbard that would contain it.—Percy Bysshe Shelley
Only a fool trips on what is behind him.—Iceberg Slim
Everyone with a cell phone thinks they're a photographer. Everyone with a laptop thinks they're a journalist. But they have no training, and they have no idea of what we keep to in terms of standards, as in what's far out and what's reality. And they have no dedication to truth.—Helen Thomas

Aug. 5—John Eliot (1604), James Anderson (1662), Johan Lulofs (1711), Michael Banim (1796), Ivar A. Aasen (1813), Guy de Maupassant (1850), Mary R. Beard (1876), Gertrude E. Durden Rush (1880), Conrad P(otter) Aiken (1889), John Huston, Wassely Leontief, and Francis Walder (Francis Waldburger) (1906), Jacquetta Hawkes and (Johan) Erik Lindegren (1910), Peter (Robert Edwin) Viereck (1916), Wendell E. Berry (1934), Benjamin "Bob" Clark (1939), Alexander (Keewatin) Dewdney (1941), Ron Silliman (1946), Élisabeth Vonarburg (1947), Linda Gregerson (1950), James (Miller) McLure (Jr.) (1951), David Baldacci and Tony Haynes (1960), Melissa Studdard (1969), Darryl Reuben Hall (1980).

It is better to be unhappy in love than unhappy in marriage, but some people manage to be both.—**Guy de Maupassant**

Separate we come, and separate we go, And this be it known, is all that we know.—**Conrad Aiken**

I don't try to guess what a million people will like. It's hard enough to know what I like.—**John Huston**

All right, every day ain't going to be the best day of your life, don't worry about that. If you stick to it you hold the possibility open that you will have better days.—**Wendell Berry**

It's all about Artistic Enlightenment.—**Darryl Reuben Hall**

Aug. 6—Nicolas de Malebranche (1638), Francois Fenelon (1651), Luc de Clapiers, marquis de Vauvenargues (1715), Alfred Lord Tennyson (1809), Judah Philip Benjamin (1811), Thomas Alexander Browne (1826), Paul Claudel (1868), Emanuel Querido (Joost Mendes) (1871), Charles Fort (1874), Louella Parsons (1881), Scott Nearing (1883), John Middleton Murry (1889), Vladimir M. Kirshon (1902), M. Revis (Willem Fisherman) (1904), Norma (Holzmann) Farber (1909), Sol Adler and James Lees-Milne (1908), Herbert Rolland "H. R." Percy (1920), Christa Reinig (1926), J. O. Jeppson (Janet Opal Jeppson; Janet Asimov) and Norman Wexler (1926), Jean Carrière (1928), Vim Karénine (b. Antony de Vial) (1933), Piers Anthony (Piers Anthony Dillingham Jacob) and Diane di Prima (1934), Robert Lee "Rob" Penny (1941), Katsuhiko Takahashi (1947), Mary di Michele (1949), Kristyn Dunnion (1969), M. Night Shyamalan (1970), Paolo Tadini Bacigalupi (1972).

Words, like nature, half reveal and half conceal the soul within.—Alfred Lord Tennyson

Normally I work out a general summary of what I mean to do, then start writing, and the details can be different from my anticipation. So there is considerable flow, but always within channels.—Piers Anthony

I love my stories being multi-layered, and coming at it from different angles, so that you don't understand the film's true emotional motivation until the very end.—M. Night Shyamalan

Aug. 7—Alonso de Ercilla y Zúñiga (1573), Robert Dudley (1574), Georg Stiernhielm (1598), Daniel W. Wyttenbach (1746), Joseph Rodman Drake (1795), Carl A. E. Ahlqvist (A. Oksanen) (1826), Charles Warren Stoddard (1843), Alice James (1848), Joachim Ringelnatz Hans Bötticher) (1883), Dornford Yates (Cecil William Mercer) (1885), Franz J. Weinrich (Heinrich Lerse) (1897), Louis S(eymour) B(azett) Leakey (1903), Cees Buddingh' (1918), Jan Walravens (1920), M. J. bin Gorion (1921), Felice Bryant and David R(oosevelt) Bunch (1925), Stanley Victor "Stan" Freberg and Sue Kaufman (1926), Laurence Joel "Larry" Eigner (1927), Betsy (Cromer) Byars and Romeo Muller (1928), Luther Dixon and Charles E. Rice (1931), Jerry (Eugene) Pournelle (1933), Richard L(ouis) Tierney (1936), Garrison Keillor (1942), Richard Hague (1947), Marty Appel (1948), Anne Fadiman (1953), Linda Aksomitis (Linda Demyen) and Ron Androla (1954), Vladimir Sorokin (1955), David Duchovny (1960), Lynn Crosbie (1963), John Birmingham (1964).

What a sense of superiority it gives one to escape reading a book which everyone else is reading.—Alice James

The author knows just what he wants to illustrate and how he would like it to be done.—Louis Leakey

Humor has to surprise us; otherwise, it isn't funny. It's a death knell for a writer to be labeled a humorist because then it's not a surprise anymore.—Garrison Keillor

The most important thing when starting out with essay writing is to find a voice with which you're comfortable. You need to find a persona that is very much like you, but slightly caricatured.—Anne Fadiman

Aug. 8—Conrad Lycosthenes (1518), Jacques Basnage (1653), Francis Hutcheson (1694), Johann C. Adelung (1732), Hieronymus van Alphen (1746), Emilie Flygare-Carlén (1807), Henry Osborn (1857), Sara Teasdale (Sara Trevor Teasdale Filsinger) (1884), Donald Davidson and Carl Randau (1893), Marjorie Kinnan Rawlings (1896), Nina Berberova (1901), Wachtang Ananjan (1905), Andre Demedts and Jesse (Hilton) Stuart (1906), Arthur J. Goldberg (1908), Don Cook (1920), Michael Parkin (1922), Gertrude Himmelfarb (1922), Elis Juliana and Juri Kasakow (1927), Terry Nation (1930), Lonnie Melvin "Mel" Tillis (1932), Donald P. Bellisario (1935), Dick Allen (1939), Alurista (Alberto Baltazar Urista Heredia) and Brenda Lee Eager (1947), Richard Tuggle (1948), Sarah Dunant (1950), Randy Shilts (1951), Jostein Gaarder (1952), Elizabeth Tallent (b. Elizabeth Ann Tallent) (1954), Deborah Norville (1958), Jonathan Earl Franzen (1959) Anastasia M. Ashman (1964), Al Letson (1974).

Life is but thought.—Sara Teasdale
Writing is agony for me. I work at it eight hours every day, hoping to get six pages, but I am satisfied with three.—Marjorie Kinnan Rawlings
When you're true to who you are, amazing things happen. —Deborah Norville

Aug. 9—Arnold Fitz Thedmar (1207), Izaak Walton (1593), John Oldham (1653), Jacob Campo Weyerman (1677), Bruno Dalberg/Anonymus Belga (Petrus the Wacker van Zon) (1758), Reynaldo Hahn (1875), Eino Kaila (1890), Jean Piaget and Aloysius Michael Sullivan (1896), David de Jong (1898), Armand Salacrou (1899), Pamela Lyndon "P. L." Travers (1899), John K(ennedy) Hutchens (1905), Berta Waterstradt (1907), John Baur (1909), Robert H. van Gulik (1910), Robert McCormick (1911), Tove Jansson (1914), Enzo Biagi (1920), Philip Larkin (1922), Gerrit Kouwenaar (1923), Michiel de Ruyter (1926), Daniel Keyes (1927), Tetsuko Kuroyanagi (1933), Graeme C. Gibson (1934), Dave Godfrey (1938), John (Herbert) Varley (1947), Jonathan Kellerman (1949), Peter Schmuck (1955), Reetika Gina Vazirani (1962), Chris Cuomo (1970), James Kim (1971), Gene Luen Yang (1973).

A writer is, after all, only half his book. The other half is the reader and from the reader the writer learns.—P. L. Travers

A writer and nothing else: a man alone in a room with the English language, trying to get human feelings right.—John K. Hutchens

I can't understand these chaps who go round American universities explaining how they write poems: It's like going round explaining how you sleep with your wife.—Philip Larkin

Aug. 10—Philipp Nicolai (1556), Eliza Frances Andrews (1840), Abai Ibragim Kunanbaiuli or Kunanbaev (1845), J. Scott Lidgett (1854), Lawrence Binyon (1869), Herbert Clark Hoover (1874), Alfred Döblin (1878), Emanuel Morgan (Harold Witter Bynner) (1881), Panait Istrati (1884), Voranc Prezikov (Lovro Kuhar) (1893), Michail M. Soschtschenko (1895), Piet(er O.) Bakker (1897), Francis Reginald "Frank" or "F. R." Scott (1899), Curt Siodmak (1902), (Joseph)Ward Moore (1903), A. N. Sherwin-White (1911), Jorge Amado and Angus Campbell (1912), Alastair Webster Mackie (1925), Saeedi Sirjani, Adam Smith (George Jerome Waldo Goodman), and Barry Unsworth (1930), Émile Martel (1941), Richard L. Kenney (1948), Mark Doty (1953), Suzanne (Marie) Collins (1962), Andrew Sullivan (1963), Christian Bök (1966), Jake Adam York (1972).

It is a paradox that every dictator has climbed to power on the ladder of free speech. Immediately on attaining power each dictator has suppressed all free speech except his own.—Herbert Hoover
Even a man who is pure in heart,
And says his prayers by night
May become a Wolf when the Wolfbane blooms
And the autumn Moon is bright.
—Curt Siodmak
Into the paradise of euphony, the good poet must introduce hell. Broken paradises are the only kind worth reading. — Mark Doty

Aug. 11—Thomas Betterton (1635), Octavia Walton Le Vert (b. Octavia Celestia Valentine Walton) (1811), Charlotte Mary Yonge (1823), Robert Green Ingersoll (1833), Alfred Coville (1860), Ernst Stadler (1883), Hugh MacDiarmid (Christopher Murray Grieve) (1892), Eiji Yoshikawa (1892), Louise Bogan (1897), Enid Blyton (1897), Hugo Buchthal (1909), Alphonse de Waelhens (1911), Prem Bhatia (1911), Angus Wilson (1913), Raymond Roseliep (1917), Alexander Murray Palmer "Alex" Haley (1921), Mavis Leslie de Trafford Gallant (1922), Carl Rowan (1925), Fernando Arrabal (1932), Jerry Falwell (1933), André Dubus II (1936), Dennis Schmitz and Taki Theodoracopoulos (1937), Bapsi Sidhwa (1938), Marilyn Vos Savant (Marilyn Mach) (1946), Hulk Hogan (Terry Gene Bollea) (1953), David Henry Hwang (1957), Serge Patrice Thibodeau (1959).

Actors speak of things imaginary as if they were real, while you preachers too often speak of things real as if they were imaginary. —Thomas Betterton

It's silly to suggest the writing of poetry as something ethereal, a sort of soul-crashing, emotional experience that wrings you. I have not fancy ideas about poetry. It doesn't come to you on the wings of a dove. It's something you work hard at.—Louise Bogan

Either you deal with what is the reality, or you can be sure that the reality is going to deal with you.—Alex Haley

I love short stories because I believe they are the way we live. They are what our friends tell us, in their pain and joy, their passion and rage, their yearning and their cry against injustice.—André Dubus

Aug. 12—Johann Heinrich Acker (1647), John Balguy (1686), Martin Gerbert (von Hornau) (1720), Robert Southey (1774), Elizabeth Oakes Smith (1806), Macellus Emants (1848), Johannes P. Kelly (Kellij) and Edith M(atilda) Thomas (1854), Katharine Lee Bates (1859), Jacinto Benavente y Martínez (1866), Edith Hamilton (1867), Émile (Chénin) Moselly (12 August 1870), Mary Roberts Rinehart (1876), Marguerite "John" Radclyffe-Hall (1880), Frank Arthur Swinnerton (1884), Keith Murdoch and Lily Ross Taylor (1886), Zerna Sharp (1889), Alfred Kantorowicz (1899), Peter Ambrose Cyprian Luke (1919), Donald Justice, twins Norris Dewar McWhirter and Alan Ross McWhirter (1925), Wallace Markfield (1926), Mary Ann Hoberman (1930), William Goldman (1931), William Charles "Bill" Kloefkorn (1932), Brian Doyle and Karl Mickel (1935), Geoff Hamilton (1936), Walter Dean Myers (1937), Réjean Ducharme (1941), Birk Sproxton (1943), Sue Monk Kidd and Tim Wynne-Jones (1948), Jim Beaver (1950), Gish Jen (b. Lillian Jen) and Ann M. Martin (1955), Chris Bohjalian (1962), Cheryl Kaye Tardif (1963), Katherine "Kate" J. Boo (1964), Anthony Swofford (1970).

It is with words as with sunbeams - the more they are condensed, the deeper they burn.—Robert Southey
     A people's literature is the great textbook for real knowledge of them. The writings of the day show the quality of the people as no historical reconstruction can.—Edith Hamilton
     I think reading is a gift. It was a gift that was given to me as a child by many people, and now as an adult and a writer, I'm trying to give a little of it back to others. It's one of the greatest pleasures I know.—Ann M. Martin

Aug. 13—William Caxton (1422), Johann A. Quenstedt (1617), William Wotton (1666), Nikolaus Lenau (1802), Vladimir Odoevsky (1803), George Grove and Joseph Alberdingk Thijm (Pauwels Foreestier) (1820), Goldwin Smith (1823), Giovanni Verga (1840), Arthur S(herburne) Hardy (1847). Rudolf Georg Binding and William A. Craigie (1867), Salomon "Sam" de Wolff (1878), Jacqueline (Pierrette) R. van Stuwe (Eline vav Stuwe) (1881), Ferdinand Sassen (1894), Max Croiset (1912), Madhur Jaffrey (1933), David Crane (1957), George Packer (1960), Tom Perrotta and Kate Walbert (1961), Amélie Nothomb (1967), Will Clarke (1970), Molly Henneberg (1973).

I wish it to be distinctly understood that I have always been a mere amateur in music. I wrote about the symphonies and concertos because I wished to try to make them clear to myself and to discover the secret of the things that charmed me so; and from that sprang a wish to make other amateurs see it in the same way.—George Grove

I'm not sure that it's possible to write a novel about people who don't transgress or stumble, people who don't surprise themselves with the things they do, people who can explain all their actions with perfect logical consistency. At least it's not possible for me to write that sort of novel.—Tom Perrotta

I'm not someone who revises. It's always the first movement, it's that. It's an instinct. Either it works straight away, or it won't ever work.—Amélie Nothomb

Aug. 14—Fra Paolo Sarpi (Paulus Venetus) (1552), Robert Hayman (1575), William Hutchinson (1786), Méric Casaubon (1599), Letitia Elizabeth Landon (1802), Park Benjamin Sr. (1809), Walter Besant (1836), Henry Duff Trail (1842), Ernest Thompson Seton (1860), Ernest (Lawrence) Thayer (1863), John Galsworthy (1867), Sibilla Aleramo (Rina Faccio) (1876), Harald Kidde (1878), Gisela Richter (1882), James Pitman (1901), Ethel Lois Payne (1911), Eva Strittmatter (1912), B. A. Santamaria (1915), Russell Baker (1925), Alice Adams (1926), René Goscinny (1926), Frederic Raphael (1931), Lee Hoffman (Shirley Bell Hoffman) (1932), Alexei Panshin (1940), Alfred Corn (1943), Stephen Glenn "Steve" Martin and Cheryl Waltz (1945), Philip F. Deaver (1946), Danielle Steel (Danielle Fernandes Dominique Schuelein-Steel) (1947), Gary Larson (1950), Cliff Johnson (1953), Stephen Sachs (1959), Brannon Braga (1964), Jaimie McEvoy (1965), Silvio Horta (1974).

I did not begin to write novels until I had forgotten all I had learned at school and college.—John Galsworthy

Americans like fat books and thin women.—Russell Baker

The real joy is in constructing a sentence. But I see myself as an actor first because writing is what you do when you are ready and acting is what you do when someone else is ready.—Steve Martin

Aug. 15—Luigi Pulci (1432), Bartol Kašić (1575), Gilles Ménage (1613), Matthias Claudius (1740), Napoléon Bonaparte (1759), Walter Scott (1771), Thomas De Quincey (1785), Julia (Strudwick) Tutwiler (1841), E. Nesbit (Edith Nesbit Bland) (1858), Johan(nes) B. Schepers (1865), Sri Aurobindo (1872), Aleksandar Belic (1876), Edna Ferber (1885), Thomas Edward "T. E." Lawrence (1888), Jan Brzechwa (1898), Hans Lorbeer (1901), Jan R. T. Campert (1902), Peter Nicholson Gunn (1914), Alma Gardeslan and Kamiel van Baelen (1915), Aleks Çaçi (1916), Benedict Kiely (1919), Shimon Peres (Szymon Persky) (1923), Robert Oxton Bolt and Phyllis Schlafly (1924), Robert L(ull) Forward (1932), Rodney J. "Rod" Anderson and Vernon (Eulion) Jordan Jr. (1935), Janusz A. Zajdel (1938), Linda Ellerbee (1944), Alastair Sweeny (1946), Ann Biderman (1951), Stieg Larsson and Mary Jo Salter (1954), Victor Shenderovich (1958), Rob Thomas (1965), Ben Affleck (Benjamin Géza Affleck-Boldt) (1972), Kiese Laymon (1974), Robert Macfarlane (1976).

A journalist is a grumbler, a censurer, a giver of advice, a regent of sovereigns, a tutor of nations. Four hostile newspapers are more to be feared than a thousand bayonets.—Napoléon Bonaparte

Life can't ever really defeat a writer who is in love with writing, for life itself is a writer's lover until death—fascinating, cruel, lavish, warm, cold, treacherous, constant.—Edna Ferber

In real life, people are integrated into society. That's what happens in my books as well. Minor characters don't just walk in and spout lines, they interact and have an effect on the events. It's not an isolated universe.—Stieg Larsson

Aug. 16—Emilie Juliane of Schwarzburg-Rudolstadt (1637), Jean de La Bruyère (1645), Vincenzo Coronelli (1650), Wilhelm Wundt (1832), Justus van Maurik (1846), Arthur Achleitner (1858), Jules Laforgue (1860), Ferdinand C. S. Schiller (1864), Antonio Nobre (1867), Bernarr Macfadden (Bernard Adolphus McFadden) (1868), Pierre H. Ritter Jr. (1882), Hugo Gernsback (Hugo Gernsbacher) (1884), Harold Rudolf "Hal" Foster (1892), Albert Cohen (1895), Georgette Heyer, Eli Siegel, and Wallace Henry Thurman (1902), William Keepers Maxwell Jr. (1908), Ralph (Barker) Gustafson (1909), Menachem Begin (1913), Charles Bukowski (1920), Louis E. Lomax (1922), Millôr Fernandes (1923), Lewis Barrett "Lew" Welch Jr. (1926), Maurice Kenny (1929), Robert Culp (1930), Reiner Kunze (1933), Diana Wynne Jones (1934), Andrew J(efferson V.) Offutt (1937), Pan Bouyoucas (1946), James Cameron and Benjamin Alire Sáenz (1954), Steve Carell (1962), Jessie Chandler (1968).

What description of clouds and sunsets was to the old novelist, description of scientific apparatus and methods is to the modern Scientific Detective writer.—Hugo Gernsback

I think myself I ought to be shot for writing such nonsense . . . But it's unquestionably good escapist literature, and I think I should rather like it if I were sitting in an air-raid shelter or recovering from flu.—Georgette Heyer

He asked, "What makes a man a writer?"

"Well," I said, "it's simple. You either get it down on paper, or jump off a bridge."—Charles Bukowski

Aug. 17—Johann V Andreae (1586), Josef Dobrovský (1753), Davy Crockett (1786), William Knox (1789), Fredrika Bremer (1801), Johannes H. Scholten (1811), Charlotte (Louise Bridges) Forten Grimké (1837), Wilfrid Scawen Blunt (1840), Luis N. F. Varela (1841), Violet Paget (Vernon Lee) (1856), Geneva Grace "Gene" Stratton-Porter (1863), Jesse Lynch Williams (1871), Clara (G. Meijer-)Wichmann (1885), Kurt Hiller (1885), Marcus Garvey (1887), Erik A. Blomberg (1894), Henry P. de Vries (1896), Gerard Schmook (1898), Janet (Loxley) Lewis (1899), Mary Cain (1904), Roger Peyrefitte (1907), Jan Lode Cantens (1911), Safa Khulusi (1917), Paul Wiens (1922), March Laumer (1923), Evan S. Connell and John A. Emmens (1924), John (Clendennin Talbot Burne) Hawkes (Jr.) (1925), Jean Poiret and David (Arthur) Watmough (1926), Ted Hughes (1930), Vidiadhar Surajprasad "V. S." Naipaul (1932), Herta Müller (1953), Jonathan (Earl) Franzen (1959), Kevin Max (1967), Nicola Kraus (1974).

Be always sure you are right - then go ahead.—Davy Crockett

A reading man and woman is a ready man and woman, but a writing man and woman is exact.—Marcus Garvey

What I felt was, if you spend your life just writing fiction, you are going to falsify your material. And the fictional form was going to force you to do things with the material, to dramatize it in a certain way. I thought nonfiction gave one a chance to explore the world, the other world, the world that one didn't know fully.—V. S. Naipaul

Aug. 18—Nur ad-Din Abd ar-Rahman Jami (1414), Marko Marulić Splićanin (1450), Jean Bolland (1598), Willem J.F. Nuyens (1823), Robert Williams Buchanan (1841), Ahad Haam (1856), Johan E. Elias (1875), Nettie Palmer (1885), Nico J. Polak (1887), Victor Barbeau (1896), Glenn Albert Black (1900), Edgar Faure and Armijn Pane (1908), David (Francis) Dodge (1910), Elsa Morante (1912), Zdzisław Żygulski Jr. (1921), Alain Robbe-Grillet (1922), Brian W(ilson) Aldiss (1925), Rosalynn Smith Carter (1927), Roman Polanski (1933), Vincent Bugliosi (1934), William George Rushton (1937), Graham Diamond (1949), Denis Leary (1957), Bob Woodruff (1961), Brian Michael Bendis (1967), Greg Dean Schmitz (1970), Nicole Krauss (1974).

Man, by his very nature, tends to give himself an explanation of the world into which he is born. And this is what distinguishes him from the other species. Every individual, even the least intelligent, the lowest of outcasts, from childhood on gives himself some explanation of the world. And with it he manages to live. And without it, he would sink into madness.—Elsa Morante

The true writer has nothing to say. What counts is the way he says it.—Alain Robbe-Grillet

I write what I think is funny and I write from a sense of popping a balloon or a sense of injustice, whether it's about yourself, or whether it's about something else. It's my worldview; it doesn't mean that everybody has to agree with it.—Denis Leary

Aug. 19—Marqués de Santillana (1398), Lodovico Guicciardini (1521), Paulus Merula (1558), John Dryden (1631), Eustace Budgell (1686), Samuel Richardson (1689), Pierre-Jean de Béranger (1780), James Hall (1793), Minna Canth (1844), Harold (Henry) Frederic(k) (1856) Edith Nesbit (1858), Hippolyte Delehaye (1859), Maurice Barres (1862), Arthur Waley (1889), Arnoldt Bronnen (1895), Vladimir M. Kirshon and Ogden Nash (1902), James Gould Cozzens (1903), Josephine Jacobsen (1908), Quentin Bell (1910), Ring Lardner Jr. (1915), Gene Roddenberry (1921), Gwendoline Butler (1922), Claude Gauvreau (1925), David Guy "D. G." Compton (1930), Bodil Malmsten (1944), William Jefferson "Bill" Clinton (1946), Joe Cottonwood and William Mastrosimone (1947), Jennie Bond and Mary Doria Russell (1950), Ingrid Rowland (1953), Li-Young Lee (1957), Sohrab Homi Fracis (1958), Asa Nonami (1960), Jonathan Coe (1961).

Words are but pictures of our thoughts.—John Dryden
I would live all my life in nonchalance and insouciance, Were it not for making a living, which is rather a nouciance.—Ogden Nash
Show me someone you think is "a simple man," and I'll show you that still waters run deep. Show me someone who thinks of himself as a simple man, and I'll show you someone who's deluding himself.—Sohrab Homi Fracis

Aug. 20—Peter Opmeer (1526), Thomas Corneille (1625), Bolesław Prus (1847), Innokenti F. Annenski (1856), Jakub Bart-Ćišinski (1856), Shaul Chernikhovski (1875), Edgar A(lbert) Guest (1881), Austin Tappan Wright (1883), Dino Campana (1885), Paul Tillich (1886), Howard Phillips "H. P." Lovecraft (1890), Tarjei Vesaas (1897), Vilhelm Moberg (1898), Hanns Lilje (1899), Salvatore Quasimodo (1901), Jean Gebser (1905), Jeanne Stern (1908), William Lindsay Gresham (1909), Jacqueline Susann (1918), Vasily Aksyonov (1932), (Barbara) Anne Cameron (1938), Robin Oakley (1941), Jo Ramirez (1941), Connie Chung (1946), Heather McHugh (1948), Chase Twichell (1950), Greg(ory Dale) Bear (1951), Lenny Henry (1958), Patricia Rozema (1958), Greg Egan and James Rollins (James Paul Czajkowski) (1961), Pedro Gomez (1962), Ibolya "Ibi" Kaslik (1973), twins Michael and Matthew Dickman, Marianne Garvey, and Marcus Mastin (1975).

I couldn't live a week without a private library—indeed, I'd part with all my furniture and squat and sleep on the floor before I'd let go of the 1500 or so books I possess.—H. P. Lovecraft

The Resistance is a moral certainty, not a poetic one. The true poet never uses words in order to punish someone. His judgment belongs to a creative order; it is not formulated as a prophetic scripture.—Salvatore Quasimodo

Dialogue is not just quotation. It is grimaces, pauses, adjustments of blouse buttons, doodles on a napkin, and crossings of legs.—Jerome Stern

Aug. 21—Francois de Sales (1567), Hubert Gautier (1660), Lucretia W. van Winter-van Merken (1721), Jernej Kopitar (1780), Jules Michelet (1798), Leonid N. Andrejev (1871), Miriam Allen deFord (1888), Roark Bradford and Raymond Herreman (1896), Roy K. Marshall and Miguel Torga (Adolfo Correia da Rocha) (1907), M. M. Kaye (1908), Anthony Boucher (William Anthony Parker White) (1911), Victor Rosow (1913), John Francis "Jack" Buck (1924), Joseph Charles "X. J." Kennedy (1929), Joseph (Prince) McElroy (1930), Melvin "Block" Van Peebles (1932), Mart Crowley (1935), Robert Stone (1937), Hugh (Hamilton) Wilson (1943), Peter Weir (1944), Margo Kane (1951), Ivan Stang (1953).

I like poems where you don't really know whether to laugh or cry when you read them. — X.J. Kennedy

Life is a means of extracting fiction.—Robert Stone

I loved Sherlock Holmes as a kid, but I remember being disappointed when he'd come up with these simple explanations for these complex mysteries.—Peter Weir

Aug. 22—Georges de Scudéry (1601), Jean Renaud de Segrais (1624), James Kirke Paulding (1778), John Hill Burton (1809), B. Amalie Skram-Alver (1846), George Herriman (1880), Gorch Fock (1880), Dorothy (Rothschild) Parker (1893), Roy Armstrong (1902), René Wellek (1903), Stojan T. Daskalov (1909), Julius J. Epstein (1909), Edith Porada (1912), Mary McGrory (1918), Pierre A. Lauffer (1920), Ray(mond Douglas) Bradbury and Wolfdietrich Schnurre (1920), Peter Kane Dufault and Gerald Long (1923), James Kirkwood (1924), Irmtraud Morgner (1933), E. Annie Proulx (1935), Herbert R. Kohl (1937), Uğur Mumcu and Stanley Ray "Stan" Tiner (1942), Rafi Zabor (b. Joel Zaborovsky) (1946), Sekou Sundiata (b. Robert Franklin Feaster) and Susan Joan Wood (1948), Þórarinn Eldjárn (1949), Will Shetterly (1955), Regina (Annette) Taylor (1960), Alfred Gough and Joshua Ozersky (1967), Charlie Connelly (1970).

Write a short story every week. It's not possible to write 52 bad short stories in a row.—Ray Bradbury

In a rough way the short story writer is to the novelist as a cabinetmaker is to a house carpenter.—Annie Proulx

Is art influential? It can be—'Uncle Tom's Cabin' rallied abolitionists, and 'The Jungle' provoked the demand for a safer food industry.—Will Shetterly

Aug. 23—Fulvio Testi (1593), Jakob F. Fries (1773), Juliusz Slowacki (1809), Moritz B. Cantor (1829), James De Mille (1833), William Southam (1843), William Ernest Henley (1849), Arnold Toynbee (1852), Marcel Schwob (1867), Edgar Lee Masters (1868), Alexander Grin (1880), Will Cuppy (1884), Jo Sternheim (1887), A(lfred) Lichtenstein and Geoffrey Cust Faber (1889), Cecil Rolph Hewitt (1901), Mauritius van Haegendoren (1903), Arthur Adamov (1908), Albert Alberts and James Vincent "J. V." Cunningham (1911), Jara Ribnikar (1912), Pierre Gauvreau (1922), Ephraim Kishon (1924), Mark Russell (Mark Ruslander) (1932), Roy Strong (1935), Lewis Nordan (1939), Nelson (Richard) DeMille (1943), Willy Russell (1947), Andrei Pleşu (1948), John Bauldie (1949), James Hynes (1955), Mary Zimmerman (1960), Roger Avary (1965), Jeremy Schaap (1969), Christian Beranek (1974).

Men there have been who have done the essayist's part so well as to have earned an immortality in the doing; but we have had not many of them, and they make but a poor figure on our shelves. It is a pity that things should be thus with us, for a good essayist is the pleasantest companion imaginable.—William Ernest Henley

Those who first oppose a good work, seize it and make it their own, when the cornerstone is laid and memorial tablets are erected.—Edgar Lee Masters

The trouble with the dictionary is that you have to know how a word is spelled before you can look it up to see how it is spelled.—Will Cuppy

The publisher is a middleman, he calls the tune to which the whole of the rest of the trade dances; and he does so because he pays the piper.—Geoffrey Faber

Aug. 24—Albrecht van Eyb (1420), John Taylor (1580), Robert Herrick (1591), Kozma Prutkov (Aleksey Konstantinovich Tolstoy Alexander Pushkin) (1817), Max Beerbohm (1872), Jean Rhys (1890), Jean Rhys (Ella Williams) (1894), Stanton A(rthur) Coblentz (1896), Malcolm Cowley (1898), Jorge Luis Borges, Johan J. Fabricius, and Ruth Schaumann (1899), Fernand Braudel (1902), Alice B(radley) Sheldon and James Tiptree Jr. (1915), Howard Zinn (1922), Arthur Jensen (1923), David Ireland, Harry Markowitz, and William V. Shannon (1927), John Alan Lee (1933), Rosmarie (Sebald) Waldrop (1935), Antonia Susan "A. S." Byatt (1936), Mason Williams (1938), Sharon Butala (Sharon Annette LeBlanc) (1940), Howard Jacobson (1942), Paulo Coelho (1947), Alexander "Sandy" McCall Smith (1948), T(im) D. White (1950), Orson Scott Card and Oscar (Jerome) Hijuelos (1951), Michael Dale "Mike" Huckabee (1955), Stephen Fry (1957), Christopher John "Chris" Offutt (1958), Denis Thériault (1959), Dana Gould (1964), David Khari Webber "Dave" Chappelle (1973), John (Michael) Green (1977).

They tell you that you'll lose your mind when you grow older. What they don't tell you is that you won't miss it very much. —Malcolm Cowley

When writers die they become books, which is, after all, not too bad an incarnation.—Jorge Luis Borges

Metaphors have a way of holding the most truth in the least space.—Orson Scott Card

I would always be that same maddening, monstrous mixture of pedantry, egoism, politeness, selfishness, kindliness, sneakiness, larkiness, sociability, loneliness, ambition, ordered calm and hidden intensity. I would cover my life with words. I would spray the whole bloody world with words.—Stephen Fry

Aug. 25—Johann G. von Herder (1744), Antoine Louis Léon de Richebourg de Saint-Just (1767), Cornelis J. van Assen (1788), Baron Bunsen (1791), John Neal (1793), Henrik Hertz (1797/98), Bret Harte (1836), Louise J. Gautier (1846), George Parsons Lathrop (1851), Waldo (David) Frank (1889), Alberto Savinio (Andrea de Chirico) (1891), Kjeld Abell and Luella Sanders Creighton (Bruce) (1901), Arpad Elo (1903), Mollie Panter-Downes (1906), J. B. Charles (Willem H. Nagel) (1910), Ed Lacy (Leonard "Len" S. Zinberg) (1911), Ralph Allen and Walt Kelly (1913), Brian Moore (1921), Mac Hyman (1923), Thea Astley (1925), Dominique Fernandez (1929), Diana Norman (1933), Charles Wright (1935), Carolyn (Gimpel) Hart (1936), Virginia Euwer Wolff (1937), Frederick Forsyth (1938), Carol Bolt (1941), Howard Jacobson (1942), Bill Holm (1943, Conrad Moffat Black and Sherley Anne Williams (1944), Father Goose (Charles Ghigna) (1946), Martin Amis (1949), Han Nolan (1956), Timothy Nicholson (1964), Marti Noxon (1964).

It is not good enough for things to be planned—they still have to be done; for the intention to become a reality, energy has to be launched into operation.—Walt Kelly

When you're a writer you no longer see things with the freshness of the normal person. There are always two figures that work inside you.—Brian Moore

Several people, not just reviewers, took me to task for writing about what they called the working classes—something I've been doing for 40 years. I thought that was contemptible—what do they want to do, ghettoize the working class as a subject? Can you only write about your own class? I've written about royalty, am I not allowed to do that?—Martin Amis

Aug. 26—William Joseph Behr (1775), Jacobus J. Backer (1825), Aleksander Kuprin (1870), Zona Gale (1874), John Buchan (1875), Guillaume Apollinaire and Philip Moeller (1880), Johannes Lindeboom (1882), Earl Derr Biggers (1884), Jules Romains (1885), Emmy van Lokhorst (1891), Ferdinand Bruckner (Theodor Tagger) (1891), Caroline Pafford Miller (1903), Christopher (William Bradshaw) Isherwood (1904), Marguerite Vivian Young (1908), Julio (Jules Florencio) Cortázar (1914), Humphrey Searle (1915), Allan Leslie Merson (1916), Brant Parker (1920), Ben Bradlee (1921), Irving R. Levine (1922), Jack Hirshleifer, Alain Peyrefitte, and Sangharakshita (Dennis Philip Edward Lingwood) (1925), Gordon Greig (1931), Arthur Gordon Clough (1934), Cornelis B. Vaandrager (Cor Vaan) (1935), Cornelia J. "Corry" Arends (1944), Alan Davies (1951), Lynn Carol "Nikky" Finney (1957), Eric D. Snider (1974).

I don't know of a better preparation for life than a love for poetry and a good indigestion.—**Zona Gale**

Every man at the bottom of his heart believes that he is a born detective.—**John Buchan**

Skill alone cannot teach or produce a great short story, which condenses the obsession of the creature; it is a hallucinatory presence manifest from the first sentence to fascinate the reader, to make him lose contact with the dull reality that surrounds him, submerging him in another that is more intense and compelling.—**Julio Cortázar**

Aug. 27—Johann Georg Hamann (1730), Herman Muntinghe (1752), Anne-Francois Mellinet (1768), Georg Wilhelm Friedrich Hegel (1770), Edward Beecher (1803), Hermann Kipper (1826), Albijn van de Abeele (1835), Manuel Acuna (1849), James Henry Breasted, Iwan Franko, and Emmuska Orczy (1865), Amado Nervo (Juan C. Ruiz de Nervo) (1870), Theodore (Herman Albert) Dreiser (1871), Lloyd Cassel Douglas (1877), Owen (McMahon) Johnson (1878), Ad van Emmenes (1897), Cecil Scott "C. S." Forester (1899), Xavier Villaurrutia (1903), Norah Lofts (1904), Donald McKenzie MacKinnon (1913), Catherine Marshall (1914), Walter W. Heller (1915), Jack (Clifford) Smith (1916), David Rowbotham (1924), Ira (Marvin) Levin and Owens Lee Pomeroy (1929), Antonia (Margaret Caroline) Fraser (1932), Kerstin Lillemor Ekman (Hjorth) (1933), Michael Holroyd and Frank Yablans (1935), Desmond O'Grady (1935), Dennis Cooley and F. Armstrong Green (1944), Lary Crews (1946), Paul Reubens (1952), Gjertrud Schnackenberg (1953), Tom Lanoye (1958), Jeanette Winterson (1959), Jill Lepore (1966).

Words are but the vague shadows of the volumes we mean. Little audible links, they are, chaining together great inaudible feelings and purposes.—Theodore Dreiser

It is a mistake to think that books have come to stay. The human race did without them for thousands of years and may decide to do without them again.—C. S. Forester

I'd rather be caught holding up a bank than stealing so much as a two-word phrase from another writer.—Jack Smith

It is easier to live a long and happy life than to write well. —F. Armstrong Green

Nostalgia is like a grammar lesson:? You find the present tense; but the past perfect!?—Owens Lee Pomeroy

Aug. 28—Rhazes (Mohammad-e Zakariā-ye Rāzi) (865), Johann Wolfgang von Goethe (1749), Antoine A. Cournot (1801), Jones Very (1813), William Robertson Davies (1913), (Joseph Thomas) Sheridan le Fanu (1814), Vance Palmer (1885), Ludwig Turek (1898), Cornelis J. Kelk and Paul Henry Lang (1901), John Betjeman (1906), Robert Merle and Roger Tory Peterson (1908), Tjalling Koopmans (1910), William Robertson Davies (1913), C. Wright Mills and John Holbrook "Jack" Vance (1916), Hélène Baillargeon (1916), Fernando Fernán Gómez (1921), Janet Frame (1924), Arkadi N. Strugazki (1925), Carlene Polite (1932), Alan Emlyn Williams (1935), Maurizio Costanzo (1938), Charles Potts (1943), André Brassard (1946), Vonda N(eel) McIntyre (1948), Dianne Warren (1950), Rita Dove (1952), Arthur Holden (1959), Dennis Bock (1964), Sheryl Kara Sandberg (1969).

Persons born with a talent they are meant to use will find their greatest happiness in using it.—Johann Wolfgang von Goethe
Too many people in the modern world view poetry as a luxury, not a necessity like petrol. But to me it's the oil of life.—John Betjeman
There are times when I think that the reading I have done in the past has had no effect except to cloud my mind and make me indecisive.—Robertson Davies
Writing a novel is not merely going on a shopping expedition across the border to an unreal land: it is hours and years spent in the factories, the streets, the cathedrals of the imagination.—Janet Frame

Aug. 29—Janus Pannonius (1434), John Locke (1632), Giambattista Casti (1724), Raphael G. Kiesewetter (1773), Oliver Wendell Holmes Sr. (1809), Anna Ella Carroll (1815), Edward Carpenter (1844), Caroline Mays Brevard (1860), Maurice (Polydore Marie Bernard) Maeterlinck (1862), Valery Nicolas Larbaud (1881), William Force Stead and Ehm Welk (1884), Marquis James (1891), Preston Sturges (Edmund P. Biden) (1898), Ernst Kreuder (1903), Joseph Wechsberg (1907), Denys Hay (1915), Leo Horn (1916), (Richard) "Mr." Blackwell, Emile Habibi, and John Edward Williams (1922), George Markstein (1926), Dorothy Tennov (1928), Thom Gunn (1929), Lise Payette (1931), Hugo Brandt Corstius (1935), John S. McCain III (1936), Karen Hesse (1952), Nancy (Lindsay Jones) Holder (1953), Kathleen Alcalá and Michael P(aul) Kube-McDowell (1954), Steve Yarbrough (1956), Michael (Joseph) Jackson (1958), Elizabeth Brown (1963), Chieu Luu (1979).

Many people die with their music still in them. Why is this so? Too often it is because they are always getting ready to live. Before they know it, time runs out.—Oliver Wendell Holmes

Deep feeling doesn't make for good poetry. A way with language would be a bit of help.—Thom Gunn

People are often unreasonable, irrational, and self-centered. Forgive them anyway. If you are kind, people may accuse you of selfish, ulterior motives. Be kind anyway. If you are successful, you will win some unfaithful friends and some genuine enemies. Succeed anyway.—Elizabeth B. Brown

Aug. 30—Mohammed (580), David Hartley (1705), Bonifacio Asioli (1769), Mary Wollstonecraft Shelley (1797), Aleksandr I. Polezjajev (1804), Pierre Jules Theophile Gautier (1811), Paul Hazard (1878), Meijer de Hond (1882), Adam Kuckhoff (1887), John Gunther (1901), Elizabeth Longford (Elizabeth Pakenham, Countess of Longford) (1906), Donald Bisset (1910), Ben Cami (1920), Jack (Barry) Ludwig (1922), Charmian Clift (1923), Laurent de Brunhoff (1925), Ruth Westerheimer (1928), Warren Burger (1930), Fabrizia Ramondino (1936), Wlliam Craig "Bill" Berkson (1939), Larry (Alfred) Woiwode (1941), Rick Salutin (1942), Robert Crumb (1943), Molly Ivins (1944), Lewis Black (1948), Anna Politkovskaya (1958), Guy A. Lepage (1960), Lisa Ling (1973).

My dreams were at once more fantastic and agreeable than my writings.—Mary Shelley

Satire is traditionally the weapon of the powerless against the powerful.—Molly Ivins

Anybody who likes writing a book is an idiot. Because it's impossible; it's like having a homework assignment every stinking day until it's done. And by the time you get it in, it's done and you're sitting there reading it, and you realize the 12,000 things you didn't do. I mean, writing isn't fun. It's never been fun.—Lewis Black

Aug. 31—Elizabeth Stuart Phelps/Mary Adams (Elizabeth Stuart Phelps Ward) (1844), Nathan Haskell Dole (1852), Maria Montessori (1870), George Al Sarton (1884), DuBose Heyward (1885), Ramon de Basterra (1888), Albert Facey and Charles Reznikoff (1894), Félix-Antoine Savard (1896), Marianne Bruns (1897), (Rollie) Lynn Riggs (1899), (Isadore) "Dore" Schary (1905), Sal Tas (1905), William Shawn (1907), William Saroyan (1908), Daniel Schorr (1916), Amrita Preetam (1919), Warren Miller (1921), Serafina K. "Sera" Anstadt (1923), Jeremy Stephen Maas (1928), Julio Ramon Ribeyro (1929), Dan Rather (1931), Benito Wogatzki (1932), (Franklin) Robert Adams (1933), Clyde Bolton and Marva (Delores Knight) Collins (1936), Martin Bell and Elizabeth Forsythe Hailey (1938), Dennis (Beynon) Lee (1939), Lorenzo Thomas (1944), Michael Andre, Jerome Corsi, and Lowell Ganz (1946), György Károly (1953), Raymond P. Hammond (1964), Kenneth Oppel (1967), G. Willow Wilson (1982).

The **true portrait of a man is a fusion of what he thinks he is, what others think he is, what he really is and what he tries to be. —Dore Shary**
The most solid advice for a writer is this, I think: Try to learn to breathe deeply, really to taste food when you eat, and when you sleep really to sleep. Try as much as possible to be wholly alive with all your might, and when you laugh, laugh like hell. And when you get angry, get good and angry. Try to be alive. You will be dead soon enough. —William Saroyan
"Look at all the Eastern writers who've written great Western literature. Kazuo Ishiguro. You'd never guess that The Remains of the Day or Never Let Me Go were written by a Japanese guy. But I can't think of anyone who's ever done the reverse—any Westerner who's written great Eastern literature. Well, maybe if we count Lawrence Durrell—does the Alexandria Quartet qualify as Eastern literature?"
"There is a very simple test," said Vikram. "Is it about bored, tired people having sex?"
"Yes," said the convert, surprised.
"Then it's western."—G. Willow Wilson

Born in September

Sept. 1—Wilhelmus Kist (1758), Emanuel Schikaneder (Johann Schickeneder) (1751), Mrs. Sigourney (Lydia [Howard Huntley] Sigourney) (1791), Jacobus J. Cremer (1827), Innokenty Annensky (1855), Henry E(dwin) Baker Jr. (1857), Marie Bankhead Owen (1869), Ismar Elbogen (1874), Edgar Rice Burroughs (1875), Rex (Ellingwood) Beach and Blaise Cendrars (Frederic Sauser-Hall) (1887), Otto Eissfeldt (1887), Arthur (William) Upfield (1890), Harold (Albert) Lamb (1892), Lucile Saunders McDonald (1898), Walter Reuther (1907), Monica Sone (Kazuko Itoi) (1919), Hubert Lampo (1920), Willem Frederik Hermans (1921), Theo H. Joekes (1923), James (Crerar) Reaney (1926), Alan (Morton) Dershowitz (1938), Gwendolyn (Margaret) MacEwen (1941), Carolyn Janice "C. J." Cherryh (1942), Mustafa Balel and Scott Spencer (1945), Darlene (Alice Barry) Quaife (1948), Timothy Zahn (1951), Kenny Mayne (1959), Jesse (Oren) Kellerman (1978), Michael Lista (1983).

We speak of educating our children. Do we know that our children also educate us?—Lydia Sigourney

I write to escape; to escape poverty.—Edgar Rice Burroughs

It is perfectly okay to write garbage—as long as you edit brilliantly.—C. J. Cherryh

Sept. 2—William Somervile (1675), Johann F. von Cronegk (1731), Caroline von Schelling (Michaelis) (1763), Esteban Echeverría (1805), William Seymour Tyler (1810), Ernst Curtius (1814), Eugene Field (1850), Jules-Paul Tardivel (1851), Paul Bourget (1852), Hans Jæger (1854), Frank Laubach (1884), Joseph Roth (1894), Andreas Embirikos (1901), Johan Daisne (Herman Thiery) (1912), Cleveland Amory (1917), Allen Drury (1918), Sidney C. Phillips Jr. (1924), Peter Mansfield (1928), William Packard (1933), Grady (Lee) Nutt (1934), Harry Northup (1940), Myrna Kostash (1944), Victor-Lévy Beaulieu (1945), Donald Margulies (1954), John S. Hall (1960), Mark Leiren-Young (1962), Chris Kuzneski (1969), Fuminori Nakamura (1977), Brendan Gall (1978).

Ideas came with explosive immediacy, like an instant birth. Human thought is like a monstrous pendulum; it keeps swinging from one extreme to the other.—Eugene Field

Be kind, be decent, be generous, be tolerant, compassionate, and understanding. Be fast to praise, slow to judge. Remember, we're all human, and don't cast the first stone.—Allen Drury

Laughter is the hand of God on the shoulder of a troubled world.—Grady Nutt

Sept. 3—Karl von Bonstetten (1745), John Humphrey Noyes (1811), Sarah Orne Jewett (1849), Wilhelm Bousset (1865), Bessie Annie Elizabeth Delany (1891), Sally Benson (b. Sara Mahala Redway Smith) (1897), Willem Kooiman (1903), Loren Eiseley (1907), Violet Kazue de Cristoforo (1917), Edwin Honig (1919), Marguerite Higgins (1921), Mort Walker (1923), John R(obert) Jones and Alison Lurie (1926), Caryl Churchill and Cherry Barbara Grimm (Lockett) (1930), Sergei Dovlatov (1941), Mick Farren (1943), Peter Morris (1946), Timothy M. "Tim" McGuire (1953), Adam Brooks (1956), Spike Feresten (1964), Jeffrey Stanley (1967), Kiran Desai (1971).

The thing that teases the mind over and over for years, and at last gets itself put down rightly on paper—whether little or great, it belongs to Literature.—Sarah Orne Jewett

It is frequently the tragedy of the great artist, as it is of the great scientist, that he frightens the ordinary man.—Loren Eiseley

Everything I know, I write about. My only research is what I did.—Mort Walker

Sept. 4—Constantine Huygens (1596), Bernardus Bosch (1746), Francois René de Chateaubriand (1768), Friedrich August von Alberti (1795), Phoebe Cary (1824), Geert A. D. Wumkes (1869), Harold MacGrath (1871), Robert J(ames) C(ampbell) Stead (1880), Antonin Artaud (1896), Paul Osborn (1901), Mary Renault (Eileen Mary Challans) (1905), Hendrikus G. "Han" Hoekstra and Wayne D. Overholser (1906), Maurice Ashley (1907), Richard (Nathaniel) Wright (1908), Alexander Liberman (1912), Robert (Augustine) W(ard) Lowndes (1916), Paul Harvey (Paul Harvey Aurandt) (1918), Craig Claiborne (1920), Per Olof Sundman (1922), Joan Delano Aiken and Harold Livingston (1924), Forrest Carter (Asa Earl Carter) (1925), Craig Claiborne (1929), Clive (William John) Granger (1934), Yann Queffélec (1949), Damon Wayans (1960), Dora Malech (1981).

An original writer is not one who imitates nobody, but one whom nobody can imitate.—François-René de Chateaubriand

Death comes not to the living soul, nor age to the loving heart.—Phoebe Cary

I would hurl words into this darkness and wait for an echo, and if an echo sounded, no matter how faintly, I would send other words to tell, to march, to fight, to create a sense of hunger for life that gnaws in us all.—Richard Wright

Sept. 5—Tommaso Campanella (1568), Gottfried Arnold (1666), Lukas Fencer (1688), Robert Fergusson (1750), August Wilhelm Schlegel (1767), Richard Chenevix Trench (1807), Aleksei K. Tolstoi (Kozjma Prutkov) (1817), Goffredo Mameli (1827), Otto E. Deutsch (1883), Sarvepalli Radhakrishnan (1888), (Joseph) Hamilton Basso (1904), Arthur Koestler (1905), Semjon I. Kirsanov (1906), Nicanor Parra (1914), Frank Shuster and Frank (Garvin) Yerby (1916), Luis Alcoriza (1918), Margaretha D. Ferguson-Wigerink (1920), Justin Kaplan and Jos Vandeloo (1925), Paul Volcker (1927), Ward S. Just (1935), Jonathan Kozol (1936), Dario Bellezza (1944), James R. Benn (1949), Cathy Guisewite and Paul William Roberts (1950), Frederick Kempe (1954), Lauren B. Davis (1955), Graham John Yost (1959), Christopher Nolan (1965), Vincent Lam (1974).

Grammar is the logic of speech; even as logic is the grammar of reason.—Richard C. Trench

A writer's ambition should be to trade a hundred contemporary readers for ten readers in ten years' time and for one reader in a hundred years' time.—Arthur Koestler

I used to be adjective happy. Now I cut them with so much severity that I find I have to put a few adjectives back.—Frank Yerby

My mother had always taught me to write about my feelings instead of sharing really personal things with others, so I spent many evenings writing in my diary, eating everything in the kitchen and waiting for Mr. Wrong to call.—Cathy Guisewite

Sept. 6—Mozes Mendelssohn (1729), Laurence Eusden (bapt. 1688), Frances Wright (1795), Catharine (Esther) Beecher (1800), Horatio Greenough (1805), Johanna D. Courtmans-Berchmans (1811), Nicolae Filimon (1819), Louis (F.H.) Apol (1850), Zelia Nuttall (1857), Frank H(amilton) Spearman (1859), Jane Addams (1860), Rodolfo Lenz (1863), Felix Salten (Siegmund Salzmann) (1869), Franz T. Csokor (1885), Arthur Cheney Train (1875), Howard Pease (1894), Mario Praz (1896), Marc Bernard and Julien Green (1900), Karlo Arvi Kivimaa (1904), Lawrence Clark Powell (1906), Elizabeth Morna MacTaggart Ferrars (1907), Anthony (Richard) Wagner (1908), Barbara (Ann Pinson) Guest (1920), Carmen Laforet and Robert Millar (1921), Robert M. Pirsig (1928), Kyotaro Nishimura (Kihachiro Yajima) (1930), David Allan Coe and Dan Cragg (1939), Gordon DeMarco (1944), Jeff Foxworthy (1958), Simon Reeve (1961), Alice Sebold (1963), Robert Budde (1966), Christopher Brookmyre and Paul Rea (1968), Paul Miller (1970), China Miéville (1972).

As liberty and intelligence have increased the people have more and more revolted against the theological dogmas that contradict common sense and wound the tenderest sensibilities of the soul. —Catharine Beecher

Writing is a solitary occupation. Family, friends, and society are the natural enemies of a writer. He must be alone, uninterrupted, and slightly savage if he is to sustain and complete an undertaking. —Lawrence Clark Powell

I don't know why my brain has kept all the words to the Gilligan's Island theme song and has deleted everything about triangles.—Jeff Foxworthy

The relationship with the words someone uses is more intimate and integrated than just a quick read and a blurb can ever be. This intimacy—the words on the page being sent back and forth from engaged editor to open author—is unique in my experience.—Alice Sebold

Sept. 7—Elizabeth I (1533), George-Louis Leclerc, comte de Buffon (1707), Willem Bilderdijk (1756), Hermann Heinrich Gossen (1810), Jean E. "Adriaan" van Bevervoorde (1819), Tristan Bernard (1866), Camilod d'Almeida Pessanha (1867), Margot S.E. Scharten-Antink (1869), Aleksander Kuprin (1870), Thomas Curtis (1870), C.J. Dennis (1876), Constantly W. L. Scheurleer (1881), (Harry) Sinclair Lewis and Elinor (Morton Hoyt) Wylie (1885), Edith L. Sitwell (1887), Bruce F. Cummings (1889), Manuel Komroff (1890), Jessica Nelson North (1891), (Janet Miriam Holland) Taylor Caldwell (1900), Margaret Landon (1903), Anthony Quayle and Oswald Szemerenyi (1913), Herbert Delauney "Bill" Hughes (1914), Harri Webb (1920), Virginia Van der Veer Hamilton and MacDonald Harris (Donald Heiney) (1921), Eric Hill and Benjamin Saltman (1927), Lloyd (Anthony) Pye Jr. (1946), Barry Siegel (1949), (Margaret) Peggy (Ellen) Noonan (1950), Charlotte Agell (1959), Lois-Ann Yamanaka (1961), Jennifer Egan (1962), Annie Martin (1981).

Monarchs ought to put to death the authors and instigators of war, as their sworn enemies and as dangers to their states.
—Elizabeth I
When audiences come to see us authors lecture, it is largely in the hope that we'll be funnier to look at than to read.—Sinclair Lewis
My relatives used to laugh when I talked of being a writer.
—Taylor Caldwell

Sept. 8—Ludovico Ariosto (1474), Alfonso Salmeron (1515), Marin Mersenne (1588), Johann Friedrich Gronovius (1611), Francois-Thomas the Baculard d'Arnaud (1718), Anna K. Emmerick/ Emmerich (1774), Nicolai Grundtvig (1783), Eduard Mörike (1804), Charles-Étienne Brasseur de Bourbourg (1814), Frédéric Mistral (1830), Wilhelm Raabe (Jakob Corvinus) (1831), Joaquin Miller (Cincinnatus Heine Miller) (1837), Adolfo Albertazzi (1865), Alfred Jarry (1873), Siegfried L. Sassoon (1886), Willem F.J. Pijper (1894), Sara García (1895), Howard Dietz (1896), Anthonie Donker (Prof. N. Donkersloot) (1902), Gianni Brera (Giovanni Luigi Brera) (1919), Isaac Sidney "Sid" Caesar (1922), Grace Metalious (Marie Grace de Repentigny) (1924), Robert W. Firestone (1930), Michael Frayn (1933), Jack Prelutsky (1940)), Nancy Ann Dibble (1942), Ann Beattie and Marianne Wiggins (1947), Lynn/Marilyn (Lorraine) Abbey (1948), Christopher Klim (1962), Richard Van Camp (1971, Sarah Kucserka (1976), a.rawlings (Angela Rawlings) (1978).

Comedy has to be based on truth. You take the truth and you put a little curlicue at the end.—Sid Caesar

I'm a lousy writer; a helluva lot of people have got lousy taste. —Grace Metalious

It seems to me that the problem with diaries, and the reason that most of them are so boring, is that every day we vacillate between examining our hangnails and speculating on cosmic order.—Ann Beattie

Sept. 9—Clemens Brentano (1778), Richard Chenevix Trench (1807), Ellen Call Long (1825), Lev Nikolayevich "Leo" Tolstoy (1828), Joseph H. Shorthouse (1834), Gentil T. Antheunis (1840), (James) Maurice Thompson (1844), Houston S. Chamberlain (1855), Mary Hunter Austin (1868), Delilah L. Beasley (1872), Adelaide Crapsey (1878), John Hall Wheelock (1886), James Hilton (1900), Marya Zaturenska (1902), Phyllis (Ayame) Whitney (1903), Brahmarishi Hussain Sha (1905), Leon Edel (1907), Cesare Pavese (1908), Paul Goodman (1911), Bernard Bailyn and Manolis Glezos (1922), Louise Abeita Chewiwi (E-Yeh-Shure or Blue Corn) and Annie Kriegel (Annie Becker) (1926), Gopal Baratham (1935), Linda Alouise Gregg (1942), Frank Richard (Aloysius Jude) Maloney (1945), Christopher Francis Palmer (1946), Bob Shacochis (1951), Kimberly Willis Holt (1960), Jennifer Egan (1962), Caroline Adderson (1963), Aleksandar Hemon (1964), Adam Sandler (1966), Anthony Shadid (1968), Chace Ambrose (1976), Zoe (Swicord) Kazan (1983).

One ought only to write when one leaves a piece of one's own flesh in the inkpot, each time one dips one's pen.—Leo Tolstoy

What women have to stand on squarely is not their ability to see the world in the way men see it, but the importance and validity of their seeing it in some other way.—Mary Hunter Austin

Most writers are in a state of gloom a great deal of the time; they need perpetual reassurance.—John Hall Wheelock

When you [as a biographer] see that many letters and that many documents and gotten that far into the situation, you are likely to see your subject as a relative.—Leon Edel

It rarely adds anything to say, 'In my opinion'—not even modesty. Naturally a sentence is only your opinion; and you are not the Pope.—Paul Goodman

Sept. 10—Hannah Webster Foster (1758), Jacques Boucher de Crèvecœur de Perthes (1788), Giuseppe Gioacchino Belli (1791), Isaac Kauffman Funk and Charles Peirce (1839), Jeppe Aakjær (1866), Georgia B. D. Camp Johnson (1877), Georgia (Blanche) Douglas (Camp) Johnson (1880), Euphemia "Phemia" Molkenboer (1883), Berthold Altaner (1885), Carl Clinton Van Doren (1885), H. D. (Hilda Doolittle) (1886), Ian (Lancaster) Fleming (1888), Franz Werfel (1890), Kavi Samrat Viswanatha Satyanarayana (1895), Georges Bataille (1897), Toivo R. Pekkanen (1902), Cyril Connolly (1903), Waldo Wedel (1908), Brother Antonius (William Everson) (1912), Franco Fortini and Miguel Serrano (1917), Lex van Delden (1919), Leo P(atrick) Kelley and Jean Vanier (1928), Robert "Bo" Goldman (1932), Charles Kuralt (1934), Mary Oliver (1935), Jared Diamond (1937), John Curl (1940), Stephen Jay Gould (1941), Neale Donald Walsch (1943), Zhang Chengzhi (1948), William James "Bill" O'Reilly (1949), Gerry Conway (1952), Andreï Sergeyevich Makine (1957), Chris Columbus (1958, Zachariah Wells (1976).

Writing. Love is writing.—H.D.
I consider myself kind of a reporter—one who uses words that are more like music and that have a choreography. I never think of myself as a poet; I just get up and write.—Mary Oliver
The most erroneous stories are those we think we know best—and therefore never scrutinize or question.—Stephen Jay Gould

Sept. 11—Bernardo Accolti (Unico Aretino) (1458), Pierre de Ronsard (1523), Thomas Erpenius (van Erpe) (1584), Elizabeth Singer Rowe (1674), James Thomson (1700), Johann Bernhard Basedow (1723), Johann J. Angel (1741), Joanna Baillie (1762), Aleksandr I. Polezjajev (1804), Fitz Hugh Ludlow (1836), Vjenceslav Novak (1859), Juhani Aho (1861), O. Henry (William Sydney Porter) (1862), Rainis (Jānis Pliekšān) (1865), David Herbert "D. H." Lawrence (1885), William Thomas Walsh (1891), Theodor Adorno (1903), Oonah (Browne) McFee (1916), Jessica (Lucy) Mitford (1917), (Edward) Reed Whittemore (Jr.) (1919), Alfred Slote (1926), David S. Broder (1929), Hans-Ulrich Wehler (1931), William Luther Pierce (1933), Leon Rooke (1934), Thomas K(incaid) McCraw (1940), Gerome Ragni (1942), Lise Blouin (1944), Stephen Osborne (1947), Jani Allan (1953), James S. Shapiro (1955), Tony Gilroy (1956), James McBride (1957)[, Phoef Sutton (1958), Philip Ardagh (1961), Dave Bidini and Patrick McWilliams (1963), John Schofield (1965), Maria Bartiromo (1967), Paul Mayeda Berges (1968), Markos Moulitsas (1971).

I'll give you the whole secret to short story writing. Here it is. Rule 1: Write stories that please yourself. There is no Rule 2.—O. Henry

It is quite true, as some poets said, that the God who created man must have had a sinister sense of humor, creating him a reasonable being, yet forcing him to take this ridiculous posture, and driving him with blind craving for this ridiculous performance. —D. H. Lawrence

You may not be able to change the world, but you can at least embarrass the guilty.—Jessica Mitford

Sept. 12—Peter Dens (1690), Johann Heinrich Jung (1740), Julien Auguste Pélage Brizeux (1803), James Hall (1811), Charles Dudley Warner (1829), Henry Louis "H. L." Mencken (1880), Daniel Jones (1881), Elsa Triolet (Ella Yurevna Kagan) (or Sept. 24) (1896), Marya Zaturenska (1902), Joe Lederer (1907), Louis MacNeice (1907), Will Henry/Clay Fisher (Henry Wilson Allen) (1912), Kenneth Lo (1913), Rais Amrohvi (1914), Frank McGee (1915), Christian Geel (1917), Jan W. Schulte Nordholt (1920), Stanisław Lem and Frank McGee (1921), Jackson Mac Low (1922), Kristin Elaine Hunter (Kristin Hunter Eggleston) (1931), Alan Isler, Jaegwon Kim, and Nellie Wong (1934), Tom Mandel (b. Thomas Oskar Poeller) (1942), Michael Ondaatje (1943), Walter E. "W. E." Butts (1944), Kevin Major (1949), Jeff Jarvis and Michael Wex (1954), Paul Bellini (1959), James Frey (1969).

People always overdo the matter when they attempt deception. —Charles Dudley Warner

Historian: an unsuccessful novelist.—H. L. Mencken

A writer uses a pen instead of a scalpel or blow torch.—Michael Ondaatje

Sept. 13—John Leland (1502), Arnold Ruge (1802), Nicolaas Beets (Hildebrand) (1814), Olivier Gloux (Aimard) (1818), Marie von Ebner-Eschenbach (1830), Johannes de Koo (1841), Ralph Connor (Charles William Gordon) (1860), Otakar Brezina (Vaclav I. Jebavy) (1868), Sherwood Anderson (1876), John Boynton "J. B." Priestley (1894), Julian Tuwim (1894), Anton Constandse (1899), Hermine Heijermans (1902), Benjamin Appel (1907), Leonard Geoffrey Feather (1914), John Malcolm Brinnin and Roald Dahl (1916), Mary Midgley (Scrutton) (1919), Reninca (Renée Lauwers) (1923), Adrienne Kennedy (1931), Judith Martin (1938), Larry (Melvin) Speakes (1939), Mildred D(eLois) Taylor (1943), Ronald "Ron" Allen (1947), Tõnu Õnnepalu (1962), Tavis Smiley (1964), E. Lockhart (Emily Jenkins) (1967).

That in the beginning when the world was young there were a great many thoughts but no such thing as truth. Man made the truths himself and each truth was a composite of a great many vague thoughts. All about in the world were truths and they were all beautiful.—Sherwood Anderson

A novelist who writes nothing for 10 years finds his reputation rising. Because I keep on producing books they say there must be something wrong with this fellow.—J. B. Priestley

For email, the old postcard rule applies. Nobody else is supposed to read your postcards, but you'd be a fool if you wrote anything private on one.—Judith Martin

Sept. 14—Heinrich Cornelius Agrippa (1486), Claudio Aquaviva (1543), Francisco de Quevedo (1580), Thomas Baker (1656), (Friedrich Wilhelm Heinrich) Alexander (Freiherr) von Humboldt (1769), Marquis Gino Capponi (1792), John Gould (1804), Theodor Storm (1817), Ivan Pavlov (1849), (Hannibal) Hamlin Garland (1860), Metropolitan Benjamin (Fedchenkov) and Paul Fechter (1880), Martin Dibelius (1883), Ernest Nash (1898), Anton Zischka (1904), Peter Scott (1909), Mae Boren Axton and Robert McCloskey (1914), Abioseh Nicol (1924), Martin Caidin (1927), Al(bert) Shanker (1928), Larry Collins (1929), Anne Bernays (1930), Ivan Klima (1931), Hans Faverey, Sarah Kofman, Kate Millett (1934), Leo H. Ferrier (1940), Bernard MacLaverty (1942), Joan Thirkettle (1947), Geraldine Brooks (1955), Kazuhiro Kiuchi (1960), Shūichi Yoshida (1968), Jeremy Dunham (1976).

What you believe someone else can or can't do hasn't got beans with the doing. Or lack of doing. Just go back through your history books and you'll discover that just about everything you take for granted today in your daily lives was absolutely impossible not so many years ago.—Martin Caidin

It sounds shameful, but on my best days I write only about three or four hours.—Anne Bernays

My sister said, You're making it hard for all us housewives in Nebraska.—Kate Millett

Sept. 15—François de La Rochefoucauld (1613), Jean-Sylvain (1736), James Fenimore Cooper (1789), James Gates Percival (1795), Willem J. van Zeggelen (1811), Adeline Dutton Train Whitney (1824), Heinrich von Treitschke (1834), Emilia Pardo Bazan (1851), Charles E. Vicomte de Foucauld (1858), Nicolaus Adriani (1865), Petr Bezruc (Vladimir Vasek) (1867), Sharat Chandra Chattopadhyay (1876), Jean/Hans Arp (1886), Robert Benchley (1889), Claude McKay (Festus Claudius McKay) (1889), Agatha Christie (Agatha Mary Clarissa Miller) (1890), Paul Reps (1895), Philippe Hériat (Raymond Gérard Payelle) and John J. Slauerhoff (1898), Gerd Gaiser (1908), Richard Baerlein (1910), Adolfo Bioy Casares and Ernest van den Haag (1914), Ismail Yasin (1915), Julius "Nipsey" Russell (1918), Nelson Gidding (1919), Lucebert (Lubertus Jacobus Swaanswijk) (1924), Leland Hickman (1934), Jacques d'Ancona (1935), Marjorie (Stibbards) Harris and Robert Lucas Jr. (1937), Charles L. Mee (1938), Breyten Breytenbach (1939), Anne Moody (b. Essie Mae Moody) and Norman (Richard) Spinrad (1940), Quinnug Fawcett et al. (Chelsea Quinn Yarbro) (1942), Oliver Stone and Howard Waldrop (1946), Loren D. Estleman and Sky Lee (1952), Christopher Willard (1960), Jim Curtiss (1969).

The common faults of American language are an ambition of effect, a want of simplicity, and a turgid abuse of terms.—James Fenimore Cooper

I am more the inspirational type of speller. I work on hunches rather than mere facts, and the result is sometimes open to criticism by purists.—Robert Benchley

The best time to plan a book is while you're doing the dishes.— Agatha Christie

The writer comes up against the misconception that he's needed only for his manual ability to translate other people's experience into words. The non-writer's illusion is, "I am just as good, I have just as much to say, more to say, but I'm missing a few technical details." —Ernest van den Haag

Sept. 16—Traversari Ambrosius (1386), Abu al-Faiz ibn Mubarak Faizi (1547), Samuel Coster (1574), Engelbert Kaempfer (1651), Henry St. John, 1st Viscount Bolingbroke (1678), Johann N. Tetens (1736), Thomas Barnes (1785), Orestes Augustus Brownson (1803), Francis Parkman (1823), Robert Barr (1849), Alfred Noyes (1880), Clive Bell (1881), T. E. Hulme (1883), Karen Horney (1885), Frans Eemil Sillanpää (1888), Gwen Bristow (1893), Andre Cheron (1896), H. A. Rey (1898), Vladimír Holan (1905), (Hans J. M.) Fernand Lodewick (1909), Wilfred Burchett (1911), Félicien Marceau (1913), Laurence J. Peter (1919), Dusty Hughers (1921), John Knowles (1926), Robert (Harold) Schuller (1916), Samuel Menashe (b. Samuel Menashe Weisberg) (1925), Lady Gwen Thompson (Phyllis Thompson) (1928), Richard (Norman) Perle (1941), James Alan McPherson (1943), Pierre Nepveu (1946), Enrique Krauze (1947), Henry Louis Gates Jr. (1950), Nancy Huston (1953), Michael (Angel) Nava (1954), Kurt Busiek (1960), Walt Becker (1968), Justin Haythe (1973).

Only reason can convince us of those three fundamental truths without a recognition of which there can be no effective liberty: that what we believe is not necessarily true; that what we like is not necessarily good; and that all questions are open.—Clive Bell

Life itself still remains a very effective therapist.—Karen Horney

Censorship is to art as lynching is to justice.—Henry Louis Gates Jr.

Sept. 17—Gilbert Burnet (1643), Durastante Natalucci (1687), Gottlieb W. Rabener (1714), Johann August Apel (1771), Edward William Lane (1801), Émile Augier (1820), Edouard Pailleron (1834), Clemens Baeumker (1853), Hans Muller (1854), Frank D(awson) Adams (1859), Owen Seaman (1861), William Carlos Williams (1883), Bastiaan de Gaay Fortman (1884), Abel J. Herzberg (1893), Martha Ostenso (1900), John Creasey and William Wister Haines (1908), Ove J. Abildgaard and Mary (Florence Elinor) Stewart (1916), Vance Nye Bourjaily and Antonio Agostinho Neto (1922), Hiram King "Hank" Williams (1923), Robert B(rown) Parker (1932), Ken Kesey (1935), Chet Raymo and Mischa de Vreede (1936), Albertine Sarrazin (1937), Carl Dennis (1939), Cynthia Flood (1940), Rita Rudner (1955), Brian Andreas (1956), Sean B. Carroll (1960), Wendy Northcutt (1963), Sarah Selecky (1974).

. . . I myself never quite feel that I know what I am talking about—if I did, and when I do, the thing written seems nothing to me. However, what I . . . allow to survive I always feel is worth while and that nobody else has ever come as near as I have to the thing I have intimated if not expressed.—William Carlos Williams

Never buy an editor or publisher a lunch or a drink until he has bought an article, story or book from you. This rule is absolute and may be broken only at your peril.—John Creasey

The best way of forgetting how you think you feel is to concentrate on what you know you know.—Mary Stewart

I think the most important thing about learning comedy is to start from who you are. If you begin the process by imitating what you perceive to be a comedy rhythm, you will get laughs sooner, but you will not be unique.—Rita Rudner

Sept. 18—Claudio Achillini (1574), Samuel Johnson (1709), Jean Allamand (1713), Tomas de Iriarte (1750), Justinus A. C. Kerner (1786), Johann D. Passavant (1787), Hermann Kutter (1863), Clark Wissler (1870), Johannes Anker Larsen (1874), Milan Rakic (1876), Grey Owl (Archibald Belaney) (1888), William March (b. William Edward Campbell) (1893), John Mens (1897), Semjon I. Kirsanov (1906), Catharine (Drew) Gilpin Faust (1947), Marilyn Lorraine "Lynn" Abbey (1948), Anna Deavere Smith and Helene Weijel (1950), Alberto Álvaro Ríos (1952), Kristine "Kris" Radish (1953), Chris Hedges (1956), Rob Brettle and Daniel Kingsley "Dan" Povenmire (1963).

Authors and lovers always suffer some infatuation, from which only absence can set them free.—Samuel Johnson

If you would the truth oppose By quotations, you will find Plenty; but, when all is done, Though they're many, truth is one.—Tomas de Iriarte

The failure to dissect the cause of war leaves us open for the next installment.—Chris Hedges

Sept. 19—Leo VI Sophos (866), (David) Hartley Coleridge (1796), Louis Joseph Vance (1879), Sarah Delany (1889), Rachel (Lyman) Field and Cornelis Rijnsdorp (1894), Ignazio Buttitta (1899), Pieter John Bouman (1902), Karen Aabye and Bergen Evans (1904), Mika Waltari (1906), William Golding (1911), Hilda Morley (1916), Paulo Freire (1921), Damon (Francis) Knight (1922), James Lipton (1926), Jean-Claude Carrière (1931), Mike Royko (1932), Gilles Archambault (1933), J(ohn) Gordon Melton (1942), Murray Silverstein (1943), Nancy Pickard (1945), Thomas H. Cook, Tanith Lee, and Howard W. Robertson (1947), Lesley Richards (Laurie R. King) (1952), Ken Rosenthal (1962), Patrick Marber (1964), Soledad O'Brien (1966), Sarah Fox (1973), Jimmy Fallon (1974).

No man was ever yet a great poet, without at the same time being a profound philosopher.—Hartley Coleridge

Authors are magpies, echoing each other's words and seizing avidly on anything that glitters.—Bergen Evans

My yesterdays walk with me. They keep step, they are gray faces that peer over my shoulder.—William Golding

Forty years ago, we were on the tail of the Front Page era. There was a different point of view. Reporters and editors were more forgiving of public people. They didn't think they had to stick someone in jail to make a career.—Mike Royko

I just love writing. It's magical, it's somewhere else to go, it's somewhere much more dreadful, somewhere much more exciting. Somewhere I feel I belong, possibly more than in the so-called real world.—Tanith Lee

Sept. 20—Francisco Esteban Acuña de Figueroa and Job Durfee (1790), Sergei T. Aksakov (1791), Peter of Limburg Brouwer (1795), Ernesto Teodoro Moneta and Petroleum V. Nasby (David Ross Locke (1833), Lubor Niederle (1865), Upton (Beall) Sinclair (1878), John G. van Dillen (1883), Maxwell Perkins (1884), Fjodor I. Panfjorov (1896), Elliot Nugent and Leo Strauss (1899), Stevie Smith and Cesare Zavattini (1902), Alexander Mitscherlich (1908), Marianne Kunvari (1912), Geraldine Clinton Little (1923), Donald Hall (1928), Gary Jennings (1928), Anne Meara (1929), Keith J. Roberts (1935), Pia Lindstrom (1938), Jude Deveraux (b. Jude Gilliam) (1947), George R(aymond) R(ichard) Martin (1948), James P(aul) Blaylock (1950), Javier Marías (1951), Deborah Roberts (1960), Rachel Rose (1970), Michael Koryta (1982), David Allen (1985), Melvin "LaThomas" Brimm (1987).

It is difficult to get a man to understand something when his salary depends upon his not understanding it.—Upton Sinclair

All poetry has to do is to make a strong communication. All the poet has to do is listen. The poet is not an important fellow. There will also be another poet.—Stevie Smith

I would also suggest that any aspiring writer begin with short stories. These days, I meet far too many young writers who try to start off with a novel right off, or a trilogy, or even a nine-book series. That's like starting in at rock climbing by tackling Mt. Everest. Short stories help you learn your craft.—George R.R. Martin

Sept. 21—Francis Hopkinson (1737), Sophia Amelia Peabody Hawthorne (1809), Edmund Gosse (1849), Cyriel Buysse (1859), James E. Talmage (1962), Herbert George "H. G." Wells (1966), Henri Béraud (1885), Sergei Yesenin (1895), Tushar Kanti Ghosh (1898), Luc Haesaerts (1899), Helen Foster Snow (1907), Charles Martin "Chuck" Jones (1912), Ulrich Ernst Simon (1913), William (Edward) Brandon (1914), Françoise Giroud (1916), Aya Zikken (1919), Mario Bunge (1919), Fazlur Rahman Malik (1919), J. Troplong "Jay" Ward (1920), Collin Wilcox (1924), Bernard Williams (1929), Romulus (Zachariah) Linney (IV) (1930), Melvin Van Peebles (1932), Leonard Cohen (1934), Bill Kurtis (1940), Charles Carroll "Charlie" Finn (1941), Flannie Flagg (Patricia Neal) (1944), Donald William "Don" Felder, Stephen (Edwin) King, and Marsha Norman (1947), William James "Bill" Murray (1950), Marta Fran Kauffman (1956), Ethan (James) Coen (1957), Vanessa Grigoriadis (1973).

No passion in the world is equal to the passion to alter someone else's draft.—H. G. Wells

Strangely enough, the first character in Fried Green Tomatoes was the cafe, and the town. I think a place can be as much a character in a novel as the people.—Fannie Flagg

People want to know why I do this, why I write such gross stuff. I like to tell them I have the heart of a small boy—and I keep it in a jar on my desk.—Stephen King

Sept. 22—Claudius Galenus (130), Philipp Nikodemus Frischlin (1547), Barthold Heinrich Brockes (1680), Philip Dormer Stanhope, 4th Earl of Chesterfield (1694), Jean-Étienne Guettard (1715), John Home (1722), Quintin Craufurd (1743), Theodore Edward Hook (1788), Wilhelm Wattenbach (1819), Theodore Winthrop (1828), Ferenc Herczeg (1863), Louis Van Deyssel (1864), Eleanor Hallowell Abbott (1872), Asser B. Kleerekoper (1880), Erich von Stroheim (1885), Frank Sullivan (1892), Babette Deutsch (1895), F. R. Boschvogel (French L. J. Ramon) (1902), Phyllis Hartnoll (1906), Dannie Abse (1923), Rosamunde Pilcher (1924), Irving Feldman (1928), Fay Weldon (1931), Gail Dianne Bowen (Bartholomew) (1942), Robert Morace (1947), Anne Laurel Carter and Geoff Gilpin (1953), Tim Miller (1958), Diogo Mainardi (1962), Cusi Cram (1967), S. Bear Bergman (1974), Shane McCrae (1975).

When you get to the footnote at the bottom of the page, like as not all you find is *ibid*. *Ibid* is a great favorite of footnote-mad authors. It was a great favorite of Gibbon. How come fiction writers do not need footnotes?—Frank Sullivan

Poetry is important. No less than science, it seeks a hold upon reality, and the closeness of its approach is the test of its success. —Babette Deutsch

There is no magic in all the world like that magic when you sell your first bit of writing.—Rosamunde Pilcher

Novelists . . . fashioning nets to sustain and support the reader as he falls helplessly through the chaos of his own existence.—Fay Weldon

Sept. 23—Euripides (480 BCE), Daniel von Czepko (1605), Adrian "Aart" van Wijck (1641), Jeremy Collier (1650), William Wallace (1768), Karl T. Korner (1791), William H. McGuffey (1800), Grace Greenwood (Sara Jane Clarke Lippincott) (1823), William Archer (1856), Kirke La Shelle (1862), John Lomax (1870), Frantisek Kupka (1871), Gerhard Kittel (1888), Walter Lippmann (1889), Kornelis H. Miskotte (1894), Jaroslav Seifert (1901), Meyer Schapiro (1904), Charles Stewart Almon Ritchie (1906), Dominique Aury (1907), Elliot Roosevelt (1910), Ghulam Mustafa Khan (1912), Philip Owen Arnould Sherrard (1922), John Okada (1923), Denis Twitchett (1925), Sehba Akhtar (1930), Ruud van den Hende (1931), Per Olov Enquist (1934), Jacques Poulin (1937), Mary Kay Place (1947), Jerry B(ruce) Jenkins (1949), George C(ostello) Wolfe (1954), Peter David (1956), Scott Shaw (1958), Amelia Ellis (1977), Nathan Jendrick (1984).

Question everything. Learn something. Answer nothing.—Euripides

A man may as well expect to grow stronger by always eating as wiser by always reading.—Jeremy Collier

The difference between a live play and a dead one is that in the former the characters control the plot, while in the latter the plot controls the characters.—**William Archer**

When all men think alike, no one thinks very much.—Walter Lippmann

Sept. 24—Horace Walpole (1717), William Lisle Bowles (1762), Richard Henry Wilde (1789), William Evans Burton (1804), Ramón de Campoamor y Campoosorio (1817), Cyprian K. Norwid (1821), Pieter Louis Tak (1848), George Frederick Cameron (1854), Samuel Rutherford Crockett (1860), C. F. Ramuz (1878), Herman Bouber (1885), Alan Herbert (1890), F(rancis) Scott Fitzgerald (1896), Gerald Warner Brace and John Faulkner (John Wesley Thompson Falkner III) (1901), Cao Yu (1910), Ian Serraillier and Robert Lewis Taylor (1912), Woodrow (Wilson) Rawls (1913), Margarita J. Aliger (1915), Richard Hoggart (1918), Harold (Edwin) Standish (1919), Ladislav Fuks (1923), Józef Krupiński (1930), Brian Glanville and Anthony Newley (1931), John Brunner (Kilian Houston) (1934), Robert Kelly (1935), Yves Navarre (1940), Rhys Bowen (Janet Quin-Harkin) (1941), Lou Dobbs and David A(llen) Drake (1945), Stephen Jones (1954), John Logan (1961), Michael J. Varhola (1966), Cheril N. Clarke (1980), Szilvia Molnar (1984), Eleanor Catton (1985).

Plot, rules, nor even poetry, are not half so great beauties in tragedy or comedy as a just imitation of nature, of character, of the passions and their operations in diversified situations.—Horace Walpole

Writers aren't people exactly. Or, if they're any good, they're a whole lot of people trying so hard to be one person.—F. Scott Fitzgerald

The saddest thing about myself is that I never read a book. I never got the habit.—Anthony Newley

Sept. 25—Mark Zuesius Boxhorn (1612), Mercy Otis Warren (1728), William Lisle Bowles (1762), Charles Robert Maturin (1782), Felicia Dorothea Hemans (Felicia Dorothea Browne) (1793), (Wilhel) Mina J. P. R. Kruseman (1839), Archibald Henry Sayce (1845), Hans Vaihinger (1852), Lope K. Santos (1879), Lu Xun (1881), John Howard Lawson (1886), George Douglas Howard Cole and C. K. Scott-Moncrieff (1889), Gregory "Greg" Clark (1892), Elsa Triolet (1896), William Faulkner (b. William Cuthbert Falkner) (1897), Ernst von Salomon (1902), Nahman Avigad and Walter Wellesley "Red" Smith (1905), Madeleine Bourdouxhe and Phyllis Pearsall (1906), Mary (Oliver) C(labaugh) Wright (1917), Akimitsu Takagi (1920), Remy C. de Kerckhove (1921), Ronald William George "Ronnie" Barker (1929), Barbara Walters (1929), Sheldon Allan "Shel" Silverstein (1930), Manouchehr Atashi (1931), Timothy Severin (1940), Aram Saroyan (1943), John Weidman (1946), Jim Murphy (1947), Eric (Ellis) Overmyer (1951), Cherríe Lawrence Moraga (1952), Ron Rash (1953), Kai Starr (Kaichi Satake) (1964), Mickey Zetts (1971), Emily K(athryn) Michael (1987).

You believe in freedom of speech for communists because what they say is true. You do not believe in freedom of speech for fascists because what they say is a lie.—John Howard Lawson

Everything goes by the board: honor, pride, decency . . . to get the book written. If a writer has to rob his mother, he will not hesitate; the *Ode on a Grecian Urn* is worth any number of old ladies.—William Faulkner

The world may be full of fourth-rate writers but it's also full of fourth-rate readers.—Barbara Walters

Short fiction is the medium I love the most, because it requires that I bring everything I've learned about poetry—the concision, the ability to say something as vividly as possible—but also the ability to create a narrative that, though lacking a novel's length, satisfies the reader.—Ron Rash

Sept. 26—Francis of Assisi (Giovanni Francesco di Bernardone) (1181), Moses Mendelssohn (1729), Isvar Chandra Vidyasagar (1820), Ivan S. Aksakov (1823), Irving Addison Bacheller (1859), Max Ehrmann (1872), Petko J. Todorov (1879), Anna M. F. "Annie" Wageningen-Salomons (1885), Edwin Keppel Bennett (1887), J(ames) Frank Dobie and Thomas Stearns "T. S." Eliot (1888), Martin Heidegger (1889), Milos Crnjanski (1893), Victor O. Stomps (1897), Gerhard Nebel (1903), Anthony F. Blunt (1907), Ernst Schnabel (1913), Matilde Camus (1919), Buland Al Haidary and Clair Huffaker (1926), Marie Therese Veronica "Terry" Goulet and Raphael Samuel (1934), Gloria E(vangelina) Anzaldúa (1942), Andrea Dworkin (1946), Patrick J. Geary (1948), Jane Smiley and Minette Walters (1949), Tom Quirke (1951), Cecil Foster and Anne (Barrett) Rouse (1954), Will Self (1961), Scott Heim (1966), Anthony Shadid (1968), Orville Lloyd Douglas (1976).

Preach the Gospel at all times and when necessary use words. —Francis of Assisi

Writing everyday is a way of keeping the engine running, and then something good may come out of it.—T. S. Eliot

Sometimes, a novel is like a train: the first chapter is a comfortable seat in an attractive carriage, and the narrative speeds up. But there are other sorts of trains, and other sorts of novels. They rush by in the dark; passengers framed in the lighted windows are smiling and enjoying themselves.—Jane Smiley

Sept. 27—(Johann Nepomuk Cosmas) Michael Denis (1729), Lucretia Maria Davidson (1808), Henri Frédéric Amiel (1821), Robert Wilson Ewing I (1859), Porsteinn Erlingsson (1858), Alexander Cohen (1864), Tryggve Andersen (1866), Grazia Deledda (1871), Cyril M. Scott (1879), Cid Ricketts Sumner (1890), Joannes D. M. Cornelissen (1893), Vjekoslav Kaleb (1905), William Empson (1906), James Myers "Jim" Thompson (1906), Francis Ambrière (1907), Giles William Playfair (1910), Catherine (Sarah Wood) Marshall (LeSourd) (1914), Louis (Stanton) Auchincloss (1917), Coral Eswyn (Ellinor) Lyster, (1923), Josef Škvorecký and Bernard Waber (1924), Roberta (Leah Jacobs) Gellis (1927), Oliver E. Williamson (1932), George R(ichard) D(onald) Goulet (1933), Barbara Howar (1934), Dick Schaap (1934), Gordon Honeycombe (1936), Carol Lynn Pearson (1939), Kay Ryan (1945), Jim Shooter (1951), Katie Fforde (1952), Barron Lerner (1960), Irvine Welsh (1961).

I came up with new leads for game stories by being observant and clever, by using the many gifts of the English language to intrigue and hook a reader.—Dick Schaap

There's an old Jewish saying: An enemy is someone whose story you do not know.—Carol Lynn Pearson

It seems like many people think that if you drive yourself crazy, then you can write. I'm absolutely not interested in that. It made sense to me to be as whole and well as I could be, and as happy. I wanted to see what a fortunate life would produce. What writing would come out of a mind that didn't try to torment itself? What did I have to know? What did I have to do rather than what can I torment and bend myself into doing? What was the fruit on that tree?—Kay Ryan

Sept. 28—Confucius (551 BCE), Alessandro Tassoni (1565), Vredius (Olivier de Wree) (1596), William Jones (1746), Prosper Mérimée (1803), Arnold Henry Guyot (1807), Freidrich Engels (1820), Francis Turner Palgrave (1824), Friedrich A(lbert) Lange (1828), Rudolf Baumbach (1840), Georges Clemenceau (1841), Henry Arthur Jones (1851), Thomas F. Tout (1855), Edward Herbert Thompson and Kate Douglas Wiggin (1856), Barry E. Odell Pain (1864), James Edwin Campbell (1867), Waclaw Rawicz (Berent) (1873), Stanner E. V. Taylor (1877), Eugenio d' Ors y Rovira (1882), H. C. McNeile/Sapper (Herman Cyril McNeile) (1888), Elmer Rice (1892), Charles Petrie (1895), Muchtar Auesow (1897), Ellis Peters et al. (Edith Mary Ellis Peters Pargeter) (1913), Harold Taylor (1914), Howard Gerald "Jerry" Clower (1926), Thomas J.J. Altizer (1927), Michael G(reatrex) Coney (1932), Rosario Ferré (1938), George Greenstein (1940), Marcia Muller and Simon Winchester (1944), Gillian Rose (1947), Carolyn Forché and John (Thomas) Sayles (1950), Wei Chen (1951), Christopher (Taylor) Buckley (1952), Joel Rane (1965), Ben Greenman (1969).

You cannot open a book without learning something. —Confucius

It does make a difference what you call things.—Kate Douglas Wiggin

To be perfectly honest the old habits, specifically deadlines, still very much inform what I do. I am brutally disciplined about getting manuscripts in on time.—Simon Winchester

Sept. 29— Miguel de Cervantes Saavedra (varied birthdates) (1547), Elizabeth Cleghorn Gaskell (1810), Herbert Agar (1897), Lanza del Vasto (Giuseppe Giovanni Luigi Enrico Lanza di Trabia) (1901), Reginald Victor Jones (1911), Elizabeth Peters/ Barbara Michaels (Barbara Mertz) (1927), Ankie (Johanna A. Hoving) Peypers (1928), Colin Dexter (1930), Robert Benton (1932), Stuart M. Kaminsky (1934), Ingrid Noll (Ingrid Gullatz) (1935), Molly Haskell (1939), d.a. levy (Darryl Alfred Levey) and Stojan "Steve" Tesich (1942), Richard J(ohn) Evans (1947), Andrés Caicedo (1951), Peter Murray Hautman (1952), Michael (Coleman) Talbot (1953), Mariela Griffor (1961).

From reading too much, and sleeping too little, his brain dried up on him and he lost his judgment.—Miguel de Cervantes

I'll not listen to reason . . . reason always means what someone else has got to say.—Elizabeth Gaskell

I think that you've got to be prepared to write a load of nonsense to start with and then you can tart it up. The business of getting going, getting started, is enormously important, and this can be physical. *Solvitur Ambulando* as the Romans used to say, which means the solution comes through walking.—Colin Dexter

But one of the attributes of love, like art, is to bring harmony and order out of chaos, to introduce meaning and affect where before there was none, to give rhythmic variations, highs and lows to a landscape that was previously flat.—Molly Haskell

Sept. 30—Jalal al-Din Muhammad Rumi (1207), Geronimo Mercuriali (Geronimo Mercuriali) (1530), Stanisław Konarski (1700), Étienne Bonnot de Condillac (1715), Ferdinand von Saar (1833), Gipsy, Gitano, and E. Prezcier (Wilhelmina Elizabeth Lensing Drucker (1847), Hermann Sudermann (1857), Margaret Widdemer (1884), William Matthew Scott (1893), Edgar Parin d'Aulaire (1898), Hendrik Marsman (1899), Michael Powell (1905), Michael Innes (John Innes Mackintosh Stewart) (1906), Joseph A. Kramm (1907), Oliver Charles Anderson (1912), Eileen Zhang Ailing Chang (1921), Truman Capote (1924), Gwyn A. Williams (1925), William Stanley "W. S." Merwin (1927), Eliezer "Elie" Wiesel (1928), Shintaro Ishihara (1932), Jonathan Gash (John Grant) (1933), Robert (Allan) Caro (1935), Jurek Becker (1937), Donald George "Don" Gutteridge (1937), bpnichol (Barrie Phillip Nichol) (1944), Larry Patrick Levis (1946), Stephen Michael "S. M." Stirling (1953), Elizabeth Sims (1957), Ari Behn (1972), Ta-Nehisi Coates (1975), Téa Obreht (Tea Bajraktarević) (1985).

I believe more in the scissors than I do in the pencil.—Truman Capote

Poetry is like making a joke. If you get one word wrong at the end of a joke, you've lost the whole thing.—W. S. Merwin

The Theory of Sexual Understanding is mine. I created it. It works between a man and a woman. It's this: Everything's up to her.— Jonathan Gash (as Lovejoy)

The craft of writing as the art of thinking. Poetry aims for an economy of truth - loose and useless words must be discarded, and I found that these loose and useless words were not separate from loose and useless thoughts.—Ta-Nehisi Coates

Born in October

Oct. 1—William Beckford (1760), Vincenzo Cuoco (1770), Sergey Aksakov (1791), Daniel Pierce Thompson (1795), Rufus Choate (1799), Lars Levi Laestadius (1800), Edward Coote Pinkney (1802), Charles Cros (1842), Annie Besant (Wood) (1847), Israel Querido (1872), Louis Untermeyer (1885), Ahmad Amin (1886), Blanche (Marie Louise) Oelrichs (1890), Faith Baldwin and Wesley Wilson (1893), Ernest (James) Haycox (1899), John Lorne Campbell (1906), Fletcher Knebel (1911), Daniel J(oseph) Boorstin (1914), René A. de Rooy (1917), David Herbert Donald (1920), James Earl "Jimmy" Carter (1924), William H. Rehnquist (1924), Tim O'Brien (1946), Isaac Bonewits (1949), John Hegley (1953), Jonathan Sarfati (1964), Chris Reason (1965), Jon Guenther (1968), Rodney Kite-Powell (1973).

Write out of love, write out of instinct, write out of reason. But always for money.—Louis Untermeyer

Time is a dressmaker specializing in alterations.—Faith Baldwin

Best-Sellerism is the star system of the book world. A "best-seller" is a celebrity among books. It is known primarily (sometimes exclusively) for its well-knownness.—Daniel J. Boorstin

Fiction is a lie that is told in the service of truth.—Tim O'Brien

Oct. 2—Andreas Gryphius (1616), François-Timoléon de Choisy (1644), Edward Burnett Tylor (1832), Julius von Sachs (1832), Louis A. Ranvier (1835), Mohandas Karamchand Gandhi (1869), Wallace Stevens (1879), Julius Henry "Groucho" Marx (1890), Louis Lebeer (1895), Fjodor I. Panfjorov (1896), (Ignatius) Roy(ston Dunnachie) Campbell (1901), (Henry) Graham Greene (1904), Jack Finney (1911), Jack Parsons and Bernarr Rainbow (1914), Edmund Crispin (Robert Bruce Montgomery/Bruce Montgomery) (1921), Jan Morris (1926), Clay Felker (1928), Ronald C. "Ron" Offen (1930), Rex Reed and Lloyd Turner (1938), John Sinclair (1941), Franklin Rosemont (1943), Vernor (Steffen) Vinge (1944), Gene Weingarten (1951), Tara Moss (1973).

Outside of a dog, a book is a man's best friend. Inside of a dog it's too dark to read.—Groucho Marx
Translations, like wives, are seldom faithful if they are in the least attractive.—Roy Campbell
Writing is a form of therapy; sometimes I wonder how all those who do not write, compose or paint can manage to escape the madness, the melancholia, the panic fear which is inherent in the human situation.—Graham Greene

Oct. 3—Fulke Greville Brooke (1554), Johann P. Uz (1720), George Bancroft (1800), Mikhail Yurevich Lermontov (1814), Stijn Streuvels (Frank Lateur) (1871), Sophie Treadwell (1885), Alain-Fournier (Henri Alban Fournier) (1886), Carl von Ossietzky (1888), Cv Ossietzky (1889), Gerardo Diego (1896), Louis Aragon (1897), Leo McCarey (1898), Thomas (Clayton) Wolfe (1900), David (Alexander Reginald) Herbert (1908), Angeles Alvarino Deleira and James Herriot (James Alfred Wight) (1916), John Boyd (Boyd Bradfield Upchurch) (1919), Harvey Kurtzman (1924), Eugene Louis "Gore" Vidal (1925), Judith Johnson Sherwin (1936), Jack Hodgins (1938), Barrett Watten (1948), Bernard Cooper (1951), Rob Liefeld (1967), Sara Zarr (1970).

The reason a writer writes a book is to forget a book and the reason a reader reads one is to remember it.—Thomas Wolfe

I love writing about my job because I loved it, and it was a particularly interesting one when I was a young man. It was like holidays with pay to me.—James Herriot

For every Scott Fitzgerald concerned with the precise word and the selection of relevant incident, there are a hundred American writers, many well-regarded, who appear to believe that one word is just as good as another and that everything which occurs to them is worth putting down.—Gore Vidal

Oct. 4—Robert Bellarmine (Roberto Francesco Romolo Bellarmino) (1542), Francisco de Rojas Zorrilla (1607), Francois P.G. Guizot (1787), John Richardson (1796), Jeremias Gotthelf (Albert Bitzius) (1797), Juliette Adam-Lamber (1836), Mary Elizabeth Braddon (1837), Frederic Remington (1861), Edward Stratemeyer (1862), Max Halbe (1865), Hugh McCrae (1876), Damon Runyon (1880), Francis Bull (1887), Robert Lawson (1892), Joseph F. "Buster" Keaton (1895), Sergei Jessenin (1895), Bona Arsenault (1903), James B. Pritchard (1909), Brendan Gill (1914), Koos Schuur (1915), Julia (Woolfook) Cunningham (1916), Charlton Heston (1923), Donald J. Sobol (1924), Alvin Toffler and Torben Ulrich (1928), Rudy (Henry) Wiebe (1934), Sally Mary Caroline Belfrage (1936), Jackie Collins (1937), Roy Blount Jr. and Anne Rice (1941), Lee (Knowlton) Blessing (1949), Bakhytzhan Kanapyanov and Gregory White Smith (1951), Pierre Yergeau (1957), Kazuki Takahashi (1961), Shannon (Dawn Marie) Bramer (1973).

Self-assertion may deceive the ignorant for a time; but when the noise dies away, we cut open the drum, and find it was emptiness that made the music. — Mary Elizabeth Braddon

I loved words. I love to sing them and speak them and even now, I must admit, I have fallen into the joy of writing them.—Anne Rice

English is an outrageous tangle of those derivations and other multifarious linguistic influences, from Yiddish to Shoshone, which has grown up around a gnarly core of chewy, clangorous yawps derived from ancestors who painted themselves blue to frighten their enemies.—Roy Blount Jr.

Oct. 5—Paul Fleming (1609), John Glas (1695), Jonathan Edwards (1703), Denis Diderot (1713), Victor de Riqueti, marquis de Mirabeau (1715), Bernhard (Placidus Johann Nepomuk) Bolzano (1781), John Addington Symonds (1840), Guido von List (1848), Ludwig Borchardt (1863), John Erskine (1879), Teresa de la Parra (1889), Kasimir Edschmid (Karl E. Schmidt) (1890), Remington Kellogg (1892), Walter Bedell "Beetle" Smith (1895), Leopold Kohr (1906), Flann O'Brien (Brian Ó Nualláin) (1911), Stetson Kennedy (1916), Robert Feenstra (1920), Stig H. Dagerman (1923), Bill Dana (William Szathmary) and Jose Donoso (1924), Landis Everson (1926), Louise Fitzhugh (1928), Vaclav Havel (1936), Marie-Claire Blais (1939), Adam Hochschild and Nick Piombino (1942), Robert P(eebles) Arthur (1943), Zahida Hina (1946), Mei-mei Berssenbrugge (1947), Zoran Živković (1948), Peter Ackroyd and Bill James (1949), Edward P(aul) Jones (1950), Clive Barker (1952), Matthew Kauffman (1961), Steven Laffoley (1965).

It is great to get praise from the lips of taciturnity.—John Addington Symonds

Oral history represents a democratization of the history-telling process . . . this thing of having history recorded from on high for us, instead of doing it for ourselves, has proven to be a risky business. We need to have history from the bottom up.—Stetson Kennedy

It may seem unfashionable to say so, but historians should seize the imagination as well as the intellect. History is, in a sense, a story, a narrative of adventure and of vision, of character and of incident. It is also a portrait of the great general drama of the human spirit. —Peter Ackroyd

Oct. 6—J. W. Richard Dedekind (1831), Giuseppe Cesare Abba (1838), Albert Jeremiah Beveridge (1862), Bo Hjalmar Bergman (1869), Mikhail Kuzmin (1872), Martín Luis Guzmán Franco (1887), Maria Dabrowska (1889), Caroline (Ferguson) Gordon (1895), Horst Lange (1904), Anthony Cuthbert Baines (1912), Meret Oppenheim (1913), Thor Heyerdahl (1914), Stanley (Bernard) Ellin (1916), Shana Alexander (1925), Fred Graham (1931), Gloria Lane (1932), Louis Begley and Horst Bingle (1933), Dennis (Graham) Holt (1942), Gerry Adams (1948), (Glen) David Brin (1950), Ayten Mutlu (1952), Peter (Gregory) McGehee (1955), Kathleen Webb (1956), Joseph Finder (1958).

A well-composed book is a magic carpet on which we are wafted to a world that we cannot enter in any other way.—Caroline Gordon

There's no doubt that scientific training helps many authors to write better science fiction. And yet, several of the very best were English majors who could not parse a differential equation to save their lives.—David Brin

I would argue that coffee has been far more important to literature than alcohol.— Joseph Finder

Oct. 7—John Marston (1576), Herbert "Herbie" Coleridge (1830), Bronson Howard (1842), James Whitcomb Riley (1849), Niels Bohr (1885), Henry A. Wallace (1888), Meyer Levin (1905), Helen Clark MacInnes (1907), Anni Blomqvist (1909), Simon Carmiggelt (1913), Margarita J. Aliger, Harry J(oseph) Boyle, and Charles (Bradley) Templeton (1915), Walt W. Rostow (1916), George Duby (1919), John Arthur Giles Gere (1921), Ronald David "R. D." Laing (1927), Sohrab Sepehri (1928), Robert Westall (1929), Imamu Amiri Baraka (Everett Leroi Jones) (1934), Thomas M. Keneally (1935), Joanna (McClelland) Glass (1936), Clive James and Wentworth M. Johnson (1939), Oliver L. North (1943), Diane Ackerman (1948), David Adams Richards (1950), Natsuo Kirino (1951), Martyn Harris (1952), Jo (Linda Susenbach) Kittinger (1955), Steven Erikson (Steve Rune Lundin) (1959), Kevin Gerard Boyle (1960), Dan Savage (1964), Sherman (Joseph) Alexie (Jr.) (1966).

When you awaken some morning and hear that somebody or other has been discovered, you can put it down as a fact that he discovered himself years ago—since that time he has been toiling, working, and striving to make himself worthy of general discovery. —James Whitcomb Riley

The range of what we think and do is limited by what we fail to notice. And because we fail to notice that we fail to notice, there is little we can do to change; until we notice how failing to notice shapes our thoughts and deeds.—R. D. Laing

The artist's role is to raise the consciousness of the people. To make them understand life, the world and themselves more completely. That's how I see it. Otherwise, I don't know why you do it.—Amiri Baraka

Oct. 8—Philipp von Zesen (1619), Benito Jerónimo Feijóo y Montenegro (1676), José de Cadalso y Vázquez (1741), William John Swainson (1789), Philarete Chasles (1798), Francisque Sarcey (1828), Edgar (Evertson) Saltus (1855), John Cowper Powys (1872), Edmund Clarence Stedman (1833), Jeanne G. van Schaik-Willing (1895), Rouben Mamoulian (1897), Walter Lord (1917), Frank (Patrick) Herbert (1920), Andrei Donatovich Sinyavsky (1925), Patrick Davis Smith (1927), Yulian Semyonovich Semyonov (Yulian Semyonovich Lyandres) (1931), Rona Barrett (1936), David Willis (1938), Harvey Pekar (1939), Bronte Woodard (1940), Cornelius Crane "Chevy" Chase and Robert Lawrence "R. L." Stine (1943), Benjamin Cheever (1948), Shenaaz Nanji (1954), Steve Coll, Neile Graham, and Bret Lott (1958), Edward Ball (1959), François Pérusse (1960), Laura Pedersen (1965), Matt Damon (1970).

To read great books does not mean one becomes 'bookish'; it means that something of the terrible insight of Dostoyevsky, of the richly-charged imagination of Shakespeare, of the luminous wisdom of Goethe, actually passes into the personality of the reader; so that in contact with the chaos of ordinary life certain free and flowing outlines emerge, like the forms of some classic picture, endowing both people and things with a grandeur beyond what is visible to the superficial glance.— John Cowper Powys

I never earned a dollar that was not somehow through writing. —Walter Lord

Read. Read. Read. Just don't read one type of book. Read different books by various authors so that you develop different styles.—R. L. Stine

Oct. 9—Jan III van Foreest (1586), Richard Blackmore (1654), Gian M. Crescimbeni (1663), Elizabeth Chase (Akers) Allen (1832), Stephanus J. du Toit (1847), Edward William Bok (1863), Ivo Andrić and Marina Tsvetaeva (1892), Mário Raul de Morais Andrade (1893), Bruce Catton (1899), Quintin McGarel Hogg (1907), Harry Hooton (1908), E. Howard Hunt Jr. (1918), Jens Bjørneboe (1920), William Edward "Bill" Tidy (1933), Jill Ker Conway (1934), Brian Blessed (1937), James H(owe) McClure and Pierre Mertens (1939), John (Winston) Lennon (1940), Jean-Jacques Schuhl (1941), Pierre Turgeon and Anthony Nicholas "Tony" Zappone (1947), Murdoch (Maclean) Burnett (1953), Guillermo del Toro Gómez (1964), William Joseph Alexander (1976).

A young person, to achieve, must first get out of his mind any notion either of the ease or rapidity of success. Nothing ever just happens in this world.—Edward William Bok

An adult life . . . is a slowly emerging design, with shifting components, occasional dramatic disruptions, and fresh creative arrangements.—Jill Ker Conway

I put things down on sheets of paper and stuff them in my pockets. When I have enough, I have a book.—John Lennon

Oct. 10—Aleksis Kivi (Stenvall) (1834), Fridtjof (Wedel-Jarlsberg) Nansen (1861), Louise Mack (1870), Arthur Talmage Abernethy (1872), George Cabot "Bay" Lodge (1873), Ferdinand Bordewijk (1884), Walter (Arthur Alexander) Anderson (1885), Rie Cramer (Marie Holman) (1887), Ivo Andric (1892), R. K. Narayan (Rasipuram Krishnaswami Iyer Narayanaswami) (1906), Edward (Alexander) McCourt (1907), Mercè Rodoreda (1908), Luc van Brabant (1909), Charles Henry Madge (1912), Claude Simon (1913), Jean Gimpel (1918), Boeli (Willem C.) van Leeuwen (1922), Kildare (Robert Eric) Dobbs (1923), James Clavell (1924), Harold Pinter and Mustafa Zaidi (1930), Gerald Masters (1933), Lily Tuck (1938), Kenule Beeson Saro-Wiwa (1941), James Edward Marshall and Roy Akira Miki (1942), Frederick Barthelme (1943), Linda Rogers and Renier S. Schoeman (1944), Scott Spencer (1945), Nora Roberts et al. (Eleanor Marie Robertson) (1950), Daniel Pearl (1963), Amanda Filipacchi and Jonathan Littell (1967), Margaret Robertson Ferguson and Geoffrey Sauer (1968), Jun Lana (1972), Noah Cicero (1980).

Our lives improve only when we take chances - and the first and most difficult risk we can take is to be honest with ourselves.—Walter Anderson

All stories have a beginning, a middle and an ending, and if they're any good, the ending is a new beginning.—James Clavell

The past is what you remember, imagine you remember, convince yourself you remember, or pretend you remember.—Harold Pinter

If I could think, maybe I wouldn't write.—Scott Spencer

Oct. 11—Andreas Gryphius (1616), Samuel Clarke (1675), Adriaan van den Ende (1768), Steen Steensen Blicher (1782), Albartus Telting (1803), C. F. Meyer (1825), Hans E. Kinck (1865), Stefan O. Iosif (1875), Gertrud von Le Fort (1876), Stark Young (1881), Hans Kelsen and Stark Young (1881), Will Vesper (1882), (Anna) Eleanor Roosevelt (1884), François Mauriac (1885), Roman (Osipovich) Jakobson (1896), Joseph Auslander (1897), Joseph (Wright) Alsop (V) (1910), Frances Thames (1917), Charles Frederick "Fred" Bodsworth (1918), Elmore (John) Leonard (Jr.) (1925), Cynthia Propper Seton (1926), Daniel Quinn (1935), Richard Henry Wilde "R. H. W." Dillard and Margaret Coel (1937), David (William) McFadden (1940), William Corbett (1942), John (Vivian Drummond) Nettles (1943), Thomas Boswell (1947), Douglas Wilson (1950), Anne (Teresa) Enright and Richard Paul Evans (1962), Claudia Palacios (1977).

You must do the things you think you cannot do.—Eleanor Roosevelt

I write whenever it suits me. During a creative period I write every day; a novel should not be interrupted. When I cease to be carried along, when I no longer feel as though I were taking down dictation, I stop.—François Mauriac

I try to leave out the parts that people skip.—Elmore Leonard

I'm always impressed with the way the writers find new and creative ways of killing people. But my favourite has to be the hat pin through the ear.—John Nettles

Oct. 12—Walter T. Watts-Dunton (1832), George Washington Cable and Charles King (1844), Jacobus of Looy and August Sauer (1855), (Edward Alexander) Aleister Crowley (1875), Louis Hémon (1880), Paula von Preradović (1887), Eugenio Montale (1896), Dirk A. M. Binnendijk (1902), Lester Dent and Ding Ling (1904), Paul Engle and Ann (Lane) Petry (1908), Zellig S. Harris and Dorothy (Kathleen May) Livesay (1909), Robert (Stuart) Fitzgerald (1910), Alice Childress (1916), Borden Deal (1922), Charles Gordone (1925), Ralph Pomeroy (1926), Thomas Burnett Swann (1928), Robert Coles (1929), Dick Gregory (1932), Joan Clark (MacDonald) (1934), James (Arthur) Crumley (1939), Lewis MacAdams (1944), Patricia Roth Schwartz (1946), Chris Wallace (1947), Soji Shimada (1948), Richard Price (1949), William Stener "Will" Ferguson (1964), Brian Kennedy (1966).

Happiness is to take up the struggle in the midst of the raging storm and not to pluck the lute in the moonlight or recite poetry among the blossoms.—Ding Ling

In *Country Place*, I tried to *underwrite* . . . . I tried to get into the style something of the surface quiet of a small country town—a slowness of tempo . . . absorbed almost unconsciously.—Ann Lane Petry

I don't need all that much—I just need to know who my characters are and what kind of jam they're going to get into, and I'll write myself out of their jam.—Richard Price

Oct. 13—John Hervey (1696), Ecco Epkema (1759), William Motherwell (1797), Thomas Haynes Bayly (1797), Jules Quicherat (1815), William Kirby (1817), Mary Henrietta Kingsley (1862), Sasha Cherny (1880), George Bacovia (Vasiliu) (1881), Conrad (Michael) Richter (1890), Arnaud Wendell "Arna" Bontemps (1902), Jutta Hecker (1904), Werner Reinowski (1908), Herblock (Herbert L. Block) (1909), Ernest K(ellogg) Gann (1910), Robert Walker (1918), Lenny Bruce (Leonard Alfred Schneider) and Frank D. Gilroy (1925), John Herbert (John Herbert Brundage) (1926), Richard Joseph Howard (Richard Joseph Orwitz) (1929), Janice Elliott (1931), Jean Edward Smith (1932), Hugo Young (1938), Richard Joseph Howard (1929), Paul Simon (1942), Mike Barnicle (1943), John Patrick Shanley (1950), Claude Ribbe (1954), Christopher Carl "Chris" Carter (1957), Colin Channer (1963), Serena Altschul (1970).

A certain sort of friendship soon arose between the Fans and me. We each recognized that we belonged to that same section of the human race with whom it is better to drink than to fight.—Mary Henrietta Kingsley

If it's good, they'll stop making it.— Herblock

A person who's going to be famous usually drops a few clues by the time they're twenty-one.— Frank D. Gilroy

Satire is tragedy plus time. You give it enough time, the public, the reviewers will allow you to satirize it. Which is rather ridiculous, when you think about it.—Lenny Bruce

Oct. 14—Maurice de Plessys (1864), Masaoka Shiki (1867), Margarete Susman (1874), (Stella Maria Sarah) Miles Franklin (1879), Otto V. Ekelund (1880), Katherine Mansfield (1888), Paul de Keyser (1891), e. e. cummings (1894), William Edwards Deming (1900), Willem A Wagenaar (1901), Hannah Arendt (1906), Barend Barendse (1907), Ruth Hale (1908), Dorothy Kingsley (1909), C. Everett Koop (1916), John Dean III (1938), James Richard Hougan (1942), Katha Pollitt (1949), Carole Malone and Beth Taylor (1954), Stephen A. Smith (1967).

Looking back, I imagine I was always writing. Twaddle it was too. But better far write twaddle or anything, anything, than nothing at all.—**Katherine Mansfield**

If a poet is anybody, he is somebody to whom things made matter very little—somebody who is obsessed by Making. —**e. e. cummings**

Storytelling reveals meaning without committing the error of defining it.—**Hannah Arendt**

Oct. 15—Publius Vergilius "Virgil" Maro (70 BCE), Robert Herrick (1674), Allan Ramsay (1686), Clément Juglar (1819), Alfred Meissner (1822), Helen (Maria) Hunt Jackson (b. Helen Maria Fiske) (1830), Isabella Lucy Bell Bishop (1831), Friedrich Nietzsche (1844), George Foot Moore (1851), Jaime de Magalhes Lima (1859), Kido Okamoto (Keiji Okamoto) (1872), Arthur B(enjamin) Reeve (1880), Pelham Grenville "P. G." Wodehouse (1881), S. S. Van Dine (Willard Huntington Wright) (1888), Alfred Neumann (1895), Bernard von Brentano and Enrique Jardiel Poncela (1901), James (Howell) Street (1903), Charles Percy "C. P." Snow (1905), Varian Fry (1907), John Kenneth Galbraith (1908), Robert Trout (1909), Arthur Schlesinger Jr. (1917), Robert Edwin Lee (1918), Edwin C(harles) Tubb (1919), Mario (Gianluigi) Puzo (1920), Agustina Bessa-Luís (1922), Italo Calvino and Eugene Corbett "Gene" Patterson (1923), Marguerite Andersen and Alexander Kent (Douglas Edward Reeman) (1924), Paul-Michel Foucault and Evan Hunter/Ed McBain (Salvatore Albert Lombino) (1926), Mary Perot Nichols (1927), Fereydun M. Esfandiary (1930), Paul (Roose-Evans) Foster (1931), Riekus Waskowsky (1932), Fanny Howe (1940), Gloria Escomel (1941), John Murrell (1945), Kim (Robert) Stafford (1949), Sarah Margaret "Fergie. Duchess of York" Ferguson and Emeril Lagasse (1959), Glen Downey (1969).

Dancing in all its forms cannot be excluded from the curriculum of all noble education; dancing with the feet, with ideas, with words, and, need I add that one must also be able to dance with the pen? —Friedrich Nietzsche

When something can be read without effort, great effort has gone into its writing.—Enrique Jardiel Poncela

There are days when the result is so bad that no fewer than five revisions are required. In contrast, when I'm greatly inspired, only four revisions are needed.—John Kenneth Galbraith

Oct. 16—Charles C. Dassoucy (1605), Noah Webster (1758), William Buell Sprague (1795), Vicente Riva Palacio (1832), Oscar (Fingal O'Flahertie Wills) Wilde (1854), Daisy May Bates (Margaret Dwyer) (1859), John Bagnell "J. B." Bury (1861), Jesse Edward Grinstead (1866), Helge Rode (1870), Armin T. Wegner (1886), Walter Burgwyn Jones and Eugene O'Neill (1888), William O. Douglas (1898), Cecile de Brunhoff (1903), Cleanth Brooks and Dino Buzzati (1906), Roger Vailland (1907), Frank O'Rourke and George Turner (1916), Kathleen Winsor (1919), Günter Grass (1927), William Luce (1931), Shirlee (Smith) Matheson (1943), Paul (Landry) Monette (1945), Robert Bringhurst and Suzanne Somers (Suzanne Marie Mahoney) (1946), Elinor Lipman (1950), Meg Rosoff (1956), Timothy Francis "Tim" Robbins (1958), Marc Levy (1961), Kenneth Lonergan (1962), Jonathan Patrick Lamas (1974).

The difference between journalism and literature is that journalism is unreadable and literature is not read.—Oscar Wilde

Obsessed by a fairy tale, we spend our lives searching for a magic door and a lost kingdom of peace.—Eugene O'Neill

For me, writing, drawing, and political activism are three separate pursuits; each has its own intensity. I happen to be especially attuned to and engaged with the society in which I live. Both my writing and my drawing are invariably mixed up with politics, whether I want them to be or not.—Günter Grass

Oct. 17—Nathan Field/Feild (1587), Simon van Leeuwen (1626), Jupiter Hammon (1711), Jacques Cazotte (1719), John Wilkes (1725), John Bowring (1792), Georg Büchner (1813), Emanuel Geibel (1815), Elinor Glyn (1864), Alfred Polgar (1875), Mildred Knopf (1898), Simon Vestdijk (1898), (Arthur) Yvor Winters (1900), Nathanael West (1903), Jerry Siegel (1914), Arthur Miller (1915), Sumner Locke Elliott (1917), Miguel Delibes and Hobart Freeman (1920), George Mackey Brown (1921), Jimmy Breslin (1930), Robert Atkins (1930), Ernst Hinterberger (1931), Barend P. Tammeling (1934), Leslie Allan "Les" Murray (1938), Drusilla Modjeska (1946), Robert Jordan et al. (James Oliver Rigney Jr.) (1948), Jorge M. Pérez and Nick Tosches (latter b. Oct. 17 or 23) (1949), Wally Lamb and David Adams Richards (1950), Ron Drummond, Mark Peel, and Richard Roeper (1959), Norm Macdonald (1963), Mark Gatiss (1966), Rick Mercer (1969), Ariel Levy (1974), Ian Rogers (1976), Tarell Alvin McCraney (1980), Randall Munroe (1984).

Everything that I write will be signed with my name.—Elinor Glyn
The structure of a play is always the story of how the birds came home to roost.—Arthur Miller
Rage is the only quality which has kept me, or anybody I have ever studied, writing columns for newspapers.—Jimmy Breslin

Oct. 18—Pius II (Aenea S. Piccolomini) (1405), Justus Lipsius (Joost Lips) (1547), Giambattista Marini (1569), Lars Johnstown (Lasse Lucidor) (1638), Charles le Beau (1701), Pierre Choderlos de Laclos (1741), Adolfs Muller and Heinrich von Kleist (1774), Thomas Love Peacock (1785), Henry Taylor (1800), Elizabeth Fries Lummis Ellet (1818), Helen (Maria) Hunt Jackson (1831), Henri Bergson (1859), Arie de Jong and Logan Pearsall Smith (1865), Ernst Didring (1868), James Truslow Adams (1878), Maxwell Struthers Burt (1882), Fannie Hurst (1889), Harold Lenoir "H. L." Davis (1894), Raymond Brulez (1895), Isabel Briggs Myers (1897), Abbott Joseph "A. J." Liebling (1904), Norberto Bobbio (1909), Jesse Helms (1921), Frank Liedel (Leo van Assche) (1924), Thomas Millar (1926), Esther R. Hautzig (1930), Katherine Kurtz (1944), James Robert Baker and Barry Gifford (1946), Ntozake Shange (1948), Wendy Wasserstein (1950), Terry McMillan (1951), Chuck Lorre (Charles Michael Levine) and Bảo Ninh (1952), David Twohy (1955), Milčo Mančevski (1959), Hiram Frederick "Rick" Moody III (1961), Beth Hirsch (1967).

On the whole . . . publishers have nothing to say to poets, regarding them as unprofitable people.—Henry Taylor

A book that furnishes no quotations is no book—it is a plaything.—Thomas Love Peacock

What I like in a good author is not what he says, but what he whispers.—Logan Pearsall Smith

The real reason for comedy is to hide the pain.—Wendy Wasserstein

Oct. 19—Marsilio Ficino (1433), Thomas Browne (1605), Leigh Hunt (1784), Annie S. Peck (1850), George Albert Boulenger (1858), Vincas Kreve-Mickievicius (1882), Louis Mumford (1895), Salimuzzaman Siddiqui (1897), Miguel Ángel Asturias Rosales (1899), Patrick Cairns "Spike" Hughes (1908), Subrahmanyan Chandrasekhar (1910), Hilde Spiel (1911), Vasco Pratolini (1913), Vinicius de Moraes (1913), Louis Althusser (1918), Pandurang Shastri "Dada-ji" Athavale (1920), Jack Anderson (1922), Joel Feinberg and Edward Lewis Wallant (1926), John le Carré (David John Moore Cornwell) (1931), Renata Adler and Nicholas Palmer (1937), James Beeland "Jim" Rogers Jr. and Andrew (Henry) Vachss (1942), John Lithgow (1945), Philip Pullman (1946), Deborah Blum (1954), Ray Richmond (1957), Doug Kirby (1957), John Bloom (Joe Bob Briggs) (1958), Susan Straight (1960), Tracy Chevalier (1962), Jon Favreau (1966), Randolph Severn "Trey" Parker III (1969), Jason Reitman (1977).

It is books that teach us to refine our pleasures when young, and to recall them with satisfaction when we are old.—Leigh Hunt

It's part of a writer's profession, as it's part of a spy's profession, to prey on the community to which he's attached, to take away information—often in secret—and to translate that into intelligence for his masters, whether it's his readership or his spy masters. And I think that both professions are perhaps rather lonely.—John le Carré

I try to write 1,000 words a day—about three pages. When I reach 1,000 words I feel good. Less than that: a failure. More than that: tired.—Tracy Chevalier

Oct. 20—Giovanni Rucellai (1475), Belle van Zuylen (1740), George Ormerod (1785), Karl Andree (1808), Thomas Hughes (1823), Alphonse Allais (1854), Arthur Rimbaud (1854), John Dewey (1859), Nellie (Letitia Mooney) McClung (1873), Samuel Flagg Bemis (1891). Charley Chase (Charles Joseph Parrott) (1893), Marnix Gijsen (baron Jan-Albert Goris) (1899), Ellery Queen co-author Frederic Dannay (1905), Robert Lochner (1918), Hans Warren (1921), Pierre Laporte and Kati Rekai (1921), Joe Minogue and Philip (Glenn) Whalen (1923), Robert Louis Peters (1924), Art Buchwald (1925), Oskar Pastior (1927), Michael McClure (1932), Robert Pinsky (1940), Connie Chung, Lewis Grizzard, and Elfriede Jelinek (1946), David Profumo (1955), Lynn Flewelling (b. Lynn Elizabeth Beaulieu) and Viggo (Peter) Mortensen (Jr.) (1958), Michelle Malkin (1970).

Remember there's always a voice saying the right thing to you somewhere if you'll only listen for it.—Thomas Hughes

The last thing a young artist should do in poetry or any other field is think about what's in style, what's current, what are the trends. Think instead of what you like to read, what do you admire, what you like to listen to in music. What do you like to look at in architecture? Try to make a poem that has some of those qualities. —Robert Pinsky

Yankees don't understand that the Southern way of talking is a language of nuance. What we can do in the South is we can take a word and change it just a little bit and make it mean something altogether different.—Lewis Grizzard

Oct. 21—Samuel Taylor Coleridge (1772), Alphonse-Marie Louis de Lamartine (1790), Petrus P.M. Alberdingk Thijm (1827), William McKendree "Will" Carleton (1845), Edmondo de Amicis (1846), George P. Gooch (1873), Albert Aftalion (1874), Egon Joseph Wellesz (1885), Gerrit Engelke (1890), Rampo Edogawa (1894), Gerhard von Rad (1901), Edmond (Moore) Hamilton (1904), Patrick Kavanagh (1904), Nikos Engonopoulos (1907), Martin Gardner (1914), Claire Sterling (1919), Fran Landesman (1927), Ursula K(roeber) Le Guin (1929), James H. "Simon" Gray (1936), Win(fred) Blevins (1938), Frances FitzGerald (1940), Marina Ripa and David Stuart Walls (1941), Larry Kane (1942), Tariq Ali (1943), Ai Ogawa (Florence Anthony) (1947), Shaye Cohen (1948), Benjamin "Bibi" Netanyahu (1949), Patti Ann Davis (Patti Reagan) and Allen Hoey (1952), Carrie (Frances) Fisher (1956), Gaétan Soucy (1958), Marc (Alan) Fein (1967), Zephyr (Rain) Teachout (1971), Robert Paul Weston (1975).

A poet ought not to pick nature's pocket. Let him borrow, and so borrow as to repay by the very act of borrowing. Examine nature accurately, but write from recollection, and trust more to the imagination than the memory.—Samuel Taylor Coleridge

A man is original when he speaks the truth that has always been known to all good men.—Patrick Kavanagh

If science fiction is the mythology of modern technology, then its myth is tragic.—Ursula K. Le Guin

Oct. 22—William the Troubador (William IX, Duke of Aquitaine) (1071), Johann Reinhold Forster (1729), Carlos Wilcox (1794), Leconte de Lisle (1818), E(dward) Phillips Oppenheim (1866), Ivan Bunin (1870), Karl B. Adam (1876), Adolf A. Joffe (1883), Parker Fennelly (1891), (Arthur) Burton Rascoe (1892), Damaso Alonso (1898), Edward R. Stettinius (1900), Sidney Kingsley (1906), Helmut Gollwitzer (1908), John Gould (1908), Doris (May) Lessing (Tayler) (1919), Georges Brassens (1921), Jan A. de Jonge (1926), David (Mansfield) Bromige (1933), Max Apple (1941), Elizabeth Grace Hay (1951), Bonnie M. Anderson (1955), Arto Salminen (1959).

What no wife of a writer can ever understand is that a writer is working when he's staring out of the window.—Burton Rascoe

I don't know much about creative writing programs. But they're not telling the truth if they don't teach, one, that writing is hard work, and, two, that you have to give up a great deal of life, your personal life, to be a writer.—Doris Lessing

Our great American writers were all newspaper people.—John Gould

Oct. 23—Juan de la Cueva (1543), Peter Burmannus Secundus (Pieter Burman) (1713), H. Benjamin Constant (de Rebeque) (1767), John Russell Bartlett and Adalbert Stifter (1805), Margaret Fuller (Sarah Margaret Fuller Ossoli) (1810), Francis Hopkinson Smith (1838), Robert (Seymour) Bridges (1844), John Herbert Quick (1861), Molly Elliot Seawell (1860), Neltje Blanchan (1865), Arthur Henry Gooden (1879), Archibald (Hamilton) Rutledge (1883), Genevieve Holden (Genevieve Long Pou) (1919), Ned Rorem (1923), Johnny Carson (1925), Philip Lamantia (1927), Michael Crichton (1942), Brian Ross (1948), Nick Tosches (1949), Michael Eric Dyson (1958), Nancy (Ann) Grace, Sam Raimi, and Alfred Matthew "Weird Al" Yankovic (1959), Randy Pausch (1960), Laurie Halse Anderson (1961), Gordon Korman (1963), Augusten Burroughs (1965), Michael George "Mike" Dupée (1966), Aravind Adiga (1974), Masiela Lusha (1985).

Never use a big word when a little filthy one will do.—Johnny Carson

Books aren't written—they're rewritten. Including your own. It is one of the hardest things to accept, especially after the seventh rewrite hasn't quite done it.—Michael Crichton

When people don't express themselves, they die one piece at a time.— Laurie Halse Anderson

Oct. 24—Antonie van Leeuwenhoek (1632), Pierre François Xavier de Charlevoix (1682), Alban Butler (1710), Dorothea von Schlegel (Brendel Mendelssohn) (1763), Sarah Josepha Hale (1788), (Graf) August von Platen-Hallermünde (1796), Alexandra David-Néel (1868), Hermann Claudius (1878), Ernest Claes (1885), Delmira Augustini (1886), Bibhutibhushan Mukhopadhyay (1894), Moss Hart (1904), Sheila (Martin) Watson (1909), Armand Lanoux (1913), Bob Kane (Robert Kahn) and Marghanita Laski (1915), Denise Levertov (1923), Gabriel Laub (1928), Hubert Aquin, James Brosnan, and Yordan Radichkov (1929), Norman Rush (1933), Katherine (Karen) Dunn (1945), Martin "Marty" Baron (1954), Dale Maharidge (1956), Jaime Garzón (1960), Dave Meltzer (1961), Ted Dekker (1962), George Noriega (1966), Robert Wilonsky (1968), Emma Donoghue (1969).

I am also a writer. That is a fact not known by the public in general.—Bob Kane

But peace, like a poem,/ is not there ahead of itself,/ can't be imagined /before it is made,/ can't be known except/ in the words of its making,/ grammar of justice,/ syntax of mutual aid.—Denise Levertov

The great thing about a short story is that it doesn't have to trawl through someone's whole life; it can come in glancingly from the side.—Emma Donoghue

Oct. 25—James Beattie (1735), Benjamin Constant (1767), John P(endleton) Kennedy (1795), Thomas Babington Macaulay (1800), Maria van Ackere-Doolaeghe (1803), Max Stirner (Johann Kaspar Schmidt) (1806), Pavel Melnikov (1818), Gleb Uspensky (1843), Rebecca Agatha Armour (1845), Dragutin Gorjanovic-Kramberger (1856), Stephanie H. (Lapidoth-)Swarth (1859), Eduardo Barrios (1884), Francois Pauwels (1888), Richard E. Byrd (1888), Henry Steele Commager and (Charles) Leslie McFarlane (1902), Edmond Pidoux (1908), John Berryman (1914), Brian Malzard Foss (1921), Peter Rohmkorf (1929), Harold Brodkey (b. Aaron Roy Weintraub) (1930), Martin John Gilbert (1936), Anne Tyler (1941), Selly Fernandes (1943), Daniel Mark Epstein (1948), J. A. Adande (1970), Zadie Smith (1975).

The artist is extremely lucky who is presented with the worst possible ordeal which will not actually kill him. At that point, he's in business.—John Berryman

I was standing in the schoolyard waiting for a child when another mother came up to me. Have you found work yet? she asked. Or are you still just writing?—Anne Tyler

Tell the truth through whichever veil comes to hand—but tell it. Resign yourself to the lifelong sadness that comes from never being satisfied.—Zadie Smith

Oct. 26—Dimitrie Cantemir (1673), Charles Sprague (1791), Philip Pendleton Cooke (1816), Elizabeth Payson Prentiss (1818), Will Allen Dromgoole (1860), Andrei Bely (Boris Nikolaevich Bugaev) (1880), Napoleon Hill (1883), E. Runar Schildt (1888), Karin Maria Boye (1900), Beryl Markham (1902), Sidney Kingsley (1906), Sorley MacLean Somhairle MacChaluim (1911), Stuart J(ames) Byrne (1913), Frances Scott "Scottie" Fitzgerald (1921), Jan Wolkers (1925), John Arden (1930), Ulrich Plentzdorf (1934), Thomas Nicholas Meschery (b. Tomislav Nikolayevich Meshcheryakov) (1938), Steven Kellogg (1941), Pat Conroy, Demetris Th. Gotsis, and John C. McAdams (1945), Hillary Rodham Clinton, Trevor Joyce, and Kenzo Kitakata (1947), Andrew Motion (1952), Jennifer Roberson (1953), Rita Wilson (Margarita Ibrahimoff) (1956), Jim Butcher (1971), Pack Beauregard "Beau" Willimon (1977).

Think twice before you speak, because your words and influence will plant the seed of either success or failure in the mind of another.—Napoleon Hill
The sated day is never first/ The best day is a day of thirst/ Yes, there is goal and meaning in our path—/ but it is the way that is the labour's worth.—Karin Boye
I've never cackled with laughter at a single line I've ever written. None of it has given me pleasure.—Pat Conroy

Oct. 27—Hester Chapone (1727), Klas (Pontus) Arnoldson (1844), Theodore Roosevelt (1858), George Middleton (1880), Enid Bagnold (1889), Frances Crane (1890), Graciliano Ramos and Victor E. van Vriesland (1892), Johan G. Dancer (1893), James Alexander Cowan (1901), Dylan Thomas (1914), Kazimierz Brandys (1916), Kocheril Raman "K. R." Narayanan (1920), Warren Allen Smith (1921), Gilles Vigneault (1928), Nawal el-Saadawi (1931), Victoria Lucas (Sylvia Plath) (1932), Cornelius Mahoney "Neil" Sheehan (1936), John Cleese (Cheese) (1939), Maxine Hong Kingston (1940), Judith Ann "J. A." Jance (1944) John Kane (1945), Terry Anderson (1947), Frances Ann "Fran" Lebowitz (1950), Robert Polito (1951), Jaq D. Hawkins (1956), Jade Arcade (1971).

These poems, with all their crudities, doubts, and confusions, are written for the love of Man and in praise of God, and I'd be a damn' fool if they weren't.—**Dylan Thomas**

And by the way, everything in life is writable about if you have the outgoing guts to do it, and the imagination to improvise. The worst enemy to creativity is self-doubt.—**Sylvia Plath**

I think you can write very good comedy without a partner, but what I love about it, working with a partner, is that you get to places you'd never get on your own. It's like when God was designing the world and decided we couldn't have children without a partner; it was a way of mixing up the genes so you'd get a more interesting product.—**John Cleese**

I hate writing. I will do anything to avoid it. The only way I could write less was if I was dead.—**Fran Lebowitz**

Oct. 28—Desiderius Erasmus (1466), Nicholas Brady (1659), Cornelius Mathews (1817), Ivan Turgenev (1818), Anna Elizabeth Dickinson (1842), Pío Baroja (1872), Gilbert Hovey Grosvenor (1875), Velimir Khlebnikov (1885), Eduard J. Dijksterhuis and Ludwig Strauss (1892), Eileen Shanahan (1901), Evelyn A. Waugh (1903), John Harold Hewitt (1907), Jonas Salk (1914), Jessie Kesson (1916), Harvey Swados (1920), Ian Hamilton Finlay (1925), John Hollander (1929), Virginia (Rudd) Lanier (1930), Richard Lush (1934), William W(allace) Johnstone and Anne Perry (1938), Susan Harris (1940), David C. Carpenter (1941), Caroline (Mary) Moorehead (1944), Sharon Thesen (1946), Bob Dolman (1949), Carolyn Coman and Joe R(ichard) Lansdale (1951), Desmond Child (b. John Charles Barrett) (1953), Andy Richter (1966), Uwe Tellkamp (1968), Ayad Akhtar and Albert Watkins "Watt" Key Jr. (1970), Jessica Care Moore (1971), Jamie DeWolf (1977).

When I get a little money, I buy books, and if any is left, I buy food and clothes.—Desiderius Erasmus

There are no poetic ideas; only poetic utterances.—Evelyn Waugh

You start at the end, and then go back and write and go that way. Not everyone does, but I do. Some people just sit down at the page and start off. I start from what happened, including the why. —Anne Perry

Oct. 29—Jacques Amyot (1513), Pierre François Xavier de Charlevoix (1682), Martin Folkes (1690), James Boswell (1740), Ľudovít Štúr (1815), Harriet Powers (1837), Conrad Haebler (1857), Guillermo Valencia (1873), Jean Giraudoux (1882), Claire Goll (1890), Alamo Boyd/Jackson W. Horne (Allan Rucker Bosworth) (1901), Fredric (William) Brown (1906), Alfred Jules "A. J."Ayer (1910), Bernard Gordon (1918), William Henry "Bill" Mauldin (1921), Wendell Givens (1922), Desmond Bagley (1923), Zbigniew Herbert (1924), Dominick Dunne (1925), Lee Child (Jim Grant) (1954), Boy Abunda (1955), Ann-Marie MacDonald and David Remnick (1958), Nancy Werlin (1961), Daniel J. Bernstein (1971), Mohsen Emadi (1976).

A good pun may be admitted among the smaller excellencies of lively conversation.—James Boswell

I would like to thank the people who encouraged me to draw army cartoons at a time when the gag man's conception of the army was one of mean ole sergeants and jeeps which jump over mountains.—Bill Mauldin

I made no pretense of doing balanced reporting about murder. I was appalled by defense attorneys who would do anything to win an acquittal for a guilty person.—Dominick Dunne

Oct. 30—Enrico C. Davila (1576), Paul Pellisson (1624), Richard Brinsley Sheridan (1751), André Chénier (1762), Philippe-Joseph Aubert de Gaspé (1786), Rinse Posthumus (1790), Andrew P. Canova (1835), William G. Sumner (1840), Gertrude (Franklin Horn) Atherton (1857), Lena Christ and Elizabeth Madox Roberts (1881), Ezra (Loomis) Pound (1885), Zoë Akins (1886), Georg Heym (1887), Willi Apel and Jan M. Romein (1893), Kostas Karyotakis (1896), Alexander Gode (Alexander Gottfried Friedrich Gode-von-Aesch) (1906), Sol Tax (1907), Miguel Hernadez Gilabert (1910), Marius Hendrikus Flothuis and James Laughlin (1914), Fred Friendly (1915), Timothy (Irving Frederick) Findley (1930), Barun De (1932), Robert Allan Caro and Agota Kristof (1935), Rudolfo Anaya (1937), Leland H. Hartwell (1939), Larry (Alfred) Woiwode (1941), Barbara Wiedemann (1945), Andrea Mitchell (1946), Dennis Covington (1948), Charles Martin Smith (1953), Andy Archer (1957), Bryden MacDonald (1960), Leo Yankevich (1961), Andrew Solomon (1963), Lizette Alvarez (1964).

You write with ease to show your breeding, but easy writing's curst hard reading.—Richard Brinsley Sheridan
Literature is news that STAYS news.—Ezra Pound
A composite is a euphemism for a lie. It's disorderly. It's dishonest and it's not journalism.—Fred W. Friendly

Oct. 31—Philippe de Vitry (1291), Caesar Baronius (1538), Denzil Holles (1599), John Evelyn (1620), (Anne) Claude (de Tubières Grimoard de Pestels Levieux) de Lévis (1692), Laura Maria Caterina Bassi (1711), Christopher Anstey (1724), Leonor de Almeida marquesa de Alorna (1750), Jean Louis van Aelbroeck (1755), John Keats (1795), Krišjānis Barons (1835), Mary E(leanor) W(ilkins) Freeman (1852), Johann Peter Adolf Erman (1854), David Graham Phillips (1867), Seerp Anema (1875), Eduard van Oort (1876), Nelson Harding (1879), Julia (Mood) Peterkin (1880), Marc Elder (Marcel Tendron) (1884), Courtney Ryley Cooper (1886), Napoleon Lapathiotis and George Hubert Wilkins (1888), Basil Henry "B. H." Liddell Hart (1895), Alfred Sauvy (1898), Charles Drummond de Andrade (1902), Dale Evans (Lucille Wood Smith) (1912), William Hardy McNeill (1917), Ian (Pretyman) Stevenson (1918), Magnus Wenninger (1919), Dick Francis (1920), Henry Reymond Fitzwalter "H. R. F." Keating (1926), Andrew Sarris (1928), Dan Rather (1931), Katherine Womeldorf Paterson (1932), Michael Landon (1937), Parnell Hall (1944), John Candy and Jane Pauley (1950), Annie Finch (1956), Sam Tanenhaus (1955), Neal Stephenson (1959), Joseph Boyden (1966), Roger Lima (1974), Seth Abramson (1976), Irina Denezhkina (1981).

I saw Hamlet Prince of Denmark played; but now the old plays begin to disgust this refined age.—John Evelyn

Poetry should surprise by a fine excess and not by singularity, it should strike the reader as a wording of his own highest thoughts, and appear almost a remembrance.—John Keats

I'm not driven by killer ambition. I'm not a workaholic. I'm a good team player. I don't have to be captain, but I do want to play on a winning team.—Jane Pauley

Born in November

Nov. 1—Étienne de La Boétie (1530), Pierre Pithou (1539), Georg Philipp Harsdorffer (1607), Nicolas Boileau Despréaux (1636), John Strype (1643), Florent Carton Dancourt (1661), Paul Daniel Longolius (1704), Christopher Brennan (1870), Stephen Crane (1871), Sholem Asch and Grantland Rice (1880), Hermann Broch (1886), David Jones (1895), Edmund Blunden (1896), Naomi Mitchison (1897), (Francis) Gerard (Luis) Fairlie (1899), Nordahl Grieg (1902), Jean Tardieu (1903), Henri Troyat (1911), Carlos A. Nicolaas (1915), Margaret Taylor Burroughs, Zenna (Chlarson) Henderson, and Richard Warrington Baldwin "R. W. B" Lewis (1917), John Secondari (1919), James J. Kilpatrick (1920), Ilse Aichinger (1921), Gordon R(upert) Dickson and Edward A. de Jongh (1923), Robert N. Rapoport (1924), Rudy (Herman R.) Kousbroek (1929), Albert Ramsdell "A. R." Gurney (Jr.) (1930), Edward Said (1935), William Melvin Kelley (1937), William (Helmuth) Heyen (1940), Go Osaka (1943), Richard Samet "Kinky" Friedman and Lee Smith (1944), Kim Krizan and Louise Boije af Gennäs (1961).

Half of tradition is a lie.—Stephen Crane
Writing comes more easily if you have something to say. —Sholem Asch
You are meant to play the ball as it lies, a fact that may help to touch on your own objective approach to life.—Grantland Rice

Nov. 2—Peter S. Lotichius (Peter Lotz) (1528), Jules Amédée Barbey D'Aurevilly (1808), George Sorel (1847), Leo Perutz (1882), Martin (Archer) Flavin (1883), Eddy (Charles E.) du Perron (1899), Gyula Illyés (1902), Daniil (Leonidovich) Andreev (1906), Odysseas Elytis (Odysseas Alepoudellis) (1911), Dale Wasserman (1914), Jorge de Sena (1919), Harold (Andrew) Horwood (1923), Paul Johnson (1928), Patrick Joseph "Pat" Buchanan (1938), Jim Forest (1941), Shere Hite (Shirley Diana Gregory) (1942), Michelle Cliff (1946), Thomas Mallon (1951), Dale Brown (1956), Lynn Nottage (1964), JT LeRoy (Laura Victoria Albert) (1965).

The life of the hero of the tale is, at the outset, overshadowed by bitter and hopeless struggles; one doubts that the little swineherd will ever be able to vanquish the awful Dragon with the twelve heads. And yet, . . . truth and courage prevail and the youngest and most neglected son of the family, of the nation, of mankind, chops off all twelve heads of the Dragon, to the delight of our anxious hearts. This exultant victory, towards which the hero of the tale always strives, is the hope and trust of the peasantry and of all oppressed peoples. This hope helps them bear the burden of their destiny.—Gyula Illyés

A publisher once told me, "Writing books is hard—almost as hard as selling them."—Jim Forest

I often tell people who want to write historical fiction: don't read all that much about the period you're writing about; read things from the period that you're writing about. There's a tendency to stoke up on a lot of biography and a lot of history, and not to actually get back to the original sources.—Thomas Mallon

Nov. 3—Lucan (39), Benvenuto Cellini (1500), Renatus Rapinus (René Rapin) (1621), August G. Meissner (1753), William Cullen Bryant (1794), John Esten Cooke (1830), Isabella Macdonald Alden (1841), Isabella "Belle" Kendrick Abbott (1842), Johann Peter Kirsch (1861), Vilhjalmur Stefansson (William Stephenson) (1879), Adrian P. "Apie" Prince (1884), Samuil Marshak (1887), Harry Stephen Keeler (1890), Andre Malraux (1901), William Donald Campbell (1905), James (Barrett) Reston (1909), Dean Riesner (1918), Oodgeroo Noonuccal (1920), Anton (Olmstead) Myrer (1922), Dieter Wellershoff (1925), D. James Kennedy (1930), Terrence McNally and Jean Rollin (1938), Terrence McNally (1939), Martin Cruz Smith and Thomas Weatherly Jr. (1942), Joe Queenan (1950), Massimo Mongai (1950), Felix R. de Rooy (1952), Roseanne Barr (1952), Dennis Miller (1953), Hal Hartley (1959).

Often the difference between a successful person and a failure is not one has better abilities or ideas, but the courage that one has to bet on one's ideas, to take a calculated risk—and to act.—Andre Malraux

Ever since I was a girl, I have written about one to five pages every day—on napkins, on scrap paper, in notebooks and tablets, on the walls in my room as a teenager, and in orange paint on the cheap white plastic blinds in my room.—Roseanne Barr

I rant, therefore I am.—Dennis Miller

Nov. 4—William Habington (1605), Augustus Montague Toplady (1740), James Montgomery (1771), Aleksander A. Bestuzhev-Marlinsky (1797), Aleardo (Gaetano) Aleardi (1812), Samuel Minturn Peck (1854), Eden Phillpotts (1862), George Edward "G.E." Moore (1873), William Penn Adair "Will" Rogers (1879), Klabund (Alfred Henschke) (1890), Carlos Pellicer (1899), Lucreţiu Pătrăşcanu (1900), Spyridon Marinatos (1901), Walter Bauer and Tadeusz Żyliński (1904), Martin Raschke (1905), Bob Considine (1906), Jean-Jacques Gautier (1908), Ciro Alegría (1909), Jack Rose (1911), Alistair Cameron Crombie (1915), Walter Cronkite (1916), Georges Papy (1920), Eugene (Bondurant) Sledge (1923), Hannah (Adelle Finegold) Weiner (1928), David Shipman (1932), Judith Herzberg (1934), Charles Kenneth "C. K." Williams (1936), Marlene Jobert (1943), Charles Frazier (1950), John Stigall (1951), Marvel Williamson (1953), Marc Awodey (1960), Jon Robin Baitz (1961), Richard "Rick" Yancey (1962), Matthew Tobin "M. T." Anderson (1968).

> But books there are with nothing fraught,—
> Ten thousand words, and ne'er a thought;
> Where periods without period crawl,
> Like caterpillars on a wall,
> That fall to climb, and climb to fall;
> While still their efforts only tend
> To keep them from their journey's end.
> —James Montgomery

The worst thing that happens to you may be the best thing for you if you don't let it get the best of you.—Will Rogers

I do the same things I did when I was 12 years old: I ride bikes, I read books, I walk in the woods. And I listen to music.—Charles Frazier

Nov. 5—Joachim Camerarius (Jr.) (1534), Philippe du Plessis (1549), Philippe de Mornay (1549), Isaac de Benserade (1613), John Brown (1715), James Beattie (1735), Pieter Nieuwland (1764), Etienne P. de Senancour (1770), Washington Allston (1779), Moritz Szeps (1835), Ruy Barbosa (de Oliveira) (1849), Ella Wheeler Wilcox (1850), Eugene V(ictor) Debs (1855), Ida Tarbell (1857), George A. Malcolm (1881), James Elroy Flecker (1884), Will Durant (1885), Willis Richardson (1889), John Burdon Sanderson "J. B. S." Haldane (1892), Henri (E. J. A.) de Page (1894), Charles (Gordon) MacArthur (1895), Philip MacDonald (1900), George Lowthian Trevelyan and Fred Lawrence Whipple (1906), Hasan Askari (1919), Douglass North (1920), Thomas Flanagan and Ian Arthur Hoyle Munro (1923), John (Peter) Berger and Leo Derksen (1926), Linwood Vrooman "Lin" Carter and Clifford (Michael) Irving (1930), Christopher Wood (1935), Arthur Ira "Art" Garfunkel (1941), Sam Shepard (Samuel Shepard Rogers III) and Friedman Paul Erhardt "Chef Tell" (1943), Bob Weltlich (1944), Richard Holmes (1945), Larry Dane Brimner (1949), Stuart Havelock Hollingdale (1951), Joyce Maynard and Deborah Wiles (1953), Karan Thapar (1955), Atul Gawande (1965).

You may choose your words like a connoisseur, And polish it up with art, But the word that sways, and stirs, and stays, Is the word that comes from the heart.—Ella Wheeler Wilcox

Writing for the theatre is so different to writing for anything else. Because what you write is eventually going to be spoken. That's why I think so many really powerful novelists can't write a play—because they don't understand that it's spoken—that it hits the air. They don't get that.—Sam Shepard

You write about what you know, and you write about what you want to know.—Joyce Maynard

Nov. 6—Thomas Kyd (bapt.) (1558), Colley Cibber (1671), Louis Racine (1692), George Back (1796), Pavel Melnikov (1818), Jonas Lie (1833), Francis Ellingwood Abbot (1836), Charles Dow (1851), John Phillip Sousa (1854), Marie Bregendahl (1867), Eugen (Samuilovich) Varga (1879), Robert Musil and Chris van Abkoude (1880), Harold Ross (1892), August Defresne (1893), Fibber McGee (Jim Jordan) (1896), Carl Rakosi (1903), Fanny Leys (1908), Benny Marshall (1919), James (Ramon) Jones (1921), K. Schippers (Gerard Stigter) (1936), Randel (McCraw) Helms (1942), Sally (Margaret) Field (1946), Dr. Beach (Stephen Parker Leatherman) (1947) (Richard) Ernest Thompson (1949), David Unger (1950), John Falsey (1951), Michael Cunningham (1952), Catherine Crier (1954), Maria (Owings) Shriver (1955), Colson Whitehead (1969).

That that is good for the body is likewise good for the soul. —Thomas Kyd

Prithee don't screw your wit beyond the compass of good manners.—Colley Cibber

I asked Ring Lardner the other day how he writes his short stories, and he said he wrote a few widely separated words or phrases on a piece of paper and then went back and filled in the spaces. —Harold Ross

. . . [T]he quality which makes a man want to write and be read is essentially a desire for self-exposure and is masochistic. Like one of the guys who has a compulsion to take his thing out and show it on the street.—James Jones

Nov. 7—Muhammad ibn Hazm (994), Gédéon Tallemant des Réaux (1619), William Stukeley (1687), Johannes G. Schnabel (1692), Friedrich Leopold Graf zu Stolberg (1750), Fritz Reuter (1810), Karel J. Erben (1811), Andrew Dickson White (1832), Auguste Villiers de l'Isle-Adam (1838), Edwin Herbert Hall (1855), Bipin Chandra Pal (1858), Leonora Speyer (von Stosch) (1872), Leon Trotsky (Leib Davidovitsj Bronstein) (1879), Mark Aldanov (Landau) (1886), Esdras Minville (1896), Ruth Pitter (1897), Mark Aleksandrovich Aldanov (1889), Margaret Kernochan Leech (1893), Donald Benson "Don" Blanding (1894), Albert Helman (Lodewijk "Lou" Lichtveld) (1903), Konrad Lorenz (1903), Jan Vercammen and Margaret Barbara Lambert (1906), Maurits Mok (1907), Walter Shlomo Gross (1911), Albert Camus (1913), Raphael Aloysius "R. A." Lafferty (1914), Philip Morrison (1915), William Franklin "Billy" Graham Jr. (1918), Matthew Coady (1923), Wolf Mankowitz (1924), William Wharton (Albert William Du Aime) (1925), Horace E. "Steve" Carter Jr. (1929), Beverly Dahlen (1934), Willibrordus S. Rendra (1935), Guido Provoost (1940), Stan Rice and Jean Shrimpton (1942), Stephen Greenblatt and Michael Spence (1943), Chrystos and Dale Zieroth (1946), Guy Gavriel Kay (1954), Hilary Thayer Hamann and Phyllis Nagy (1962), Bryant Harrison McGill (1969).

Are you really going to see [C. S.] Lewis? One of the few people it's worth getting excited over, I think. I know he is a good poet. I daresay he never heard of me, but I wish you would tell him that his work is the joy of my life.—Ruth Pitter

Every artist preserves deep within him a single source from which, throughout his lifetime, he draws what he is, and what he says. When the source dries up, the work withers and crumbles. —Albert Camus

Almost everybody will listen to you when you tell your own story.—Billy Graham

Nov. 8—Julian of Norwich (1342), Teofilo Folengo (1491), Pierre Bayle (1647), Edmond Halley (1656), Johann Ulrich von Cramer (1706), Sarah Fielding (1710), Roger de Beauvoir (Eugene Auguste Roger de Bully) (1806), Girolamo / Jeromin de Rada (1814), Owen Meredith (Edward R. L. Bulwer-Lytton) (1831), Abraham "Bram" Stoker (1847), René (Raphael) Viviani (1863), William King Baggot (1879), Hermann Rorschach (1884), Hans Cloos (1885), René Maran (1887), Photios Kontoglou (1895), Dorothy Day (1897), Margaret (Munnerlyn) Mitchell (1900), Marius Grout (1903), Cedric Belfrage (1904), Martha Gellhorn and Raja Rao (1908), Katharine Hepburn (1909), Peter Weiss (1916), Fred Cogswell (1917), Purushottam Laxman "P. L." Deshpande (1919), Christiaan Barnard and Hiroshi Kashiwagi (1922), Robert Cleckler "Bobby" Bowden and António Castanheira Neves (1929), Benjamin William "Ben" Bova (1932), David Jessel and Alice (Elizabeth) Notley (1945), Luci Tapahonso (1953), David Bret, Timothy Egan, and Kazuo Ishiguro (1954), Richard Curtis (1956), Craig Chester (1965), Gordon Ramsay (1966), Courtney Thorne-Smith (1967), Kevin Young (1970), Vanesa Littlecrow (1973), Masashi and Seishi Kishimoto (1974), Lauren Oliver (b. Laura Suzanne Schechter) (1982).

If modesty and candor are necessary to an author in his judgment of his own works, no less are they in his reader.—Sarah Fielding

The world can forgive practically anything except people who mind their own business.—Margaret Mitchell

Life is to be lived. If you have to support yourself, you had bloody well better find some way that is going to be interesting. And you don't do that by sitting around.—Katharine Hepburn

Nov. 9—Martin Chemnitz (1522), Menso Alting (1541), Paul Aler (1656), Mark Akenside (1721), Benjamin Banneker (1731), Julie de Lespinasse (1732), Thomasine Christine Gyllembourg-Ehrensvard (1773), Elijah P(arish) Lovejoy (1802), Ivan Turgenev (1818), Matthias de Vries (1820), Émile Gaboriau (1832), Mary Hallock Foote (1847), Maud Howe Elliott (1854), Emmanuel K. de Bom (1868), Bohdan Lepky (1872), Otfrid Foerster (1873), Allama Iqbal (1877), Velimir Khlebnikov (1885), Ed Wynn (Isaiah Edwin Leopold) (1886), Owen Barfield (1898), Erika Mann (1905), Hendrik van Randwijk (1909), Tabish Dehlvi (1911), Spiro (Theodore) Agnew (1918), Ivo (Rudolph) Jarosy (1921), Raymond Devos and Imre Lakatos (1922), James (Marcus) Schyler (1923), Alistair Horne (1925), Anne Sexton (1928), Marc Favreau and Imre Kertész (1929), Marian Christy (1932), Ronald Harwood (Horwitz) and Carl Sagan (1934), Bob Graham (1936), Roger McCough (1937), Ti-Grace Atkinson (1938), Paul Cameron (1939), Frederick Arthur "F. A." Nettelbeck (1950), Bill Mantlo (1951), Ellen McLaughlin (1957), Jackie Kay (1961), Louis Émond (1969), William Rivers Pitt (1971).

A poet must be a psychologist, but a secret one: he should know and feel the roots of phenomena but present only the phenomena themselves in full bloom or as they fade away.—Ivan Turgenev

The beautiful feeling after writing a poem is on the whole better even than after sex, and that's saying a lot.—Anne Sexton

But the fact that some geniuses were laughed at does not imply that all who are laughed at are geniuses. They laughed at Columbus, they laughed at Fulton, they laughed at the Wright Brothers. But they also laughed at Bozo the Clown.—Carl Sagan

Nov. 10—Martin Luther (1483), Laurentius Paulinus Gothus (1565), Jacob Cats (1577), Ninon de l'Enclos (Anne de Lenclos) (1620), John Bevis (1695), William Hogarth (1697), Adam Gottlob Moltke (1710), Oliver Goldsmith (1730), Granville Sharp (1735), Frederich von Schiller (1759), Vladimir (Ivanovich) Dal (1801), Jose Hernandez (1834), Henry Eyster Jacobs (1844), Josiah Royce (1855), Winston Churchill of the U.S. (1871), (Nicholas) Vachel Lindsay and Patrick Pearse (1879), Aart A. van Schelven (1880), Max Mell (1882), Olaf Bull (1883), Jan van Nijlen (1884), Arnold Zweig (1887), John P. Marquand (1893), Murk Ozinga (1902), John Moore (1907), Robert A. Arthur Jr. and Paweł Jasienica (1909), Karl (Jay) Shapiro (1913), Oda Blinder (Yolanda Corsen) (1918), Doris (Hilda) Anderson (1921), W. E. B. Griffin (William Edmund Butterworth III) (1929), J. California Cooper (Joan Cooper) (1931), Robert F. Engle (1942), Jack Ketchum (Dallas William Mayr) and David Stockman (1946), Aaron Brown (1948), Debra Hill (1950), Anne Lamott (1954), James Chapman and Roland Emmerich (1955), Mohsen Badawi (1956), Mark (David) Danner (1958), Linda Cohn (1959), Neil (Richard MacKinnon) Gaiman (1960), Jeanine Tesori (1961).

The multitude of books is a great evil. There is no measure of limit to this fever of writing; everyone must be an author, some for some kind of vanity to acquire celebrity and raise a name, others for the sake of lucre or gain.—Martin Luther

I wrote the scenes . . . by using the same apprehensive imagination that occurs in the morning before an afternoon's appointment with my dentist.—John Marquand

To be a good writer, you not only have to write a great deal but you have to care. You do not have to have a complicated moral philosophy. But a writer always tries, I think, to be a part of the solution, to understand a little about life and to pass this on.—Anne Lamott

A short story is the ultimate close-up magic trick—a couple of thousand words to take you around the universe or break your heart.—Neil Gaiman

Nov. 11—Bernardo Tasso (1493), Paracelsus (Philippus Aureolus Theophrastus Bombastus von Hohenheim) (1493), Joachim Hopperus (Hoppers) (1523), Martin Ruland the Younger (1569), George Savile, 1st marquis of Halifax (1633), Yen Jo-chue (1636), Johann Albert Fabricius (1668), Firmin Abauzit (1679), Carl Peter Thunberg (1743), Fyodor (Mikhailovich) Dostoyevsky (1821), Thomas Bailey Aldrich (1836), Anna Katharine Green (1846), Alfred Hermann Fried (1864), Nils Kjaer (1870), George S. Patton (1885), Alceu Amoroso Lima (1893), Gordon W. Allport (1897), Hugo Enomiya-Lassalle (1898), F(rancis) Van Wyck Mason (1901), Alger Hiss and John Henry Constantine "J. H. C." Whitehead (1904), Felix Pollak (1909), Yisrael Eldad (1910), Peter Black (1913), E. V. Cunningham/Walter Ericson (Howard [Melvin] Fast) (1914), (Edward) William Proxmire (1915), Eladio Rusconi (1916), (Dallas) Mack/McCord Reynolds (1917), Kalle Päätalo (1919), Kurt Vonnegut Jr (1922), Jonathan (Harshman) Winters (III) (1925), H. M. Enzensberger and Carlos Fuentes (1929), Alicia (Suskin) Ostriker (1937), William Matthews (1942), Trevor Ferguson and Callum Alexander MacDonald (1947), Mircea Dinescu (1950), Judith Ariana Fitzgerald (1952), Mary Gaitskill (1954), Stanley Tucci (1960), Max Mutchnick (1965), David L. Cook (1968), Lee Battersby (1970), Jennifer Celotta (1971), Donari Braxton (1982).

Man is fond of counting his troubles, but he does not count his joys. If he counted them up as he ought to, he would see that every lot has enough happiness provided for it.—Fyodor Dostoevsky

So Friar Jerome began his Book. / From break of dawn till curfew-chime / He bent above the lengthening page, / Like some rapt poet o'er his rhyme.—Thomas Bailey Aldrich

Who is more to be pitied, a writer bound and gagged by policemen, or one living in perfect freedom who has nothing more to say?—Kurt Vonnegut

Writing is a struggle against silence.—Carlos Fuentes

Nov. 12—Juana Ines de La Cruz (1651), Jacobus Bellamy (1757), Elizabeth Cady Stanton (1815), Bahá'u'lláh (Mírzá Ḥusayn-ʿAlí Núrí) (1817), Anton Kerner von Marilaun (1831), John William Strutt, 3rd Baron Rayleigh (1841), Oskar Panizza (1853), Ben Travers (1886), Anne Parrish (1888), Sálim (Moizuddin Abdul) Ali (1896), Abraham J. D. van Oosten (1898), George (Hill) Dillon (1906), Hans Werner Richter (1908), William Thomas Pennar Davies and Luc Estang (Lucien Bastard) (1911), Edward Cornelis Florentius Alfonsus "Henricus" Schillebeeckx (1914), Roland Barthes (1915), Charlotte MacLeod (1922), Vicco von Bülow (Bernhard Victor Christoph Carl von Bülow) (1923), Michael Ende (1929), Tonke Dragt (1930), John Metcalf (1938), Wallace (Michael) Shawn (1943), Johnny van Doorn "Johnny the Selfkicker" (1944), Michael (Lawson) Bishop and Tracy Kidder (1945), Luigi Jannuzzi (1952), Katharine Weber (1955), Andrée A. Michaud (1957), Nick Stellino (1958), Bertice Berry (1960), Jonathan Nossiter (1961), Mariella Frostrup, Neal Shusterman, and Naomi Wolf (1962), Charles Evered (1964), Ian Bremmer (1969).

I probably have a higher opinion of my writing than the average person, at least when I'm in a good mood, but I don't really think of my plays as only being relevant to a particular month or year. —Wallace Shawn

At first, I spend about four hours a day writing. Toward the end of a book, I spend up to 16 hours a day on it, because all I want to do is make it good and get it done.—Tracy Kidder

For all the power of video and film, I am not giving up my pen. I am just much more likely to try to link essays to webcasts or videos. The best way for these two media to move forward, to inform and make change, is in tandem; together they are more than the sum of their parts.—Naomi Wolf

Nov. 13—Augustine of Hippo (354), Johann Eck (1486), Cyril Lucaris (1572), Charles Simon Favart (1710), William Shenstone (1714), Esaias Tegnér (1782), Edward John Trelawny (1792), Petar II Petrovic Njegos (1813), James (Clerk) Maxwell (1831), Ignacio M. Altamirano (1834), Joseph F. Smith (1838), Robert Louis Stevenson (1850), Louis D(embit) Brandeis (1856), Abraham Flexner and Bert Leston Taylor (1866), Helene Stöcker and Ariadna Tyrkova-Williams (1869), Max Dehn (1878), Vera (Louise) Caspary (1899), Gustav Heinrich Ralph "G. H. R." von Koenigswald (1902), Thomas Head Raddall (1903), Josef B. Kjellgren (1907), C. Vann Woodward (1908), Paul de Vree (1909), William Bradford Huie (1910), George Parkin Grant (1918), Motooer'sura (1924), Inez van Dullemen (1925), Fred R(oy) Harris and Nico Scheepmaker (1930), Garry (Kent) Marshall (1934), Peter Arnett (1934), George Leonard Carey and Thomas Augustine "Gus" Martin (1935), Wanda Coleman (1946), Gérald Godin (1938), George V. Higgins (1939), Arnold Rampersad (1941), John Steffler (1947), Robert Hilles (1951), Whoopi Goldberg (Caryn Johnson) and Jon Jefferson (1955), Ronald Shusett (1957), Edwin "Rick" Bakker (1961), Thilo Timothy Newman (1963), Ayaan Hirsi Ali (1969), Rivkah (1981).

He is smitten on the brain,—he reads and writes verses! I caught him in the act! Fools might say he was inspired; but I know it is the first and worst symptom of lunacy. All other maniacs have lucid intervals; some are curable; but the madness of poets, dogs, and musicians, is past hope. Earth possesses no remedy, science no cure.—Edward John Trelawny

Fiction is to the grown man what play is to the child; it is there that he changes the atmosphere and tenor of his life.—Robert Louis Stevenson

We're born with success. It is only others who point out our failures, and what they attribute to us as failure.—Whoopi Goldberg

Nov. 14—Janus Secundus (1511), Marie François Xavier Bichat (1771), Adam Gottlob Oehlenschläger (1779), Charles Lyell (1797), August F. Pott (1802), Jacob Abbott (1803), Robert J. Fruin (1823), August Senoa (1838), Frederick Jackson Turner (1861), Robert Smythe Hichens (1864), Jakob Schaffner (1875), René de Clerq (1877), Leopold Staff (1878), Jawaharlal Nehru (1889), Carlo E. Gadda and Evert S.J. Kruythoff (1893), Harold Collett Dent (1894), Walter Freeman (1895), Benjamin Fondane (1898), Aaron Copland (1900), Marya Mannes and Dick Powell (1904), Sanoesi Pane (1905), Louise Brooks (1906), Astrid Lindgren (1907), Harrison E. Salisbury (1908), Joseph R. McCarthy (1909), Norman MacCaig and Eric Lawson Malpass (1910), Eric John Crozier (1914), Edward Digby Baltzell (1915), Sherwood Schwartz (1916), Boutros Boutros Ghali (1922), Ornelio Martina (1930), Inger Frimansson (1944), Patrick Jake "P. J." O'Rourke (1947), Douglas Glover (1948), Carol Matas (1949), Cara Black (1951), Liaquat Ahamed (1952), Condoleezza Rice (1954), Gail Kathryn Anderson-Dargatz (1963), David Lindsay-Abaire (1969), Brad Vice (1973).

All my major works have been written in prison. . . . I would recommend prison not only to aspiring writers but to aspiring politicians, too.—Jawaharlal Nehru
Timing and arrogance are decisive factors in the successful use of talent.—Marya Mannes
When you say the name Gilligan, you know who that is. If a show is good, if it's written well, you should be able to erase the names of the characters saying the lines and still be able to know who said it. If you can't do that, the show will fail.—Sherwood Schwartz
Being a humorist is not a voluntary thing. You can tell this because in a situation where saying a funny thing will cause a lot of trouble, a humorist will still say the funny thing. No matter how inappropriate.—P. J. O'Rourke

Nov. 15—Madeleine de Scudéry (1607), Hermann von der Hardt (1660), Christoph von Graffenried (1661), Louis Bertrand Castel (1688), Eusebius Amort (1692), F. William Herschel (1738), Johann C. Lavater (1741), Joseph Quesnel (1746), Michel Chasles (1793), Aleksei N. Apuchtin and May Agnes Fleming (1840), Adolf Bartels amd Gerhart (Johann Robert) Hauptmann (1862), Cornelia Sorabji (1866), B. M. Bower (Bertha Muzzy Sinclair or Sinclair-Cowan) (1871), Robert (Pellevé de La Motte-Ango, marquis) de Flers (1872), Schack August Steenberg Krogh (1874), Franklin P. Adams (1881), Felix Frankfurter (1882), René Guénon (1886), Georgia O'Keefe (1887), Marianne Moore (1887), René Maran (1887), Richmal Crompton (1890), Erwin (Johannes Eugen) Rommel (1891), W. Averell Harriman (1891), Antoni Słonimski (1895), Sacheverell Sitwell (1897), Willy Alfredo (Willem Jue) (1898), George Bagby (Aaron Marc Stein) (1906), Astrid (Anna Emilia) Lindgren (1907), Arthur Haulot (1913), Lewis Elliott Chaze (1915), Giorgio Manganelli (1922), Yuli Daniel (1925), Thomas Williams (1926), James Graham "J. G." Ballard (1930), Jan Terlouw (1931), Jack Burns (1933), Ted Berrigan (1934), Gustaf Sobin (1935), Wolf Biermann (1936), Carole Nelson Douglas and Daniel (Manus) Pinkwater (1941), Alamgir Hashmi (1951), Georgie Born (1955), Nancy A. Henry and Ian Reid (1961), Tim Butcher and François Ozon (1967), James (Winston) Brady (1968), J. Mills Goodloe (1971), Sascha Rothchild (1976).

Having imagination, it takes you an hour to write a paragraph that, if you were unimaginative, would take you only a minute. Or you might not write the paragraph at all.—Franklin P. Adams

If technique is of no interest to a writer, I doubt that the writer is an artist.—Marianne Moore

A childhood without books—that would be no childhood. That would be like being shut out from the enchanted place where you can go and find the rarest kind of joy.—Astrid Lindgren

Nov. 16—Joost van den Vondel (1587), John Chardin (Jean-Baptiste Chardin) (1643), Abraham Alewijn (1684), Peter Andreas Heiberg (1758), Petronella Moens (1762), Louis-Honoré Fréchette (1839), W(illiam) C(hristopher) Handy (1873), Alexander A. Block (1880), Henri (Ferdinand M.J.) Bosco (1888), George S. Kaufman (1889), George Seldes (1890), Guo Moruo (1892), Eduard Bagritsky (Dzhubin) (1895), Michael Arlen (1895), Oswald Mosley (1896), Joan Lindsay (1896), Eddie Condon (1904), Frederik van der Meer (1904), Anton (Tom) Koolhaas (1912), Jean (Guttery(Fritz (1915), (Charles) Daws(on) Butler (1916), José Saramago (1922), Tamar (Renate Rubinstein) (1929), (Albert) Chinụa(lụmọgụ) Achebe (1930), Elizabeth Drew (1935), Robert Nozick (1938), Hugo Dittberner (1944), Ebby Thust (1947), Bonnie Greer (1948), William Kent Krueger and John Swartzwelder (1950), Paula Vogel (1951), Candas (Jane) Dorsey and Robin McKinley (1952), Griff Rhys Jones (1953), Andrea Barrett (1954), Evan (Tlesla) Ádams and Tahir Shah (1966), Craig Arnold (1967), Danny Wallace (1976).

At dramatic rehearsals, the only author that's better than an absent one is a dead one.—George S. Kaufman

The test of literature is, I suppose, whether we ourselves live more intensely for the reading of it.—Elizabeth Drew

What I write, if you have to label it, is crossover, and I think that much of the stuff that is called children's or YA is in fact crossover and is equally valid for anyone who likes to read fantasy.—Robin McKinley

Nov. 17—Johan van Beverwijck (1594), Pierre François le Courayer (1681), Salomeja Neris (S. Bacinskaite-Buciene) (1704), August Ferdinand Möbius (1790), Titian Ramsay Peale (1799), August Wilhelm Ambros (1816), Petko Slavejkov (1827), Joseph (Jules François Félix) Babinski (1857), Martin Allerdale Grainger (1874), Grace Abbott (1878), Crane Wilbur (1886), Sigurd Wesley Christiansen (1891), Mikhail Bakhtin (1895), Gregorio López y Fuentes (1895), Lev (Semyonovich) Vygotsky (1896), Roger Vitrac (1899), Eugene Paul "E.P." Wigner (1902), Wazyk (Adam Wagman) (1905), Gerald Savory (1909), Shelby (Dade) Foote (1916), Ludwig Freiherr von Hammerstein-Equord (1919), Henri Coulette (1927), Audrey (Grace Callahan) Thomas (1935), Dahlia Ravikovitch (1936), Peter (Edward) Cook (1937), Auberon Waugh (1939), Martin Scorsese (1942), Lorne Michaels (Lipowitz) (1944), Steven E. de Souza (1947), Rick Elice (1956), Christopher Paolini (1983).

I'm going to give the people what they want. Sensation, horror, shock. Send them out in the streets to tell their friends how wonderful it is to be scared to death.—Crane Wilbur

I don't want anything to do with anything mechanical between me and the paper, including a typewriter, and I don't even want a fountain pen between me and the paper.—Shelby Foote

Anyone wishing to communicate with Americans should do so by email, which has been specially invented for the purpose, involving neither physical proximity nor speech.—Auberon Waugh

I love studying Ancient History and seeing how empires rise and fall, sowing the seeds of their own destruction.—Martin Scorsese

Nov. 18—Cornelius Broere (1803), Asa Gray (1810), Adolf Erik Nordenskiöld (1832), Cesare Lombroso (Ezechia Marco Lombroso) (1835), Dorothy Dix (Elizabeth Meriwether Gilmer) (1861), Richard Dehmel (1863), Clarence (Shepard) Day (Jr.) (1874), Arthur C(ecil) Pigou (1877), Wyndham Lewis and Jacques Maritain (1882), Frances Marion (1888), Patrick M(aynard) S(tuart) Blackett (1897), Howard Thurman (1900), George Gallup (1901), Jorgen Nielsen (1902), Klaus Mann (1906), Halldis Vesaas-Moren (1907), Friedrich Weinreb (1910), Attilio Bertolucci (1911), Jaap Meijer (Saul van Messel) (1912), Madeline DeFrees (1919), Vassilis Vassilikos (1934), Sam Abrams, Rodney Hall, and Frank Joseph Kofsky (1935), Margaret E. Atwood (1939), James Welch (1940), Alan Dean Foster (1946), Frances Fyfield (1948), Tina McElroy Ansa (1949), Michael Swanwick (1950), Dennis Foon and Justin Raimondo (1951), Alan Moore (1953), Seán Mac Falls (1957), Michael Crummey (1965), Jorge Camacho (1966), Terrance Hayes (1971).

The world of books is the most remarkable creation of man. Nothing else . . . ever lasts. Monuments fall, nations perish, civilizations grow old and die out; and, after an era of darkness, new races build others. But in the world of books are volumes that have seen this happen again and again, and yet live on, still young, still as fresh as the day they were written, still telling men's hearts of the hearts of men centuries dead.—Clarence Day

I wish I had a formula, . . . that would be kind of, you know, this is what Chapter One is always like, and this is what Chapter Two is always like. But it isn't. I just have to plunge into it. And it's usually the one. . . that the voice of sanity and reason is telling me not to write. It's usually that one that I end up writing.—Margaret Atwood

A short story. . .can be held in the mind all in one piece. It's less like a building than a fiendish device. Every bit of it must be cunningly . . . crafted to fit together perfectly and without waste so it can perform its task with absolute precision.—Michael Swanwick

Nov. 19—Lieuwe van Aitzema (1600), Michail V. Lomonosov (1711), Karl Schwarz (1812), Wilhelm Dilthey (1833), Georg Hermann Quincke (1834), Richard (Heinrich Ludwig) Avenarius (1843), John Antoine Nau (Eugène Léon Édouard Torquet) (1860), Amelia Josephine Burr (1878) Karel van den Oever (1879), Hjalmar Fredrik Elgerus Bergman (1883), Fernand Crommelynck (1886), Arthur R(obert) von Hippel (1898), (John Orley) Allen Tate (1899), Anna Seghers (Netty Radvanyi-Reiling) (1900), Jack (Warner) Schaefer (1907), Peter Drucker (1909), Adrian Conan Doyle (1910), William (Alexander) Attaway and Mary Elizabeth Counselman (1911), George E(mil) Palade (1912), Peter (Sturges) Ruckman (1921), Mark Harris, Yuri Knorozov, and (Stanley) Keith Runcorn (1922), Zygmunt Bauman (1925), Jeane J. Kirkpatrick (1926), Joanne Kyger (1934), Dick Cavett (1936), Sharon (Stuart) Olds (1942), Nigel Bennett (1949), Anthony Dey Hoagland (1953), Sam Hamm (1955), Ann Curry (1956), Annette Gordon-Reed and Charles Stuart "Charlie" Kaufman (1958), Djángo Haskins and Ryukishi (1973).

According to its doctors, my one intransigent desire is to have been a Confederate general, and because I could not or would not become anything else, I set up for poet and began to invent fictions about the personal ambitions that my society has no use for.—Allen Tate

You know the fairy tale about the man who died, don't you? He was waiting in Eternity to find out what the Lord had decided to do with him. He waited and waited, for one year, ten years, a hundred years. He begged and pleaded for a decision. Finally he couldn't bear the waiting any longer. Then they said to him: 'What do you think you're waiting for? You've been in Hell for a long time already. —Anna Seghers

Sloppy language leads to sloppy thought, and sloppy thought to sloppy legislation.—Dick Cavett

Nov. 20—Abraham de Wicquefort (1606), Avvakum Petrovich (1621), Daniel Ernst Jablonski (1660), Thomas Chatterton (1752), le doyen Bridel (Philippe Sirice Bridel) (1757), Karl Friedrich Eichhorn (1781), François-Réal Angers (1812), Selma Lagerlöf (1858), Gerard W. Kernkamp (1864), Arthur Guiterman and William H. Kilpatrick (1871), Franz Pfemfert (1879), Norman Thomas (1884), Karl von Frisch (1886), Edwin Hubble (1889), Yevgenia Ginzburg (1896), Chester Gould (1900), Wolfgang Kunkel (1902), Ishtiaq Hussain Qureshi (1903), Henri-Georges Clouzot (1907), Alistair Cooke (1908), Anna Pauline "Pauli" Murray (1910), John Frederick Nims (1913), Robert A. Bruce and Thomas (Matthew) McGrath (1916), Robert C. Byrd (Cornelius Calvin Sale Jr.) (1917), Earling Carothers "Jim" Garrison (1921), Nadine Gordimer (1923), Benoit Mandelbrot (1924), Robert Francis "Bobby" Kennedy (1925), Donald Richard "Don" DeLillo (1936), Viktoriya Tokareva (1937), George Swede (Juris Puriņš) (1940), Haseena Moin (1941), Joseph Robinette "Joe" Biden Jr. (1942), Rachid Mimouni (1945), Judy Woodruff (1946), John R(obert) Bolton (1948), Orlando Figes (1959), Larry Karaszewski (1961), Jill Thompson (1966), Sheema Kalbasi (1972).

A professional is someone who can do his best work when he doesn't feel like it.—**Alistair Cooke**

A serious person should try to write posthumously.—**Nadine Gordimer**

I don't see why it matters what is written. Not when it's about people. It can always be crossed out.—**Jill Thompson**

Nov. 21—John Bale (1495), Carolus Scribani (1561), Catharina Questiers (1637), Carlo Fragoni (1692), Voltaire (Francois-Marie Arouet) (1694), Friedrich (Daniel Ernst) Schleiermacher (1768), William Beaumont (1785), Zeng Guofan (1811), Peter A. de Genestet (1829), Benjamin Paul Blood (1832), Désiré-Félicien-François-Joseph Mercier (1851), Benedict XV (Giacomo Paolo Giovanni Battista della Chiesa) (1854), Joao da Cruz (1861), Arthur Quiller-Couch (1863), Mary Johnston (1870), Franz Hessel (1880), Harold G. Nicolson (1886), Mollie Steimer (Marthe Alperine) (1897), James Alonzo "Jim" Bishop (1907), Elizabeth George Speare (1908), Anne Bolt (1912), John Edward Boulting and Roy Alfred Clarence Boulting (1913), William C. Heine (1919), Christopher (Reuel) Tolkien (1924), Johan "Poncke" Princen (1925), Marilyn French and Laurier LaPierre (1929), Brock Brower and Revaz Dogonadze (1931), Laurence Luckinbill (1934), Tina Howe and Margaret Julia "Marlo" Thomas (1937), Richard "Dick" Marcinko (1940), Richard Denner (1941), Harold Ramis (1944), Tina Brown (1953), Kiki Carter (b. Kimberli Wilson) (1957), Moisés Kaufman (1963), Christopher Noxon (1968), Alec Brownstein (1980).

The multitude of books is making us ignorant.—**Voltaire**

Whenever you feel an impulse to perpetuate a piece of exceptionally fine writing, obey it . . . and delete it before sending your manuscript to the press.—**Arthur Quiller-Couch**

What makes a good writer of history is a guy who is suspicious. Suspicion marks the real difference between the man who wants to write honest history and the one who'd rather write a good story. —**Jim Bishop**

My books are water; those of the great geniuses are wine— everybody drinks water.—**Marilyn French**

I always claim that the writer has done 90 percent of the director's work.—**Harold Ramis**

The Brazilian poet Vinicius de Moraes wrote that beauty is fundamental. Well, with the poet's permission, so is courage.—**Tina Brown**

Nov. 22—Francis Willughby (1635), Hryhorii Skovoroda (1722), George Eliot (Mary Anne Evans) (1819), Friedrich von Bernhardi (1849), Paul-Henri-Benjamin Baluet d'Estournelles, baron de Constant de Rébecque (1852), George Gissing (1857), André Gide (1869), Georges Rency (1875), Endre Ady (1877), Syed Sulaiman Nadvi (1884), Charles de Gaulle (1890), Erik Lindahl (1891), Nikolai S. Tichonov (1896), Paul Oswald Ahnert (1897), Hoagland Howard "Hoagy" Carmichael (1899), Tom Macdonald (1900), Nancy Wilson Ross (1901), James Burnham (1905), Michael Balfour (1908), Peter Woolridge Townsend (1914), Brian (Brendon Talbot) Cleeve (1921). Peter (Reginald Frederick) Hall (1930), Richard Emil Braun (1934), Terence Van "Terry" Gilliam (1940), Nicholas Dante (1941), William Kotzwinkle (1943), Valerie Wilson Wesley (1947), David Pietrusza (1949), Jamie Lee Curtis (1958), Léos Carax (1960), Mariel Hemingway and Randal L. Schwartz (1961), Victor Pelevin (1962), Jason Starr (1966), Marjane Satrapi (1969), Stel Pavlou (1970), Jennifer Nicole Mascia (1977), Alasdair Duncan (1982), Suresh Guptara and Jyoti Guptara (1988).

Correct English is the slang of prigs who write history and essays.—George Eliot
The public which reads, in any sense of the word worth considering, is very, very small; the public which would feel no lack if all book printing ceased tomorrow is enormous.—George Gissing
What would there be in a story of happiness? Only what prepares it, only what destroys it can be told.—André Gide
You get trapped by stories. Though I've got this reputation for being out of control, it's not true, it just happens to be a more interesting story than the truth.—Terry Gilliam

Nov. 23—Prospero Alpini (1553), John Wallis (1616), Jean Mabillon (1632), Johann K. Amman (1669), Thomas Birch (1705), Pierre Charles Le Monnier (1715), François-Noël "Gracchus" Babeuf (1760), Michail P. Pogodin (1800), Isaac Todhunter (1820), Johannes Diderik van der Waals (1837), Francis Saltus Saltus (1849), (Horatio) Gilbert (George) Parker (1862), Anatoly Lunacharsky (1875), Herman Baccaert and Jose Clemente Orozco (1883), Joris Vriamont (1896), Nirad C. Chaudhuri (1897), Norman Hunter (1899), Aaron Bank (1902), Nelson S. Bond and Leendert P. J. Braat (1908), Nigel Tranter (1909), Wilson Tucker (Arthur Wilson "Bob" Tucker) (1914), Patricia Kathleen "P. K." Page (1916), Hugh Joseph Charles James L'Etang (1917), Peter Strawson (1919), Paul Celan (Antschell) (1920), Gloria Whelan (1923), Colin Turnbull (1924), Christopher Logue (1926), Guy Davenport (1927), Jerrold Lewis "Jerry" Bock (1928), Hal Lindsey (1929), Ali Shariati (1933), Rita Rossi Colwell and Robert Towne (1934), Robert Barnard (1936), (b. William Frederick "Bill" Bissett (1939), Joe Eszterhas and Jose Torikens (1944), Bruce Vilanch (1948), Gayl Jones (1949), David Lerner (1951), Steven (Karl Zoltán) Brust (1955), Robin (René) Roberts (1960), Keith Ablow (1961), Jennifer Michael Hecht (1965), Hamid Hassani and Kirsty Young (1968).

A creative man is motivated by the desire to achieve, not by the desire to beat others.—Colin Turnbull

If you have a good ear for dialogue, you just can't help thinking about the way people talk. You're drawn to it. And the obsessive interest in it forces you to develop it. You almost can't help yourself.—Robert Towne

If you look at a testimony of love from 2,000 years ago it can still exactly speak to you, whereas medical advice from only 100 years ago is ridiculous.—Jennifer Michael Hecht

Nov. 24—Charles, Duke of Orléans (1394), Juan Martínez de Jáuregui y Aguilar (1583), Etienne Baluze (1630), Baruch "Benedict" de Spinoza (1632), Willem Bachiene (1712), Laurence Sterne (1713), Thomas Dick (1774), Ludwig Bechstein (1801), Carlo Collodi (Carlo Lorenzini) (1826), Frances (Eliza) Hodgson Burnett (1849), Harry Thurston Peck (1856), Scott Joplin (1868), Alben W. Barkley (1877), Mark N. Tod (1878), Al Christie (1881), Margaret Caroline Anderson (1886), Dale Carnegie and Fredrick Willius (1888), Cissy van Marxfield (Setske Beek-de Haan) (1889), Ward Morehouse (1899), Jerzy (Bonawentura) Toeplitz (1900), Fernand Braudel (1902), Harry Kemelman (1908), Hotze de Roos (1909), Bernardus Maria Ignatius "Bernard" Delfgaauw and Garson Kanin (1912), Forrest J. Ackerman (1916), John Silverlight (1919), John V(liet) Lindsay (1921), William F. Buckley Jr. and Alun Owen (1925), Paul Blackburn, Tsung-Dao "T. D." Lee, and Alan Owen (1926), Ahmadou Kourouma (1927), Martin Charnin (1934), Eric (Hamilton) Wilson (1940), William "Billy" Connolly Jr. and Marlin Fitzwater (1942), Jules Deelder, Claudia Dreifus, and Ibrahim Gambari (1944), Caroline Courtney, Melinda Wright, Lydia Hitchcock, Penny Jordan, and Annie Groves (Penelope "Penny" Jones Halsall) (1946), Spider Robinson (1948), Arundhati Roy and Mark Winegardner (1961), Peter (Franz) Schweizer (1964), Gregory Pardlo (1968), Marlon James (1970), Kevin Loring (1974), Thomas Kohnstamm (1975).

All things excellent are as difficult as they are rare.—Baruch Spinoza

I chose to write the kind of romance I love best—one with a sheikh hero.—Penny Jordan

I do what I do, and write what I write, without calculating what is worth what and so on. Fortunately, I am not a banker or an accountant. I feel that there is a time when a political statement needs to be made and I make it.—Arundhati Roy

Nov. 25—Toegye (Yi Hwang) (1501), Joost de Damhoudere (1507), Lope Felix de Vega (1562), Gerhard Tersteegen (1697), Jean-François Séguier (1703), Charles-Michel de l'Épée (1712), Gustaf Fredrik Gyllenborg (1731), Mary Anne Schimmelpenninck (1778), Julius Robert von Mayer (1814), John Bigelow (1817), Franjo Racki (1828), Andrew Carnegie (1835), Hugo Verriest (1840), Ernst Schröder (1841), Karl F. Benz (1844), José Maria de Eça de Queiroz (1845), Carrie (Amelia Moore) Nation (1846), Alfred Capus (1858), Alphonso J. "Al" Jennings (1863), Ben(jamin Barr) Lindsey (1869), Winthrop Ames and Maurice Denis (1870), Harley Granville-Barker (1877), Georg Kaiser (1878), Elsie J. Oxenham and Leonard S. Woolf (1880), John XXIII (Angelo Giuseppe Roncalli) (1881), Harvey Spencer Lewis (1883), Nikolai Vavilov (1887), Isaac Rosenberg (1890), Helen Hooven Santmyer (1895), Virgil Thomson (1896), William Riley "W. R." Burnett (1899), Ba Jin (Li Yaotang) (1904), Hugh Davson (1909), Leon Poliakov (1910), Jack Davies and Lewis Thomas (1913), Léon Zitrone (1914), Ann Stanford (1916), Takaaki Yoshimoto (1924), Poul (William) Anderson and Murray Schisgal (1926), Ella Leffland (1931), Martin Feldstein (1939), Gerald Seymour and Riaz Ahmed Gohar Shahi (1941), Rosa Von Praunheim (Holger Bernhard Bruno Mischwitzky) (1942), Julie Smith and Ben Stein (1944), Alexis Wright (1950), Charlaine Harris Schulz (1951), (Jayson) Tyler Brûlé (1968), Eliot Schrefer (1978).

The grinding of the intellect is for most people as painful as a dentist's drill.—Leonard Woolf

We live with our archetypes, but can we live in them?—Poul Anderson

We have to think big. We have to imagine big, and that's part of the problem. We're letting other people imagine and lead us down what paths they want to take us. Sometimes they're very limited in the way their ideas are constructed. We need to imagine much more broadly. That's the work of a writer, and more writers should look at it.—Alexis Wright

Nov. 26—Princess Catherine of Portugal (1436), William Derham (1657), Pedro de Peralta y Barnuevo (1663), Jean Jacques d'Ortous de Mairan (1678), Theophilus Cibber (1703), William Cowper (1731), Charles-Joseph Panckoucke (1736), Georg Forster (1754), Ellen Gould White (1827), Mary Edwards Walker (1832), William Barclay "Bat" Masterson (1853), Ferdinand de Saussure (1857), (Mark) Aurel Stein (1862), Herman Gorter (1864), Edmond Fleg(enheimer) (1874), Mihály Babits (1883), Heinrich Brüning (1885), Albert Dieudonné (1889), Norbert Wiener (1894), Karl Ziegler (1898), George Emlyn Williams (1905), Ruth Myrtle "R. M." Patrick (1907), Eugène Ionesco (1909), Samuel "Sammy" Herman Reshevsky (1911), Eric Sevareid (1912), Owen (Vincent) Dodson (1914), Frederik Pohl (1919), Paul T.B. Rodenko (1920), Françoise Gilot (1921), Charles M. Schulz (1922), Adolfo Perez Esquivel (1931), Margaret Boden (1936), Rod(ney) Jory (1938), George F. Jewsbury (1941), Marilynne (Summers) Robinson (1943), Andreas Schroeder (1946), David Poyer (1949) Rosalind "Roz" Chast (1954), Tracy (Raye) Hickman (1955), Nico Slothouwer (1956).

Knowledge is proud that it knows so much; wisdom is humble that it knows no more.—William Cowper
The idea that myth is the opposite of knowledge, or the opposite of truth, is simply to disallow it. It is like saying poetry is the opposite of truth.—Marilynne Robinson
It is no accident that every human culture passes on its values in the form of story.—David Poyer

Nov. 27—Robbert Robbertsz (le Canu) (1563), Pierre Dupuy (1582), Valerius Andreas (Walter Driessens) (1588), Friedrich Rudolf Ludwig Canitz (1654), Anders Celsius (1701), Robert Lowth (1710), Paul van Hemert (1756), Joachim George le Sage ten Broek (1775), Frances Anne "Fanny" Kemble (1809), Bankim Chandra Chatterji (1838), Aleksei N. Apuchtin (1840), Jose Asunción Silva (1865), Charles A. Beard, Eugene Walter, and Chaim Weizmann (1874), Wladyslaw Orkan (Szmaciarz-Smreczynsky) (1875), Jatindramohan Bagchi (1878), Pedro Salinas y Serrano (1892), Giovanni B. Angioletti and Fredric Warburg (1896), Marie-Angele "Jovette" Alice Bernier (1900, L(yon) Sprague de Camp (1907), James (Rufus) Agee and Anatoly Maltsev (1909), Fe del Mundo (1911), Yves Thériault (1915), Francis Dayle "Chick" Hearn (1916), John Richard Ravensdale (1920), Ole Sarvig (1921), Ernie Wise (Ernest Wiseman) (1925), Barbara Anderson and John Maddox (1925), Kirby Doyle (b. Stanton Doyle) (1932), Jacques Godbout (1933), Gail Sheehy (1937), Ingrid Pitt (1937), Bruce Lee (Lee Jun-fan) (1940), Marilyn Hacker (1942), Nicole Brossard (1943), Teri Lynn DeSario (1951), Bill Nye (William Sanford "Bill" Nye) (1955), Caroline Bouvier Kennedy-Schlossberg (1957), Kevin Henkes (1960), Steve Oedekerk (1961).

There is no mistaking the dismay on the face of a writer who has just heard that his brain child is a deformed idiot.—L. Sprague de Camp

Creativity can be described as letting go of certainties.—Gail Sheehy

To be a poet is to place pleasure, beauty and sensual delights front and centre, it means having a predilection for debauchery.—Nicole Brossard

Nov. 28—Pietro Sforza (1607), John Bunyan (1628), William Blake (1757), Luke Howard (1772), (Georg Christian) August Kestner (1777), Victor Cousin (1792), Carl Jonas Love Almqvist (1793), John Lloyd Stephens (1805), Friedrich Engels (1820), James Allen (1864), Louis Dantin (Eugène Seers) (1865), Vincent O'Sullivan (1868), Jozef van Mierlo (1878), Alexander A. Block (1880), Stefan Zweig (1881), John Willard (1885), Gregorio Perfecto (1891), Brooks Atkinson (1894), Dawn Powell (1896), Uno Choyo and Marcus (Aurelius) Goodrich (1897), Yuri N. Libedinski (1898), Victor Jory (1902), Nancy Mitford (1904), Alberto Moravia (Pincherle) (1907), Claude Lévi-Strauss, Mary Oppen, and Richard Pitts Powell (1908), Václav Renč (1911), Owen (Vincent) Dodson (1914), Helen Delich Bentley (1923), Arthur Melvin Okun (1928), George Ramsay Cook, Rinus Ferdinandusse, and Dervla Murphy (1931), Terence Frisby (1932), Randolph Stow (1935), Gary Hart (Gary Warren Hartpence) (1936), Kenneth Wayne "Ken" Brewer (1941), Rita Mae Brown (1944), Susan Spencer (1946), Agnieszka Holland, Alan (Paige) Lightman, and Bruce Vilanch (1948), Victor Ostrovsky and Paul (Allen Wood) Shaffer (1949), Ed Harris (1950), Diedre Murray (1951), Jeffrey Byron (1955), Alfonso Cuarón (1961), Paul Dinello and Jon Stewart (Jonathan Stuart Leibowitz) (1962), Erwin Mortier (1965), Samuel Lincoln "Sam" Seder (1966), Eka Kurniawan (1975).

Good plays drive bad playgoers crazy.—Brooks Atkinson
The ratio of literacy to illiteracy is constant, but nowadays the illiterates can read.—Alberto Moravia
Virginia Woolf said that writers must be androgynous. I'll go a step further. You must be bisexual.—Rita Mae Brown
Writing never had the immediate gratification I was looking for.—Paul Shaffer

Nov. 29—Joachim Vadian (Joachim von Watt) (1484), John Ray (1627), Pierre André Latreille (1762), Andres Bello (1781), Amos Bronson Alcott (1799), Wilhelm Hauff (1802), Christian Doppler (1803), Gottfried Semper (1803), Wendell Phillips (1811), Fran Miklošič (1813), George Brown and (William) Ellery Channing (1818), Jean-Martin Charcot (1825), Louisa May Alcott (1832), Ludwig Anzengruber (1839), Ambrose Fleming (1849), Grace (Elizabeth) King (1851), Theodor Escherich (1857), (Edward) Alan Sullivan (1868), Andre Lichtenberger (1870), Anna Bahr-Mildenburg (1872), (António Caetano de Abreu Freire) Egas Moniz (1874), Francis Dodd (1874), Philip L. Carret (1896), Emiel van Hemeldonck (1897), Clive Staples "C. S." Lewis (1898), Carlo Levi (1902), Georges Poulet (1902), Charles S(tanley) Strong and Luis (d'Antin) Van Rooten (1906), Nagerkoyil Sudalaimuthu "Kalaivanar" Krishnan (1908), Rupert Davies (1909), Edith Tilton Penrose (1914), Taisen Deshimaru (1914), Merle (Robert) Travis (1917), Herb Shriner (Herbert Arthur Schriner) (1918), Madeleine L'Engle (Franklin) (1918), Kahil Gibran (1922), Paul Martin Simon (1928), Shintaro "Katsu-shin" Katsu (Toshio Okumura) (1931), Jacques Chirac (1932), David Reuben (1933), William Weaks "Willie" Morris (1934), Diane Ladd (b. Rose Diane Ladner) (1935), Gerti Tetzner (1936), Margaret "Maggie" Thompson (1942), Sue Miller (1943), David Kirby (1944), Silvio Rodríguez (1946), Petra Kelly (Petra Karin Lehmann) (1947), Garry Shandling (1949), Kevin O'Donnell Jr. (1950), Christine Pascal (1952), Joel (David) Coen (1954), Léo (Gordon) Laporte (1956), Mario Petrucci (1954), Cork Graham (1964), Sarah Jones (1973), Jennifer Lynette "Jenn" Sterger (1983).

Good books, like good friends, are few and chosen; the more select, the more enjoyable.—Louisa May Alcott

He that uses many words for the explaining any subject doth, like the cuttlefish, hide himself for the most part in his own ink. —John Ray

Sleep on your writing; . . . review it of an afternoon; digest it after a meal; let it sleep in your drawer a twelvemonth; never venture a whisper about it to your friend, if he be an author especially. —A. Bronson Alcott

Nov. 30—Veronica Gambara (1485), Andrés de Urdaneta (1498), Andrea Palladio (Andrea di Pietro della Gondola) (1508), Philip Sidney (1554), Louis-Sébastien Le Nain de Tillemont (1637), Jonathan Swift (1667), John Toland (1670), Ernst Chladni (1756), Jędrzej Śniadecki (1768), Louise-Victorine Ackermann and Hermann Kurz (1813), (Christian Matthias) Theodor Mommsen (1817), Mary Langdon/ Sydney A. Story Jr. (Mary Hayden [Green] Pike) (1824), Ernest H. Baillon (1827), Jedediah Hotchkiss (1828), Mark Twain (Samuel Langhorn Clemens) (1835), Jozsef Kiss (1843), Jagdish Chandra Bose (1858), Dr. John Alexander McCrae (1872), Winston (Leonard Spencer) Churchill and Lucy Maud "L. M." Montgomery (1874), Edgar D. Adrian (1889), Oege Bakker (1890), Israel Joshua Singer (1893), Donald Ogden Stewart (1894), Korneel Goossens and Geoffrey (Edward West) Household (1900), Philip Burton (1904), John Dickson Carr (1906), Jacques Barzun (1907), Paul Frederic Bowles (1910), Gordon Parks (1912), John K. M. McCaffery (1913), Robert Lax (1915), John Franklin Bardin (1916), Jan Elburg (Joannes Gommert Elburg) and Anne S. Wadman (1919), Eugene Ferdinand Walter Jr. (1921), Shirley (Anita St. Hill) Chisholm and Allan Sherman (1924), Leo Connellan (1928), G(eorge) Gordon Liddy (1930), Margot Zemach (1931), Abbot Howard "Abbie" Hoffman (1936), Adeline Yen Mah and Richard Threlkeld (1937), Milton Terrence "M. T." Kelly (1946), Sergio Badilla Castillo and David Mamet (1947), Keith Giffen (1952), Joël Champetier and Colin Mochrie (1957), Lorraine Kelly (1959), Daniel Keys Moran (1962), Lee Klein and Ben Stiller (1965), Wil Mara and David Nicholls (1966), David Auburn (1969), Nicole Blackman (1971), Emil Steiner (1978).

Books, the children of the brain.—Jonathan Swift
Writing is easy. All you have to do is cross out the wrong words. —Mark Twain

Writing a book is an adventure. To begin with it is a toy and an amusement. Then it becomes a mistress, then it becomes a master, then it becomes a tyrant. The last phase is that just as you are about to be reconciled to your servitude, you kill the monster and fling him to the public.—Winston Churchill

Born in December

Dec. 1—Anna Comnena (1083), Tadeáš Hájek (1525), Philippus Rovenius (Filips van Rouveen) (1573), Nicolas-Claude Fabri de Peiresc (1580), A. L. Karschin (1722), Nikolai Mikhailovich Karamzin (1766), Francis Fisher Browne (1843), Julia Ann (Davis) Moore (1847), George Sterling (1869), Valery Bryusov (1873), Willem E. Crown, Pierre Kemp, and Rex (Todhunter) Stout (1886), Ernst Toller (1893), Henry Williamson (1895), Charles G(randison) Finney (1905), Jan Koplowitz (1909), Pierre Martory (1920), George Harry Bowering and Woody Allen (Allan Stewart Konigsberg) (1935), John Crowley (1942), Tahar Ben Jelloun and Daniel Pennac (1944), Bette Midler (1945), John Schlimm (1971), Suzy Kassem (1975), Joel A. Sutherland (1980).

A character who is thought-out is not born, he or she is contrived. A born character is round, a thought-out character is flat.—Rex Stout

Authors are ordinary people who usually start to live apart, in the imagination, because they don't fit in with normal, healthy people. —Henry Williamson

I don't want to achieve immortality through my work. I want to achieve it through not dying.—Woody Allen

Writing a book is not as tough as it is to haul thirty-five people around the country and sweat like a horse five nights a week.—Bette Midler

Dec. 2—Carlin (Carlo Antonio Bertinazzi) (1710), Robert Bloomfield (1766), Francis Jammes (1868), Nikos Kazantzákis (1885), Rewi Alley (1897), Emery Bonett (Felicity Winifred Carter) (1906), Hy Gardner (1908), Helen Adam (1909), Russell Lynes (1910), Gerald Allan "Jerry" Sohl Sr. (1913), Adolph Green (1914), Jon Silkin (1930), David Hackett Fischer (1935), John B. Balaban (1943), Botho Strauß (1944), Bob Perelman (1947), T. Coraghessan Boyle (1948), Fae Myenne Ng (1956), James Brock, Eric L. Harry, and George Saunders (1958), Ann Patchett (1963).

No author dislikes to be edited as much as he dislikes not to be published.—Russell Lynes

I'd read somewhere that nine out of ten adults in Alaska had a drinking problem. I could believe it. Snow, ice, sleet, wind, the dark night of the soul: what else were you supposed to do?
—T. Coraghessan Boyle

When you read a short story, you come out a little more aware and a little more in love with the world around you.—George Saunders

I don't write for an audience, I don't think whether my book will sell, I don't sell it before I finish writing it.—Ann Patchett

Dec. 3—France Preseren (1800), Joseph Conrad (Józef Teodor Konrad Korzeniowski) (1857), J(ohn Brown) Gordon Coogler (1865), Kate O'Brien (1897), Eli Mandel (1922), Francisco Sionil José (1924), Morley Torgov (1927), Jean-Luc Godard (1930), Franz Josef Degenhardt (1931), Alfred (Fox) Uhry (1936), Walter A(llen) McDougall (1946), Melvin Kenneth "Mel" Smith (1952), Patrick Chamoiseau (1953), Sheree Fitch (1956), Hermann Heijermans (1964).

History repeats itself, but the special call of an art which has passed away is never reproduced. It is as utterly gone out of the world as the song of a destroyed wild bird.—Joseph Conrad

A story should have a beginning, a middle, and an end . . . but not necessarily in that order.—Jean Luc Godard

It's a pragmatist's business, comedy. Start off with good intentions and references to the Pompidou Centre and you end up with boiled sweets and a pantomime cow.—Mel Smith

Dec. 4—Heinrich Meibom (1555), Jean Chapelain (1595), Gasparo Gozzi (1713), Emil Aarestrup (1800), Frances Power Cobbe (1822), Samuel Butler (1835), Hannes Thordur Hafstein (1861), Rainer Maria Rilke (1875), Katharine Susannah Prichard (1883), Douwe Hermans Kiestra (Harm Harmstra) (1899), Cornell (George Hopley-) Woodrich (1903), Jo Boer (1907), John W. Pritchard (Ian Wallace) (1912), Ely Jacques Kahn Jr. (1916), Sigrid de Lima (1921), Anne (Carroll) George (1927), Ronald Balfour "Ronnie" Corbett (1930), Douglas Maitland Gibson (1943), Anne (Carroll) Bell (1927), and Ursula Krechel (1947), Steven Jay "Jesse" Bernstein (1950), Jeramy Dodds (1974).

Books are like imprisoned souls till someone takes them down from a shelf and frees them.—Samuel Butler

Find out the reason that commands you to write; see whether it has spread its roots into the very depth of your heart; confess to yourself you would have to die if you were forbidden to write.
—Rainer Maria Rilke

Don't sacrifice your life to work and ideals. The most important things in life are human relations. I found that out too late.
—Katharine Susannah Prichard

Dec. 5—Janus Dousa, (Johan van de Does) (1545), Fyodor Ivanovich Tyutchev (1803), Afanasy Fet (1820), Christina Rossetti (1830), Alice Brown (1857), Condé Benoist Pallen (1858), Antti Aarne (1867), Ellis Parker Butler (1869), Celia Dropkin (1887), (Lady Huxley) Juliette Baillot (1896), Nunnally Johnson (1897), Walter Elias "Walt" Disney (1901), Abraham L. Polonsky (1910), Hans Hellmut Kirst (1914), Wladimir Fjodorowitsch Tendrjakow (1923), John A(lfred) Williams (1925), Leonard R. N. Ashley (1928), Joan Didion (1934), Calvin Trillin (1935), James Lee Burke (1936), Horst Bastian (1939), Hanif Kureishi (1954), Lydia Millet (1968).

A dramatic writer should never tell anything he can show.—Nunnally Johnson

Was it only by dreaming or writing that I could find out what I thought?—Joan Didion

I actually think of being funny as an odd turn of mind, like a mild disability, some weird way of looking at the world that you can't get rid of.—Calvin Trillin

Anna Karenina is just a story about a woman falling in love with a bloke who is not her husband. It's gossip, rubbish—on the other hand, it's the deepest story there could be about social transgression, about love, betrayal, duty, children.—Hanif Kureishi

Dec. 6—Elizabeth Carter (1717), S. von Laroche (1731), Thomas Ingoldsby (Richard Harris Barham) (1788), Susanna (Strickland) Moodie (1803), James Gordon (1833), William S(urrey) Hart (1864), Albrecht Schaeffer (1885), Joyce Kilmer (1886), F. Osbert S. Sitwell (1892), O. W. Cisek (1897), Mary Ethel Barnard (1909), William P(eter) McGivern (1918), Donald (Lamont) Jack (1924), Peter Handke (1942), John Reynolds Gardiner (1944), Linda Barnes (1949), Tomson Highway (1951), Arthur Golden (1956) Julia (Mae Spicher) Kasdorf (1962).

> 'Twas now the very witching time of night,
> When churchyards groan, and graves give up their dead,
> And many a mischievous, enfranchised sprite
> Had long since burst his bonds of stone or lead,
> And hurried off, with schoolboy-like delight,
> To play his pranks near some poor wretch's bed,
> Sleeping, perhaps serenely as a porpoise,
> Nor dreaming of this fiendish Habeas Corpus.
> —Thomas Ingoldsby

The only reason a road is good as every wanderer knows Is just because of the homes, the homes, the homes to which one goes.—Joyce Kilmer

The only difference between an artist and a lunatic is, perhaps, that the artist has the restraint or courtesy . . . to conceal the intensity of his obsession from all except those similarly afflicted.—Osbert Sitwell

Dec. 7—Allan Cunningham (1784), Paul Adam (1862), Cale Young Rice (1872), Willa (Sibert) Cather (1873), Akiko Yosano (1878), Joyce Cary (1888), Matthew Heywood Campbell Broun (1888), John R(oberts) Tunis (1889), Jacques Gans (1908), John Victor Maxwell "Max" Braithwaite (1911), Leigh (Douglass) Brackett (1915), Jean-Paul Audet (1918), Tatamkulu Afrika (1920), Noam Chomsky (1928), Christopher (Robin) Nicole (1930), Kumar Shahani (1940), Susan Isaacs (1943), Lucy (Angela) Hughes-Hallett (1951), Guillermo Verdecchia (1962), John Joseph "J. R." Moehringer (1964), Nikola Wapzarow (1975).

The average editor can't help feeling that telling a writer to do something is almost the same thing as performing it himself. —Heywood Campbell Broun

There are only two or three human stories, and they go on repeating themselves as fiercely as if they had never happened before.—Willa Cather

A novel should be an experience and convey an emotional truth rather than arguments.—Joyce Cary

Books. It's that simple. A book is the only real escape from this fallen world. Aside from death.—J. R. Moehringer

Dec. 8—Horace (Quintus Horatius Flaccus) (65 BCE), John Althuysen (1715), Johann G. von Zimmermann (1728), Henry Timrod (1829), Bjørnstjerne Bjørnson and George Alfred "G. A." Henty (1832), Georges Feydeau (1862), John Cowper "J. C." Powys (1872), Padraic Colum (1881), Kenneth (Lewis) Roberts (1885), W(illiam) Hervey Allen (1889), James (Grover) Thurber and Elzie Crisler "E. C." Segar (1894), Josephine Bell (Doris Bell Collier) (1897), Richard (Dafydd Vivian) Llewellyn (Lloyd) (1906), Stephen (Caroyl) Shadegg (1909), Jura Soyfer (1912), Delmore Schwartz (1913), Ernest Lehman and George Scheuer (1915), Carmen Martín Gaite (1925), Clysle Julius "C. J." Stevens (1927), Goffredo Parise (1929), John Morressy and Sherwin Bernard Nuland (Shepsel Ber Nudelman) (1930), Jim Morrison (1943), James (Vincent) Tate (1943), John Banville (1945), Ron Hansen (1947), Mary (Catherine) Gordon (1949), William McGuire "Bill" Bryson (1951), Ann (Hart) Coulter (1961).

Let it be kept until the ninth year, the manuscript put away at home: you may destroy whatever you haven't published; once out, what you've said can't be stopped.—Horace

The devoted writer of humor must continue to try to come as close to the truth as he can, even if he gets burned in the process, but I don't think he will get too badly burned. His faith in the good will, the soundness, and the sense of humor of his countrymen will always serve as his asbestos curtain.—James Thurber

All poets' wives have rotten lives Their husbands look at them like knives.—Delmore Schwartz

It was actually a women's writing group I belonged to in graduate school that gave me the courage to move from poetry to fiction.—Mary Gordon

Dec. 9—John Milton (1608), George Grossmith (1847), Joel Chandler Harris (1848), Laura Goodman Salverson (1890), Leonie Fuller Adams (1899), Lawrence Edward Watkin (1901), Dalton Trumbo (1905), Herbert Huncke (1915), Wolfgang Hildesheimer (1916), Jan Křesadlo (1926), Buck Henry (Henry Zuckerman) (1930), (Erman) Louie Clay (b. Erman Louie Crew Jr.) (1936), Allan Reed Folsom (1941), Joe McGinniss (1942), Ki Longfellow (1944), Susanna Moore (1945), Ann Hood (1956).

As good almost kill a man as kill a good book: who kills a man kills a reasonable creature, God's image, but he who destroys a good book, kills reason itself, kills the image of God, as it were, in the eye.—John Milton

Watch out when you're getting all you want. Fattening hogs ain't in luck.—Joel Chandler Harris

What comes, is called.—Ki Longfellow

Dec. 10—Giovanni Battista Guarini (1538), Agatha "Aagje" Deken (1741), Nikolai A. Nekrassow (1821), George MacDonald (1824), Emily Dickinson (1830), Edward Eggleston (1837), Rudolf W. Canne (1870), Alfred Francis Kreymborg (1883), Nelly Sachs (1891), Gertrud Kolmar (1894), Christopher (Grant) La Farge and Karl H. Waggerl (1897), Yuri N. Libedinski (1898), William Plomer (1903), Michael Blankfort and (Margaret) Rumer Godden (1907), Jim Kjelgaard (1910), Chester Robert "Chet" Huntley (1911), Jorge Semprun (1923), Carolyn (Ashley) Kizer (1925), Ronald Dworkin (1931), Walter B. Edgar (1943), Thomas Lux (1946), August Kleinzahler (1949), Jacquelyn Mitchard (1956).

If I read a book and it makes my whole body so cold no fire can ever warm me, I know that is poetry. —Emily Dickinson

For a dyed-in-the-wool author nothing is as dead as a book once it is written . . . . She is rather like a cat whose kittens have grown-up. While they were a-growing she was passionately interested in them but now they seem hardly to belong to her—and probably she is involved with another bunch of kittens as I am involved in other writing.—Rumer Godden

You write for the people in high school who ignored you. We all do.—Carolyn Kizer

I do a great deal of research. I don't want anyone to say, "That could not have happened." It may be fiction, but it has to be true. —Jacquelyn Mitchard

Dec. 11—Apostolo Zeno (1669), Max von Schenkendorf (1783), Christian Dietrich Grabbe (1801), Alfred de Musset (1835), Kemal Bey (1840), Volgin (Georgi Valentinovich Plechanow) (1856), Subramanya Bharathy (1882), Frederick William Wallace (1886), Paul Kornfeld (1889), Harriet Stratemeyer Adams (1892), Nils J. E. Ferlin (1898), Robert Henriques (1905), Birago Diop (1906), Ronald McKie (1909), Willard R(ichardson) Espy (1910), Vincent Henry Kemp and Naguib Mahfouz (1911), Aleksandr (Isayevich) Solzhenitsyn (1918), Joe Masteroff (1919), Grace Paley (1922), Jerome Rothenberg (1931), Keith Waldrop (1932), Earnest P. van Altena (1933), James "Jim" Harrison (1937), Thomas Francis "Tom" McGuane III (1939), Pauline Gedge (1945), David Mason (1954), Lani Brockman (1956), Cesare Dominic "Chez" Pazienza (1969).

Great artists have no country.—Alfred de Musset

Calvin Trillin once proposed that "the advance for a book should be at least as much as the cost of the lunch at which it was discussed." When he asked an editor what he thought of this formula, he was told that it was "unrealistic."—Willard Espy

"The Immigrant Story," which took me about twenty-five years to write, was a very simple story, but I couldn't think of how to tell it. Then twenty years after I started it, I found this one page and realized it was going to be the story. That's the only way you get it sometimes.—Grace Paley

The novelist who refuses sentiment refuses the full spectrum of human behavior, and then he just dries up. Irony is always scratching your tired ass, whatever way you look at it. I would rather give full vent to all human loves and disappointments, and take a chance on being corney, than die a smartass.—Jim Harrison

I like young girls. Their stories are shorter.—Tom McGuane

Dec. 12—Peter Rabus (1660), William Lloyd Garrison (1805), Gustave Flaubert (1821), Maurice Donnay (1859), Arthur Brisbane and Paul Elmer More (1864), Rose Emily "Lola" Ridge (1873), Rachel Crothers (1878), Scofield Thayer (1889), Mulk Raj Anand and Manès Sperber (1905), Armand H. F. Boni (1909), Kenneth Lawrence Beaudoin (1913), Eugene (Leonard) Burdick (1918), Ahmad Shamlou (1925), Donald Eugene "Don" Pendleton (1927), Tschingis Aitmatow (1928), John Osborne (1929), and Bill Beutel (1930).

Writing is a dog's life, but the only life worth living.—Gustave Flaubert

A good friend can tell you what is the matter with you in a minute. He may not seem such a good friend after telling.—Arthur Brisbane

I never deliberately set out to shock, but when people don't walk out of my plays I think there is something wrong.—John Osborne

Dec. 13—Carlo Gozzi (1720), (Christian Johann) Heinrich Heine (1797), Emily Carr (1871), Marcus Cook "Marc" Connelly (1890), Drew Pearson (1896), Jewgeni Petrow (1903), (Willis) Todhunter Ballard and John Piper (1903), Kenneth Patchen (1911), Alan L. Bullock (1914), Ross MacDonald (Kenneth Millar) (1915), John (Marsden) Ehle (Jr.) (1925), James (Arlington) Wright (1927), W. Gordon Smith (1928), Jack Hirschman (1933), Thomas Wakefield (1935), Michael C. Ford (1939), Modris Eksteins (1943), Lise Bissonnette (1945), Charles Upton and Tom Walmsley (1948), Roberta Ann "R. A." MacAvoy (1949), Anne-Marie Alonzo (1951), Jean Rouaud (1952), Emma Bull and Tamora Pierce (1954), Scott McPherson (1959), James Twining (1972).

Wherever they burn books they will also, in the end, burn human beings.—Heinrich Heine

There are so many little dyings every day, it doesn't matter which one of them is death.—Kenneth Patchen

We writers, as we work our way deeper into our craft, learn to drop more and more personal clues. Like burglars who secretly wish to be caught, we leave our fingerprints on broken locks, our voiceprints in bugged rooms, our footprints in the wet concrete. —Ross MacDonald

Dec. 14—Nostradamus (Michel de Nostredame) (or b. Dec. 21) (1503), Aphra Behn (1640), Daniel Neal (1678), Charles Wolfe (1791), Mary Tappan Wright (1851), Salvador Diaz Miron (1853), Alexander V. Amfiteatrov (1862), Regina Ullmann (1884), Jane Cowl (1884), Paul Eluard (1895), Shirley (Hardie) Jackson (1916), Ann (Wood) Waldron (1924), Ernest Dinwoodie Pickering (1928), George Furth (George Schweinfurth) (1932), Ellen Willis (1941), Antony (James) Beevor (1946), Boudewijn Buch (1948), Wade Davis and Joe Toplyn (1953), Gary Ferris (1957), Kelley Armstrong and Ewa Białołęcka (1968), Corey James Hodges (1970).

The present time, together with the past, shall be judged by a great jovialist.—Nostradamus

I have always loved to use fear, to take it and comprehend it and make it work and consolidate a situation where I was afraid and take it whole and work from there.—Shirley Jackson

The handles (of a scene) are the one or two most distinctive people or things in the picture and the action that those people or things are performing. This descriptive sentence will bridge the *visual* picture and a *verbal* punch line, i.e., the funny caption.—Joe Toplyn

Dec. 15—J. F. Beck (1720), Emilio Jacinto (1875), Ferdinand Hardekopf (1876), Hans Carossa (1878), Pieter C. A. Geyl (1887), David (Thompson Watson) McCord (1897), (James) Maxwell Anderson and Artturi A. Leinonen (1888), Betty Smith (Elisabeth Lillian Wehner) (1896), John Glassco (1909), Nicholas P. Dallis (1911), Muriel Rukeyser (1913), Shan-ul-Haq Haqqee (1917), Edna O'Brien (1932), Ronald William Loewinsohn and John (Thomas) Sladek (1937), Lee Aronsohn (1952), J. M. DeMatteis and Robert Charles Wilson (1953), Mike McAlary (1957).

If you practice an art, be proud of it and make it proud of you. It may break your heart, but it will fill your heart before it breaks it; it will make you a person in your own right.—Maxwell Anderson
The universe is made of stories, not of atoms.—Muriel Rukeyser
Writing is like carrying a fetus.—Edna O'Brien

Dec. 16—Louis-Jules Mancini-Mazarini (1716), Elizabeth Carter (1717), Jane Austen (1775), Mary Russell Mitford (1787), Arlo Bates (1850), Eugene Demolder and John Fox Jr. (1862), George Santayana (1863), Paul Neuhuys (1897), Noel Coward (1899), Victor S. Pritchett (1900), Margaret Mead (1901), Rafael Alberti (1903), Piet Hein (1905), Theodore Weiss (1916), Arthur C. Clarke (1917), Pierre Chany (1922), Tip (Silvio A.) Marugg (1923), Warren Adler, Peter (Malcolm de Brissac) Dickinson, and Randall Garrett (1927), Philip K. Dick (1928), Ann Copeland (Virginia Walsh Furtwangler) (1932), Karleen Bradford (1936), Lesley Stahl (1941), Peter Seaton (1942), Steven Bochco (1943), Adriaan van Dis (1946), Joanne Arnott and Allen Kurzweil (1960), Dan Le Batard (1968), Juan Gómez-Jurado (1977).

The person, be it gentleman or lady, who has not pleasure in a good novel, must be intolerably stupid.—Jane Austen
Short stories can be rather stark and bare unless you put in the right details. Details make stories human, and the more human a story can be, the better.—V. S. Pritchett
Politicians should read science fiction, not westerns and detective stories.—Arthur C. Clarke

Dec. 17—Thomas Tickell (1685), Gabrielle Émilie Le Tonnelier de Breteuil, marquise du Châtelet (1706), John Almon (1737), Thomas Chandler Haliburton (1796), Gergely Czuczor (1800), John Greenleaf Whittier (1807), Rose Terry Cook (1827), Jules de Goncourt (1830), Émile Faguet (1847), Ford Madox Ford (1873), Hans Henny Jahnn (1894), Simon Drach (1902), Erskine Caldwell (1903), Christianna Brand (1907), Penelope Fitzgerald (1916), Charlotte Jay (Geraldine Halls (1919), Jacques Borel (1925). Jeremy Brooks (1926), Marilyn Beck and George (Smith) Lindsey (1928), William Safire (1929), Yvonne Keuls (1931), Paul Snoek (1933), Frank Martinus Arion (1936), Bertha Harris and John Kennedy Toole (1937), Kåre Valebrokk (1940), Jack L(aurence) Chalker and Theodore Rosengarten (1944), Chris Matthews and Jacqueline Wilson (1945), Eugene Levy (1946), Nadia Janice Brown (1973).

The best of a book is not the thought which it contains, but the thought which it suggests; just as the charm of music dwells not in the tones but in the echoes of our hearts.—John Greenleaf Whittier

Only in grammar can you be more than perfect.—William Safire

However, no two people see the external world in exactly the same way. To every separate person a thing is what he thinks it is—in other words, not a thing, but a think.—Penelope Fitzgerald

Dec. 18—Knud L. Rahbek (1760), Yakov Petrovich Polonsky (1819), Charles Alexandre Chatrian (1826), Lyman Abbott (1835), Saki (Hector Hugo Munro) (1870), Christopher Fry (1907), Abe Burrows (b. Abram Solman Borowitz) and John Henry Reese (1910), Helen Vlachos (1911), Alfred Bester (1913), Vintilă Horia (1915), Ossie Davis (1917), Sterling Lanier (1927), Michael J(ohn) Moorcock (1939), Jack Carroll "Jay" Haldeman II (1941), Michael Davidson (1944), Steven Spielberg (1947), Leonard (Michael) Maltin (1950), Lenore Hart and Daniel Poliquin (1953), Amy M. "A. M." Homes and Thomas Strittmatter (1961), Miles Marshall Lewis (1970), Barkha Dutt (1971).

The young have aspirations that never come to pass, the old have reminiscences of what never happened.—Saki

In tragedy every moment is eternity; in comedy, eternity is a moment.—Christopher Fry

Any form of art is a form of power; it has impact, it can affect change—it can not only move us, it makes us move.—Ossie Davis

Dec. 19—Su Tung-p'o (1036), Manuel Bretón de los Herreros (1796), George L. Aiken (1830), Italo Svevo (1861), Eleanor (Emily) H(odgman) Porter (1868), Carter G(odwin) Woodson (1875), Frank Stuart "F. S." Flint (1885), Maurice Roelants (1895), Oliver (Hazard Perry) La Farge (1901), Theo Harych (1903), Dorothy M(arie) Johnson (1905), H(arry) Allen (Wolfgang) Smith (1906), Jean Genet and Jose Lezama Lima (1910), Adriaan van der Veen (1916), Michel Tournier (1924), Robert B(ernard) Sherman and Tankred Torst (1925), James Booth (1927), Howard Sackler (1929), Salvador Elizondo (1932), Jean-Patric Manchette (1942), Rosemary Conley and Miguel Piñero (1946), Christine Negroni (1956), Michelangelo Signorile (1960), Brandon Sanderson and Jon Smith (1975), Patrick Casey (1978).

Those who have no record of what their forebears have accomplished lose the inspiration which comes from the teaching of biography and history.—Carter G. Woodson

There's such a thing as too much point on a pencil.—H. Allen Smith

Worse than not realizing the dreams of your youth, would be to have been young and never dreamed at all.—Jean Genet

Dec. 20—Paul Melissus (Paul Schede) (1539), John Fletcher (1579), Edwin Abbott Abbott (1838), Pieter C. Boutens (1870), T. F. Powys (1875), Jan Van Oudshoorn (Jan K. Feylbrief) (1876), Max Lerner (1902), Jack Fenno (Hortense Calisher) (1911), Carl (Atwood) Elliott (1913), Aziz Nesin (1915), Joseph Payne Brennan (1918), Jack Richard "J. R." Salamanca (1922), Gloria Sawai (1932), G. Wolfgruber (1944), Andrei Codrescu (1946), Peter May (1951), Schuyler Lee "Sky" Gilbert Jr. (1952), Sandra Cisneros (1954), Nalo Hopkinson (1960), Ramon Stoppelenburg (1976).

He never is alone that is accompanied with noble thoughts.—John Fletcher

The crime of book purging is that it involves a rejection of the word. For the word is never absolute truth, but only man's frail and human effort to approach the truth. To reject the word is to reject the human search.—Max Lerner

First publication is a pure, carnal leap into that dark which one dreams is life.—Hortense Calisher

Dec. 21—Benjamin Disraeli (1804), Marion Harland (Mary Virginia Hawes Terhune) (1830), Mehmed N. Kemal (1840), James Lane Allen (1849), Isolde Kurz (1853), Gustave Kahn (1859), Albert Payson Terhune (1872), Frances Goodrich (1890), Amy Key Clarke and Rebecca West (Cicely Isabel Fairfield) (1892), Juan A. de Zunzunegui y Loredo (1901), Anthony Powell (1905), Garmt Stuiveling (1907), Seichō Matsumoto (1909), Eve Perrick (1916), Heinrich Böll (1917), Richard Hugo and Intizar Hussain (1923), Edward Hoagland (1932), Kelly Cherry (1940), James Sallis (1944), Rebecca Anne "Becky" Allison (1946), Erica Hayden (1982).

When I want to read a good book, I write one.—Benjamin Disraeli

Journalism: an ability to meet the challenge of filling the space.—Rebecca West

People think that because a novel's invented, it isn't true. Exactly the reverse is the case. Biography and memoirs can never be wholly true, since they cannot include every conceivable circumstance of what happened. The novel can do that.—Anthony Powell

The persistent problem with my writing is that I never know how something is going to come out; even when I write a short review, I always have to start over. I have no mastery. But it's actually beneficial—it prevents things from becoming routine.—Heinrich Böll

Dec. 22—Jean(-Baptiste) Racine (1639), Hermann Samuel Reimarus (1694), James Oglethorpe (1696), Johann Sebastian Welhaven (1807),Thomas Wentworth Higginson (1823), Justin M'Carthy (1830), Charles Stuart Calverley (1831), Mark Rutherford (1831), Jose Maria de Heredia (1842), George (Robert) Gissing (1857), Manuel Gutiérrez Nájera (1859), Sara Jeannette Duncan (1861), Frantisek X. Salda (1867), Edwin Arlington Robinson (1869), Filippo Tommaso Marinetti (1876), Endre Ady (1877), Charles Vildrac (1882), Mikha`il Na'imah (1889), Nikolay Semyonovich Tikhonov (1896), Evelyn (Sybil Mary) Eaton (1902), Kenneth Rexroth (1905), Doris Miles Disney (1907), Jack Richard "J. R." Salamanca and Calder Willingham (1922), Donald (Douglas) Harington and Tomás Rivera (1935), James Burke (1936), Martin (Gerald) Sherman (1938), Anne Chislett (1942), Brian (Charles) Daley (1947), David Gilmour (1949), Charles de Lint and Frederick "Fred" Stenson (1951), Susan Powter (1957), David S. Goyer (1965).

Human language may be polite and powerless in itself, uplifted with difficulty into expression by the high thoughts it utters, or it may in itself become so saturated with warm life and delicious association that every sentence shall palpitate and thrill with the mere fascination of the syllables . . . . There may be phrases which shall be palaces to dwell in, treasure-houses to explore; a single word may be a window from which one may perceive all the kingdoms of the earth and the glory of them. Oftentimes a word shall speak what accumulated volumes have labored in vain to utter: there may be years of crowded passion in a word, and half a life in a sentence.—Thomas Wentworth Higginson

The basic line in any good verse is cadenced . . . building it around the natural breath structures of speech.—Kenneth Rexroth

When you read a book, you hold another's mind in your hands.—James Burke

Dec. 23—Martin Opitz (1597), Ippolit Bogdanovich (1743), Sara Coleridge (1803), Charles-Augustin Sainte-Beuve (1804), Samuel Smiles (1812), Jan Jakob Lodewijk ten Kate (1819), Mathilde Wesendonk (1828), Vladimir Nemirovitch-Dantshenko (1858), Henri Pirenne and John Alfred "J. A." Spender (1862), Albert Ehrenstein (1886), Friedrich Wolf (1888), Giuseppe Tomasi di Lampedusa (1896), Norman (Fitzroy) Maclean (1902), Manuel Lopes (1907), Dino Risi (1916), Calder (Baynard) Willingham (Jr.) (1922), Leonard Stern (1923), Robert Bly (1926), Margaret Olwen MacMillan (1943), Ilchi Lee (1950), Carol Ann Duffy (1955), Naoyuki Uchida (1960), Donna Tartt (1963), Tim Fountain (1967), Carson Cistulli (1979).

The experience gathered from books, though often valuable, is but the nature of learning; whereas the experience gained from actual life is one of the nature of wisdom.—Samuel Smiles

If you are getting the worst of it in an argument with a literary man, always attack his style. That'll touch him if nothing else will. —J. A. Spender

Eventually, all things merge into one, and a river runs through it.—Norman Maclean

[W]here a man's wound is, that is where his genius will be. —Robert Bly

Dec. 24—Philip Warwick (1609), George Crabbe (1754), Selam III (1789), A. Eugene Scribe (1791), Adam B. Mickiewicz (1798), Matthew Arnold (1822), Lydia Koidula (1843), Henriette G. A. Roland Holst-van der Schalk (1869), Émile Nelligan (1879), Juan Ramon Jiménez (1881), James Hadley Chase (1906), Lucille M. Nixon (1908), Fritz (Reuter) Leiber (Jr.) (1910), Malcolm MacEwen (1911), Mary Higgins Clark (Mary Theresa Eleanor Higgins Clark Conheeney) (1927), Walter Abish (1931), James (Karl) Bartleman (1939), Michael Nicholas Pocalyko (1954), Adam Haslett (1970), Stephenie Meyer (1973), Evan (Lionel Richard) Osnos (1976).

Books cannot always please, however good; Minds are not ever craving for their food.—George Crabbe

For the creation of a masterwork of literature two powers must concur, the power of the man and the power of the moment, and the man is not enough without the moment.—Matthew Arnold

The first four months of writing the book, my mental image is scratching with my hands through granite. My other image is pushing a train up the mountain, and it's icy, and I'm in bare feet.—Mary Higgins Clark

Dec. 25—Lady Grizel Baillie (1665), William Collins (1721), Dorothy Wordsworth (1771), Fernán Caballero (Cecilia Francisca Josefa de Arrom) (1796), Alexandros Rhizos Rhankaves (1810), Isabella Valancy Crawford (1846), Alfred Kerr (1867), Gustav Davidson (1895), Quentin Crisp (1908), Henri Nannen (1913), Rod Serling (1924), Carlos Castaneda and Joseph Nicholas "Joe" Gores (1931), Phyllis Rowland (1932), Anne Roiphe (1935), Hilary Spurling (1940), Sanders Anne Laubenthal (1943), Lex Hixon (1941), Alexandre Trudeau (1973), Sheila Heti (1976).

When a writer becomes a reader of his or her own work, a lot can go wrong. It's like do-it-yourself dentistry.—William Collins

An autobiography is an obituary in serial form with the last installment missing.—Quentin Crisp

Every writer is a frustrated actor who recites his lines in the hidden auditorium of his skull.—Rod Serling

Dec. 26—Thomas Gray (1716), Jean François de Saint-Lambert (1716), Heinrich J. von Collin (1771), Emma Dorothy Eliza Nevitte "E. D. E. N." Southworth (1819), Dion Boucicault (Dionysius Lardner Boursiquot (1820/1822), René Bazin (1853), Norman Angell (1874), Henry Miller (1891), Jean Toomer (1894), Willie Corsari, (Wilhelmina A. Schmidt) (1897), Andrew (Nelson) Lytle (1902), Alentejo Carpentier (1904), Frank Swift (1913), Stephen Valentine Patrick William "Steve" Allen (1921), Roy Vernon Scott (1927), Bahram Beizai (1938), Gérard Bouchard (1943), Jean Echenoz (1947), Bob Flanagan (1952), David (Raymond) Sedaris (1956), Andrew (Michael) Graham-Dixon (1960), Elizabeth Kostova (1964), Robert Muchamore (1972).

Poetry is thoughts that breathe, and words that burn.—Thomas Gray

One can be absolutely truthful and sincere even though admittedly the most outrageous liar. Fiction and invention are of the very fabric of life.—Henry Miller

A good [short story] would take me out of myself and then stuff me back in, outsized, now, and uneasy with the fit.—David Sedaris

Dec. 27—François Hemsterhuis (1721), Mirza Ghalib (1796), Mina Loy (b. Mina Gertrude Löwry) (1882), Louis Bromfield and Carl Zuckmayer (1896), Ingri d'Aulaire (1904), Sebastian Haffner (1907), Louis J. H. C. A. de Bourbon (1908), Charles Olson (1910), Elizabeth Smart (1913), Giuseppe Berto (1914), William Howell Masters (1915), Onni Palaste (1917), Agnes Nixon (1927), Wilfrid (John Joseph) Sheed (1930), Peter T. "P. T." Deutermann (1941), Cokie Roberts (1943), Juan Felipe Herrera (1948), David Baker (1954, Gerina Dunwich (1959), Kevin Patterson (1964), Sarah Vowell (1969).

One-half of life is luck; the other half is discipline—and that's the important half, for without discipline you wouldn't know what to do with luck.—Carl Zuckmayer

One reason the human race has such a low opinion of itself is that it gets so much of its wisdom from writers.—Wilfrid Sheed

History is full of really good stories. That's the main reason I got into this racket: I want to make the argument that history is interesting.—Sarah Vowell

Dec. 28—Antoine Furetière (1619), Hermanus J. Abbring (1787), Catharine Maria Sedgwick (1789), Jeremiah Clemens (1814), Prentiss Ingraham (1843), John W. Fortescue (1859), Harry B(ache) Smith (1860), Félix E. Vallotton (1865), Christian D.F.L. Leipoldt (1880), Frank Butler (1890), Mortimer J. Adler and Shen Congwen (1902), Murray Burnett (1910), Stan Lee (b. Stanley Martin Lieber) (1922), Simon Raven (1927), Jesse Hill Ford and Janet (Louise Swoboda) Lunn (1928), Roy Hattersley and Manuel Puig (1932), Charles (McColl) Portis (1933), Herbert George "Herb" Gardner and Alasdair Gray (1934), Janet Hough Bryant and Richard Sudhalter (1938), Max Hastings (1945), Ian Buruma (1951), Gilles Leroy (1958), Andy McNab (Steven Billy Mitchell) (1959), Martine Robine (1965).

In the case of good books, the point is not to see how many of them you can get through, but how many can get through to you. —Mortimer Adler

I used to be embarrassed because I was just a comic-book writer while other people were building bridges or going on to medical careers. And then I began to realize: entertainment is one of the most important things in people's lives. Without it they might go off the deep end. I feel that if you're able to entertain people, you're doing a good thing.—**Stan Lee**

I would be miserable if I went to bed without having written 1,000 words about something.—Max Hastings

Dec. 29—Archibald Alison (1792), William Ewart Gladstone (1809), Carmen Sylva (Elisabeth of Wied) (1843), Oscar Williams (Oscar Kaplan) (1900), Charles L(eonard) Harness and Robert Ruark (1915), Dobrica Cosic (1921), William (Thomas) Gaddis (Jr.) (1922), William Pfaff (1928), Peter Meinke (1932), Bertha "Thea" Bowman, (1937), Robert J. Conley, Peter Koelewijn, and Brigitte Kronauer (1940), Douglas Porch (1944), Paul Rudnick (1957), Robert Louis Tewdwr Moss (1961). Ashleigh Banfield (1967), Danny R. McBride and Bryan Penberthy (1976).

Books are a delightful society. If you go into a room filled with books, even without taking them down from their shelves, they seem to speak to you, to welcome you.—William Ewart Gladstone

Life is an art in which too many remain only dilettantes. —Carmen Sylva

If they keep exposing you to education, you might even realize some day that man becomes immortal only in what he writes on paper, or hacks into rock, or slabbers onto a canvas, or pulls out of a piano.—Robert Ruark

Every poem, formal or free, has an ideal shape, and the job of the poet is to find it.—Peter Meinke

Dec. 30—Vincenzo da Filicaja (1642), Theodor Fontane (1819), Charles Edward Caryl (1841), Heinrich Hart (1855), Rudyard Kipling (1865), Stephen (P. H. Butler) Leacock (1869), Helen von Kolnitz Hyer (1896), Alfredo Bracchi (1897), Paul Frederic Bowles (1910), Elyne Mitchell (1913), and Alfred Wellington "A. W." Purdy (1918), Jane (Gillson) Langton (1922), Sara A. Lidman (1923), Edsel Ford (1928), Rosalind Hurley (1929), Richard Christ (1931), Glenda Adams (1939), Vladimir Bukovsky and Matthew "Matt" Cohen (1942), Janko Prunk (1942), Patricia Lee "Patti" Smith (1946), Lewis Shiner (1950), Melissa Fay Greene and Somtow Sucharitkul (S.P. Somtow) (1952), Harald Schmautz and Meredith Vieira (1953), Douglas Coupland (1961), Joshua Clover (b. Joshua Miller Kaplan) (1962), Chandler Burr (1963).

> I keep six honest serving men
> (They taught me all I knew).
> Their names are What and Why and When
> and How and Where and Who.
> —Rudyard Kipling

If you can take pleasure in the act of writing, it'll be a lot easier on your mental health in the long run.—Lewis Shiner

Storytelling is ultimately a creative act of pattern recognition. Through characters, plot and setting, a writer creates places where previously invisible truths become visible. Or the storyteller posits a series of dots that the reader can connect.—Douglas Coupland

Dec. 31—G. A. Burger (1747), José Mariá de Heredia y Campuzano (1803), Pliny Earle (II) (1809), James Thomas Fields (1817), Giovanni Pascoli (1855), Alfredo Panzini (1863), Lawrence Beesley (1877), Horacio Quiroga (1878), George Sylvester Viereck (1884), Frances Steloff (1887), Jacob Israel de Haan (1881), Max Lamberty (1893), Tadeusz Breza (1905), Dal Stivens (1911), Sam Ragan (1915), Dieter Noll (1927), Veijo Meri (1928), Bob Shaw (1931), Edward (Heward) Bunker (1933), Rolf Haufs (1935), Nicolas Born (1937), Eleanor Taylor Bland (1944), Constance Elaine Trimmer "Connie" Willis (1945), Susan Shwartz (1949), Val (Edward) Kilmer (1959), Nicholas Sparks (1965), Hiromi Goto (1966), Junot Díaz (1968), Joe Craig (1981), Lauren (Danielle) Drain (1985).

Writing the last page of the first draft is the most enjoyable moment in writing. It's one of the most enjoyable moments in life, period.—Nicholas Sparks

I believe that anyone who doesn't read remains dumb. Even if they know how, failing to regularly ingest the written word dooms them to ignorance, no matter what else they have or do.—Edward Heward Bunker

We get so many people saying short fiction is not economical, that it doesn't sell; but there are so many of us enjoying writing it and reading it. So it's wonderful to be around people who love short fiction too—it's like hanging around with my tribe.—Junot Diaz

Astrology for Wordsmiths[6]

Everyone needs help in telling the future, including writers, editors, poets, columnists, and freelancers. We have made an extensive review of the predictive value of tea leaves, Delphic oracles, numbers, fortune-tellers, swamis, and astrologers from the East or the West, and we find our methodology will work as well as any other system.

GEMINI (May 22–June 21): When you are going to your favorite bookstore or library branch, be careful at the traffic light closest to where you live. Especially look out for a maroon Ford Expedition that typically runs that red light.

CANCER (June 22–July 23): It's fine to listen to books on tape, but, when you are approaching a busy intersection near your home, be on the alert for a vehicle in front of you suddenly hitting the brakes while a Ford Expedition is blasting through the intersection.

LEO (July 24–Aug. 23): Your friends will be talking to you about car accidents and what-not. Notice the excitable tone they use. Wouldn't that tone help to jazz up that weak character in the chapter you are writing?

VIRGO (Aug. 24–Sept. 23): In your home office, you have dozens of notebooks or legal pads in which you have sketched out ideas or extracts of possible novels, stories, or poetry. Go to your first notebook and actually type up a story. Print it out.

LIBRA (Sept. 24–Oct. 23): Quit waiting for inspiration to write. Sit at one spot for an hour for three or four times a week. Do not check out your friends' Facebook pages (nor yours). Do not email friends or pay bills online. If you have pondered and cogitated but have still struck out, then repeatedly write any sentences: "It was a dark and stormy

---

[6] This piece originally appeared in *The Write Stuff* and then in the collection *Shoot-Out with a Wild-Eyed Moderate* (Amazon/Kindle, 2012).

night," "Leslie couldn't think of what to write," etc. Eventually add a "when-clause" ("…when lightning struck the tower clock," "…when a black bird flew into the room and settled on his stack of DVDs").

SCORPIO (Oct. 24–Nov. 22): In your 400-page manuscript, you have given the thoughts of 48 characters. Cut out 95 to 99 percent of those interior sections. You may need to go into the heads of two or three protagonists, but not many more, especially since you are writing a cookbook. Besides, who cares what a rutabaga thinks?

SAGITTARIUS (Nov. 23–Dec. 21): Learn how to use *The Oxford English Dictionary* and keep up with when words came into use. For example, your manuscript has a minister in the 1850s referring to someone as a "scumbag." Since that expression is slang for a condom and its contents, a preacher probably wouldn't use such words.

CAPRICORN (Dec. 22–Jan. 20): Your lucky numbers are 0 1 2 3 4 5 6 7 8 9, used in various combinations. Use these in lotteries until your number wins. Hire a secretary to type up your boxes and boxes of hand-written stuff. If your winnings are high enough, buy yourself a publishing house.

AQUARIUS (Jan. 21–Feb. 19): When you obsess about why you can't get down to writing, watch the video *My Left Foot*. Christy Brown was born severely handicapped, and Daniel Day-Lewis shows us how Brown grew up to paint and write successfully even though he could only move (what else?) his left foot. There are NO excuses for not writing.

PISCES (Feb. 20–March 20): It's time to quit using your *Writer's Market for 1887*. Use later editions or even magazines' websites to determine the names of the editors who should receive submission. Oh, yes: Quit trying to sell your article on "The Comeback of the Bustle."

ARIES (March 21–April 20): Write a nostalgic piece on your first Ram pickup. Don't include everything you did in the back of the truck if you are writing for grocery store mags. The article could also be about any other eight-cylinder pickup you've had.

TAURUS (April 12–May 21): If you are reading the 13th book about Quagmark the Robotic Doofus, you may not have noticed that the creator, Sri Lanka's eccentric Drawoh Nosned, started repeating himself in his third book. Try expanding your reading.

SPECIAL TO STEPHANIE: When the moon is waxing, revise what you wrote in the days before. Duct-tape the wee one in your household to a banister. If the mischief-maker has put a hamster in your desk drawer, increase the amount of duct-tape.

Astrology for Wordsmiths Rides Again

Wait a day after reading the previous guide to the stars and future, and then act on the following advice.

CANCER (June 22–July 23): Max of this sign has asked, "<u>WHAT</u> is <u>GOING ON</u> in my <u>WRITING</u>????!!!!" (And so on in a similar vein.) Max, you are not a typographer so knock it off. If you can't stop underlining, bold-facing, and punctuating madly, take a walk around a lake or stream at the closest park to you. If that does not work, stick your head in the water for thirty minutes.

LEO (July 24–Aug. 23): Purchase several containers of epoxy. Stroll around a nearby park or by a beach, a river, or a stream as you listen to your favorite book. If you see an anxious Cancer making exclamation points in a notebook, apply the epoxy to his fingers.

VIRGO (Aug. 24–Sept. 23): Quit imitating Faulkner. You're irritating your writing group and scaring the seagulls along the beaches.

LIBRA (Sept. 24–Oct. 23): On the other hand, minimalism isn't always ideal. Considering your poem, "Redneck and RC Cola":

> **Hick** UP

Isn't that more decoration than art?

SCORPIO (Oct. 24–Nov. 22): Let's see: Your protagonist looks like a teenager who only takes night classes, but he's a really sweet vampire who's in love with Britney, whose mother manages a blood bank. He quits his job sucking groceries, er, sacking groceries at the Piggly Wiggly to become a clerk at the blood bank. Wow, totally original.

SAGITTARIUS (Nov. 23–Dec. 21): What's this with arrows? You write scripts about Green Arrow (who's owned by DC). You do novels about Robin Hood. Your characters wear Arrow shirts and drive Pierce

Arrows. For starters, try using .45-calibre automatics and see where that takes you.

CAPRICORN (Dec. 22–Jan. 20): Your poems about camels don't seem to go anywhere. Since you are born under the sign of the goat, you should try sonnets to goats. Try a villanelle on the theme of "Do not go *ba-a-a-a*-ing into that good pasture."

AQUARIUS (Jan. 21–Feb. 19): There's a difference between informal and formal writing. The latter does not mean you wear a top hat, tux, and cane.

PISCES (Feb. 20–March 20): You haven't had a single piece of writing accepted by editors during the past year. It probably would help if you sent out something for them to consider. (Just a thought.)

ARIES (March 21–April 20): You've been misplacing your iKeys, iDevices, and iSocks, but you shouldn't misplace your modifiers in your writing. "Having frozen in the refrigerator, my father took out some cubes"—who froze in the fridge?

TAURUS (April 12–May 21): Don't be bullheaded about holding onto your favorite lines past their times of usefulness. Besides, "it was the goodest of times, it was the worstest of times" is both derivative and ungrammatical.

GEMINI (May 22–June 21): ~~In this modern complex world we live in~~ today, **we need to scratch out words that aren't necessary.**

SPECIAL TO GEORGINA: If you are tattooing "carpe diem" on your face, why not use 12- to 14-point type instead of 72 point? If you use 72 points for the letters, folks will only be seeing "CARP" on your face since the rest will be under your hair.

"Lights, Camera, Action, Scribble!"[7]

Filmmakers in Hollywood and Britain have often used writers as characters and have labored to come up with exciting visuals as the scribes create their novels, plays, or poems.

Writers pace the seashore and wrinkle their brows to come up with ideas, and the 100-piece orchestra saws its strings a little off camera while the waves lash against the shore.

The movies usually do not show what writers actually do, which is read a lot, scrunch over and write with a quill or a keyboard, grimace at what they have written, frown at rejection slips, smile occasionally at an acceptance, and revise, revise, revise.

So, film buffs everywhere, let's quiz you on movies about writers, but we make a few restrictions:

The movies in the quiz have to be theatrical films about real poets, novelists, or playwrights; and they shouldn't include any films by Ken Russell.

Okay, on second thought, we will let the late Ken Russell play, too, even with the nudity, drugs, and rats he likes to use.

First, a warm-up: What American writer is most likely to appear as a character in a film set before 1900? That, of course, would be Mark Twain, who even appeared twice on *Star Trek: The Next Generation*. (Don't ask.) Edgar Allan Poe, of course, comes in second, thanks to walk-ons in various horror flicks.

A second warm-up: Until recently, what major British writer is *least* likely to appear as a character in historic films? Among the titans of Brit Lit, William Shakespeare was seldom used until *Shakespeare in Love*. In *Anonymous*, Roland Emmerich tried to make the case that Edward de Vere was the true author of Shakespeare's plays. He wasn't, but the effort in advocating for de Vere at least kept Emmerich from stealing his neighbors' hubcaps.

Now let's go for the questions that count:

1. Two poets are enjoying themselves in Switzerland, making up spooky stories and swapping ideas. One poet's new wife is only eighteen and has a yearning to write. Name films involving any of the three main writers. (10

---

[7] This piece originally appeared in *The Write Stuff* and then in the collection *Gunfight with a Wild-Eyed Moderate* (Amazon/Kindle, 2014).

points for each film named)

2. A woman with an unhappy marriage leaves the North and settles in a swampy area of Florida, where she realizes the story potential of the rustic setting. (10 points)

3. The Irishman is immobilized by cerebral palsy, but finally gets movement in a foot, so he paints and even writes a novel. (10 points)

4. He's witty, but also the social conscience of France in the 18th Century. Knowing the danger of dissent, he lives next to the Swiss border in case he needs to make a run for it. In his old age, the Parisians finally celebrate him and his work . . . and the parties kill him of the old duffer. (10 points)

5. Although continually fighting and being arrested for theft, he was well-beloved by Parisians during the reign of Louis XI. (10 points each)

6. A British science-fiction writer is chasing after Jack the Ripper in a time-machine. (10 points)

7. A British poet lives with her maiden aunt in the 20th Century. (10 points)

8. The French woman uses a male penname for her novels and stories and is in love with a pianist-composer. (10 points for each)

9. An old bachelor in Britain has spent his life with his writing until an American divorcee comes along. They marry and live happily until illness strikes her. (10 points)

10. This film is about the last years of a British writer of "dirty novels." (10 points)

11. Inspired by the example of sports writer Paul Gallico (who boxed with Jack Dempsey to see what it was like), this Ivy League writer convinces a professional football team to let him take some snaps in a game. (10 points)

12. Karen Blixen marries for convenience and moves to Nairobi, where she falls in love with an Englishman and pursues her writing career. (10 points)

13. A playwright, novelist, and all-around wit defends his reputation in a libel suit, but loses and winds up in jail for sexual deviance. (10 points for each)

14. The Persian poet gave us the lines "a loaf of bread, a jug of wine, and thou" and inspired a silly film, even though he was a great mathematician, astronomer, free thinker and epigrammatist. (10 points)

15. He made it through the Civil War, wrote lots of weird short stories and devilish definitions, and then disappeared in Mexico in 1913. Perhaps Pancho Villa's troops got him. Or maybe it was an *X-Files* case that would have interested Mulder and Scully. (10 points)

16. This fabulist and long-time slave from Samos in the sixth century BCE goes a-wooing in a film that will tell you more about Hollywood musicals than about the Greeks. (10 points)

17. Controversy and a passion for art followed this Japanese writer after

World War II. Also, an actor, playwright, director, and militarist, he commits a ritual suicide in 1970. (10 points)

18. While in a Spanish prison, the author passes the time by writing, supposedly prompted by prisoners to come up with an entertaining tale. (10 points)

19. He writes hard-boiled detective stories and novels and is in love with a playwright. (10 points each)

20. A mathematician-logician is afflicted with a stammer and is drawn to the society of children, especially little girls. He writes two famous books for a Miss Liddell. (10 points for each)

Answers to the Movie Quiz

1. *Gothic* (1986), with Natasha Richardson and Julian Sands, shows the danger of turning Ken Russell loose with undeveloped film and a script supposedly about Lord Byron, Percy Shelley, Mary Shelley, and Dr. John Polidori back in 1816. The film is a mess historically since it is doubtful that any woman in the party crawled around nude with a rat in her mouth, and Russell probably had a bad trip, too. Polidori was inspired to write *The Vampyr* (which some want to credit to Byron), but Mary's creation was more powerful.

Haunted Summer (1988), with Phillips Anglim and Laura Dern, does a little better job of telling about that encounter. However, *The Bride of Frankenstein* (1935) is a better all-around film than *Gothic* or *Haunted Summer*. It opens with Mary getting ideas for what became *Frankenstein: A Modern Prometheus*. Elsa Lanchester played Mary and the Bride. Other films: Lord Byron is featured in *Lady Caroline Lamb* (1972) and *Bad Lord Byron* (1951).

2. *Cross Creek* (1983) starred Mary Steenburgen as Marjorie Kinnan Rawlings, with Malcolm McDowell doing a cameo as Scribner's legendary editor Maxwell Perkins.

3. *My Left Foot* (1989) features Daniel Day-Lewis as the Dublin author Christy Brown.

4. *Voltaire* (1933) features George Arliss playing the author of *Candide* and finally being feted in the capital when he is an old man. The parties prove too exhausting and kill off the old fellow.

5. François Villon, poet and scoundrel, was the subject of *The Vagabond King* (1956), with Kathryn Grayson, Oreste, Rita Moreno, and others, and *If I Were King* (1938), with Ronald Colman and Basil Rathbone.

6. Not very biographical or historical, but generally fun, *Time After Time* (1979) features Malcolm McDowell as H. G. Wells, with David Warner playing the Ripper. Wells, author of *The Time Machine*, has become as useful as Mark Twain to some SF story-tellers and even appeared several times as a character on ABC's *Lois and Clark*.

7. *Stevie* (1978) featured Glenda Jackson as Yorkshire-born Stevie Smith, with Mona Washbourne playing the aunt. The diminutive Florence Margaret Smith was nicknamed "Stevie," after a jockey. The film is based on the play by Hugh Whitemore.

8. Merle Oberon plays George Sand in *Song to Remember* (1945), with Cornel Wilde as Frederic Chopin, but a better version may be *Impromptu* (1991), with Judy Davis, Hugh Grant, Mandy Patinkin, Emma Thompson and others.

9. Anthony Hopkins played long-time bachelor C. S. Lewis in *Shadowlands* (1994), whose script was by playwright William Nicholson. Debra Winger played the love interest, and Edward Hardwicke was Lewis' brother Warnie.

10. Ian McKellen portrayed the ailing D. H. Lawrence in *Priest of Love* (1985), with Janet Suzman playing his wife Frieda during his last years when *Lady Chatterley's Lover* was published.

11. Alan Alda played George Plimpton in *The Paper Lion* (1968), which also featured Alex Karras and Sugar Ray Robinson.

12. She adopts the penname Isak Dinessen and is played by Meryl Streep in *Out of Africa* (1985).

13. That's Oscar Wilde, of course, who often crops up in films: e.g., *Oscar Wilde* (1960), with Robert Morley in the title role; *The Trials of Oscar Wilde* (1960), with Peter Finch as the Wilde man. Oh, and someone let Ken Russell loose again, so we wind up with *Salome's Last Dance* (1988), which has Oscar lounging in a knocking-shop, where his play is about to be performed (and where he will be arrested by and by). Stephen Fry portrayed the title role in *Wilde* (1998), which co-starred Jude Law and Vanessa Redgrave.

14. *Omar Khayyam* (1957) featured Cornel Wilde[8] as the author of *The Rubaiyat*. It also starred Debra Paget, John Derek, and Raymond Massey. (10 points)

15. Ambrose Bierce, played by Gregory Peck, is the subject of *Old Gringo* (1989). It also featured Jane Fonda as an American spinster.

16. *A Night in Paradise* (1946) was supposedly about Aesop of fables fame. It starred Merle Oberon, Turhan Bey (as Aesop), Gale Sondergaard, Ray Collins, and Ernest Truex.

17. *Mishima* (1985) is a stylized drama about Yukio Mishima.

18. Miguel de Cervantes, of course, was the creator of Don Quixote, and the film is *The Man of La Mancha* (1972), with Peter O'Toole playing Cervantes and Quixote.

19. Jason Robards plays Dashiell Hammett in *Julia* (1977), with Jane Fonda as Lillian Hellman and Vanessa Redgrave as her radical friend in the 1930s. *Hammett* (1983) is a piece of fiction about Hammett's involvement in a real-life mystery. It stars Frederic Forest, Peter Boyle, and Elisha Cook.

---

[8] No relation to Oscar since he was born Kornél Lajos Weisz.

20. Ian Holm played Reverend Charles Dodgson, or Lewis Carroll, in *Dreamchild* (1985), which features Alice (Coral Browne) coming to America in the 1930s in her 80s and remembering some scenes that make today's viewers uncomfortable.

Scores:

250-290, You do not watch any network TV, you do not read, and you are going to too many Ken Russell films;

210-240, You have an excellent memory and you are probably avoiding Ken Russell flicks;

150-200, You are probably reading more than the average bear;

50-140, You are either reading a whole lot or you only go to the movies to see *Star Trek Degenerations*;

10-40, You only go to flicks like *Animal House*, *Porky's*, and *Jackass*.

Tidbits and Titillating Trivia

A journey into the births and advice of famous and obscure writers offers fascinating discoveries that are mixed in with the near-template information about writers and poets on university and college faculties. Human nature requires that the research has to pause if a mesmerizing detail pops up. Mixed in with these discoveries are the memorable facts that we carry around about various scribblers, and it's disconcerting at times when we have to move fact into the myth category.

Let's begin with **William Shakespeare**, whom the reader will find listed among the April 23 births. Actually, we are not sure exactly when he was born. We do know that he was baptized on April 26 in 1564 and that (hmm, hang on here) he died on April 23 in 1616. Some followers of the Bard reasoned, "If you are born on one day, then you are likely baptized three days later. So that would mean he was born and died on the same day of a month. Isn't that a great symmetry?" The Bard could have been born and baptized on April 21, 22, 23, or 24.

Churches back then in England and Europe permitted their parishioners to lie in the earth until they had turned to bones. Then the bones were removed and spread along passage- and walk-ways, making the churches ossuaries. The Bard didn't like the notion of being dug up and perhaps sniffed at by dogs, so he paid £440 to be safely planted inside the church in Stratford-upon-Avon and added this epitaph for his tomb (rendered here with modern spelling):

> *Good friend, for Jesus' sake forbear,*
> *To dig the dust enclosed here.*
> *Blessed be the man that spares these stones,*
> *And cursed be he that moves my bones.*

Shakespeare's sister was buried in a churchyard but didn't have a potent epitaph (or £440) to ward off bone collectors. So her skeleton was collected and dispursed.[9] Apparently, Shakespeare shouldn't feel so smug because

---

[9] Don't you hate it when that happens?

recent scientific probings have revealed the Bard is missing his skull.[10]

Readers and writers today seldom discuss **Melville Davisson Post** (Ap19), but the West Virginian was a prolific writer of true crime and mysteries, with his Sherlock being Uncle Abner. He exited the literary scene in 1930 when he died after falling off a horse. He may have influenced **William Faulkner** (S25), who used recurring character Gavin Stephens as a detective in *Knight's Gambit*. Oh, an inebriated Faulkner also fell from a horse in 1959 but survived until a heart attack took him out in 1962.

David Graham Phillips (O31) was a handsome muckraker and novelist (*Susan Lenox: Her Fall and Rise*). That narrative was done as a movie starring Greta Garbo and Clark Gable. However, another of his novels, *The Fashionable Adventures of Joshua Craig*, obsessed a mentally deranged man who believed that the novel libeled his family and his sister. The man shot Phillips, shouting, "There you go!" After shouting, "And here I go!", he then shot himself.

Visitors to Westminster Abbey will notice many effigies, especially of **Elizabeth I** (S7) and **Mary Queen of Scots** (D8), plus cenotaphs for various military men who may have gone down with their ships. You will spot the **Poets' Corner**, so named because **Geoffrey Chaucer** (a.k.a. the Father of English Literature) was buried there in 1400. You will spot a stone honoring **Ben Jonson** (c.Jn11) and may not realize he is buried in an upright position. You will also locate a stone memorializing **William Shakespeare**, but he is actually buried in his church in Stratford-upon-Avon.

Francis Hopkinson Smith (O23) boasted an impressive, Friedrich Nietzsche-like moustache, but he was a Renaisance man. All right, to be exact, he was a Victorian Age man. He was an engineer who built the foundation for the Statue of Liberty. He was an award-winning painter, and he wrote novels, short stories, and travel books.

For early women American writers, most of us know of **Harriet Beecher Stowe** (Jn14), even though we don't read *Uncle Tom's Cabin*. We hardly discuss a woman who wrote sixty novels, **Emma Dorothy Eliza Nevitte Southworth** (D26). Her clever parents must have known she would need a penname, so she was able to use her initials and call herself **"E. D. E. N." Southworth**.[11]

We know **Louisa May Alcott** (N29) and we do read *Little Women* and *Little Men*. With scant biographical information about her, we may

---

[10] The skull of the composer Mozart is probably still missing. (They keep doing DNA studies on the possible skulls that might be his.) Mozart wasn't buried in a pauper's grave. Instead, he faced what happened to Shakespeare's sister. After so many years in the earth in the ground for commoners, his bones were dug up, and who knows what happened?

[11] If you think your new-born daughter will become an author, why not name her Bestseller Andrea Jones?

erroneously assume she was married and had a passel of children. Under the penname A. M. Barnard, she also wrote fiery novels about wronged women seeking revenge (think of them as PG-13 or R rated). She is buried in the **Author's Ridge** section of Sleepy Hollow Cemetery in Concord.

Elizabeth Stuart Phelps Ward (Ag31) stands out as a nineteenth-century freethinker. Her books and novels advocated progressive programs in women's issues. In her forties, she even married a man seventeen years younger than she.

Nathaniel Hawthorne (Jy4) and **Frederic Jesup Stimson** (Jy20) had something in common: Both were diplomats. Since Hawthorne had written a campaign biography for future president Franklin Pierce, he was rewarded with the position of United States consul in Liverpool, the most lucrative position at the time. Stimson became the first envoy to Argentina to have the office title of "Ambassador." But wait, there's more. **James Weldon Johnson** (Jn17) was appointed by President Theodore Roosevelt as the U.S. consul in Venezuela and Nicaragua. We mainly know **Washington Irving** (Ap3) as the author of "The Legend of Sleepy Hollow" and "Rip van Winkle," but, to make ends meet and to network with other writers, he was a secretary/aide de camp for the Ambassador in England and later a minister to Spain.

Grace Zaring Stone (Ja9) was a novelist and short story writer who was married to the commander of an aircraft carrier during World War II. When she wrote the novel *Escape* in 1939, she used the penname Ethel Vance in order to protect her daughter Eleanor (later Baroness Zgismond Perényi), who was living under Nazi occupation.

In the mystery section of libraries and bookstores, readers will see the name of **Phyllis A. Whitney** (S9) and may not realize a couple of interesting facts: She was born in Japan of American parents, and she lived to be 104 years old.

Carl Rakosi (N6) was the last surviving member of a group of poets known as the Objectivists. Like Ms. Whitney above, he made it to 104 years old and was still giving readings in his nineties.

Herman Wouk (My27), 101 years old at this writing, is closing in on Whitney and Rakosi. He is most noted for his novel (and later play and film) *The Caine Mutiny*. But in his advanced years, he published *The Language God Talks: On Science and Religion* (2010, non-fiction), *The Lawgiver* (2012, fiction), and *Sailor and Fiddler: Reflections of a 100-Year Old Author* (2015, non-fiction).

Theodore Winthrop (S22) was unknown as a writer during his thirty-two years on earth. As a Union major, he unfortunately was killed on June 10, 1861, at the Battle of Big Bethel[12] (a few weeks before the First Battle of Bull Run). The operation was botched, but Winthrop tried to rally his troops

---

[12] Also known as the Battle of Bethel Church or the Battle of Big Bethel.

by saying, "One more charge, boys, and the day is ours." It wasn't, and a bullet to the heart took him out entirely. His sister saw to the publication of his novels, poetry, and prose.

Constance Fenimore Woolson (Mr5) was the grandniece of James Fenimore Cooper. She wrote novels, short stories, and poetry. At the age of fifty-three, while suffering from depression and influenza, she fell (or jumped?) from a window in Venice, Italy, and died. She was buried in Rome's Protestant Cemetery, which is also the resting place for **John Keats** (O31) and **Percy Shelley** (Au4).

Frank Yerby (S5) was born in Augusta, Georgia, and became the first African American writer to become a millionaire with his writing and the first one to have his novel snatched up by Hollywood. Frustrated by the racial tensions and restrictions in the U.S., he moved to Spain for the rest of his life.

Florida's **Harry Whittington** (F4) was king of the paperback writers but didn't develop a name "trademark" because he used so many pseudonyms, including Ashley Carter (for a "slave-gothic" in the manner of Yerby), Curt Colman, John Dexter, Tabor Evans, Whit Harrison, Robert Hart-Davis, Kel Holland, Harriet Kathryn Myers, Suzanne Stephens, Blaine Stevens, Clay Stuart, Hondo Wells, Harry White, Hallam Whitney, Henri Whittier, and J. X. Williams. The Ocala native said he worked for thirty years before he became aware of this maxim: No one could make a living as a writer in the U.S.

Who remembers **Susan Glaspell** (Jy1) today? She was a best-selling author who won the Pulitzer Prize. As she had a major impact on American drama, she wrote nine novels, fifteen plays, fifty short stories, and a biography. A prominent British critic recently called her "American drama's best-kept secret."

The criminal careers of **Al Jennings** (N25) and **William Sydney Porter** (S11) intersected when they met in prison. Jennings had been a train robber, while Porter was arrested for embezzling from a bank.[13] Porter turned to writing and became famous as **O. Henry**. Jennings turned to the movies and was a consultant on *The Great Train Robbery*. He later became a cowboy actor and wrote stories about crooks and an autobiography, *Through the Darkness with O. Henry*.

Another writer who served time in prison was **Julian Hawthorne** (Jn22), son of Nathaniel. Perhaps through carelessness, he was arrested with a colleague for mail fraud and served a year in the Atlanta Penitentiary. Formerly he had written about his father's works, but the time in jail

---

[13] He was doing a payday loan from the cash drawer but fell victim to a surprise audit before he could put it back.

convinced him to write a book opposing prison terms for criminals.[14]

A year before he died, **Madison Cawein** (Mr23) published a poem in a periodical edited by **Ezra Pound** (O30). Its title? *The Waste Land.* Was it the spark that encouraged **T. S. Eliot** (S26) to tackle the same subject?

Who was the first poet laureate of any American state? That would be **Ina Donna Coolbrith** (My10) of California.

What do Nobel Prize winning author **Pearl S. Buck** (Jn26) and Western novelist **Zane Grey** (Ja31) have in common? Yes, both were born with the name "Pearl." He started life as Pearl Zane Gray, but his family preferred the surname to be spelled "Grey." For some reason, the manly young man dropped "Pearl" and used "Zane" as his first name.[15]

A reader would think that a distant cousin of **Mark Twain** just might take to the pen or quill himself. That is exactly what happened with **Jeremiah Clemens** (D28). A native of Huntsville, Alabama, he was an attorney and a newspaper editor, but he made it into this collection because of his novels: *Bernard Lyle* (1853), *Mustang Grey* (1857), *The Rivals* (1859), and *Tobias Wilson* (published posthumously in 1865). He was opposed to secession and walked a tightrope concerning his loyalties during the Civil War.

Since writers are often gloomy cusses who dwell on early deaths, they shake their heads at the brief times alloted to **John Keats** (TB), **Thomas Chatterton** (suicide), **Henry Kirke White** (TB), and **Lucretia Maria Davidson** (TB). Lucretia was only sixteen. A play is begging to be written with the title *Death Comes to the Romantic Rhymsters.* That is because the five major Romantic poets were born in this order: **William Wordsworth**, **Samuel Taylor Coleridge**, **Lord Byron**, **Percy Shelley**, and **John Keats**. Ironically, they died in the reverse order: Keats, Shelley, Byron, Coleridge, and Wordsworth.

Writers often go down in ships at sea. For example, **Jacques Futrelle** (Ap9), a mystery writer from Pike County, Georgia, went down on the *Titanic* in 1912, while **Elbert Hubbard** (Jn19) perished in 1915 when the *Lusitania* was torpedoed by the Germans.

One adventurer, **Richard Halliburton** (Ja9), had a junk built in China while the Asian war with Japan was going on in the late Thirties. He was going to voyage across the Pacific to San Francisco, where *The Sea Dragon* would be part of the Golden Gate International Exposition. During a storm, other vessels noticed that the *Sea Dragon* was in trouble and offered help, but Halliburton continued on. The junk sank in the storm, but one conspiracy theory said that Halliburton had been captured by the Japanese, as had supposedly happened to **Amelia Earhart** (Jy24).

Another who went down at sea was **Percy Shelley** (Au4) and his two

---

[14] If I were convicted of some crime, that certainly would be my position.

[15] "You better not smile when you call me 'Pearl,' Podner."

crewmen on the *Don Juan* in the summer of 1822. Shelley's boat was top heavy with sails, so he could race Byron's *Bolivar* when good weather permitted. Apparently, during a storm, the boat tipped, and everyone drowned. Bodies were washed ashore, buried quickly on the beach to avoid spreading disease. Eventually Shelley's friends discovered that some bodies had been found and buried until the required cremation could be arranged. Although the creatures of the deep had eaten away Shelley's face and hands, they found a volume of poems by John Keats in his pocket and knew they had found the poet. One summer day, his friends gathered with a portable furnace and cremated what they could. The ritual was taking longer than Lord Byron liked, so he cooled off by swimming out to the *Bolivar*. Another Romantic, **Leigh Hunt** (O19), could not bear to watch his friend burned and remained in the carriage. Meanwhile, an Indiana Jones-style friend, **Edward John Trelawny** (N13), stayed through the whole ordeal, and, when he saw that Shelley's heart had not been turned to ashes, he extracted the cardial briquette, which he eventually gave to Mary Shelley. She kept it with her for the rest of her life, eventually giving it to their son, who had it buried with himself. The ashes of Shelley were collected and interred at Rome's Protestant Cemetery, with this epitaph:

Nothing of him that doth fade
But doth suffer a sea-change
Into something rich and strange

Those words were certainly kinder than what the Tory newspaper, *The Courier*, wrote when it heard of the poet's death:

Shelley, the writer of some infidel poetry,
has been drowned, *now* he knows
whether there is God or no.

The novelist and adventurer Trelawny had the last laugh in life's wheel of fortune. He came from a family of long-livers and made it to eighty-eight.[16]

In contrast to Shelley's epitaph, Keats' final words stated:

Here lies One whose
Name is Writ in Water.

Will Shakespeare Hays (Jy19) was a poet and song-writer in the 19th Century. His work was often confused with that of Stephen Foster, since

---

[16] "When Trelawny died in 1881, they had to beat his liver to death with a stick." That would have been an English music-hall joke back then.

both wrote for minstrel shows. His friends called him "Shakespeare" because he was scribbling all the time, so he legally made it part of his name. Still unsettled is his claim that he wrote the lyrics for "Dixie." (The actual melody came from a variety of sources.)

Jane Johnston Schoolcraft (Ja31) deserves attention because she was an early woman writer in the U.S. and was the earliest known American Indian literary writer. Her name, *Bamewawagezhikaquay*, may be translated as "Woman of the Sound [that the stars make] Rushing Through the Sky."

A New Englander would automatically know that many famous writers are buried on **Author's Ridge**, part of the Sleepy Hollow Cemetery in Concord, Massachusetts. Buried there are members of the **Alcott** family, **William Ellery Channing** (Transcendentalist and poet), **Ralph Waldo Emerson**, **Daniel Chester French** (sculptor of the Lincoln Memorial), **Nathaniel Hawthorne**, **Sophia Hawthorne** (artist and wife of Hawthorne), **Richard Marius** (Reformation historian and Southern novelist), **Elizabeth Peabody** (education reformer), **Franklin Benjamin Sanborn** (author and social reformer), **Henry David Thoreau** (American Transcendentalist, philosopher, essayist, and lecturer), **Mary Colman Wheeler** (founder of the Wheeler School), and other notables.

In closing for this edition, the reader will find **William Barclay Masterson** (N26) listed among the writers. He is better known for his nickname **"Bat" Masterson**. Although he wasn't as elegant as the character portrayed by Gene Barry in the old TV series, Masterson did indeed have a history as a gunman or lawman, then as a gambler, briefly an editor, and finally as a reporter and columnist for twenty years. He died of a massive heart attack while working at his desk of the *New York Morning Telegraph* . . . a fitting end for any writer.

About the Author

Thanks to his father's jobs in newspaper circulation departments and then as a U.S. Navy photographer, Howard Denson moved from one part of the South to another. Finally, the Jasper, Alabama native settled in Jacksonville, Florida, during the administration of what he calls Saint Richard the Reluctant Confessor.

At what is now Florida State College at Jacksonville, he taught composition, literature, and creative writing, plus humanities courses in the ancient world and Middle Ages, the Renaissance to the modern world, art appreciation, and American art and culture.

For over two decades, he was involved in a town-and-gown writers' conference, the Florida First Coast Writers' Festival. He also attended similar conferences at Samford University, Birmingham-Southern College, the University of Florida, and especially at St. Petersburg's excellent Florida Suncoast Writers' Conference.

He has been an editor and/or contributor to *The State Street Review*, *Kalliope*, *Asheville Poetry Review*, *The Penchant*, *The International Journal of Elvisology and the Elvisian Era*, *The Write Stuff*, *The FCCFF Update*, and *Kassandra's Kitchen*. He helped coordinate or judge contests in novels, short fiction, poetry, and plays.

He and his smarter bride of over forty years Michele Boyette currently have several four-legged children: the meowers, Eddie, Miss Peepers, Billy, Mercutio, Wally, Frieda, and Amber; and the barkers, Mr. Darcy and Daphne.

His website: http://howarddenson.webs.com

www.ingramcontent.com/pod-product-compliance
Lightning Source LLC
Chambersburg PA
CBHW071327280526
45787CB00001B/13